PRAYER RAIN

DR. D. K. OLUKOYA
MFM MINISTRIES
NIGERIA

© 1999 - **Prayer Rain**
Dr. D. K. Olukoya

A publication of
MOUNTAIN OF FIRE AND MIRACLES MINISTRIES

13, Olasimbo Street, off Olumo Road,
(By UNILAG Second Gate), Onike, Iwaya
P. O. Box 2990, Sabo, Yaba, Lagos, Nigeria.
☎ 01-868766
E-Mail: mfm@micro.com.ng
mfm@nigol.net.ng

ISBN 978-0615900018

Cover Illustration by - **Sister Shade Olukoya**

All Scriptures are quoted from the King James Version of the Bible

First Edition February 1999
Second Edition March 2002
Third Edition February 2003
Fourth Edition December 2003
Fifth Edition June 2004
Sixth Edition August 2004
Sevrnth Edition August 2005
Eighth Edition March 2006
Ninth Edition November 2006
Tenth Edition April 2008

III

DEDICATION

This book, Prayer Rain, is dedicated to late Apostle Joseph Ayodele Babalola, a minister of God, who understood the power of prayer. He was a man mightily used by God to ignite the fire of the first Christian revival in this country in the nineteen thirties.

Brother J. A. and his team of aggressive prayer warriors entered forbidden forests, silenced demons that demanded worship, paralysed deeply-rooted, anti-gospel activities. Sometimes, beginning from the highest places, they emptied hospitals by the healing power of the Lord Jesus Christ, rendered witchdoctors jobless, and they started the first indigenous Holy-Ghost filled church in Nigeria. So far - and we stand to be corrected - none has equalled, let alone surpassed this humble Brother in the field of aggressive evangelism in this country.

CONTENTS

VI

IX

INTRODUCTION

Prayer is a gift to you and a privilege. The gift is offered to all and all may become the wielders of the great power in prayer. However, the fact remains that the power of prayer is least exercised by the average believer. You will do well to learn the art of warfare prayer. The present temperature of the prayer of many christians needs to rise if they expect serious breakthroughs.

The prayer points in this book are targeted at certain needs so that as you are praying you will not be beating the air. This is how to go use the book:

1. Locate your area of need by looking at the table of contents.

2. Select appropriate scriptures promising you what you desire. Meditate on them and let them sink into your spirit.

3. Go about the prayers in any of the following ways as led by the Holy Spirit:

   a. Three days' night vigil, i.e praying from 10 P.M. to 5 A.M. three consecutive nights.

   b. Three days' fast (breaking daily), i.e. praying at intervals and breaking the fast at 6.00 P.M. or 9.00.P.M. daily.

   c. Seven days' night vigil, i.e. praying from 10 P.M. to 5 A.M. seven consecutive nights.

   d. Seven days' fast (breaking daily), i.e. praying at intervals and breaking the fast at 6.00 P.M. or 9.00.P.M. daily.

   e. Three or more days of dry fast .i.e praying and fasting three or more days without any food or drink.

4. Pray aggressively.

NOTE: Spend part of vigil or fasting praying in the Spirit - Praying in the Spirit is an ability to pray in tongues as given utterance by the Holy Spirit. To pray in the Spirit, you must have been baptised in the Holy Ghost (not water baptism) - 1 Cor. 14:15.

You will be victorious in Jesus' name.

FOR SPIRITUAL GROWTH

John 3:30

- *For all believers who desire meaningful spiritual growth in their walk with God.*

There is no height you cannot attain in the spirit if only you are ready to take the bull by the horn; do away with every form of hindrance and follow the principles of spiritual growth laid down in God's word.

Hebrews 5:12: *"For when for the time ye ought to be teachers, ye have need that one teach you again which be the first principles of the oracles of God; and are become such as have need of milk and not of strong meat."*

Jesus expects each believer to grow to the level where he can teach others. In many of the Epistles, the believer is encouraged to grow in grace and in the knowledge of Christ (2 Peter 3:18). When a believer refuses to grow, he remains a spiritual babe who is unskillful in the WORD. Such baby christians need milk and not strong meat.

When we as believers, begin to apply the truth we know in our lives, we will begin to grow and our knowledge of Christ will also increase. Paul encourages the believer to be "rooted and built up in Him" (Col. 2:7). As believers, we draw our nutrients from Him, i.e. Jesus Christ.

As you pray these prayer points for spiritual growth, the Holy Spirit will draw you into a deeper and fulfilling relationship with Christ.

- *Scripture for meditation*

Phil. 3:10,14: *That I may know him, and the power of his resurrection, and the fellowship of his sufferings, being made conformable unto his death; . . . I press toward the mark for the prize of the high calling of God in Christ Jesus.*

Make these confessions to establish your identity in Christ Jesus.

I am not what the world thinks or says I am. I am not what the devil or the kingdom of darkness says, imagines or has designed me to be. I am not the picture of what my idolaterous forefathers wished I should be. I am not what the unregenerated mind of any friend thinks I am. I am not what my father and mother think or want me to be. I am not what my village wickedness, household wickedness and environmental wickedness want me to be. I am not a picture of what the national economy and institutionalised wickedness has restructured the people to be. I am not what I think I am. I am what the Word of God says I am. I am an express image of Jehovah God on earth. I am fashioned after the likeness of the Creator of the heaven and earth.

I am regenerated by the blood of Jesus. I am ransomed from the powers of death and hell. I am blood washed. I am redeemed. I am justified by Christ. I am made to be the righteousness of God through Christ. I am a believer of the Word of Truth. I am born again. I am heaven-bound; my citizenship is in heaven. I am seated with Christ in heavenly places far above principality and powers. I am a priest and a king ordained by Christ to rule here on earth. I am the fear and the dread of God against the kingdom of darkness. I am a dwelling place of the Holy Spirit of God. I am built up together and attached with other children of God into a holy habitation of God.

The word of God says, I am a royal priesthood, I am a holy nation, I am a chosen generation, and a peculiar person to the nation. I am special in the sight of God. The Bible says because I believe and receive Jesus Christ, power has been given to me to become a son of God, and I am empowered to trample upon serpents and scorpions and all the powers of the enemy. I am empowered to use the name of Jesus to cast out demons and heal the sick. I am empowered to bind, to loose and to decree things and the Bible says wherever my voice is heard no one can ask me why. I do these things for my voice is the voice of a king that is full of authority.

I am commanded and empowered by my God to subdue and to exercise dominion. For I am made a little lower than the angels and God has crowned me with glory and honour and has also made me to have dominion over all the works of His hands. The devil that was against my authority as a God's representative on earth has been destroyed by Christ and once again; the keys of the kingdom of heaven are given to me and because I am a member of the body of Christ, which is the Church, the gates of hell cannot prevail against me.

I am a branch in the vine; Jesus Christ is the true vine because I abide in Him. I am full of the fruit of the Spirit. I am full of love, joy, peace, longsuffering, kindness, goodness, faithfulness, gentleness, self-control. Because the grace of God is upon my life as the light of His glory, I am full of divine favour; I am a partaker of all heaven's spiritual blessings.

I am an overcomer; the Bible says whosoever is born of God overcomes the world, and this is the victory that overcomes the world, even my faith. In faith I overcome ungodly worry, anxiety, heaviness of spirit, sorrow, depression, lust of the eyes and lust of the flesh. In faith I have overcome all the tricks of the devil, for it is written, greater is Jesus Christ that dwells in me than the devil that is in the world. No weapon that is formed against me shall prosper. In righteousness I am established; I am far from oppression, for I shall not fear and from terror for it shall not come near me. The Lord shall cover me with His feathers, because I have made Him my dwelling place. Evil shall not befall me; I shall tread upon the Lion and the Cobra and surely the Lord will always deliver me from the snare of the fowlers.

God has made me a beneficiary of divine health through the stripes that were laid on Jesus Christ. Through Jesus Christ I have right standing with God. Through Jesus Christ I have access to the throne grace of God, to find peace with God. I have prosperity for God will no longer withhold any good thing from me.

I have spoken with the tongue of the learned and as it is written, I shall be justified by the words of my mouth. I ask that the word of God I have confessed begin to transform me to the original image God designed me to be in His book. I ask that the blood of Jesus wipe away every mark of reproach whether physical or spiritual. I ask for the blood of Jesus to erase every evil and negative name I was ever called. I nullify every negative report ever made about me. I cease to be a picture of failure. I cease to be abased, rejected, forsaken, desolate and downcast. I begin to manifest *expressly every good thing God has written about me in book. I begin to look fearfully and wonderfully made. I begin to operate at the head and not the tail. I begin to be a true worshiper of Jehovah El shaddai and I begin from now to continually praise Him and confess positively.*

- **PRAISE WORSHIP**

1. O Lord, comfort my heart.
2. O Lord, establish me in every good work.
3. O Lord, establish me in every good word.
4. God of peace, sanctify me wholly, in the name of Jesus.
5. Father Lord, let my body, soul and spirit be preserved blameless unto the coming of our Lord Jesus Christ, in the name of Jesus.
6. Let me be filled with the knowledge of His will, in Jesus' name.
7. Let me be filled with all wisdom and spiritual understanding, in the name of Jesus.
8. Father Lord, help me to walk worthy of, and pleasing to the Lord, in the name of Jesus.
9. Father Lord, make me be fruitful in every good work, in Jesus' name.
10. O Lord, increase me in the knowledge of God.
11. O Lord, strengthen me mightily.
12. Father Lord, let me be filled with the spirit of wisdom and understanding in the knowledge of Christ, in the name of Jesus.
13. Father Lord, let the eyes of my understanding be enlightened, in the name of Jesus.
14. Father Lord, let me be strengthened with might by His Spirit in the inner man, in the name of Jesus.
15. Father Lord, let Christ dwell in my heart by faith, in Jesus' name.
16. Father Lord, let me be rooted and grounded in love, in Jesus' name.
17. Lord, let me be filled with all the fullness of God.
18. God, help me comprehend the breadth, length, depth and height of

the love of Christ, in the name of Jesus.

19. Let the word of the Lord have free course and be glorified in me, in the name of Jesus.

20. Let the Lord of peace give me peace in all areas of life, in the name of Jesus.

21. Let utterance be given unto me to make known the mystery of the Gospel, in the name of Jesus.

22. O Lord, perfect what is lacking in my faith.

23. O Lord, perfect Your good work in me.

24. O Lord, make me perfect unto Your good work.

25. O Lord, enrich me in all utterance and knowledge.

26. Let the grace of the Lord Jesus Christ be with me, in Jesus' name.

27. Father Lord, inject into me your spiritual vitamins that will make me spiritually healthy, in the name of Jesus.

28. Father Lord, inject into me spiritual vitamins that will boost my appetite to eat Your word, in the name of Jesus.

29. Father Lord, infuse into my blood spiritual vitamins that will produce hungerand thirst for prayers in me, in the name of Jesus.

30. Let God inject into me spiritual vitamins that will clear my vision and strengthen its clarity, in the name of Jesus.

31. Lord God, inject into me spiritual vitamins that will sustain me in evil days.

32. Lord God, inject into me divine immunity that will always kill spiritual germs and evil deposits in me.

33. Lord God, inject into me the spiritual energy that will make me tirelessly with You.

34. Lord God, feed me with the foods of the champions.

35. Lord God, boost my energy to run the race set before me.

36. I receive the comforting anointing and power in the Holy Ghost, in the name of Jesus.

37. I receive the unsearchable wisdom in the Holy Ghost, in the name of Jesus.

38. I take the shield of faith to quench every fiery dart of the enemy, in the name of Jesus.

39. I run into the name of the Lord which is a strong tower and I am safe, in the name of Jesus.

40. Father Lord, always make me drink from Your everlasting well of joy, in the name of Jesus.

41. Thank God for the new spiritual height He has lifted you to.

POWER AGAINST DESERT SPIRITS

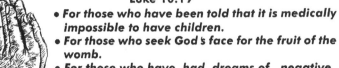

Luke 10:19
- *For those who have been told that it is medically impossible to have children.*
- *For those who seek God's face for the fruit of the womb.*
- *For those who have had dreams of negative surgical operation performed on their reproductive organs.*

Desert spirits are satanic powers responsible for keeping a person in an awful state of barrenness or unfruitfulness. It is your responsibility as a child of God, to take up the weapons of God and fight against these wicked spirits. There are spiritual weapons that have been made available to you by Christ. Use these weapons and victory will surely be yours, in Jesus' name.

Romans 4:19: *"And being not weak in faith, he considered not his own body now dead, when he was about an hundred years old, neither yet the deadness of Sarah's womb."*

I don't think your case can be as impossible or as ridiculous as the situation Abraham and Sarah found themselves in. The Bible says, "It ceased to be with Sarah after the manner of women." (Genesis 18:11) Sarah was 90 years old, her menstruation had stopped, yet "the God which quikeneth the dead, and calleth those things which be not as though they were" (Rom 4:17) stepped into her situation and made the impossible, possible.

The Bible says in Hebrews 11:11: "Through faith also Sarah herself received strength to conceive seed and was delivered of a child when she was past age, because she judged him faithful who had promised."

I don't know what the doctors have told you but I will advise you to ignore that medical report. Don't be weak in faith. Stand on the **WORD** of God that says, "There shall nothing cast their young nor be barren in thy land" Exodus 23:26.

As you pray these prayers in faith, the 'God which quickeneth the dead and calleth those things which be not as though they were' will step into your situation and endue you with strength to conceive and be delivered of a child. You will bring forth your own Isaac, so that those who hear will rejoice with you. (Genesis 21:6).

● *Make these powerful confessions and personalise them.*

Ps. 31:2: *Bow down thine ear to me; deliver me speedily: be thou my strong rock, for an house of defence to save me.*

Ps. 143:7: *Hear me speedily, O LORD: my spirit faileth: hide not thy face from me, lest I be like unto them that go down into the pit.*

Isa. 58:8: *Then shall thy light break forth as the morning, and thine health shall spring forth speedily: and thy righteousness shall go before thee; the glory of the LORD shall be thy rereward.*

Luke 18:8: *I tell you that he will avenge them speedily*

Ps. 102:2: *Hide not thy face from me in the day when I am in trouble; incline thine ear unto me: in the day when I call answer me speedily.*

Jer. 1:12: *Then said the LORD unto me, Thou hast well seen: for I will hasten my word to perform it.*

Jer. 29:11: *For I know the thoughts that I think toward you, saith the LORD, thoughts of peace, and not of evil, to give you an expected end.*

Ps. 56:9: *When I cry unto thee, then shall mine enemies turn back: this I know; for God is for me.*

Mal. 4:2: *But unto you that fear my name shall the Sun of righteousness arise with healing in his wings; and ye shall go forth, and grow up as calves of the stall.*

Gal. 3:13-14: *Christ hath redeemed us from the curse of the law, being made a curse for us: for it is written, Cursed is every one that hangeth on a tree: That the blessing of Abraham might come on the Gentiles through Jesus Christ; that we might receive the promise of the Spirit through faith.*

Col. 2:14-15: *Blotting out the handwriting of ordinances that was against us, which was contrary to us, and took it out of the way, nailing it to his cross; And having spoiled principalities and powers, he made a shew of them openly, triumphing over them in it.*

Matt. 8:17: *That it might be fulfilled which was spoken by Esaias the prophet, saying, Himself took our infirmities, and bare our sicknesses.*

Rom. 16:20: *And the God of peace shall bruise Satan under your feet shortly. The grace of our Lord Jesus Christ be with you. Amen.*

Matt. 3:10: *And now also the axe is laid unto the root of the trees: therefore every tree which bringeth not forth good fruit is hewn down, and cast into the fire.*

I Jn. 3:8b: *For this purpose the Son of God was manifested, that he might destroy the works of the devil.*

2 Tim. 4:18: *And the Lord shall deliver me from every evil work, and will preserve me unto his heavenly kingdom: to whom be glory for ever and ever. Amen.*

Jesus is Lord over my spirit, soul and body for the word of God tells me that at the name of Jesus every knee shall bow. I can do all things through Christ who strengthens me. The Lord is my shepherd, I shall not want. Jesus has delivered me from the powers of darkness and has translated me into the kingdom of His Dear Son. In Jesus I have redemption through His shed blood and also the forgiveness of my sins. Jesus has blotted out the handwriting of ordinances that was against me which was contrary to me, and took it out of the way nailing it to His cross. I am the body of Christ. I am redeemed from the curse because Jesus bore my physical and spiritual diseases in His body. I have the mind of Christ and hold the thoughts, feelings and purposes of His heart.

• PRAISE WORSHIP

1. Thank the Lord for His power to deliver from any form of bondage.
2. I confess the sins of my ancestors (list them).
3. Ask the Lord for forgiveness.
4. Ask the Lord to forgive those sins you do not know about.
5. Let the power in the blood of Jesus separate me from the sins of my ancestors.
6. I renounce any evil dedication placed upon my life, in Jesus' name.
7. I break every evil edict and ordination, in the name of Jesus.
8. I renounce and loose myself from every negative dedication placed upon my life, in the name of Jesus.

9. I command all demons associated with said dedication to leave now, in the name of Jesus Christ.

10. I take authority over all cases that are associated with this dedication, in the name of Jesus.

11. Lord, cancel the evil consequences of any broken demonic promise or dedication.

12. I take authority over all the curses emanating from breaking the vows made during this dedication, in the name of Jesus.

13. I command all demons associated with any broken evil parental vow and dedication to depart from me now, in the name of Jesus.

14. Ask the Lord to separate you completely from all the sins of your forefathers by the precious blood of Jesus.

15. Ask the Lord to remove the curse if it is from Him.

16. I command the curse of . . . to be broken, in the name of Jesus.

17. Apply the oil and command all demons associated with the curse to leave at once, in the name of Jesus.

18. I command any demon afflicting the . . . or causing . . . to leave at once, in the name of Jesus.

19. Ask the Lord to heal all the damages done.

20. I dismiss and disband from my heart every thought, image or picture of failure in these matters, in the name of Jesus.

21. I reject every spirit of doubt, fear and discouragement, in the name of Jesus.

22. I cancel all ungodly delays to the manifestations of my miracles, in the name of Jesus.

23. Let the angels of the living God roll away every stone of hindrance to the manifestation of my breakthroughs, in the name of Jesus.

24. O Lord, hasten Your word to perform it in every department of my life.

25. O Lord, speedily avenge me of my adversaries.

26. I refuse to agree with the enemies of my progress, in Jesus' name.

(Pray the next four prayer points according to the level of your faith)

27. O Lord, I desire breakthroughs concerning . . . today, in the name of Jesus.

28. O Lord, I desire breakthroughs concerning . . . this week, in the name of Jesus.

29. O Lord, I desire breakthroughs concerning . . . this month, in the name of Jesus.

30. O Lord, I desire breakthroughs concerning . . . his year, in the name of Jesus.

31. Let there be turbulence, re-arrangement, revision, re-organisation and 're-routing' of situations and circumstances in order to give way to the manifestations of my desired miracles, in Jesus' name.

32. Let every leakage present in the container of my life be mended, in the name of Jesus.

33. I bind, plunder and render to nothing every anti-testimony, anti-miracle and anti-prosperity force, in the name of Jesus.

34. The God of Elijah who answers by fire, answer me by fire, in the name of Jesus.

35. The God who answered Moses speedily at the Red Sea, answer me by fire, in the name of Jesus.

36. The God who changed the lot of Jabez, answer me by fire, in the name of Jesus.

37. The God which quickeneth and calleth those things that be not as if they are, answer me by fire, in the name of Jesus.

38. I apply the blood of Jesus on my spirit, soul, body and womb.

39. Let the fire of God saturate my womb, in the name of Jesus.

40. Let every design against my life be completely nullified, in the name of Jesus.

41. Let all evil labels fashioned by the camp of the enemy against my life be rubbed off by the blood of Jesus.

Sing the song HOLY GHOST FIRE, FIRE FALL ON ME with full concentration and faith.

42. I vomit every satanic deposit in my life, in the mighty name of Jesus. *(You may prime the expulsion of these things by coughing slightly. Refuse to swallow any saliva coming out from the mouth)*

43. I break myself loose from the bondage of stagnancy, in the mighty name of Jesus.

44. Lord, destroy with Your fire anything that makes Your promise to fail in my life, no matter the origin.

As you pray No 45, take 3-4 deep breaths determinedly to expel and flush out spiritual contamination. Do so aggressively, in the mighty name of Jesus.

45. Let the blood, the fire and the living water of the Most High God wash my system clean from . . . pick from the under listed).

    - every unprofitable growth in my womb
    - all evil plantations
    - evil deposits from 'spirit husband'
    - impurities acquired from parental contamination
    - evil spiritual consumption
    - hidden sicknesses
    - remote control mechanisms
    - physical and spiritual incisions
    - satanic poisons
    - evil stamps, labels and links.

46. Let every area of my life become too hot for any evil to inhabit, in the name of Jesus.

47. You evil growth in my life, be uprooted, in the name of Jesus.

48. Let my body reject every evil habitation, in the name of Jesus.

49. O Lord, reverse all evil arrangements attached consciously or unconsciously to my life.

50. I reject all evil manipulations and manipulators, in Jesus' name.

51. I break the powers of the occult, witchcraft and familiar spirits over my life, in the name of Jesus.

You can prime the expulsion of the following things by heaving deeply and applying little force upon the lower part of the abdomen.

52. I deliver and pass out any satanic deposit in my intestine, in the name of Jesus.

53. I deliver and pass out any satanic deposit in my reproductive organs, in the name of Jesus.

54. I deliver and pass out any satanic deposit in my womb, in the name of Jesus.

55. *In the Name of Jesus, I Declare Before All the Forces of Darkness, "Jesus Christ Is Lord over Every Department of My Life."*

56. You foreign hand laid on my womb, release me, in Jesus' name.

57. In the name of Jesus, I renounce, break and loose myself from all

- demonic holds   - psychic powers
- bonds of physical illness   - bondage

58. In the name of Jesus, I break and loose myself from all evil curses, chains, spells, jinxes, bewitchments, witchcraft or sorcery, which may have been put upon me.

59. Let a creative miracle take place in my womb and reproductive system, in the name of Jesus.

60. Father, I ask You, in the name of Jesus Christ, to send out Your angels and have them unearth and break all evil storage vessels fashioned against me.

61. I loose myself from every evil influence, dark spirit and satanic bondage, in the name of Jesus.

62. I confess and declare that my body is the temple of the Holy Spirit, redeemed, cleansed, and sanctified by the blood of Jesus Christ.

63. I bind, plunder and render to naught every strongman assigned to my

womb, reproductive system and marital life, in Jesus' name.

64. God who quickens the dead, quicken my womb and reproductive system, in the name of Jesus.

65. I release myself from the hold of the spirits of sterility, infertility and fear, in the name of Jesus.

66. All spirits rooted in fornication, come out of my womb with all your roots, in the mighty name of our Lord Jesus.

67. All spirits rooted in sexual perversion, come out of my womb with all your roots, in the mighty name of Jesus.

68. All spirits rooted in spirit husband, come out of my womb with all your roots, in the mighty name of our Lord Jesus.

69. All spirits rooted in masturbation, come out of my womb with all your roots, in the mighty name of our Lord Jesus.

70. All spirits rooted in guilt, come out of my womb with all your roots, in the mighty name of our Lord Jesus.

71. All spirits rooted in pornography, come out of my womb with all your roots, in the mighty name of our Lord Jesus.

72. Sing this song: *There is power mighty in the blood* . . .

73. I reverse every evil manipulation carried out against my womb using my menstrual pads or dates, in the name of Jesus.

74. I divorce every satanic marriage to my father, in the name of Jesus.

75. I release myself from every inherited womb malformation, in the name of Jesus.

76. Lord, grant unto my womb the power to retain, maintain and safely deliver my babies in the name of Jesus.

77. Let the blood of Jesus sanitise my womb and anoint it, in the name of Jesus.

78. I command all satanic networks against my being fruitful to be completely broken, in the name of Jesus.

79. I break every anti-marriage and anti-pregnancy curse, in the name of Jesus.

80. I bind every spirit of abortion and miscarriage, in Jesus' name.

81. Jesus, I thank You for the good testimonies that will follow this prayer.

● **DAILY EXERCISE:**

A. *Speak to your womb to retain and maintain the pregnancy till birth.*

B. *Barricade your spirit with the hedge of fire and the blood of Jesus.*

C. *Bind household strongmen from both sides of the family.*

D. *Command the spirit of abortion and miscarriage to depart from the womb.*

E. *Command the spirit of death to depart from the womb.*

F. *Thanksgiving.*

FOR PROFITABLE SALES

Deut. 28:13

- *For all Christian traders and businessmen.*
- *When you want your wares to sell.*
- *When you notice a lull in your profit-margin.*
- *When you wish to create market-hunger for your products.*

God has ordained that you should be the foremost dealer in your line of merchandise in the market. Don't be deceived by the enemy, rise up today and possess your possession. We are given an example in Genesis 26:13: *"And the man waxed great, and went forward, and grew until he became very great"*

This is how the Bible describes the wealth of Isaac. At this point in time Isaac was in Gerar in the Philistine. Although there was famine, yet Isaac prospered. The NIV Bible says. "The man became rich, and his wealth continued to grow until he became very wealthy." The reason for this supernatural growth is found in the preceding verse it says, "the Lord blessed him."

What a simple and profound statement! To bless means to empower to prosper! This basically means that the Lord empowered Isaac to prosper till he became very wealthy.

Are you running your business in a way God can bless you? Deuteronomy 8:18 says, "Thou shalt remember the Lord thy God; for it is he that giveth thee power to get wealth..."

Check your life. Check the way you are running your business. As you pray these prayers with clean hands and a pure heart (Psalm 24:4), the God that empowers to get wealth will step into your business and grant you profitable sales.

• CONFESSIONS

Ps. 46:1: *God is our refuge and strength, a very present help in trouble.*

Heb. 1:14: *Are they not all ministering spirits, sent forth to minister for them who shall be heirs of salvation?*

Phil. 4:19: *But my God shall supply all your need according to his riches in glory by Christ Jesus.*

Num. 6:25: *The LORD make his face shine upon thee, and be gracious unto thee:*

Deut. 28:13: *And the LORD shall make thee the head, and not the tail; and thou shalt be above only, and thou shalt not be beneath; if that thou hearken unto the commandments of the LORD thy God, which I command thee this day, to observe and to do them:*

Dan. 1:17: *As for these four children, God gave them knowledge and skill in all learning and wisdom: and Daniel had understanding in all visions and dreams.*

Ps. 5:12: *For thou, LORD, wilt bless the righteous; with favour wilt thou compass him as with a shield.*

Ps. 119:165: *Great peace have they which love thy law: and nothing shall offend them.*

● **PRAISE WORSHIP**

1. Father, I dedicate and consecrate these products to You, in the name of Jesus.

2. Lord, bless the efforts of all who are involved in selling my products.

3. Lord, give my representatives favour with the customers.

4. Father, help my salesmen to understand the needs of my customers, in the name of Jesus.

5. Lord, help my sales representative never to indulge in profiteering, but always to efficiently present my products and services.

6. Father, let the Holy Spirit teach me sales promotion and techniques for increasing sales.

7. Lord, help me to always remain ahead and not behind.

8. Lord, help me to offer my products in the proper way.

9. Lord, grant my salesmen favour to make profitable sales.

10. Almighty Father, initiate a hunger and demand for my goods and services, in the name of Jesus.

11. Lord, open new doors and provide new markets for my goods and services.

12. Lord, help me to increase sales and add new markets daily.

13. I retrieve my products from every evil attack, in Jesus' name.

14. I break every curse of failure upon the sales of my products, in the name of Jesus.

15. I command the devil to take off his legs from my goods and services, in the name of Jesus.

16. Let the rod of iron fall on any strange money passed to me, in the name of Jesus.

17. I use the blood of Jesus Christ to wash my hands and my products clean today, in the name of Jesus.

18. Let there be a breakthrough for me in my transactions, in the name of Jesus.

19. Lord, let me have the spirit of favour in all my business transactions.

20. I ask for the release of prosperity on the sales of my products, in the name of Jesus.

21. Let all demonic hindrances to the sales of my products be totally paralysed, in the name of Jesus.

22. I break every circle of sales failure upon my products, in the name of Jesus.

23. Let my products be shielded away from all evil observers, in the name of Jesus.

24. Father, let Your angels lift up my products on their hands so that they do not strike their feet against a stone, in the name of Jesus.

25. I remove my products from the dominion of the powers of darkness, in the name of Jesus.

26. Let my products become a channel of blessings and a foundation of life for other businesses, in the name of Jesus.

27. I command my money being caged by the enemy to be completely released, in the name of Jesus.

28. Lord, give me supernatural breakthroughs in all my present business proposals.

29. I bind and put to flight all the spirits of fear, anxiety and discourage-ment, in the name of Jesus.

30. Lord, let divine wisdom fall upon all those who are supporting me in selling my products.

31. I break the backbone of any spirits of conspiracy and treachery, in the name of Jesus.

32. Lord, hammer my matter into the mind of those who will assist me in selling my products so that they do not suffer from demonic loss of memory.

33. I paralyse the handiworks of all household enemies and envious agents against my selling my products, in the name of Jesus.

34. You devil, take your legs away from the top of my finances, in the mighty name of Jesus.

35. Let the fire of the Holy Spirit purge my finances from any evil mark, in the name of Jesus.

36. Father, guide and direct me to rectify any problem I have with my business, in the name of Jesus.

37. Lord, forgive me for any wrong decision action or thought that I have engaged in.

38. Father, help me to see my mistakes and faults and help me to do all in my power to overcome and correct them, in Jesus' name.

39. Lord, give unto me the Eagle's eye and the eyes of Elisha to foresee market situations.

40. Lord, give me wisdom to walk out of any unfavorable business situa-tion.

41. Lord, always help me to identify evil business traps.

42. Lord, help me erect safeguards to prevent business failure.

43. Lord, help me be on the lookout for ways to provide better products and services.

44. In the mighty name of Jesus, I claim . . . (pick from the following)

- a good reputation
- divine favour with clients and customers
- abundant prosperity
- divine wisdom for those who occupy important decision-making positions
- increased sales and services, and expanded markets
- new product ideas and new servicing concepts.

45. Father Lord, I thank You for answering my prayers.

POWER AGAINST SEXUAL PERVERSION

Romans 6:14

Sexual sins open the doors for all kinds of evil spirits to enter. This prayer programme is for those:
- *Who would like to be delivered from the spiritual contamination resulting from past sexual sins.*
- *Who would like to be delivered from their present sexual lusts, enticement, and other sexual sins.*
- *Who would like to expel sexual satanic deposits acquired by sleeping with demonised people.*
- *Who had been a commercial sex worker in the past.*
- *Who frequently dream of having sex.*

Don't despair if the enemy has subjected you to such a depth of immoral degradation. You would be lifted up to the height of purity which God has purposed for you as you call upon Him to help you.

Rom. 1:22: *"Professing themselves to be wise, they became fools."*

Please, open your Bible and slowly, meditatively read Rom. 1:18-32 and Leviticus 18:1-30.

Are you surprised at the things you've just read? Indeed there is nothing new under the sun! (Ecclesiastes 1:9) Basically the laws of God concerning sexual perversion as stated in Leviticus 18 can be divided into 5 groups. They are laws against

- incest (i.e. having sex with close relatives, brothers, in law's, uncles etc., there are 20 categories of close relatives stated between verses 6 and 19)
- adultery (vs 20) - idolatry i.e. offering child sacrifices (vs 21)
- homosexuality, lesbianism, masturbation, prostitution etc (vs 22)
- bestiality (having sex with animals (vs 23)

Are you caught in the bondage of any of these? Indeed the chains of habit (perversion) are too weak to be felt till they are too strong to be broken. All kinds of sexual bondage can be broken through the power of the blood of Jesus. There is hope for you, the Bible says, "Sin shall not have dominion over you" (Rom. 6:14) because "The law of Spirit of life in Christ Jesus has set you free from the law of sin and death" (Rom 8:2).

As you pray sincerely with a contrite/repentant heart (Psalm 51:17) God will set you free from the chains of sexual perversion.

• CONFESSION

Gal. 5:24: *And they that are Christ's have crucified the flesh with the affections and lusts.*

• PRAISE WORSHIP

1. Thank God for His power to deliver from every bondage.

2. I break myself from every spirit of sexual perversion, in the name of Jesus.

3. I release myself from every spiritual pollution emanating from my past sins of fornication and sexual immorality, in Jesus' name.

4. I release myself from every ancestral pollution, in Jesus' name.

5. I release myself from every dream pollution, in the name of Jesus.

6. I command every evil plantation of sexual perversion in my life to come out with all its roots, in the name of Jesus.

7. Every spirit of sexual perversion working against my life, be paralyzed and get out of my life, in the name of Jesus.

8. Every demon of sexual perversion assigned to my life, be bound, in the name of Jesus.

9. Father Lord, let the power of sexual perversion oppressing my life receive the fire of God and be roasted, in the name of Jesus.

10. Every inherited demon of sexual perversion in my life, receive the arrows of fire and remain permanently bound, in the name of Jesus.

11. I command every power of sexual perversion to come against itself, in the name of Jesus.

12. Father Lord, let every demonic stronghold built in my life by the spirit of sexual perversion be pulled down, in the name of Jesus.

13. Let every power of sexual perversion that has consumed my life be shattered to pieces, in the name of Jesus.

14. Let my soul be delivered from the forces of sexual perversion, in the name of Jesus.

15. Let the Lord God of Elijah, arise with a strong hand against every

spirit wife / husband and all the powers of sexual perversion, in the name of Jesus.

16. I break the hold of any evil power over my life, in Jesus' name.

17. I nullify every effect of the bite of sexual perversion upon my life, in the name of Jesus.

18. Every evil stranger and all satanic deposits in my life, I command you to be paralyzed and to get out of my life, in the name of Jesus.

19. Holy Ghost fire, purge my life completely, in the name of Jesus.

20. I claim my complete deliverance from the spirit of fornication and sexual immorality, in the name of Jesus.

21. Let my eyes be delivered from lust, in the name of Jesus.

22. As from today, let my eyes be controlled by the Holy Spirit, in the name of Jesus.

23. Holy Ghost fire, fall upon my eyes and burn to ashes every evil force and all satanic power controlling my eyes, in Jesus' name.

24. I move from bondage to liberty in every area of my life, in the name of Jesus.

25. Thank God for answers to your prayers.

ATTACKING THE ENEMY OF YOUR CALLING

Isaiah 59:19

Specifically designed for ministers. To be used when:
- *Things are not moving in your ministry.*
- *There is a satanic gang-up in your ministry.*
- *Your ministerial life is being attacked by disappointments, frustrations and division.*
- *Signs and wonders completely elude your ministry.*
- *You are unable to focus your attention on what God expects you to do.*
- *You want to sharpen your spiritual sword.*

You must be wary of the fact that the enemy is all out to frustrate your calling, but the moment you resist him through aggressive prayer, God would be at hand to bail you out.

2 Timothy 4:5: *"But watch thou in all things, endure afflictions, do the work of an Evangelist, make full proof of your Ministry."*

In the epistles, Paul the Apostle often encourages his readers to fulfil their Ministry e.g. Col. 4:17. In his letter to his son Timothy, he gives him three keys to a successful ministry.

Key 1: Watch thou in all things. Jesus said we must watch and pray (Matt. 26:41). This means there is no room for slumber or resting. We must be alert. The Bible says, "be sober, be vigilant; because your adversary the devil, as a roaring lion, walketh about seeking whom he may devour" (1 Peter 5:8). We have to make sure we do not give the devil a foothold in our lives. We must examine ourselves daily whether we are still in the faith (2 Corinthians 13:5). We have to live holy and blameless lives because our God is holy.

Key 2: Endure afflictions. Persecution will always arise because of the work of God. Jesus said, "in the world you shall have tribulation but be of good cheer; I have overcome the world" (John 16:37). This is a promise of tribulation and affliction, but we must bear it and encourage ourselves so we can grow unto maturity (James 1:4 NIV)

Key 3: Do the work of an evangelist. Whatever the Lord has called you to do, make sure you labour to fulfil it. You might not be an evangelist,. Your Ministry could be teaching, singing or church planting. Whatever it is, you must work at it. You must take it more serious than you take your secular job.

In the parable of the unfaithful servant (Matthew 24:45-51), we see a careless man who did not fulfil his call being thrown where there was weeping and gnashing of teeth!

Beloved, as we use these three keys, I pray the Lord will fortify our inner man with fire so we can attack the enemies of our calling.

● CONFESSION

Matt. 16:18: *And I say also unto thee, That thou art Peter, and upon this rock I will build my church; and the gates of hell shall not prevail against it.*

● PRAISE WORSHIP

1. I destroy the power of every satanic arrest in my life, in the name of Jesus.

2. All satanic-arresting agents, release me, in the name of Jesus.

3. I command every spiritual contamination in my life to receive cleansing by the blood of Jesus.

4. Let the brush of the Lord scrub out every dirty in my spiritual pipe, in the name of Jesus.

5. I destroy everything that is representing me in the demonic world with the fire of God, in the name of Jesus.

6. Lord, teach me to die to self.

7. Every rusted spiritual pipe in my life, receive wholeness, in the name of Jesus.

8. I command every power, eating up my spiritual pipe to be roasted, in the name of Jesus.

9. Spirit of the living God, quicken the whole of my being, in the name of Jesus.

10. I command every hole in my spiritual pipe to be closed, in the name of Jesus.

11. O God, stretch me and renew my strength, in the name of Jesus.

12. Holy Spirit, open my eyes to see beyond the visible and make the invisible veal to me, in the name of Jesus.

13. Lord, ignite my calling with Your fire.

14. Let my spiritual pipe receive the strength of God against any contamination, in the name of Jesus.

15. Holy Spirit, open my eyes and let me have a revelation vision of Christ, in the name of Jesus.

16. O Lord, liberate my spirit to follow the leading of the Holy Spirit.

17. I receive heavenly flushing in my spiritual pipe, in Jesus' name.

18. I confess that my spiritual pipe shall be effective throughout my life, in the name of Jesus.

19. Holy Spirit, teach me to pray through problems instead of praying about them, in the name of Jesus.

20. O Lord, deliver me from the lies I tell myself.

21. Every evil spiritual padlock and chain hindering my spiritual growth, be roasted, in the name of Jesus.

22. I rebuke every spirit of spiritual deafness and blindness in my life, in the name of Jesus.

23. O Lord, deliver me from the lies the enemy tells me.

24. O Lord, empower me to resist satan so that he would flee from me.

25. I bind the strongman behind my spiritual blindness and deafness and paralyse his operations in my life, in Jesus' name.

26. I anoint my eyes and my ears with the blood of Jesus.

27. I choose to believe the report of the Lord and no other, in the name of Jesus.

28. Let the fire of the Holy Spirit melt my resistance, in Jesus' name.

29. O Lord, restore my spiritual eyes and ears.

30. Lord, anoint my eyes and my ears that they may see and hear wondrous things from heaven.

31. Let the fire of the Holy Spirit smash my pride, in Jesus' name.

32. O Lord, anoint me to pray without ceasing.

33. I send the fire of God to my eyes and ears to melt away every satanic deposit, in the name of Jesus.

34. Let my spiritual eyes and ears be wide open, in the name of Jesus.

35. In the name of Jesus, I capture every power behind all my spiritual blindness and deafness.

36. Let my spiritual sight and ear hearing drum receive healing, in Jesus' name.

37. Holy Spirit, rain on me now, in the name of Jesus.

38. Holy Spirit, uncover my darkest secrets, in the name of Jesus.

39. You spirit of confusion, loose your hold over my life, in Jesus' name

40. In the power of the Holy Spirit, I defy satan's power, in the name of Jesus.

41. Holy Spirit, pour Your healing power on me, in the name of Jesus.

42. Let the water of life flush out every unwanted stranger in my life, in the name of Jesus.

43. You enemies of the gospel in my life, be paralysed, in the name of Jesus.

44. O Lord, begin to clean away from my life all that do not reflect You.

45. Lord Jesus, nail me to Your cross.

46. I reject every spiritual pollution, in the name of Jesus.

47. Lord Jesus, break me, melt me, mould me, fill me and use me by the power of Your spirit.

48. O Lord, I lose myself in You.

49. Holy Spirit fire, ignite me to the glory of God, in Jesus' name.

50. O Lord, let the anointing of the Holy Spirit break every yoke of backwardness in my life, in the name of Jesus.

51. Let my spirit-man become divine fire, in the name of Jesus.

52. I frustrate every demonic arrest over my spirit-man, in Jesus' name.

53. Let the blood of Jesus remove any retrogressive label from every area of my life, in the name of Jesus.

54. All anti-breakthrough decrees, be revoked, in the name of Jesus.

55. Holy Ghost fire, destroy every satanic garment in my life, in the name of Jesus.

56. O Lord, give unto me the key to good success, so that anywhere I go,

the doors of prosperity will be opened unto me.

57. Let every wicked house constructed against me be demolished, in the name of Jesus.

58. Let the road close against every unprofitable visitation in my life, in the name of Jesus.

59. O Lord, establish me a holy person unto You.

60. O Lord, let the anointing to excel in my spiritual and physical life fall on me.

61. I shall not serve my enemies; my enemies shall bow down to me, in the name of Jesus.

62. I bind every desert and all poverty spirits in my life, in Jesus' name.

63. I reject the anointing of non-achievement in my handiwork, in the name of Jesus.

64. I pull down all strongholds erected against my progress, in the name of Jesus.

65. I recall all my blessings thrown into the water, the forest, any satanic bank, in the name of Jesus.

66. Holy Spirit, control my ability to frame my words, in Jesus' name.

67. I cut down the roots of all problems in my life, in Jesus' name.

68. Let all satanic scorpions be rendered stingless in every area of my life, in the name of Jesus.

69. Let all demonic serpents be rendered harmless in every area of my life, in the name of Jesus.

70. I declare with my mouth that nothing shall be impossible with me, in the name of Jesus.

71. Let the camp of the enemy be put in disarray, in Jesus' name.

72. Spiritual parasites in my life, be disgraced, in the name of Jesus.

73. Let all my Herod receive spiritual decay, in the name of Jesus.

74. O Lord, let Your favour and that of man encompass me this year, in the name Jesus.

75. Let all evil worms in any area of my life die, in the name of Jesus.
76. I reject any demonic limitation on my progress, in Jesus' name.
77. Let all evil handwriting against me be paralysed, in Jesus' name.
78. I reject the spirit of the tail, and I choose the spirit of the head, in the name of Jesus.
79. Let all those circulating my name for evil be disgraced, in the name of Jesus.
80. Lord, put into my hand the gift that will elevate my calling, in the name of Jesus.
81. Let all evil friends make mistakes that would expose them, in the name of Jesus.
82. I will not lose my calling, in the name of Jesus.
83. Let the strongmen from both sides of my family destroy themselves, in the name of Jesus.
84. Lord, teach me to be crucified with You.
85. Let not Your peace depart from me, O Lord.
86. I command every blockage in my spiritual pipe to be cleared, in the name of Jesus.
87. I refuse to wear the garment of tribulation and sorrow, in the name of Jesus.
88. Let every rebellion flee from my heart, in the name of Jesus.
89. O Lord, let the spirit that flees from sin incubate my life.
90. Let the secrets of hidden and open enemies be revealed, in the name of Jesus.
91. I claim all my rights now, in the name of Jesus.
92. I command every satanic net to receive destruction, in Jesus' name
93. Holy Ghost, grant me a glimpse of Your glory now, in Jesus' name.
94. O Lord, create in me a clean heart by Your power.
95. O Lord, renew a right spirit within me.

96. Holy Ghost, pour the Father's jealousy upon me now, in the name of Jesus.

97. I renounce all rights to anger, in the name of Jesus.

98. Holy Ghost, quicken me, in the name of Jesus.

99. O Lord, remove from me every root of irritation that keeps anger alive in me.

100. Holy Ghost, breathe on me now, in the name of Jesus.

101. I reject all thoughts that I will never change, in Jesus' name.

102. Holy Ghost, fill me that I might bring forth healing power, in the name of Jesus.

103. O Lord, produce in me the power of self-control and gentleness.

104. O Lord, I thank You for promoting me.

UPROOTING THE TREE OF NON-ACHIEVEMENT

Matthew 3:10

These are prayers to dissolve:
- *Profitless hard-work and fruitless efforts.*
- *Constant frustrations and failures in achieving anything in life.*
- *Financial coffins.*
- *Satanic embargo on progress.*
- *The tortoise and snail anointing, i.e., sluggish progress.*
- *Also for those who have been fishing and catching nothing in the ocean of life.*
- *Use when you observe that there is little or nothing to show for living.*

God is ready to assist you to uproot every tree of non-achievement in your life, provided you too are ready to do battle against it in prayer.

Eph. 2:10: *"For we are his workmanship, created in Christ Jesus unto good works which God hath before ordained that we should walk in them."*

God is not the author of failure! Everything God created was good. When He created man, the Bible says it was very good. You are God's creation! You are His workmanship. You are His master piece. You are the crown of everything God created.

When God created man, he created him in His own image and after His own likeness. He gave man dominion over all creation (Gen. 1: 26-30). He made him a little lower than the Elohim (Psalm 8:5). He made Him to reign in life by Christ Jesus (Rev. 5:10). He has created us to show forth His Praise (1 Peter 2:9).

We cannot reflect His glory when we fail. We cannot reflect His glory in lack and poverty. When society calls you a failure, you are not walking in the path God has made for you.

God's work cannot be spoiled or ruined. We need to get back to our Maker so that He will uproot every tree of non-achievement in our lives. Every failure and poverty mentality has to go. He, the master potter will remould/reshape our lives so we can reflect His glory.

• CONFESSIONS

Gal. 3:13-14: *Christ hath redeemed us from the curse of the law, being made a curse for us: for it is written, Cursed is every one that hangeth on a tree: That the blessing of Abraham might come on the Gentiles through Jesus Christ; that we might receive the promise of the Spirit through faith.*

Matt. 3:11: *I indeed baptize you with water unto repentance: but he that cometh after me is mightier than I, whose shoes I am not worthy to bear: he shall baptize you with the Holy Ghost, and with fire:*

Col. 1:13: *Who hath delivered us from the power of darkness, and hath translated us into the kingdom of his dear Son:*

Col. 2:15: *And having spoiled principalities and powers, he made a shew of them openly, triumphing over them in it.*

2 Tim. 4:18: *And the Lord shall deliver me from every evil work, and will preserve me unto his heavenly kingdom: to whom be glory for ever and ever. Amen.*

Heb. 2:15: *And deliver them who through fear of death were all their lifetime subject to bondage.*

Ps. 27:2: *When the wicked, even mine enemies and my foes, came upon me to eat up my flesh, they stumbled and fell.*

Note: ***Prayers of uprooting the tree of non-achievement have to be done aggressively and violently. No stone should be left unturned. You must hate the spirit of non-achievement with perfect hatred.***

• PRAISE WORSHIP

1. Thank God for making the provision for deliverance from any form of bondage.

2. Confess your sins and those of your ancestors, especially those sins linked to evil powers.

3. I cover myself with the blood of Jesus.

4. I release myself from any inherited bondage, in Jesus' name.

5. O Lord, send Your axe of fire to the foundation of my life and destroy every evil plantation there.

6. Let the blood of Jesus flush out from my system every inherited satanic deposit, in the name of Jesus.

7. I release myself from the grip of any problem transferred into my life from the womb, in the name of Jesus.

8. I break and loose myself from every inherited evil covenant, in the name of Jesus.

9. I break and loose myself from every inherited evil curse, in the name of Jesus.

10. I vomit every evil consumption that I have been fed with as a child, in the name of Jesus.

11. I command all foundational strongmen attached to my life to be paralysed, in the name of Jesus.

12. Let any rod of the wicked rising up against my family line be rendered impotent for my sake, in the name of Jesus.

13. I cancel all the consequences of any evil local name attached to my person, in the name of Jesus.

14. You evil foundational plantations, come out of my life with all your roots, in the name of Jesus.

15. I break and loose myself from every form of demonic bewitching, in the name of Jesus.

16. I release myself from every evil domination and control, in the name of Jesus.

17. Let every gate opened to the enemy by my foundation be closed forever with the blood of Jesus.

18. Lord Jesus, walk back into every second of my life and deliver me where I need deliverance, heal me where I need healing, transform me where I need transformation.

19. Let every evil imagination against me wither from the source, in the name of Jesus.

20. All those laughing me to scorn shall witness my testimony, in the name of Jesus.

21. Let all the destructive plan of the enemies aimed against me blow up in their faces, in the name of Jesus.

22. Let my point of ridicule be converted to a source of miracle, in the name of Jesus.

23. Let all powers sponsoring evil decisions against me be disgraced, in the name of Jesus.

24. Let the stubborn strongman delegated against me fall down to the ground and become impotent, in the name of Jesus.

25. Let the stronghold of every spirit of Korah, Dathan and Abiram militating against me be smashed to pieces, in Jesus' name.

26. Let every spirit of Balaam hired to curse me fall after the order of Balaam, in the name of Jesus.

27. Let every spirit of Sanballat and Tobiah planning evil against me receive the stones of fire, in the name of Jesus.

28. Let every spirit of Egypt fall after the order of Pharaoh, in the name of Jesus.

29. Let every spirit of Herod be disgraced, in the name of Jesus.

30. Let every spirit of Goliath receive the stones of fire, in the name of Jesus.

31. Let every spirit of Pharaoh fall into the Red Sea of its own making, in the name of Jesus.

32. Let all satanic manipulations aimed at changing my destiny be frustrated, in the name of Jesus.

33. Let all unprofitable broadcasters of my goodness be silenced, in the name of Jesus.

34. Let all leaking bags and pockets be sealed up, in Jesus' name.

35. Let all evil monitoring eyes fashioned against me be blind, in the name of Jesus.

36. Let every evil effect of any strange touches be removed from my life, in the name of Jesus.

37. I command all demonic reverse gears installed to hinder my progress to be roasted, in the name of Jesus.

38. Any evil sleep undertaken to harm me, be converted to dead sleep, in the name of Jesus.

39. Let all weapons and devices of the oppressors and tormentors be rendered impotent, in the name of Jesus.

40. Let the fire of God destroy every power operating any spiritual vehicle working against me, in the name of Jesus.

41. Let all evil advice given against my favour crash and disintegrate, in the name of Jesus.

42. Let the wind, the sun and the moon run contrary to every demonic presence in my environment, in the name of Jesus.

43. O you devourers, vanish from my labour, in the name of Jesus.

44. Let every tree planted by fear in my life dry up from the roots, in the name of Jesus.

45. I cancel all the enchantments, curses and spells that are against me, in the name of Jesus.

46. Let all iron-like curses break, in the name of Jesus.

47. Let divine tongues of fire roast any evil tongue that is against me, in the name of Jesus.

48. O Lord, I thank You very much for everything You have done for me through these prayer points.

SPIRITUAL SANITATION

Matthew 21:12

Many Christians are suffering from ancestral burdens which hinders spiritual growth. This programme is designed:

- *To help you obtain deliverance from foundational contamination and bondage.*
- *To help you obtain freedom from ancestral yokes and burdens.*
- *To clean up the unprofitable spiritual background militating against physical and spiritual progress.*

Jesus is always in the business of driving away all strange elements undertaking satanic and destructive transactions in the body, soul and spirit. He would do no less for you as you cry unto Him.

1 Pet 1:15-16: *"But as he which hath called you is holy, so be ye holy in all manner of conversation; Because it is written, Be ye holy; for I am holy."*

The Lord, knoweth them that are His! Are you a professor or a believer? Do you just claim to be a Christian, speak Christianity ('Praise God'. 'Hallelujah'. 'Thank You Jesus'.) and go through the motions others around you are going through.

God cannot be mocked. The scripture says the Lord **KNOWETH** them that are His. Does God know you? The greatest hindrance to being known by God is iniquity. Iniquity separates from God. "Behold, the Lord's hand is not shortened, that it cannot save; neither his ear heavy, that it cannot heal: But your iniquities have separated between you and your God, and your sins have hid his face from you, that he cannot hear (Isaiah 59:1,2).

The Bible says we should depart from iniquity. Also Paul says "If a man will purge himself from there, he shall be a vessel unto honour, sanctified, and meet for the master's use, and prepared unto every good work."

Prayers for spiritual sanitation, are intended to purge us, from the things that separate us from God. As you pray these prayer points, the blessings of purging stated in 2 Timothy 2:21 will manifest in your life, and you will become

- a vessel of honour
- sanctified
- usable to God
- prepared unto every good work, a workman that needs not be ashamed

• CONFESSION

2 Tim. 2:21: *If a man therefore purge himself from these, he shall be a vessel unto honour, sanctified, and meet for the master's use, and prepared unto every good work.*

• PRAISE WORSHIP

1. I release myself from every ancestral demonic pollution, in the name of Jesus.

2. I release myself from every demonic pollution emanating from my parents' religion, in the name of Jesus.

3. I release myself from every demonic pollution emanating from my past involvement in any demonic religion, in the name of Jesus.

4. I break and loose myself from every idol and related associations, in the name of Jesus.

5. I release myself from every dream pollution, in Jesus' name.

6. Let every satanic attack against my life in my dreams be converted to victory, in the name of Jesus.

7. Let all rivers, trees, forests, evil companions, evil pursuers, visions of dead relatives, snakes, spirit husbands, spirit wives, and masquerades manipulated against me in the dream, be completely destroyed by the power in the blood of the Lord Jesus.

8. I command every evil plantation in my life to come out with all your roots, in the name of Jesus! (*Lay your hands on your stomach and keep repeating the emphasized area.*)

9. All evil strangers in my body, come out of your hiding places, in the name of Jesus.

10. I disconnect any conscious or unconscious linkage with demonic caterers, in the name of Jesus.

11. Let all avenues of eating or drinking spiritual poisons be closed, in the name of Jesus.

12. I cough out and vomit any food eaten from the table of the devil, in the name of Jesus. (*Cough and vomit them out in faith. Prime the expulsion.*)

13. Let all negative materials circulating in my bloodstream, be evacuated, in the name of Jesus.

14. I drink the blood of Jesus. (*Physically swallow and drink it in faith. Keep doing this for some time.*)

15. *Lay one hand on your head and the other on your stomach or navel and begin to pray like this:* Holy Ghost fire, burn from the top of my head to the sole of my feet. *Begin to mention every organ of your body; your kidneys, liver, intestines, blood, etc. You must not rush at this level, because the fire will actually come and you may start feeling the heat.*

16. I cut myself off from every spirit of . . . (*mention the name of your place of birth*), in the name of Jesus.

17. I cut myself off from every tribal spirit and curse, in Jesus' name.

18. I cut myself off from every territorial spirit and curse, in the name of Jesus.

19. Holy Ghost fire, purge my life, in the name of Jesus.

20. I claim my complete deliverance from the spirit of . . . (*mention those things you do not desire in your life*), in the name of Jesus.

21. I break the hold of any evil power over my life, in Jesus' name.

22. Thank God for answers to your prayer.

DELIVERANCE FROM EVIL INHERITANCE

Obadiah 1:17

- *For those who are suffering from inherited sicknesses*
- *For those seeking divine touch to heal them from genetic diseases.*
- *For those who would like to break themselves free from any evil family pattern.*

As you climb your own mount Zion through violent and aggressive prayer, a new lease of life awaits you following perfect deliverance from evil inheritance.

The Bible says, *"Christ has redeemed us from the curse of the law, being made a curse for us:" (Gal. 3:13).*

The problem you are facing right now may not be your own doing. It may be as a result of an evil inheritance which can be in the form of generational or genetic problems. The Bible says that the sin of the father will be visited on his children to the fourth generation and sometimes to the tenth generation. (Read Deuteronomy 5:9,10; Exodus 20:4-6.)

Sickness and genetic diseases can be inherited. A classic example was the case of Gehazi, the servant of Elisha (2 Kings 5:27). Elisha cursed Gehazi saying, "The leprosy of Naaman shall cleave unto thee, and unto thy seed forever. And he went out from his presence a leper as white as snow."

In Deuteronomy 28:15-68, there are 112 curses pronounced by God ranging from sickness to poverty and captivity. These curses will come on a person as a result of disobedience to God's laws.

The good news is that Jesus has redeemed us, He died in our place, He bought us with His precious blood. So these curses cannot affect us again. We need to remove ourselves from every evil inheritance and confess with our mouths that we belong to the family of God.

● CONFESSION

Obad. 1:17: *But upon mount Zion shall be deliverance, and there shall be holiness; and the house of Jacob shall possess their possessions.*

● PRAISE WORSHIP

1. Thank God for making the provision for deliverance from any form of bondage.
2. I release myself from any inherited bondage, in Jesus' name.
3. O Lord, send Your axe of fire to the foundation of my life and destroy every evil plantation there.
4. Let the blood of Jesus flush out from my system every inherited satanic deposit, in the name of Jesus.
5. I release myself from the grip of any problem transferred into my life from the womb, in the name of Jesus.
6. Let the blood of Jesus and the fire of the Holy Ghost cleanse every organ in my body, in the name of Jesus.
7. I break and loose myself from every inherited evil covenant, in the name of Jesus.
8. I break and loose myself from every inherited evil curse, in the name of Jesus.
9. Pray aggressively against the following evil foundations. Pray as follows: You (*pick the under listed one by one*), loose your hold over my life and be purged away from my foundation, in the name of Jesus.

   - evil physical design
   - envious rivalry
   - evil dedication
   - demonic incisions
   - dream pollution
   - demonic sacrifice
   - wrong exposure to sex
   - demonic initiations
   - parental curses
   - demonic blood transfusion
   - demonic alteration of destiny
   - demonic marriage
   - evil laying on of hands
   - fellowship with family idols
   - exposure to evil diviners
   - inherited infirmity

- destructive effect of polygamy   - fellowship with local idols
- unscriptural manners of conception
- fellowship with demonic consultants

10. O Lord, let Your resurrection power come upon my . . . *(be specific)*.

11. I bind every spirit of death operating in my . . . *be specific)*, in the mighty name of Jesus.

12. I command every dead bone in my . . . *(be specific)* to come alive, in the name of Jesus.

13. You evil hand laid on my . . . *(be specific)*, receive the thunder and the fire of God and be roasted, in Jesus' name.

14. I command every evil monitoring gadget fashioned against my . . . *(be specific)* to be destroyed, in the name of Jesus.

15. I breathe in the life of God and I reject every spirit of death and hell, in the name of Jesus.

16. I recover every miracle that I have lost through unbelief, in the name of Jesus.

17. Father, let Your creative power operate afresh in my . . . *(be specific)*, in the name of Jesus.

18. Father, let the fire of the Holy Ghost enter into my bloodstream and cleanse my system, in the name of Jesus.

19. I release my body systems *(be specific)*, from the cage of every household wickedness, in the name of Jesus.

20. Let every information about my body systems *(be specific)*, be erased from every satanic memory, in the name of Jesus.

21. I command every evil plantation in my life, **come out with all your roots, in the name of Jesus**! *(Lay your hands on your stomach and keep repeating the emphasized area.)*

22. You evil strangers in my body, come all the way out of your hiding places, in the name of Jesus.

23. I cough out and vomit any food eaten from the table of the devil, in the

name of Jesus. (*Cough them out and vomit them in faith. Prime the expulsion.*)

24. Let all negative materials circulating in my bloodstream be evacuated, in the name of Jesus.

25. I drink the blood of Jesus. (*Physically swallow and drink it in faith. Keep doing this for some time.*)

26. Lay one hand on your head and the other on your stomach or navel and begin to pray like this: Holy Ghost fire, burn from the top of my head to the sole of my feet. *Begin to mention every organ of your body; your kidney, liver, intestine, blood, etc. You must not rush at this level, because the fire will actually come and you may start feeling the heat.*

27. I cut myself off from every spirit of . . . (*mention the name of your place of birth*), in the name of Jesus.

28. I cut myself off from every tribal spirit and curse, in Jesus' name.

29. I cut myself off from every territorial spirit and curse, in the name of Jesus.

30. Holy Ghost fire, purge my life, in the name of Jesus.

31. I claim my complete deliverance, in the name of Jesus, from the spirit of . . . (*mention those things you do not desire in your life*).

32. I break the hold of any evil power over my life, in Jesus' name.

33. I move from bondage into liberty, in the name of Jesus.

34. I release myself from every inherited disease, in Jesus' name.

35. Let the blood of Jesus correct any inherited defect in my body, in the name of Jesus.

36. Let every abnormality inside my body receive divine correction, in the name of Jesus.

37. Lord Jesus, I thank You for my deliverance.

POWER AGAINST UNREPENTANT HOUSEHOLD WICKEDNESS

Genesis 50:20; Micah 7:6-7; Matthew 10:36
You need these prayer points:
  • *When your strongest opposition is from within your own household.*
  • *When there is a gang-up against you by known enemies.*
  • *When visions, revelations and dreams show that household witches and wizards have vowed to disgrace you.*

It is an established fact in God's word that the enemy's onslaughts against you are best facilitated through your own kindred. Please, watch out and be ready to fight against the household wickedness victimising you.

The Bible says, *"And a man's foes shall be they of his own household"* (Matt. 10:36).

The above verse is clearly indicated in the life of Joseph. Out of envy and jealousy his brothers sold him into slavery. (Gen. 37:7-27). Samson, a Judge in Israel, was bound by members of his household and handed over to his enemies (Judges 15:1-13).

Household wickedness is one singular reason why most black men are in trouble today. Many people are looking for their enemies outside while they are already inside. The household enemy has bound and amputated the destiny of many.

You cannot run away from it. You need to pray violently so that you can be free from its grip. Generally it operates using familiar spirits, demonic names, placental manipulation, hair, etc. as part of its evil strategies.

As you start these prayers God will assist you to pray your way to breakthrough and, like Joseph, you will be able to say, *"But as for you, ye thought evil against me; but God meant it unto good, to bring to pass, as it is this day, to save much people alive"* (Genesis 50:20).

• CONFESSION

Obad. 1:3-4: *The pride of thine heart hath deceived thee, thou that dwellest in the clefts of the rock, whose habitation is high; that saith in his heart, Who shall bring me down to the ground? Though thou exalt thyself as the eagle, and though thou set thy nest among the stars, thence will I bring thee down, saith the LORD.*

• PRAISE WORSHIP

1. Let every evil imagination against me wither away from the root, in the name of Jesus.
2. Those laughing me to scorn shall witness my testimony, in the name of Jesus.
3. Let the destructive plan of the enemies aimed against me blow up in their faces, in the name of Jesus.
4. Let the cause of my ridicule be converted to a source of miracle, in the name of Jesus.
5. Let all powers sponsoring evil decisions against me be disgraced, in the name of Jesus.
6. Let the stubborn strongman delegated against me fall down to the ground and become impotent, in the name of Jesus.
7. Let the stronghold of every spirit of Korah, Dathan and Abiram militating against me, be smashed, in the name of Jesus.
8. Let every spirit of Balaam hired to curse me fall after the order of Balaam, in the name of Jesus.
9. Let every spirit of Sanballat and Tobiah planning evil against me receive the stones of fire, in the name of Jesus.
10. Let every spirit of Egypt fall after the order of Pharaoh, in the name of Jesus.
11. Let every spirit of Herod be disgraced, in the name of Jesus.
12. Let every spirit of Goliath receive the stones of fire, in the name of Jesus.

13. Let every spirit of Pharaoh fall into the Red Sea of their own making, in the name of Jesus.

14. Let all satanic manipulations aimed at changing my destiny be frustrated, in the name of Jesus.

15. Let all unprofitable broadcasters of my goodness be silenced, in the name of Jesus.

16. Let all leaking bags and pockets be sealed up, in Jesus' name.

17. Let all evil monitoring eyes fashioned against me,be blind, in the name of Jesus.

18. Let every evil effect of strange touches be removed from my life, in the name of Jesus.

19. I command every blessing confiscated by witchcraft spirits to be released, in the name of Jesus.

20. I command every blessing confiscated by familiar spirits to be released, in the name of Jesus.

21. I command every blessing confiscated by ancestral spirits to be released, in the name of Jesus.

22. I command every blessing confiscated by envious enemies to be released, in the name of Jesus.

23. I command every blessing confiscated by satanic agents to be released, in the name of Jesus.

24. I command every blessing confiscated by principalities to be released, in the name of Jesus.

25. I command every blessing confiscated by rulers of darkness to be released, in the name of Jesus.

26. I command every blessing confiscated by evil powers to be released, in the name of Jesus.

27. I command all my blessings confiscated by spiritual wickedness in the heavenly places to be released, in the name of Jesus.

28. I command all demonic reverse gears installed to hinder my progress, to be roasted, in the name of Jesus.

29. Any evil sleep undertaken to harm me should be converted to dead sleep, in the name of Jesus.

30. Let all the weapons and devices of my oppressors and tormentors be rendered impotent, in the name of Jesus.

31. Let the fire of God destroy the power operating any spiritual vehicle working against me, in the name of Jesus.

32. Let all the evil advice given against my favour crash and disintegrate, in the name of Jesus.

33. Let all the eaters of flesh and drinkers of blood stumble and fall, in the name of Jesus.

34. I command all stubborn pursuers to pursue themselves, in the name of Jesus.

35. Let the wind, the sun and the moon run contrary to every demonic presence in my environment, in the name of Jesus.

36. You devourers, vanish from my labour, in the name of Jesus.

37. Let every tree planted by fear in my life dry up to the roots, in the name of Jesus.

38. I cancel all enchantments, curses and spells that are against me, in the name of Jesus.

39. Let all iron-like curses break, in the name of Jesus.

40. Let divine tongues of fire roast any evil tongue against me, in the name of Jesus.

41. Let all pronouncements uttered against me by poisonous tongues be nullified, in the name of Jesus.

42. I cut myself off from every territorial spirit, in Jesus' name.

43. I loose myself from any power of witchcraft and bewitchment, in the name of Jesus.

44. I loose myself from every satanic bondage, in the name of Jesus.

45. I cancel the power of all curses upon my head, in Jesus' name.

46. I bind the strongman over my life, in the name of Jesus.

47. I bind the strongman over my family, in the name of Jesus.

48. I bind the strongman over my blessings, in the name of Jesus.

49. I bind the strongman over my business, in the name of Jesus.

50. I command the armour of the strongman to be roasted completely, in the name of Jesus.

51. I command all curses issued against me to be smashed and broken, in the name of Jesus.

52. I separate my life from all evil idols present in my place of birth, in the name of Jesus.

53. I separate my life from all evil streams present in my place of birth, in the name of Jesus.

54. I separate my life from all evil shrines present in my place of birth, in the name of Jesus.

55. Let all agents banking my blessings release them now, in the name of Jesus.

56. I destroy every evil peace, evil agreement, evil unity, evil love, evil happiness, evil understanding, evil communication and evil gathering fashioned against my life, in the name of Jesus.

57. Let every power of the oppressor rise up against each other, in the name of Jesus.

58. I disband all evil hosts gathered against my progress, in the name of Jesus.

59. Let the sorrow of the enemy upon the progress of my life remain permanent, in the name of Jesus.

60. Let all drinkers of blood and eaters of flesh hunting for my life begin to stumble and fall, in the name of Jesus.

61. I paralyse all problem expanders, in the name of Jesus.

62. I paralyse all forces behind delayed-miracles, in Jesus' name.

63. Begin to thank God.

SPEAKING DESTRUCTION UNTO EVIL GROWTH

Matthew 21:17-22

- *To dissolve fibroid, cancer and ovarian cysts and satanic growths deposited in the womb by spirit husbands.*
- *To clear all impediments in the birth canal.*

Most people do not know that the spoken word is the most powerful weapon in the world. You have the inalienable right as a child of God to use this weapon positively against the spread of evil growth and development in your life.

Jer. 23:29: *"Is not my word like as a fire? saith the LORD; and like a hammer that breaketh the rock in pieces?"*

You may say: How can my WORDS destroy this cancer or this fibroid? It is impossible. Why can't the pastor just pray for me? Why doesn't he lay hands on me or anoint me with oil?

Beloved, relax and let your mind be at rest. There is power in the word of God and God has said He will make His word in your mouth as fire (Jer. 5:14). The Bible records that Jesus, our example, healed people with His word. "When the even was come, they brought unto him many that were possessed with devils: and he cast out the spirits with his word, and healed all that were sick" (Matt. 8:16). Psalm 107:20 also says, "He sent his word and healed them and delivered them from their destruction." There is healing and deliverance in the WORD of God. The Bible says, "The weapons of our warfare are not carnal but mighty through God to the pulling down of strongholds" (2 Cor.10:4).

As you start this prayer programme, God's word in your mouth will function as fire and like a hammer and every evil growth will be supernaturally destroyed.

• CONFESSIONS

Ps. 31:2: *Bow down thine ear to me; deliver me speedily: be thou my strong rock, for an house of defence to save me.*

Isa. 58:8: *Then shall thy light break forth as the morning, and thine health shall spring forth speedily: and thy righteousness shall go before thee; the glory of the LORD shall be thy rereward.*

Luke 18:8: *I tell you that he will avenge them speedily. Nevertheless when the Son of man cometh, shall he find faith on the earth?*

Ps. 102:2: *Hide not thy face from me in the day when I am in trouble; incline thine ear unto me: in the day when I call answer me speedily.*

Jer. 1:12: *Then said the LORD unto me, Thou hast well seen: for I will hasten my word to perform it.*

Jer. 29:11: *For I know the thoughts that I think toward you, saith the LORD, thoughts of peace, and not of evil, to give you an expected end.*

Ps. 56:9: *When I cry unto thee, then shall mine enemies turn back: this I know; for God is for me.*

Mal. 4:2: *But unto you that fear my name shall the Sun of righteousness arise with healing in his wings; and ye shall go forth, and grow up as calves of the stall.*

Gal. 3:13-14: *Christ hath redeemed us from the curse of the law, being made a curse for us: for it is written, Cursed is every one that hangeth on a tree: That the blessing of Abraham might come on the Gentiles through Jesus Christ; that we might receive the promise of the Spirit through faith.*

Col. 2:14-15: *Blotting out the handwriting of ordinances that was against us, which was contrary to us, and took it out of the way, nailing it to his cross; And having spoiled principalities and powers, he made a shew of them openly, triumphing over them in it.*

Matt. 8:17: *That it might be fulfilled which was spoken by Esaias the prophet, saying, Himself took our infirmities, and bare our sicknesses.*

Rom. 16:20: *And the God of peace shall bruise Satan under your feet shortly. The grace of our Lord Jesus Christ be with you. Amen.*

Matt. 3:10: *And now also the axe is laid unto the root of the trees: therefore every tree which bringeth not forth good fruit is hewn down, and cast into the fire.*

1 Jn. 3:8: *He that committeth sin is of the devil; for the devil sinneth from the beginning. For this purpose the Son of God was manifested, that he might destroy the works of the devil.*

2 Tim. 4:18: *And the Lord shall deliver me from every evil work, and will preserve me unto his heavenly kingdom: to whom be glory for ever and ever. Amen.*

● **PRAISE WORSHIP**

1. *Spend quality time to stand against the effects of the evil fruits listed hereunder. Take one fruit at a time and be violent. If you notice any reaction, stop and deal thoroughly with it before you proceed to the next one. Pray aggressively as follows:* I speak destruction unto the fruits of . . . , in the name of Jesus.

   - blood pollution   - polygamous contamination
   - parental curses   - peppery arrows
   - open curses and threats   - marital disgrace
   - spiritual confiscation   - dream harassment
   - periodic problems   - infirmity
   - enchantment ·   - rejection

2. I recover every organ in my body from the hands of household wickedness, in the name of Jesus.

3. Every evil grip upon my life, loose your hold, in the name of Jesus.

4. I overthrow every demonic judgement directed against any organ in my body, in the name of Jesus.

5. Holy Ghost fire, destroy every garment of reproach in my life, in the name of Jesus.

6. I refuse every evil design and label placed upon my life, in the name of Jesus.

7. Any material eaten conscious or unconscious from the table of the enemy come out of my life now, in the name of Jesus.

8. I dismantle every demonic opposition to my marriage, in the name of Jesus.

9. I cast all the spirits behind my problems into the fire of judgement, in the name of Jesus.

10. Let the blood, the fire and the living water of the Most High God wash my system clean from:
    - unprofitable growth in my womb   - evil plantation
    - evil deposits from spirit husband   - satanic poisons
    - evil stamps, labels and ink
    - impurities acquired from parental contamination

11. Let every organ of my body become too hot for any evil to inhabit, in the name of Jesus.

12. Every evil growth in my life, be uprooted by fire, in Jesus' name.

13. Let my body reject every evil habitation, in the mighty name of our Lord Jesus Christ.

14. I expel any satanic deposit in my intestine, in the name of Jesus.

15. I expel any satanic deposit in my reproductive organs, in the name of Jesus.

16. I expel any satanic deposit in my womb, in the name of Jesus.

17. You foreign hand laid on my womb, release me, in Jesus' name.

18. Let a creative miracle take place in my womb and reproductive system, in the name of Jesus.

19. Father, I ask You in the name of Jesus Christ, to send out Your angels and have them unearth and destroy all evil storage vessels fashioned against me.

20. I bind and render useless every strongman assigned to my womb, reproductive system and marital life, in the name of Jesus.

21. God who quickens the dead, quicken my womb and reproductive system, in the name of Jesus.

22. I release myself from the hold of the spirits of sterility, infertility and fear, in the name of Jesus.

23. All spirits of fornication, come out of my womb with all your roots, in

the mighty name of our Lord Jesus.

24. All spirits of sexual perversion, come out of my womb with all your roots, in the mighty name of Jesus.

25. I reverse every evil manipulation done against my womb using my menstrual pads or period, in the name of Jesus.

26. I release myself from every inherited womb malformation, in the name of Jesus.

27. Let the blood of Jesus sanitise my womb and anoint it, in the name of Jesus.

28. I break every anti-marriage and anti-pregnancy curse, in the name of Jesus.

29. Lord Jesus, I thank You for given me testimonies on this issue.

POWER AGAINST EVIL MARITAL MAGNETS

Job 11:4-20

- **To stop the activities of satanic intruders into marriage.**

As you open up your heart, the Holy Ghost fire would purge out every evil marital magnet designed by the enemy to ruin your marriage.

Matthew 19:6: *"Wherefore they are no more twain but one flesh. What therefore God has joined together let no man put asunder."* God intends that a man and his wife should live together in love and unity for a life time. The marriage covenant is not to be broken for any reason.

God's original plan is that only death should separate a couple.

However, there are many forces that seek to destroy marriage. These forces can be called anti-marriage forces. They operate by planting evil marital magnets in the home.

Such magnets include activities of strange men/women, promiscuity by either partner, 'Jezebel' activities, anger and control by ungodly in-laws.

The Bible says let him that is afflicted pray. (James 5:13). If you are experiencing any of these problems pray these prayer points with holy madness. As long as you are the first and properly married wife of the man, God will fight for you!

- **CONFESSIONS**

Jer. 1:10: *See, I have this day set thee over the nations and over the kingdoms, to root out, and to pull down, and to destroy, and to throw down, to build, and to plant.*

Gen. 1:26: *And God said, Let us make man in our image, after our likeness: and let them have dominion over the fish of the sea, and over the fowl of the air, and over the cattle, and over all the earth, and over every creeping thing that creepeth upon the earth.*

Gen. 3:15: *And I will put enmity between thee and the woman, and between thy seed and her seed; it shall bruise thy head, and thou shalt bruise his heel.*

Luke 10:19: *Behold, I give unto you power to tread on serpents and scorpions, and over all the power of the enemy: and nothing shall by any means hurt you.*

Rev. 12:9-10: *And the great dragon was cast out, that old serpent, called the Devil, and Satan, which deceiveth the whole world: he was cast out into the earth, and his angels were cast out with him. And I heard a loud voice saying in heaven, Now is come salvation, and strength, and the kingdom of our God, and the power of his Christ: for the accuser of our brethren is cast down, which accused them before our God day and night.*

With my heart I believe God. I believe His word and I confess with my mouth that He is Jehovah God who created the heaven and the earth. I confess that He is the beginning and the end of all things. He was, He is and forever shall be. With God, I believe nothing shall be impossible, God has spoken once and twice I have Heard this that all power in heaven and or earth belongs to Him.

As I say this prayer and confess the word of God, I command all the spirits of distractions and hindrances to be bound, in the name of Jesus. I cast away from me every spirit of tiredness, weakness and defeat. In the mighty name of Jesus Christ, I command every knee of things in heaven, on earth and in the seas that are against this prayer to know and be bound.

I ask for the presence of God to overshadow me as the dew of Hermon and His anointing oil, which breaks the yokes, to fall on my head and run through me to wrought great deliverance. As it is written, it has to pass today that the burden of the spirit husband/wife shall be taken off my shoulders and his/her yoke off my neck and the yoke shall be destroyed by the reason of the anointing oil.

By the grace of God, I have accepted Jesus Christ and I am now saved. Jesus loves me, he shed his blood for me and washed me in that same blood, bought me back from the hand of my strong enemy and redeemed me. I am a beneficiary of every work of redemption ans restoration which Jesus finished on the cross of calvary through death Jesus destroyed him who had the power of death. Now, I shall not die but live because Jesus has become my deliverer, my defender, my protector, my high tower, my refuse, my victory, the author and the finisher of my faith. Jesus has set me free and I have received deliverance. I have been delivered from the law of sin and death. God has translated my life from the kingdom of darkness into the kingdom of His dear own son.

All power in heaven and on earth belongs to my Lord Jesus. Jesus Christ has given me authority in his name against all powers of darkness and their operations. Now, in the name of Jesus, I overcome you spirit husband/wife by the blood of Jesus. I am born of God and I have overcome the world by my faith. I am a child of light, darkness cannot overcome or comprehend me. I command all forces of spiritual marriage fashioned against me to be struck with the light of God. Light and darkness cannot dwell together, I use the word of God as my light to break the spell of the spirit husband/wife oppressing me through darkness.

In the name of Jesus Christ, I reject and break every link with the kingdom of darkness through any conscious/unconscious relationship with any spirit husband/wife. It is written, "Every tree not planted by God shall be rooted out." I uproot and destroy all evil spiritual marriages enforced against me in the kingdom of darkness. I am bought with a price. Jesus paid the price through His shed blood. The Bible says, God already predestined me to belong ti Him before the foundations of the world were laid. Jesus Christ is now my husband, Am married to Him eternally. The Bible says, whosoever defiles the temple of God shall be destroyed. I command destruction upon the spirit husband/ wife that has been stubbornly defiling me, the temple of God.

In the name of Jesus, let every spiritual dowry ever paid on me by the spirit husband be made of no effect again in my life. Let any legal ground in the form of agreement, promises, vows and covenants made on my behalf or by myself, be nullified by the precious blood of Jesus, old things have passed away; behold all things have become new. I renounce and reject every evil name given to me by the spirit husband/wife. It is written, a white stone shall be given to me, and on it is written a new name that no one else knows. I cast to the bottomless pit any evil spirit transferred into me through my contact with the spirit husband/wife physically or in my dreams. I break every rule and law binding me to him/her with the blood of Jesus. I set on fire any wedding certificate, wedding ring, gown and gifts. Let every spirit child that is between us roast now, in the name of Jesus. Let the blood of Jesus that cleanses from all impurities purge my body of every sexual pollution and contamination of the spirit husband/ wife.

Every covenant that is strongly binding me to any evil spiritual marriage, be broken. For it is written, God has made a new covenant with me and all others are old and annulled. Every curse placed upon my body, my business, my property, my home and marriage by the spirit husband/wife, loose your hold now by the blood of Jesus. Who shall curse him that the Lord has blessed. It is written, God will bless them that bless me and curse them that curse me.

Whosoever rolls a stone, it shall fall on him; and whosoever dug a pit shall fall therein. Therefore, I return to the senders all curse placed upon me and anything that pertains to me, in the name of Jesus. Every tongue rising up against me in the kingdom of darkness, I condemn you in the judgement of God.

There is no divination or enchantment against me. Let every physical and spiritual activities of land and marine witchcraft be completely wiped off by the blood of Jesus.

Let every water associated with activities of spiritual husband/wife in my dreams be polluted with the blood of Jesus. Let the fire of God destroy every workmanship of the devil fashioned against me through the operations of the spirit husband/wife. Every attack and operations of the demons of spiritual marriages lunched through eating in the dream, because impotent and of no effect. I shall eat a deadly thing and it shall not harm me.

In the name of Jesus, I use the blood of Jesus to set a boundary between me and the spirit husband/wife. Henceforth let no spirit husband/wife trouble me for I bear in my body the mark of the precious blood of the Lamb of

God. I command that the spirit husband/wife cannot steal, or kill, or destroy any good thing in my life any longer. God has raised me up to sit with Jesus Christ in heavenly places, far above principalities, powers, all dominions and all their thrones and kingdoms whether visible or invisible. Jesus is the head of all principalities and powers, and I am complete in him who is the head of all things. All the powers of darkness are under my feet. I use the power in the blood and in the name of Jesus to put a stop to all disturbances and oppressions in my dreams. I forbid all forms of sexual attacks, eating, drinking, swimming, wandering, being naked or bathing in my dreams. I shall be far from oppression and from terror, for it shall not come near me. God is my dwelling place, so shall I dwell in safety. I will always lie down, sleep and awake for the Lord sustains me. Therefore shall I not fear the powers of the night.

I prophesy that every good thing the spirit husband/wife has chased away or diverted from reaching me shall restored the ones he/she has stolen, killed or destroyed shall come back to life in my life, for Jesus has come to give me abundance of life and to restore that which the locust, the cankerworm, the palmer-worm and the grasshoppers have eaten and destroyed. Therefore I confess and receive divine restoration in my marriage, in my health, in my finances in my spiritual well-being and in all other areas of my life.

I confess and possess my total deliverance from the bondage of the spirit husband/wife, and I seal my divine freedom with the blood of Jesus.

● **PRAISE WORSHIP**

1. Thank God because He is going to intervene in your marriage through these prayer points.

2. I destroy anything that is going to stand between me and my prayers now, in the name of Jesus.

3. The anointing to pray to the point of breakthrough in my marriage, fall upon me now, in the name of Jesus.

4. Lord Jesus, I invite You to come to my aid in every difficult situation in my marriage.

5. All my matrimonial properties, which the strange woman sat upon, I withdraw them, in the name of Jesus.

6. I withdraw peace, harmony, unity, love and continuity between my husband and the strange woman, in the name of Jesus.

7. Lord Jesus, let the strange and unholy love affair between my husband and the strange woman die.

8. I withdraw the favour of my husband from the strange woman, in the name of Jesus.

9. I stand against every power of polygamy, in the name of Jesus.

10. All spiritual evil arrows fired from the strange woman presently in my marriage, loose your grip upon my marriage and go back to your sender, in the name of Jesus.

11. Let confusion be the lot of every strange woman militating against my marriage.

12. Let irreparable division be between . . . (mention the name of your husband) and . . . (mention the name of the strange woman if you know it), in the name of Jesus.

13. Angel of God, go right away and disconnect the relationship between my husband and the strange woman, in Jesus' name.

14. Every strange woman militating against my marriage, receive the judgement of God, in the name of Jesus.

15. I nullify every evil judgement that is against me in my marriage, in the name of Jesus.

16. Let all the hindrances to the manifestation of my restoration to my rightful home depart from me and my marriage, in Jesus' name.

17. Lion of Judah, consume every fake lion of the strange woman roaring against my marriage, in the name of Jesus.

18. Thunder and fire of God, begin to scatter to pieces, every stronghold of the strange woman in the heart of my husband, in Jesus' name.

19. You demons energising the relationship between my husband and

any strange woman, be rendered impotent and be roasted by the fire of God, in the name of Jesus.

20. Angels of the living God, brush off the love of the strange woman completely from the heart of my husband, in Jesus' name.

21. Lord Jesus, create a new heart in my husband.

22. Every open door that the strange woman is using to gain ground in my husband=s life and in my home, receive the blood of Jesus and be closed, in the name of Jesus.

23. God of new beginnings, begin a new thing in my marital life, in the name of Jesus.

24. Blood of the Lamb, flow into the foundation of my marital life and give it a new lease of life, in the name of Jesus.

25. Father Lord, let Your kingdom be established in my marriage, in the name of Jesus.

26. O Lord, create a wall of fire between my husband and the strange woman, so that they may be separated forever.

27. Every evil veil covering the face of my husband, receive the fire of God; and burn to ashes, in the mighty name of Jesus.

28. I recover all my legal rights as the woman of the house from the hands of the strange woman, in the name of Jesus.

29. Every trap of destruction fashioned against my husband by the strange woman, fail woefully, in the name of Jesus.

30. Let the stones of the fire of God locate the heads of my household serpents, in the name of Jesus.

31. I crush the head of the ancient serpent afflicting me and my house-hold with the shoes of iron, in the name of Jesus.

32. Let all the strongholds of the serpent and the scorpion in my house-hold receive the thunder of God and be dismantled, in the name of Jesus.

33. Let all habitation of the serpent and the scorpion in my household

become utterly desolate, in the name of Jesus.

34. Let the thunder and fire of God expose all the secret places of my household enemies and consume them all, in the name of Jesus.

35. Let every legal ground of household wickedness in my home be nullified by the blood of Jesus.

36. Let every evil association of the serpent with any member of my family, be terminated now, in the name of Jesus.

37. Let the custodian of my household serpent and scorpion fall down and die, in the name of Jesus.

38. I dismantle the head of all my Goliaths, in the name of Jesus.

39. Every power and spirit in the likeness of snakes attacking me in my dreams, be buried, in the name of Jesus.

40. Every property of the enemy in any area of my life, receive the fire of God and be melted, in the name of Jesus.

41. I challenge the root of any serpentine spirit deposit in my body to be rearranged by the fire of God, in the name of Jesus.

42. I vomit poison of the serpent and scorpion circulating in my body, in the name of Jesus.

43. Every serpentine pollution affecting my health, be flushed out of my system by the blood of Jesus.

44. Every injury inflicted on my marriage by household serpents, be healed by the blood of Jesus.

45. Every household serpent spitting on my breakthroughs, be neutralised by the blood of Jesus.

46. Every good thing in my life swallowed by the household serpent, be converted to fire and vomited into my hands, in Jesus' name.

47. Every good thing in my life paralysed by the poison of the household serpent, receive the blood of the Lamb and be made whole, in the name of Jesus.

48. Let all the activities of the serpent in every area of my life be totally

paralysed, in the name of Jesus.

49. Henceforth, let no enemy trouble me for I bear in my body the mark of the blood of the Lamb of God.

50. Father Lord, I thank you for restoring the joy of my marriage.

DELIVERANCE FROM FOUNDATIONAL BONDAGE

Psalm 11:3

- *This is recommended as the first series of prayers to be said during deliverance sessions.*
- *To obtain deliverance from foundational contamination and bondage.*
- *To release yourself from ancestral yokes and burdens.*
- *To clean up unprofitable spiritual background militating against physical and spiritual progress.*

It would do you well if you can agree with me that the problems of people stem from their foundation. Why not be up and doing and face it squarely in prayer so that you can get out of the stigma.

Ps 11:3: *"If the foundations be destroyed, what can the righteous do?"*

In architecture, the foundation is the most important part of a building. This is the part on which the whole building will rest. It has to be solid. The height of the building is determined by the foundation.

Where we get to in life depends on the kind of foundation we have. The ability to read is the foundation for further education. It is impossible for an illiterate to graduate from a university.

Many of us have foundations that will limit and hinder our physical and spiritual progress. Such foundations are the result of evil dedications and evil inheritance which have now became a bondage, limiting your success in life. The enemy of man's soul knows how to convert footholds to strongholds.

The good news is that as a believer, a born again, spirit-filled Christian, our foundation is Christ. The faulty foundation of your childhood can be repaired. As you use these prayer points, Christ Jesus will step into your life to rebuild every faulty foundation, and He will release you from every foundational bondage.

● CONFESSIONS

Gal. 3:13-14: *Christ hath redeemed us from the curse of the law, being made a curse for us: for it is written, Cursed is every one that hangeth on a tree: That the blessing of Abraham might come on the Gentiles through Jesus Christ; that we might receive the promise of the Spirit through faith.*

Matt. 3:11: *I indeed baptize you with water unto repentance: but he that cometh after me is mightier than I, whose shoes I am not worthy to bear: he shall baptize you with the Holy Ghost, and with fire:*

Col. 1:13: *Who hath delivered us from the power of darkness, and hath translated us into the kingdom of his dear Son:*

Col. 2:15: *And having spoiled principalities and powers, he made a shew of them openly, triumphing over them in it.*

2 Tim. 4:18: *And the Lord shall deliver me from every evil work, and will preserve me unto his heavenly kingdom: to whom be glory for ever and ever. Amen.*

Heb. 2:15: *And deliver them who through fear of death were all their lifetime subject to bondage.*

Ps. 27:2: *When the wicked, even mine enemies and my foes, came upon me to eat up my flesh, they stumbled and fell.*

NOTE: Prayers of release from foundational bondage have to be said aggressively. No stone should be left un-turned. You must hate the foundational bondage with perfect hatred. Scriptural fasting will enhance deliverance.

● PRAISE WORSHIP

1. Thank God for making provision for deliverance from any form of bondage.
2. Confess your sins and those of your ancestors, especially those sins linked to evil powers.
3. I cover myself with the blood of Jesus.
4. I release myself from any inherited bondage, in Jesus' name.

5. O Lord, send Your axe of fire to the foundation of my life and destroy every evil plantation.

6. Let the blood of Jesus flush out from my system every inherited satanic deposit, in the name of Jesus.

7. I release myself from the grip of any problem transferred into my life from the womb, in the name of Jesus.

8. Let the blood of Jesus and the fire of the Holy Ghost cleanse every organ in my body, in the name of Jesus.

9. I break and loose myself from every inherited evil covenant, in the name of Jesus.

10. I break and loose myself from every inherited evil curse, in the name of Jesus.

11. I vomit every evil consumption that I have been fed with as a child, in the name of Jesus.

12. I command all foundational strongmen attached to my life to be paralyzed, in the name of Jesus.

13. Let any rod of the wicked rising up against my family line be rendered impotent for my sake, in the name of Jesus.

14. I cancel the consequences of any evil local name attached to my person, in the name of Jesus.

15. Pray aggressively against the following evil foundations. Pray as follows: You (*pick the under-listed one by one*), loose your hold over my life and be purged out of my foundation, in Jesus' name.

- evil physical design	- parental curses
- envious rivalry	- demonic blood transfusion
- evil dedication	- demonic alteration of destiny
- demonic incisions	- demonic marriage
- dream pollution	- evil laying on of hands
- demonic sacrifice	- fellowship with family idols
- exposure to evil diviner	- inherited infirmity

- fellowship with local idols   - wrong exposure to sex
- demonic initiations   - destructive effect of polygamy
- unscriptural manner of conception
- fellowship with demonic consultants

16. You evil foundational plantation, come out of my life with all your roots, in the name of Jesus.

17. I break and loose myself from every form of demonic bewitchment, in the name of Jesus.

18. I release myself from every evil domination and control, in the name of Jesus.

19. Let the blood of Jesus be transfused into my blood vessel.

20. Let every gate opened to the enemy by my foundation be closed for ever with the blood of Jesus.

21. Lord Jesus, walk back into every second of my life and deliver me where I need deliverance, heal me where I need healing, transform me where I need transformation.

22. Lord Jesus, I thank You for this wonderful deliverance.

REMOVING BLOCKAGES OPERATING AT THE EDGE OF MIRACLES

Psalm 24:7

- *When success slips out of the hand with ease.*
- *For those tormented by the spirit of 'almost there but never gets there.*
- *Powerful prayers for those aiming at the top.*

The ultimate purpose of the enemy is for you to experience failure at the point where your success is approaching in order to drag the name of God to the mud. Is that the normal trend in your life? Then you need divine intervention. If only you can really pray, the Lord will reverse this trend in your life.

Psalm 138:8: *"The Lord will perfect that which concerneth me: thy mercy O Lord, endureth forever: forsake not the works of thine own hands."*

The Spirit of Pisgah is the spirit that causes one to fail at the edge of breakthroughs. It is also called the spirit of 'almost there'.

Maybe you've noticed that any time you have a business deal, everything is in place, then at the last minute things just fall apart. Or you are on a line waiting for something, when it gets to your turn they say it is finished. Or whenever you attend a job interview, at the final stage, they will say, sorry we cannot take you. These are just a few of the manifestations of the spirit of Pisgah. You see what you want, just as you are about to get it, something goes wrong.

Jesus is the only one that has the power to finish what He started. That is why the Bible says, "Looking unto Jesus, the author and the finisher of our faith" (Hebrew 12:2). The Bible also calls Him Alpha and Omega, the beginning and the ending (Revelation 1:8). He does not leave things half done, He completes and perfects everything He starts. Prayerfully commit all your projects into His hands. And as you violently pray these prayer points, the God of perfection will break the stronghold of the spirit of Pisgah that is operating in your life.

● **CONFESSION**

Ps. 24:7: *Lift up your heads, O ye gates; and be ye lift up, ye everlasting doors; and the King of glory shall come in.*

● **PRAISE WORSHIP**

1. I confess my sins of exhibiting occasional doubts.

2. Let the angels of the living God roll away the stone blocking my financial, physical and spiritual breakthroughs, in Jesus' name.

3. I bind every spirit manipulating my beneficiaries against me, in the name of Jesus.

4. I remove my name from the book of seers of goodness without manifestation, in the name of Jesus.

5. Let God arise and let all the enemies of my breakthrough be scattered, in the name of Jesus.

6. Let the fire of God melt away the stones hindering my blessings, in the mighty name of Jesus.

7. Let the cloud blocking the sunlight of my glory and breakthrough be dispersed, in the name of Jesus.

8. All secrets of the enemy in the camp of my life that are still in the darkness, let them be revealed to me now, in Jesus' name.

9. All evil spirits planning to trouble me, be bound, in Jesus' name.

10. Lord, let me not put unprofitable and heavy load upon myself, in the name of Jesus.

11. All keys to my goodness that are still in the possession of the enemy, Lord, give them unto me.

12. Open my eyes, O Lord, and let not my ways be darkened before me.

13. All my sweat on the affairs of my life will not be in vain, in the name of Jesus.

14. The pregnancy of good things within me will be not be aborted by any contrary power, in the name of Jesus.

15. Lord, turn me to untouchable coals of fire.

16. Lord, let wonderful changes begin to be my lot from this week.

17. Lord, remove covetousness from my eyes.

18. Lord, fill the cup of my life to the brim.

19. Let every power stepping on my goodness receive God's arrow of fire now, in the name of Jesus.

20. I reject every spirit of the tail in all areas of my life, in Jesus' name.

21. Thank God for the victory.

PRAYER FOR PROTECTION AND SPIRITUAL SANITATION

Psalm 121:4-8

● *For those who have ceremonies to attend or to celebrate*

There is no cause for you as a child of God, to entertain any form of fear of any danger, except you don't know how to claim your right in prayer.

At one time or the other, we will need to attend ceremonies like weddings, engagements, burial, naming, etc. Some will involve travelling, some will involve your mixing with unfriendly friends. The Bible says, if God be for us, who can be against us? God's protection in all areas for His children is sure. Remember He says, no evil shall befall you and no disease shall come near you. He shall give His holy angels charge over you, to keep you in all your ways.

No matter what happens, do not allow any form of fear to grip you. Commit everything about the occasion into the hand of God and be rest assured that it shall be well.

● **CONFESSIONS**

Rom. 9:33: *As it is written, Behold, I lay in Sion a stumbling stone and rock of offence: and whosoever believeth on him shall not be ashamed.*

Rom. 16:20: *And the God of peace shall bruise Satan under your feet shortly. The grace of our Lord Jesus Christ be with you. Amen.*

Rom. 8:31-37: *What shall we then say to these things? If God be for us, who can be against us? He that spared not his own Son, but delivered him up for us all, how shall he not with him also freely give us all things? Who shall lay any thing to the charge of God's elect? It is God that justifieth. Who is he that condemneth? It is Christ that died, yea rather, that is risen again, who is even at the right hand of God, who also maketh intercession for us. Who shall separate us from the love of Christ? shall tribulation, or distress, or persecution, or famine, or nakedness, or peril, or sword? As it is written, For thy sake we are killed all the day long; we are accounted as* *sheep for the slaughter. Nay, in all these things we are more than conquerors through him that loved us.*

Eph. 5:11: *And have no fellowship with the unfruitful works of darkness, but rather reprove them.*

Col. 1:13-15: *Who hath delivered us from the power of darkness, and hath translated us into the kingdom of his dear Son: In whom we have redemption through his blood, even the forgiveness of sins: Who is the image of the invisible God, the firstborn of every creature:*

Col. 2:14-15: *Blotting out the handwriting of ordinances that was against us, which was contrary to us, and took it out of the way, nailing it to his cross; And having spoiled principalities and powers, he made a shew of them openly, triumphing over them in it.*

Acts 27:25: *Wherefore, sirs, be of good cheer: for I believe God, that it shall be even as it was told me.*

Num. 23:23: *Surely there is no enchantment against Jacob, neither is there any divination against Israel: according to this time it shall be said of Jacob and of Israel, What hath God wrought!*

Isa. 8:8-10: *And he shall pass through Judah; he shall overflow and go over, he shall reach even to the neck; and the stretching out of his wings shall fill the breadth of thy land, O Immanuel. Associate yourselves, O ye people, and ye shall be broken in pieces; and give ear, all ye of far countries: gird yourselves, and ye shall be broken in pieces; gird yourselves, and ye shall be broken in pieces. Take counsel together, and it shall come to nought; speak the word, and it shall not stand: for God is with us.*

• PRAISE WORSHIP

1. Let every organised strategy of the hosts of the demonic world against my life be rendered useless, in the name of Jesus.
2. Let every demonic influence targeted at destroying my vision, dream and ministry receive total disappointment, in Jesus' name.
3. Let every demonic trap set against my life be shattered to pieces, in the name of Jesus.

4. All unfriendly friends militating against my life, receive commotion and be dis organised, in the name of Jesus

5. Father Lord, let my life, ministry and prayer life be extremely dangerous for the kingdom of darkness, in the name of Jesus

6. All demoniacally organised seductive appearances to pull me down, be rendered null and void, in the name of Jesus.

7. My Lord and my God, raise intercessors to stand in the gap for me always, in the name of Jesus.

8. I reject all uncontrollable crying, heaviness and regrets, in the name of Jesus.

9. Father Lord, help me so that my divine spiritual assignments shall not be transferred to another person, in the name of Jesus.

10. I command all organised forces of darkness against my life to receive commotion, lightning and thunder, in the name of Jesus.

11. All demonically organised networks against my spiritual and physical ambition, be put to shame, in the name of Jesus.

12. I command all demonic mirrors and monitoring gadgets against my spiritual life to crack to pieces, in the name of Jesus.

13. Let every ceremony on this issue be soaked in the blood of Jesus and in the fire of the Holy Ghost.

14. I paralyse any attempt by the devil to use this ceremony as a cover-up to carry out any evil assignment against my life, in the name of Jesus.

15. Confess Ps. 121:1- 8: *"I will lift up mine eyes onto the hills, from whence cometh my help. My help cometh from the LORD, which made heaven and earth. He will not suffer thy foot to be moved: he that keepeth thee will not slumber. Behold, he that keepeth Israel shall neither slumber nor sleep. The LORD is thy keeper: the LORD is thy shade upon thy right hand. The sun shall not smite thee by day, nor the moon by night. The LORD shall preserve thee from all evil: he shall preserve thy soul. The LORD shall preserve thy going out and thy coming in from this time forth, and even for evermore."*

16. Let every evil river emanating from the deceased be cut off and rendered ineffective, in the name Jesus. *(Relevant if it is a burial ceremony).*

17. I cover myself, my family and my vehicle with the blood of Jesus.

18. I fire back to the sender any planned evil arrows directed against me during the ceremonies, in the name of Jesus.

19. O Lord, let my body, soul and spirit be turned into hot coals of fire.

20. I paralyse and render impotent any negative speech, invited curses and masked evil statements against me during this ceremony, in the name of Jesus.

21. O Lord, take total control of all plans and activities, in the name of Jesus.

22. Father Lord, let all the foods and drinks that will be served receive the sanctifying power of the blood of Jesus.

23. Let Your fire of protection be upon all guests, visitors, and participants, in the name of Jesus.

24. Let Your name alone be glorified at the end of everything.

25. Begin to thank God for the victory.

DEFEATING SATANIC NETWORK

Isaiah 8:9-10

- When there is a network of evil surrounding and tormenting you.
- When you feel as if the whole world was against you.

The Lord is a man of war and would muster His superior forces to destroy any satanic network that is working against you.

Job 5:12: *"He disappointeth the devices of the crafty, so that their hands cannot perform their enterprise."*

A satanic network comes in form of widespread evil association or gang-up against a person. These evil associations are connected and their aim is to destroy God's plan and purpose in a person's life.

Satanic network is destroyed by fire prayers and Scriptural bombardment. It is necessary that one should destroy the communication system of the enemy.

As you violently take these prayer points, every satanic gathering against your life will be completely destroyed.

- **CONFESSIONs**

Rom. 9:33: *As it is written, Behold, I lay in Sion a stumbling stone and rock of offence: and whosoever believeth on him shall not be ashamed.*

Rom. 16:20: *And the God of peace shall bruise Satan under your feet shortly. The grace of our Lord Jesus Christ be with you. Amen.*

Rom. 8:31-37: *What shall we then say to these things? If God be for us, who can be against us? He that spared not his own Son, but delivered him up for us all, how shall he not with him also freely give us all things? Who shall lay any thing to the charge of God's elect? It is God that justifieth. Who is he that condemneth? It is Christ that died, yea rather, that is risen again, who is even at the right hand of God, who also maketh intercession for us. Who shall separate us from the love of Christ? shall tribulation, or* *distress, or persecution, or famine, or nakedness, or peril, or sword? As it is written, For thy sake we are killed all the day long; we are accounted as sheep for the slaughter. Nay, in all these things we are more than conquerors through him that loved us.*

Eph. 5:11: *And have no fellowship with the unfruitful works of darkness, but rather reprove them.*

Col. 1:13-15: *Who hath delivered us from the power of darkness, and hath translated us into the kingdom of his dear Son: In whom we have redemption through his blood, even the forgiveness of sins: Who is the image of the invisible God, the firstborn of every creature:*

Col. 2:14-15: *Blotting out the handwriting of ordinances that was against us, which was contrary to us, and took it out of the way, nailing it to his cross; And having spoiled principalities and powers, he made a shew of them openly, triumphing over them in it.*

Acts 27:25: *Wherefore, sirs, be of good cheer: for I believe God, that it shall be even as it was told me.*

Num. 23:23: *Surely there is no enchantment against Jacob, neither is there any divination against Israel: according to this time it shall be said of Jacob and of Israel, What hath God wrought!*

Isa. 8:8-10: *And he shall pass through Judah; he shall overflow and go over, he shall reach even to the neck; and the stretching out of his wings shall fill the breadth of thy land, O Immanuel. Associate yourselves, O ye people, and ye shall be broken in pieces; and give ear, all ye of far countries: gird yourselves, and ye shall be broken in pieces; gird yourselves, and ye shall be broken in pieces. Take counsel together, and it shall come to nought; speak the word, and it shall not stand: for God is with us.*

● PRAISE WORSHIP

1. Let every organised strategy of the hosts of the demonic world against my life be rendered useless, in the name Jesus.

2. I command all demonic spirits transferred into my life through demonic contacts to be withdrawn and be cast into fire, in the name of Jesus.

3. Let every demonic influence targeted at destroying my vision, dream and ministry receive total disappointment, in Jesus' name.

4. Let every demonic trap set against my life be shattered to pieces, in the name of Jesus.

5. I command all demonic activities against my calling to receive disgrace and commotion, in the name of Jesus.

6. All partners in demonic business militating against my life, receive commotion and be dis organised, in the name of Jesus.

7. Father Lord, let my life, ministry and prayer life be extremely dangerous for the kingdom of darkness, in the name of Jesus.

8. All demoniacally organised seductive appearance to pull me down, be rendered null and void, in the name of Jesus.

9. Father Lord, show me an immeasurable forgiveness daily in my life, in the name of Jesus.

10. Father Lord, don't terminate my divine spiritual assignments on earth, but help me to accomplish them, in the name of Jesus.

11. My Lord and my God, raise intercessors to stand in the gap for me always, in the name of Jesus.

12. Father Lord, let all the dominant spiritual gifts and talents in my life begin to function for Your glory, in the name of Jesus.

13. I reject all uncontrollable crying, heaviness and regrets, in the name of Jesus.

14. Father Lord, help me so that my divine spiritual assignments shall not be transferred to another person, in the name of Jesus.

15. I command all organised forces of darkness against my life to receive commotion, lightning and thunder, in the name of Jesus.

16. All demonic organised networks against my spiritual and physical ambition, be put to shame, in the name of Jesus.

17. I command all demonic mirrors and monitoring gadgets against my spiritual life to crack to pieces, in the name of Jesus.

18. Let the demonic computers and operators militating against my life receive destruction, in the name of Jesus.

19. Let the demonic computers and operators militating against my life receive destruction, in Jesus' name.

20. Father, don't take my life until I am able to fulfil my ministry, in the name of Jesus.

21. Thank God for disgracing your enemies.

YOU SHALL BE THE HEAD AND NOT THE TAIL

Deut. 28:13

- *Success in interviews, appointments, promotions, examinations and employments.*
- *When you want to excel and be favoured above others*
- *When you want God to take the glory in your career*

It is part of God's own agenda, for you as His child that you should tower above your contemporaries no matter how bleak the situation is.

Daniel 6:3: *"Then this Daniel was preferred above the presidents and princes, because an excellent spirit was in him, and the king thought to set him over the whole realm."*

To be the head means to be number one; to be the best or to be better than others. It also means to be of very high quality or to be unusually good.

What was it in the life of Daniel, a Jewish captive, that made the Babylonian king set him over the whole realm? What was in his life that enabled him to effectively serve two Babylonian kings and two Medo Persian kings?

In each government, Daniel was at the head. The Bible says that there was an excellent spirit in him (Daniel 5:12,14; 6:3,4) and thus no one could find any fault in him. It was this excellent spirit that made him to stand out.

As you pray these prayer points in faith, the Lord will deposit in your life an excellent spirit, that will catapult you to the position of the head.

- **CONFESSIONS**

1 Sam. 17:45-46: *Then said David to the Philistine, Thou comest to me with a sword, and with a spear, and with a shield: but I come to thee in the name of the LORD of hosts, the God of the armies of Israel, whom thou* *hast defied. This day will the LORD deliver thee into mine hand; and I will smite thee, and take thine head from thee; and I will give the carcases of the host of the Philistines this day unto the fowls of the air, and to the wild beasts of the earth; that all the earth may know that there is a God in Israel.*

I Kings 18:36-37: *And it came to pass at the time of the offering of the evening sacrifice, that Elijah the prophet came near, and said, LORD God of Abraham, Isaac, and of Israel, let it be known this day that thou art God in Israel, and that I am thy servant, and that I have done all these things at thy word. Hear me, O LORD, hear me, that this people may know that thou art the LORD God, and that thou hast turned their heart back again.*

Deut. 33:25-27: *Thy shoes shall be iron and brass; and as thy days, so shall thy strength be. There is none like unto the God of Jeshurun, who rideth upon the heaven in thy help, and in his excellency on the sky. The eternal God is thy refuge, and underneath are the everlasting arms: and he shall thrust out the enemy from before thee; and shall say, Destroy them.*

Ps. 118:10-12: *All nations compassed me about: but in the name of the LORD will I destroy them. They compassed me about; yea, they compassed me about: but in the name of the LORD I will destroy them. They compassed me about like bees; they are quenched as the fire of thorns: for in the name of the LORD I will destroy them.*

Deut. 28:13: *And the LORD shall make thee the head, and not the tail; and thou shalt be above only, and thou shalt not be beneath; if that thou hearken unto the commandments of the LORD thy God, which I command thee this day, to observe and to do them:*

Jer. 1:19: *And they shall fight against thee; but they shall not prevail against thee; for I am with thee, saith the LORD, to deliver thee.*

Nahum 1:7-8: *The LORD is good, a strong hold in the day of trouble; and he knoweth them that trust in him. But with an overrunning flood he will make an utter end of the place thereof, and darkness shall pursue his enemies.*

• PRAISE WORSHIP

1. Let all evil competitors stumble and fall, in the name of Jesus.
2. Let all my adversaries make mistakes that will advance my cause, in the name of Jesus.
3. I send confusion into the camp of all evil counselors planning against my progress, in the name Jesus.
4. I command darkness into the camp of the enemy, in Jesus' name.
5. I remove my name from the book of failure and demonic side-track, in the name of Jesus.
6. Lord, give me the power to
   - make use of the divine opportunity presented to me
   - possess more wisdom than my competitors
   - drink from the well of salvation
   - make my paths unknown to the enemy
   - always be ahead of my competitors in terms of favour and independent assessment, in the name of Jesus.
7. Let all the adversaries of my breakthroughs be put to shame, in the name of Jesus.
8. I claim the power to overcome and to excel amongst all competitors, in the name of Jesus
9. I command all human woes to find me untouchable, in Jesus' name.
10. Let any decision by any panel be favourable unto me, in the name of Jesus.
11. I remove my name from the book of failure and moving backward, in the name of Jesus
12. Let the anointing of the overcomer fall upon my life, in the name of Jesus.
13. I receive wisdom, knowledge and understanding to subdue all competitors, in the name of Jesus
14. Let every negative word and pronouncement against my success be

completely nullified, in the name of Jesus.

15. All competitors with me in this issue will find my defeat impossible, in the name of Jesus

16. Father Lord, let Your wisdom, and power be upon me in a measure that cannot be confronted, in the name of Jesus

17. I claim supernatural wisdom to answer all questions in a way that will advance my cause, in the name of Jesus.

18. Let every Achan depart from my camp, in the name of Jesus.

19. I receive the anointing for supernatural breakthrough in this matter, in the name of Jesus.

20. Thank the Lord for the answers.

VICTORY IN THE HUMAN COURT

Isaiah 54:15

- *When you want court cases decided in your favour*
- *When you have a court case*
- *When you face a panel which decides your fate*
- *When you dream of being convicted in a court room*
- *When there is a conspiracy against you and you need God's intervention.*

Remember, human jury may try to pronounce a destructive and negative sentence on you but it is the good verdict of the Lord that will stand.

Proverbs 21:1: *"The king's heart is in the hand of the LORD, as the rivers of water; he turneth it wheresoever He will."*

You must understand that there are two realms of power - the physical and the spiritual. No matter how bleak or legally impossible a case may appear in the physical, or no matter how tightly woven a conspiracy, the final power rests in the name of Jesus. That is the reason the Scripture says categorically, "Once has He spoken, twice have I heard that (ABSOLUTE) power belongs to God" (Psalm 62:11).

However, God is not an unjust God, if you have opened a door and you need some repentance to do, do it fast.

"The preparations of the heart in man and the answer of the tongue, are from the Lord" (Proverbs 16:1). As you pray these prayer points sincerely, God will cause the judge/magistrate to give a judgement that favours you.

• CONFESSIONS

Rom. 8:31-34,37: *What shall we then say to these things? If God be for us, who can be against us? He that spared not his own Son, but delivered him up for us all, how shall he not with him also freely give us all things? Who shall lay any thing to the charge of God's elect? It is God that justifieth. Who is he that condemneth? It is Christ that died, yea rather, that is risen again, who is even at the right hand of God, who also maketh intercession for us. . . . Nay, in all these things we are more than conquerors through him that loved us.*

Ps. 27:1-2: *The LORD is my light and my salvation; whom shall I fear? the LORD is the strength of my life; of whom shall I be afraid? When the wicked, even mine enemies and my foes, came upon me to eat up my flesh, they stumbled and fell.*

Isa. 8:8-10: *And he shall pass through Judah; he shall overflow and go over, he shall reach even to the neck; and the stretching out of his wings shall fill the breadth of thy land, O Immanuel. Associate yourselves, O ye people, and ye shall be broken in pieces; and give ear, all ye of far countries: gird yourselves, and ye shall be broken in pieces; gird yourselves, and ye shall be broken in pieces. Take counsel together, and it shall come to nought; speak the word, and it shall not stand: for God is with us.*

Isa. 50:7: *For the Lord GOD will help me; therefore shall I not be confounded: therefore have I set my face like a flint, and I know that I shall not be ashamed.*

Rom. 9:33: *As it is written, Behold, I lay in Sion a stumbling stone and rock of offence: and whosoever believeth on him shall not be ashamed.*

Jer. 20:11: *But the LORD is with me as a mighty terrible one: therefore my persecutors shall stumble, and they shall not prevail: they shall be greatly ashamed; for they shall not prosper: their everlasting confusion shall never be forgotten.*

Prov. 19:21: *There are many devices in a man's heart; nevertheless the counsel of the LORD, that shall stand.*

Job 5:12: *He disappointeth the devices of the crafty, so that their hands cannot perform their enterprise.*

Prov. 21:1: *The king's heart is in the hand of the LORD, as the rivers of water: he turneth it whithersoever he will.*

Ps. 24:1-2: *The earth is the LORD's, and the fulness thereof; the world, and they that dwell therein. For he hath founded it upon the seas, and established it upon the floods.*

NOTE: *These prayers will only work for those who are on the right path of justice. It will not work for purposes that are unscriptural. However, an ignorant offender may find help from using the prayers.*

• PRAISE WORSHIP

1. Thank the Lord because He is the Lord of hosts and the Man of war.

2. I claim victory over every adversary in this court case, in the name of Jesus.

3. I bind and paralyse the strongman employed or delegated to disgrace me, in the name of Jesus.

4. Let all the affairs of my life be too hot for any evil power to manipulate, in the name of Jesus.

5. O Lord, grant me and my lawyer supernatural wisdom to subdue all opposition.

6. O Lord, let it be impossible for my adversary to subdue the truth in this matter, in the name of Jesus.

7. O Lord, let me find favour in the sight of those who are responsible for judging this case.

8. I close every negative door that the enemy might want to open, using this case, in the name of Jesus.

9. You satanic agents, I command you to clear out from the pathway to my victory in this matter, in the name of Jesus.

10. I cancel any demonic decision and expectation concerning this case, in the name of Jesus.

11. Father, make it possible for me to find favour in the sight of the judge, in the name of Jesus.

12. Lord, show let me find favour, compassion and loving-kindness with the jury, in the name of Jesus.

13. Let all the demonic obstacles that have been established in the heart of anyone against my prosperity be destroyed, in the name of Jesus.

14. Lord, give all the parties concerned, dreams, visions and restless-

ness that would advance my cause.

15. I command my money being caged by the enemy to be completely released, in the name of Jesus.

16. I bind and put to flight all the spirits of fear, anxiety and discouragement, in the name of Jesus.

17. Lord, let divine wisdom fall upon all who are supporting me in these matters.

18. I break the backbone of the spirits of conspiracy and treachery, in the name of Jesus.

19. Lord, hammer my matter into the mind of those who will assist me so that they do not suffer from demonic loss of memory.

20. I paralyse the handiwork of house hold enemies and envious agents in this matter, in the name of Jesus.

21. You devil take your leg away from the top of my finances, in the mighty name of Jesus.

22. Let the fire of the Holy Spirit purge my life from any evil mark put upon me, in the name of Jesus.

23. Let the Lord confuse the tongues of those gathered to do me harm, after the order of the builders of the Tower of Babel, in the name of Jesus.

24. Let my adversaries make mistakes that will advance my cause, in the name of Jesus.

25. I command every evil power and vessel sitting on my rights and goodness to be violently overthrown, in the name of Jesus.

26. I pursue, overtake and recover my properties from the hands of spiritual Egyptians, in the name of Jesus.

27. Let every counsel, plan, desire, expectation, imagination, device and activity of the enemy against this case be rendered null and void, in the name of Jesus.

28. I terminate every journey into bondage and unfruitfulness designed

for me by the enemies of my soul, in the name of Jesus.

29. I bind every money-consuming demon attached to my finances, in the name of Jesus.

30. I refuse to be tossed about by any demonic device of the enemy to delay my miracle, in the name of Jesus.

31. Let all satanic banks and purses receive the fire of God and burn to ashes, in the name of Jesus.

32. Holy Spirit, teach me to avoid unfriendly friends and unprofitable transactions, in the name of Jesus.

33. Let all my blessings presently in the prison of the enemy begin to pursue me and overtake me as from today, in the name of Jesus.

34. Begin to thank God for the victory.

REMOVING HINDRANCES TO ADVANCEMENT AND DEMOLISHING STUMBLING BLOCKS

Psalm 24:7

● *For success in interviews, appointments, promotions, examinations and employments.*

● *When you want to excel and be favoured above others.*

● *When you want God to be glorified in your career.*

All the gates and everlasting doors which constitute hindrances and stumbling blocks to your progress in life cannot withstand the appearance of the King of Glory if you invite Him to intervene in your affairs.

Proverbs 4:18: *"But the path of the just is as the shinning light, that shineth more and more unto the perfect day."*

For every Red Sea, there is a Moses. For every wall of Jericho, there is a Joshua, and for every Goliath, there is a David. As long as you are a child of God and you are living in accordance with the word of God, whatever hindrances and stumbling blocks are placed on your path, you can surely overcome at the name of Jesus, with appropriate praying.

The Scripture says, "But they that wait upon the LORD shall renew their strength; they shall mount up with wings as eagles; they shall;; run, and not be weary; and they shall walk, and not faint" (Isa. 40:31).

Therefore, any power erecting stumbling blocks on your way, will be demolished as you pray with aggressive faith.

● **CONFESSIONS**

Ps. 34:10: *The young lions do lack, and suffer hunger: but they that seek the LORD shall not want any good thing.*

Ps 75:6: *For promotion cometh neither from the east, nor from the west, nor from the south.*

Ps 113:5,7-8: *Who is like unto the LORD our God, who dwelleth on high, He raiseth up the poor out of the dust, and lifteth the needy out of the dunghill; That he may set him with princes, even with the princes of his people.*

Phil 4:13,19: *I can do all things through Christ which strengtheneth me . . . But my God shall supply all your need according to his riches in glory by Christ Jesus.*

Gal 6:17: *From henceforth let no man trouble me: for I bear in my body the marks of the Lord Jesus.*

• PRAISE WORSHIP

1. Thank the Lord because He alone can advance you.
2. O Lord, bring me into favour with all those who will decide on my advancement.
3. O Lord, cause a divine substitution to happen if this is what will move me ahead.
4. I reject the spirit of the tail and I claim the spirit of the head, in the name of Jesus.
5. I command all evil records planted by the devil in anyone's mind against my advancement to be shattered to pieces, in Jesus' name
6. O Lord, transfer, remove or change all human agents that are bent on stopping my advancement.
7. O Lord, smoothen my path to the top by Your hand of fire.
8. I receive the anointing to excel above my contemporaries, in the name of Jesus.
9. O Lord, catapult me into greatness as You did for Daniel in the land of Babylon.
10. O Lord, help me to identify and deal with any weakness in me that can hinder my progress.
11. I bind every strongman delegated to hinder my progress, in the name of Jesus.

12. O Lord, despatch Your angels to roll away every stumbling block to my promotion, advancement and elevation.

13. Let power change hands in my place of work to the hands of the Holy Spirit, in the name of Jesus.

14. I receive the mandate to put to flight every enemy of my breakthroughs, in the name of Jesus.

15. You spirit of . . . (pick from the under listed), I bind and render you to naught in my life, in the mighty name of Jesus.

- demonic antagonism
- strife
- marginal success
- wrong words
- bad feet/bad luck
- unprofitable controversies
- demonic opinions against me
- demonic logic and unprofitable interviews
- unprofitable questions

- confusion
- mind blankness
- mind dullness
- memory failure
- evil collaborators

16. I claim the position of . . . , in the mighty name of Jesus.

17. Let the mark of the blood of Jesus, of divine favour and protection be upon my life, in the name of Jesus.

18. Praise the Lord for answered prayers.

SPIRITUAL CHECKUP
Psalm 139:23,24

- *A personal deliverance programme, especially when you are unable to contact a minister who can assist you.*
- *Also for spiritual cleansing.*

Spiritual self-examination is the greatest recipe for holiness and constant readiness for the rapture and eternal bliss with God.

2 Corinthians 13:5: *"Examine yourselves whether ye be in the faith; prove your own selves, know ye not your own selves, how that Jesus Christ is in you, except ye be reprobates."*

Many of us go for full medical check-up at least once a year. In the same way, Paul is here telling us to carry out a full spiritual check-up on our lives.

If we are effective Christians we will know. If we are stagnant we will know. We need to be honest with ourselves. We need to prove ourselves. When we are not growing, there is something wrong with our spiritual lives and we need to seriously address it with prayers. If we are truly Christians the power and the presence of God will manifest in our lives and it will continue to multiply.

As you engage in these prayers for spiritual check-up, the Lord will purge your life and draw you closer to Him.

- INSTRUCTIONS

A. *Sit comfortably.*

B. *Focus your attention on the Lord Jesus Christ.*

C. *Avoid distractions. If they come, do not concentrate on them.*

D. *Spend a few minutes in praises to the Lord.*

E. *Confess any known sin to the Lord.*

F. *Ask the Lord to bring to your memory the legal ground or the open doors that forces of spiritual wickedness are using to gain entrance into your life.*

G. Enter into this period with aggressive prayer. All prayer points are to be done with holy anger, violently and with determined aggression.

● **PRAISE WORSHIP**

1. I release myself from every ancestral demonic pollution, in the name of Jesus.

2. I release myself from every demonic pollution emanating from my parents' religion, in the name of Jesus.

3. I release myself from demonic pollution emanating from my past involvement in any demonic religion, in the name of Jesus.

4. I break and loose myself from every idol and related associations, in the name of Jesus.

5. I release myself from every dream pollution, in Jesus' name.

6. Let every satanic attack against my life in my dreams be converted to victory, in the name of Jesus.

7. Let all rivers, trees, forests, evil companions, evil pursuers, pictures of dead relatives, snakes, spirit husbands, spirit wives and masquerades manipulated against me in the dream be completely destroyed by the power in the blood of the Lord Jesus.

8. I command every evil plantation in my life, **come out with all your roots, in the name of Jesus!** (*Lay your hands on your stomach and keep repeating the emphasized area.*)

9. Evil strangers in my body, come all the way out of your hiding places, in the name of Jesus.

10. I disconnect any conscious or unconscious linkage with demonic caterers, in the name of Jesus.

11. Let all avenues of eating or drinking spiritual poisons be closed, in the name of Jesus.

12. I cough out and vomit any food eaten from the table of the devil, in the name of Jesus. (*Cough them out and vomit them in faith. Prime the expulsion.*)

13. Let all negative materials circulating in my blood stream be evacuated, in the name of Jesus.

14. I drink the blood of Jesus. (*Physically swallow and drink it in faith. Keep doing this for some time.*)

15. *Lay one hand on your head and the other on your stomach or navel and begin to pray like this:* Holy Ghost fire, burn from the top of my head to the sole of my feet. *Begin to mention every organ of your body: your kidney, liver, intestine, blood, etc. You must not rush at this level, because the fire will actually come and you may start feeling the heat.*

16. I cut myself off from every spirit of . . . (*mention the name of your place of birth*), in the name of Jesus.

17. I cut myself off from every tribal spirit and curse, in Jesus' name.

18. I cut myself off from every territorial spirit and curse, in the name of Jesus.

19. Holy Ghost fire, purge my life.

20. I claim my complete deliverance, in the name of Jesus, from the spirit of . . . (*mention those things you do not desire in your life*).

21. I break the hold of any evil power over my life, in Jesus' name.

22. I move from bondage into liberty, in the name of Jesus.

23. Jesus, I thank You for the purging and for the in-filling of Your revival fire.

TO KNOW GOD'S WILL CONCERNING ANY ISSUE

Jer. 33:3

- *To enable you take the right decision on any issue.*
- *To make you know the mind of God on any par-particular issue.*
- *To determine whether a particular thing is God's choice for you.*
- *To discover secret things beneficial or detrimental to a particular issue.*
- *To receive revelation knowledge on any issue.*
- *To know the mind of God concerning a particular issue.*

The only thing that can secure peace, joy and happiness for you amidst turbulence and vicissitudes of life is to seek to know the will of God in all areas of your life and to follow it.

Psalm 25:12: "What man is he that feareth the Lord? him shall he teach in the way he shall choose."

God desires to make his will known to man. Time and again people ask, "How can I know the will of God? God doesn't talk to me? I don't know what to do."

There are many Scriptures which show us that God sincerely wants to teach us the way we should go. God wants to patiently instruct us so we will not make mistakes. Psalm 32:8 says, "I will instruct you and teach you in the way which you should go: I will guide you with my eyes." Proverbs 3:5 commands us to "Trust in the Lord with all thine heart; and lean not unto thine own under-standing. In all thy ways acknowledge him and he shall direct thy paths."

When we come to the Lord without any idol in our hearts or preconceived ideas of what we want or how we want things to turn out, He will teach us how to choose the best.

Be still in the presence of the Lord and He will speak to you in a way you will understand. His will always aligns with His WORD.

As you pray these prayer points with an open mind, ". . . you will be filled with the knowledge of His will in all wisdom and spiritual understanding" (Col. 1:9).

NOTE: *The issue you are placing before God for direction or guid-ance must be scriptural.*

● **CONFESSIONS**

Dan. 2:22: *He revealeth the deep and secret things: he knoweth what is in the darkness, and the light dwelleth with him.*

Eph. 1:17: *That the God of our Lord Jesus Christ, the Father of glory, may give unto you the spirit of wisdom and revelation in the knowledge of him:*

Ps. 25:14: *The secret of the LORD is with them that fear him; and he will shew them his covenant.*

Deut. 29:29: *The secret things belong unto the LORD our God: but those things which are revealed belong unto us and to our children for ever, that we may do all the words of this law.*

● **PRAISE WORSHIP**

1. Thank God for the revelation power of the Holy Spirit.

2. O God, to whom no secret is hidden, make known unto me whether . . . (*mention the name of the thing*).

3. O Lord, remove from me any persistent buried grudges, enmity against anyone and every other thing that can block my spiritual vision.

4. Let every idol present, consciously or unconsciously, in my heart concerning this issue be melted away by the fire of the Holy Spirit.

5. O Lord, give unto me the spirit of revelation and wisdom in the knowledge of You.

6. O Lord, remove spiritual cataract from my eyes.

7. O Lord, forgive me for every false motive or thought that has ever been formed in my heart since the day I was born.

8. O Lord, forgive me for any lie that I have ever told against any person, system or organisation.

9. O Lord, open up my spiritual understanding.

10. O Lord, teach me deep and secret things.

11. O Lord, reveal to me every secret behind this particular issue, whether beneficial or not.

12. I refuse to fall under the manipulation of the spirits of confusion, in the name of Jesus.

13. O Lord, teach me to know that which is worth knowing and love that which is worth loving, and to dislike whatsoever is not pleasing unto You.

14. I refuse to make foundational mistakes in my decision-making, in the name of Jesus.

15. Father Lord, guide and direct me in knowing Your mind on this particular issue.

16. I stand against all satanic attachments that may seek to confuse my decision, in the name of Jesus.

17. If . . . (mention the name of the thing) is not for me, O Lord, re-direct my steps.

18. I bind the activities of . . . (pick from the list below) in my life, in the name of Jesus.

 - lust
 - ungodly infatuation
 - ungodly family pressure
 - demonic manipulation in dreams and visions
 - attachment to the wrong choice
 - confusing revelations
 - spiritual blindness and deafness
 - unprofitable advice
 - ungodly impatience

19. Lord, make Your way plain before my face.

20. O God, You who reveals secret things, make known unto me Your choice for me on this issue.

21. Holy Spirit, open my eyes and help me to make the right decision, in the name of Jesus.

22. Father Lord, I thank You for the testimonies that will follow these prayer points.

POWER FOR A NEW BEGINNING

Psalm 103:5

- *Against the spirit of stagnation.*
- *When you desire that new things should be gin in your life.*

The end of your sinful, hopeless, helpless, weary and frustrating life is a new beginning of a vi brant and existing life in Christ.

Isa. 43:19: *"Behold, I will do a new thing; now it shall spring forth; shall ye not know it? I will even make a way in the wilderness, and rivers in the desert."*

Listen to these stories. There was one woman, called May. She sobbed uncontrollably; after 35 years of marriage, her husband died. All her plans for retirement were of no use.

Two. Men are not supposed to cry; they are supposed to be strong; yet Andrew covered his face with his hands and wept bitterly because his business had collapsed. All his hand-work and all his dreams were shattered.

Three. Anne suddenly found herself jobless. Where will she start from?

Four. Paul cried out in unbelief when his fiancee called off their engagement because she had met someone else.

Your own case may be like any of the above. Whatever the situation: the death of a loved one, the collapse of a business, the loss of your job, a broken engagement or divorce, have faith in God.

Our God is faithful and He will not deny himself (2 Timothy 2:13). As long as there is life, there is hope. We do not need to be confused or afraid of the future. God is always there for us. He said, "I will not leave you or forsake you" (Hebrews 13:5). Our hope and the confidence we have in Him cannot be in vain. These prayers will bring Power for a New Beginning. He has promised, "Behold, I will do a new thing" (Isaiah 43:19). Your future is se-cured in Christ.

- **CONFESSIONS**

Isa. 43:19: *Behold, I will do a new thing; now it shall spring forth; shall ye not know it? I will even make a way in the wilderness, and rivers in the desert.*

• PRAISE WORSHIP

1. O Lord, plant good things in my life.
2. O Lord, uproot evil things from my life.
3. I cancel every unconscious negative agreement, in Jesus' name.
4. Lord, make me Your battle axe.
5. Let every spiritual weakness in my life receive termination now, in the name of Jesus.
6. Let every financial failure in my life receive termination now, in the name of Jesus.
7. Let every sickness in my life receive termination now, in the name of Jesus.
8. Let every architect of problems receive termination now, in the name of Jesus.
9. I paralyze all spiritual wolves working against my life, in the name of Jesus.
10. Let that which hinders me from greatness begin to give way now, in the mighty name of Jesus.
11. Let every imprisoned and buried potentials begin to come forth now, in the name of Jesus.
12. You unfriendly helpers, I command you, in the name of the Lord Jesus Christ, depart from me.
13. Let every negative transactions currently affecting my life negatively be canceled, in the name of Jesus.
14. I command all the dark works done against my life in the secret to be exposed and be nullified, in the name of Jesus.
15. I loose myself from any evil spirit, in the name of Jesus.
16. O Lord, if my life is on the wrong course, correct me.

17. Let every anti-progress altar fashioned against me be destroyed with the thunder fire of God, in the name of Jesus.

18. I command my destiny to change to the best, in Jesus' name.

19. Let my hand become a sword of fire to cut down demonic trees, in the name of Jesus.

20. All boasting powers delegated against me, be silenced permanently, in the name of Jesus.

21. I withdraw all my benefits from the hands of the oppressors, in the name of Jesus.

22. Let all unprofitable marks in my life be erased, in Jesus' name.

23. Let every power chasing away my blessings be paralyzed, in the name of Jesus.

24. Let every good thing eaten up by the enemy be vomited now, in the name of Jesus.

25. Let the anointing for spiritual breakthroughs fall upon me, in the name of Jesus.

26. O Lord, make me a prayer addict.

27. O Lord, ignite my prayer life with Your fire.

28. O Lord, empower my prayer altar.

29. I reject every spiritual contamination, in the name of Jesus.

30. O Lord, give me power to overcome all obstacles to my breakthroughs.

31. O Lord, give me divine prescription to my problems.

32. I break all curses of leaking blessings, in the name of Jesus.

33. Let all spiritual holes in my life be closed with the blood of Jesus, in the name of Jesus.

34. Lord, help me to locate the defect in the clay of my life.

35. Lord, let me be at the right place at the right time.

36. I disarm every household enemy today, in the name of Jesus.

37. Let my enemies pitch their tents against one another, in the name of Jesus.

38. I frustrate and disappoint every instrument of the enemy fashioned against me, in the name of Jesus.

39. I seal my victory with the blood of Jesus.

40. I thank You Lord Jesus for answering my prayers.

VICTORY TABLET
Isaiah 43:4

- *For those who have been unrighteously detained or incarcerated.*
- *For those in prison, cell or detention.*
- *For those who are being kept in prison pending the determinatio of their cases.*
- *When you dream of being locked up or arrested.*
- *When you feel caged.*

People are fond of swallowing varied forms of magical substance in the quest for victory over destructive forces; but at the end of the day, they'll discover that they are back to square one. But people who swallow the word of God and the blood of Jesus coupled with prayer are always victorious.

Acts 4:29: *"And now, Lord, behold their threatenings: and grant unto thy servants, that with all boldness they may speak thy word."*

"Why do the heathen rage and the people imagine a vain thing?" (Psalm 2:1). When unbelievers rise up against you and lock you up or detain you unrighteously, call upon the Lord.

Peter cried, "Lord, behold their threatenings." When you are being accused unjustly the Lord will fight for you. Whatever the set-up may be, the Lord will fight for you.

The apostles were locked up for healing a man. They did not do anything wrong. They were simply doing what the Lord asked them to do. This offended the religious leaders of the day. They locked Peter and John in prison. The Lord stepped into their situation and they were released. These prayer points are designed to invite the Almighty God into your situation so that He can fight for you and help you overcome!

- **CONFESSIONS**

Rev. 13:10: *He that leadeth into captivity shall go into captivity: he that killeth with the sword must be killed with the sword. Here is the patience and the faith of the saints.*

Rom. 8:31-34: *What shall we then say to these things? If God be for us, who can be against us? He that spared not his own Son, but delivered him up for us all, how shall he not with him also freely give us all things? Who shall lay any thing to the charge of God's elect? It is God that justifieth. Who is he that condemneth? It is Christ that died, yea rather, that is risen again, who is even at the right hand of God, who also maketh intercession for us.*

Ps. 27:1-2: *The LORD is my light and my salvation; whom shall I fear? the LORD is the strength of my life; of whom shall I be afraid? When the wicked, even mine enemies and my foes, came upon me to eat up my flesh, they stumbled and fell.*

Isa. 8:8-10: *And he shall pass through Judah; he shall overflow and go over, he shall reach even to the neck; and the stretching out of his wings shall fill the breadth of thy land, O Immanuel. Associate yourselves, O ye people, and ye shall be broken in pieces; and give ear, all ye of far countries: gird yourselves, and ye shall be broken in pieces; gird yourselves, and ye shall be broken in pieces. Take counsel together, and it shall come to nought; speak the word, and it shall not stand: for God is with us.*

Isa. 50:7: *For the Lord GOD will help me; therefore shall I not be confounded: therefore have I set my face like a flint, and I know that I shall not be ashamed.*

Rom. 9:33: *As it is written, Behold, I lay in Sion a stumbling stone and rock of offence: and whosoever believeth on him shall not be ashamed.*

Jer. 20:11: *But the LORD is with me as a mighty terrible one: therefore my persecutors shall stumble, and they shall not prevail: they shall be greatly ashamed; for they shall not prosper: their everlasting confusion shall never be forgotten.*

Prov. 19:21: *There are many devices in a man's heart; nevertheless the counsel of the LORD, that shall stand.*

Prov. 21:1: *The king's heart is in the hand of the LORD, as the rivers of water: he turneth it whithersoever he will.*

Job. 5:12: *He disappointeth the devices of the crafty, so that their hands cannot perform their enterprise.*

Ps. 24:1-2: *The earth is the LORD's, and the fulness thereof; the world, and they that dwell therein. For he hath founded it upon the seas, and established it upon the floods.*

NOTE: *This prayer will work only for those who are on the right path of justice. It will not work for purposes that are unscriptural. However, an ignorant offender may find help using the prayer.*

● **PRAISE WORSHIP**

1. Thank the Lord because He is the Lord of hosts and the Man of war.

2. I claim victory over every adversary in this case, in Jesus' name.

3. I bind and paralyse the strongman employed or delegated to disgrace me, in the name of Jesus.

4. Let all the affairs of my life be too hot for any evil power to manipulate, in the name of Jesus.

5. O Lord, grant me and those working for my freedom supernatural wisdom to subdue all opposition.

6. O Lord, let it be impossible for my adversary to subdue the truth in this matter.

7. O Lord, let me find favour in the sight of those who are responsible for my freedom on this matter.

8. I close every negative door that the enemy might want to open for this case, in the name of Jesus.

9. You satanic agents, I command you to clear out of from the path to my victory on this matter, in the name of Jesus.

10. I cancel any demonic decision and expectation concerning this matter, in the name of Jesus.

11. Father, make all efforts being made towards my freedom find favour in the sight of all those concerned to free me, in the name of Jesus.

12. Let every hidden secret about this matter be revealed, in the name of Jesus.

13. Let all the demonic obstacles that has been established in the heart

of anyone against my prosperity be destroyed, in Jesus' name.

14. Let every evil trap set against me fail and let the enemy fall therein, in the name of Jesus.

15. Lord, show all the parties concerned, dreams, visions and facts that would advance my cause.

16. Let every plan of the enemy to disgrace me be totally nullified, in the name of Jesus.

17. I bind and put to flight all the spirits of fear, anxiety and discouragement, in the name of Jesus.

18. Lord, let divine wisdom fall upon all who are supporting me in these matters.

19. Let there be no rest of mind for my adversaries, in Jesus' name.

20. Let evil pursue and overtake those seeking for my life, in the name of Jesus.

21. I break the backbone of spirits of conspiracy and treachery, in the name of Jesus.

22. Lord, hammer my matter into the mind of those who will assist me so that they do not suffer from demonic loss of memory.

23. I paralyse the handiwork of house-hold enemies and envious agents on this matter, in the name of Jesus.

24. You devil, take your legs away from every affair of my life, in the mighty name of Jesus.

25. Let the fire of the Holy Spirit purge my life from any evil mark put upon me, in the name of Jesus.

26. Let the Lord confuse the tongues of those gathered to do me harm, after the order of the builders of the Tower of Babel, in the name of Jesus.

27. Let my adversaries make the mistakes that will advance my cause, in the name of Jesus.

28. Let every counsel, plan, desire, expectation, imagination, device and

activity of the enemy against this matter be rendered null and void, in the name of Jesus.

29. I terminate every journey into bondage and unfruitfulness designed for me by the enemies of my soul, in the name of Jesus.

30. I bind every money-consuming demon attached to my finances, in the name of Jesus.

31. I refuse to be tossed about by any demonic device of the enemy to delay my miracle, in the name of Jesus.

32. Let God do to my adversaries what He did to the adversaries of Daniel, in the name of Jesus.

33. Holy Spirit, teach me to avoid unfriendly friends and unprofitable transactions, in the name of Jesus.

34. Father Lord, I thank You for everything You have done for me with these prayer points.

VICTORY OVER FINANCIAL HANDICAP

Malachi 3:11-12

- *When you desire dumbfounding financial break throughs*
- *When you are tired of financial embarrassments*
- *To break financial bondage*
- *Destroying satanic embargo on finances*
- *Arresting the spirit of leaking pockets*

One of the strategies of the enemy is to plague you with financial handicap in order to paralyse your potentials. You have to resist it by taking on the amour of warfare against it.

Mal. 3:10: *"Bring ye all the tithes unto the storehouse, that there may be meat in mine house, and prove me now herewith, saith the Lord of hosts if I will not open to you the windows of heaven and pour you out a blessing, that there shall not be room enough to receive it."*

Unfaithfulness in our tithes and offering is the most common cause of financial handicap. God expects that we give Him 10 per cent of our income. After paying our tithes, we are expected to give offerings. Tithes belong to God.

Unfortunately, many give to God as if they were giving alms to beggars. They murmur and grumble that, "If we give now, it is the pastor that will spend it." Many even go as far as trying to calculate what the pastor gets every week. It is a pity! All they end up doing is breaking the spiritual law of prosperity. Luke 6:38 says, "Give and it shall be given unto you good measure, pressed down and shaken together and running over, shall men give unto your bosom. For with the same measure that ye mete withal it shall be measured to you again."

The second major cause of financial handicap is giving sparingly. This is plainly stated in the above scripture. It is the same measure you give that you will be given. This fact is also buttressed by 2 Cor. 9:6, "He which soweth sparingly shall reap also sparingly;"

Beloved, if you have been stealing from God by not paying your tithes, please, for your own sake, repent. Ask God to forgive you and purpose in your heart that you will begin to pay your tithes and give offering to God and the needy. As you do this, God will (1) Open the windows of heaven for you (2) Rebuke the devourer for your sake (3) Men will call you blessed when they see God's blessings in your life. (Malachi 3:11,12).

● CONFESSIONS (Personalise them)

Phil. 4:19: *But my God shall supply all your need according to his riches in glory by Christ Jesus.*

Ps. 23:6: *Surely goodness and mercy shall follow me all the days of my life: and I will dwell in the house of the LORD for ever.*

Deut. 8:18: *But thou shalt remember the LORD thy God: for it is he that giveth thee power to get wealth, that he may establish his covenant which he sware unto thy fathers, as it is this day.*

3 Jn. 1:2: *Beloved, I wish above all things that thou mayest prosper and be in health, even as thy soul prospereth.*

Ps. 84:11: *For the LORD God is a sun and shield: the LORD will give grace and glory: no good thing will he withhold from them that walk uprightly.*

Phil. 4:13: *I can do all things through Christ which strengtheneth me.*

● NOTE:

1. *Before you begin this prayer session, carry out a search of your spiritual life. Repent from all known sins, confess such sins to the Lord and ask for forgiveness.*

2. *Have you broken the laws of divine prosperity? For example, are you faithful in your giving tithe and offerings? Have you ever used your money to sponsor evil? E.g . . ., abortion, demonic consultation, sacrifice to idols and demons? Have you been stingy when you had money? Are you guilty of abandoning your marital and family responsibilities?*

3. *After sorting out all these things with the Lord, embark on seven (7) days prayers and fasting using the under listed prayer points. The result will surprise you beyond your wildest imagination.*

● PRAISE WORSHIP

1. I command all demonic hindrances to my prosperity to be totally paralysed, in the name of Jesus.

2. Let every demonic bank keeping my finances be destroyed and re-

lease my finances, in the name of Jesus.

3. I bind every strongman holding my finances captive, in Jesus' name.

4. I possess all my possessions, in the name of Jesus.

5. I break and loose myself from every curse of financial bondage and poverty, in the name of Jesus.

6. I release myself from every conscious and unconscious covenant with the spirit of poverty, in the name of Jesus.

7. Let God arise and let every enemy of my financial breakthrough be scattered, in the name of Jesus.

8. O Lord, restore all my wasted years and efforts and convert them to blessings, in the name of Jesus.

9. Let the spirit of favour be upon me everywhere I go concerning my finances, in the name of Jesus.

10. Father, I ask You, in the name of Jesus, to send ministering spirits to bring in prosperity and funds into my finances.

11. Let men bless me anywhere I go, in the name of Jesus.

12. I release my finances from the clutches of financial hunger, in the name of Jesus.

13. I loose angels, in the mighty name of Jesus, to go and create favour for my finances.

14. Let all financial hindrances be removed, in the name of Jesus.

15. I remove my name and those of my customers from the book of financial bankruptcy, in the name of Jesus.

16. Holy Spirit, be my senior partner in my finances.

17. Every good thing presently eluding my finances should flow into it, in the mighty name of Jesus.

18. I reject every spirit of financial embarrassment, in Jesus' name.

19. Father, block every space causing unprofitable leakage to my finances, in the mighty name of Jesus.

20. Let my finances become too hot to handle for dupes and demonic

customers, in the name of Jesus.

21. Let spiritual magnetic power that attracts and keeps wealth be deposited in my finances, in the name of Jesus.

22. I release my finances from the influences, control and domination of household wickedness, in the name of Jesus.

23. Let all satanic angels deflecting blessings away from me be completely paralyzed, in the name of Jesus.

24. Let the evil effect of any strange money I have received or touched be neutralised, in the name of Jesus.

25. O Lord, teach me the divine secret of prosperity.

26. Let the joy of the enemy over my financial life be converted to sorrow, in the name of Jesus.

27. Let all my blessings held captive locally or overseas be released to me, in the name of Jesus.

28. I bind every anti-breakthrough, anti-miracle, and anti-prosperity forces, in the name of Jesus.

29. Let my finances be too hot for any evil power to sit upon, in the name of Jesus.

30. O Lord, quicken my spirit to evolve money-yielding ideas.

31. Let every spirit of debt and financial blockage be rendered impotent for my sake, in the name of Jesus.

32. O Lord, bring honey out of the rock for me and let me find the way where men say there is no way.

33. Thank the Lord for the answers.

FOR RAPID MANIFESTATION OF MIRACLES
Hab. 2:3

To be said very early morning and late in the night for seven (7) days consecutively.

- *When you feel that your breakthrough is being hindered.*

- *When you are believing the Lord for a mighty breakthrough*

If you learn to wait upon God in prayer and fasting, not minding how long it takes to get results, what would eventually follow is an avalanche of miracles in your life.

Ezekiel 12:28: *"Therefore say unto them, Thus saith the Lord God; There shall none of my words be prolonged any more, but the word which I have spoken shall be done, saith the Lord God."*

We serve a God that never comes late. He is always on time. And He makes all things beautiful in His time. (Ecclesiastes 3:11). Not in our own time. God always performs what He speaks (Ezekiel 37:14). Even if it seems like there is a delay, hang on because His words will not return to Him void. His WORD always performs that to which it is sent. (Isaiah 55:11).

Prayers for rapid manifestation of miracles, will remove any satanic delay of your expected breakthrough and God's promises. God will step into your situation and hasten His WORD to perform it (Jeremiah 1:12).

• PRAISE WORSHIP MAKE THESE POWERFUL CONFESSIONS AND PERSONALISE THEM

Ps. 31:2: *Bow down thine ear to me; deliver me speedily: be thou my strong rock, for an house of defence to save me.*

Ps. 143:7: *Hear me speedily, O LORD: my spirit faileth: hide not thy face from me, lest I be like unto them that go down into the pit.*

Isa. 58:8: *Then shall thy light break forth as the morning, and thine health* *shall spring forth speedily: and thy righteousness shall go before thee; the glory of the LORD shall be thy rereward.*

Luke 18:8: . . . *I tell you that he will avenge them speedily.*

Ps. 102:2: *Hide not thy face from me in the day when I am in trouble; incline thine ear unto me: in the day when I call answer me speedily.*

Jer. 1:12: *Then said the LORD unto me, Thou hast well seen: for I will hasten my word to perform it.*

Jer. 29:11: *For I know the thoughts that I think toward you, saith the LORD, thoughts of peace, and not of evil, to give you an expected end.*

● PRAISE WORSHIP
Sing at least seven (7) songs of praise to the Lord.

Praise Him from the bottom of your heart for answered prayers.

1. I dismiss and disband from my heart every thought, image or picture of failure on these matters, in the name of Jesus.

2. I reject every spirit of doubt, fear and discouragement, in the name of Jesus.

3. I cancel all ungodly delays to the manifestations of my miracles, in the name of Jesus.

4. Let the angels of the living God roll away every stone of hindrance to the manifestation of my breakthroughs, in the name of Jesus.

5. O Lord, hasten Your word to perform miracles in every department of my life.

6. O Lord, avenge me of my adversaries speedily, in Jesus' name.

7. I refuse to agree with the enemies of my progress, in the mighty name of Jesus.

(Say the next four (4) prayer points according to the level of your faith)

8. O Lord, I desire breakthroughs concerning . . . today, in the name of Jesus.

9. O Lord, I desire breakthroughs concerning . . . this week, in the name of Jesus.

10. O Lord, I desire breakthroughs concerning . . . this month, in the name of Jesus.

11. O Lord, I desire breakthroughs concerning . . . this year, in the name of Jesus.

12. Let there be turbulence, re-arrangement, revision, re-organisation and re-routing of situations and circumstances in order to create a path to my desired miracles, in the name of Jesus.

13. Let every hole present in the container of my life be mended, in the name of Jesus.

14. I bind, plunder and render to nothing every anti-testimony, anti-miracle and anti-prosperity forces, in the name of Jesus.

15. The God who answers by fire and the God of Elijah, answer me by fire, in the name of Jesus.

16. The God who answered Moses speedily at the Red Sea, answer me by fire, in the name of Jesus.

17. The God who changed the lot of Jabez, answer me by fire, in the name of Jesus.

18. The God which quickeneth the dead and calleth those things that be not as if they are, answer me by fire, in the name of Jesus.

19. The God of all comfort and joy, answer me by fire, in Jesus' name.

20. In the name of Jesus, let every foreign knee preventing the manifestation of my miracles in heaven, on earth and under-neath the earth, bow, in the name of Jesus.

21. I receive victory over all the forces of wickedness, in Jesus' name.

22. Let every evil force gathered against my breakthrough be completely scattered, in the name of Jesus.

23. I reject the spirit of the tail and I claim the spirit of the head, in the name of Jesus.

24. I command all evil records planted by the devil in anyone's mind against my desired miracles to be shattered to pieces, in the name of Jesus.

25. Let my path be cleared to the top by the hand of fire, in the name of Jesus.

26. Lord, catapult me into greatness as You did for Daniel in the land of Babylon.

27. Lord, help me to identify and deal with any weakness in me that can hinder the manifestation of my miracles.

28. I bind every strongman delegated to hinder the manifestations of my miracles, in the name of Jesus.

29. Let power change hands in every area of my life to the hands of the Holy Spirit, in the name of Jesus.

30. I receive the mandate to put to flight every enemy of my breakthroughs, in the name of Jesus.

31. I thank You, Lord Jesus, for given me divine victory.

DEFEATING ANTI-CONCEPTION FORCES

Deut. 7:14

- *For conception - whether problems and hin drances are identified or not*
- *When medical assistance has failed to yield results*

The promise of God concerning fruitfulness stands but for those who are still waiting for the fulfillment, it is because a unique child like Samuel would require a unique conception.

Genesis 1:28: *"And God blessed them, and God said unto them, Be fruitful, and multiply, and replenish the earth, and subdue it: and have dominion over the fish of the sea, and over the fowl of the air, and over every living thing that moveth upon the earth."*

These prayer points are designed to give you power over anti-conception forces, and break their yokes from your life! The vow of the enemy to prevent you from having children must be broken.

- **PERSONALISE THESE CONFESSIONS**

Ps. 127:3-5: *Lo, children are an heritage of the LORD: and the fruit of the womb is his reward. As arrows are in the hand of a mighty man; so are children of the youth. Happy is the man that hath his quiver full of them: they shall not be ashamed, but they shall speak with the enemies in the gate.*

Isa. 8:18: *Behold, I and the children whom the LORD hath given me are for signs and for wonders in Israel from the LORD of hosts, which dwelleth in mount Zion.*

Deut. 7:12-15: *Wherefore it shall come to pass, if ye hearken to these judgments, and keep, and do them, that the LORD thy God shall keep unto thee the covenant and the mercy which he sware unto thy fathers: And he will love thee, and bless thee, and multiply thee: he will also bless* *the fruit of thy womb, and the fruit of thy land, thy corn, and thy wine, and thine oil, the increase of thy kine, and the flocks of thy sheep, in the land which he sware unto thy fathers to give thee. Thou shalt be blessed above all people: there shall not be male or female barren among you, or among your cattle. And the LORD will take away from thee all sickness, and will put none of the evil diseases of Egypt, which thou knowest, upon thee; but will lay them upon all them that hate thee.*

● **PRAISE WORSHIP**

1. Thank the Lord for He is able to do all things.

2. Lord, forgive me all my ancestral sexual sins, in Jesus' name.

3. Let the lost glory of my family line be restored to me, in the name of Jesus.

4. I bind and paralyse the activities of the family strongman in my life, in the name of Jesus.

5. I bind and paralyse any strongman who is in charge of my womb, in the name of Jesus.

6. Let all the doorways of the enemy into my life be firmly closed, in the name of Jesus.

7. I decree the exit of all spiritual poison that entered into my womb during my wedding ceremony, in the name of Jesus.

8. Spiritual poison introduced into my womb through . . . (pick from the under listed), I command you to depart completely, in the name of Jesus.

   - eating in the dream
   - sexual intercourse in the dream
   - drinking dirty water in the dream
   - demonic contamination
   - abortion
   - masturbation
   - spiritual incision

- remote control mechanisms
- intercourse with demonic sexual partner

9. I break and cancel every curse, jinxes and spells placed on my womb, in the name of Jesus.

10. Let all the spiritual parasites which are feeding on the seeds of my womb be roasted, in the name of Jesus.

11. Lord, correct any disorder in my ovary, fallopian tube and womb, supernaturally, in the name of Jesus.

12. Let the fire and thunder of God destroy any demonic padlock used by the enemy to lock my womb, in the name of Jesus.

13. Let all the demonic eyes monitoring my body and progress receive blindness, in the name of Jesus.

14. I command all evil plantation in my womb to come out with all their roots, in the name of Jesus (*lay your hand on your womb and pray aggressively*).

15. Terminal pains around my waist and beneath my belly cease completely, in the name of Jesus.

16. Lord, activate my womb for conception.

17. Every vicious cycle of problems in my life break, in Jesus' name.

18. Evil inner voice speaking discouragement, unbelief and impossibility to my heart, be silenced, in the name of Jesus.

19. No devourer will devour the fruit of my womb, in Jesus' name.

20. I soak my womb, fallopian tube and ovary in the blood of Jesus.

21. I claim the promise of God concerning child bearing, in Jesus' name. (*Confess Psalm 127:1-5 loudly.*)

22. Praise God for answered prayers.

PRAYING FOR THE HEDGE OF THORNS

Luke 15:14-16

- *To be said violently and with aggressive faith. They must be borne out of the heart of compassion for the lost. They are not a spiritual whip to punish anyone.*

It is an acceptable biblical principle to pray for the hedge of thorns for your ungodly and wicked relations who are treading the path of destruction. If the way of the prodigal son was not hedged with thorns, he would not have remembered to come back to the father.

Acts 9:5: *"And the Lord said, I am Jesus whom thou persecutes It is hard for thee to kick against the pricks."*

God will prefer that all men be saved and come to the knowledge of the truth! This is His heartbeat: Salvation of souls.

Israel was enjoying a time of prosperity, so they forsook God and committed spiritual adultery by running after Baal and other false gods.

God said, "He would hedge their way with thorns," i.e. make things very difficult for Israel. This will cause them to come to their senses and recognise the source of their blessing. Just as in the physical a man will make life difficult for an unfaithful wife until she returns to him, God will make things difficult for man, till man returns to God.

In Paul's encounter with the Lord Jesus Christ, as he was striking the church, attacking Christ, rebelling against his Maker, he was hurting himself. God built a hedge of thorns around him and each time he struck the Church, the thorns would prick him.

These prayer points are specially designed for those who are far from the living God. Those loved ones who are into spiritual adultery, running after the gods of this age, wealth, women and worship of men.

As you faithfully bring your loved one before God, using these prayer points, God will hedge his or her way and the promise that "you and your household will be saved" (Acts 16:31) will become a reality.

● MEDITATE DEEPLY ON THIS SCRIPTURE

Hosea 2:6-15: *"Therefore, behold, I will hedge up thy way with thorns, and make a wall, that she shall not find her paths. And she shall follow after her lovers, but she shall not overtake them; and she shall seek them, but shall not find them: then shall she say, I will go and return to my first husband; for then was it better with me than now. For she did not know that I gave her corn, and wine, and oil, and multiplied her silver and gold, which they prepared for Baal. Therefore will I return, and take away my corn in the time thereof, and my wine in the season thereof, and will recover my wool and my flax given to cover her nakedness. And now will I discover her lewdness in the sight of her lovers, and none shall deliver her out of mine hand. I will also cause all her mirth to cease, her feast days, her new moons, and her Sabbaths, and all her solemn feasts. And I will destroy her vines and her fig trees, whereof she hath said, These are my rewards that my lovers have given me: and I will make them a forest, and the beasts of the field shall eat them. And I will visit upon her the days of Baalim, wherein she burned incense to them, and she decked herself with her earrings and her jewels, and she went after her lovers, and forgat me, saith the LORD. Therefore, behold, I will allure her, and bring her into the wilderness, and speak comfortably unto her. And I will give her her vineyards from thence, and the valley of Achor for a door of hope: and she shall sing there, as in the days of her youth, and as in the day when she came up out of the land of Egypt."*

● BRIEF EXPLANATION

1. *Praying for the hedge of thorns is an important aspect of spiritual warfare.*
2. *It has to be done daily.*
3. *Evil friends and strange partners will begin to avoid the person being prayed for.*
4. *The person will begin to have difficulty in finding his or her path of wickedness.*

5. *The person becomes miserable and uncomfortable until he finds the Lord.*

6. *It should be noted that the Bible says: "We are not to rescue" until the mission is accomplished.*

• PRAISE WORSHIP

1. Lord, I pray that . . . will not find peace until he returns in repentance to his/her Creator.

2. I command the ways of all unfriendly friends confusing . . . to become dark and slippery, in the name of Jesus.

3. Let the angels of God arise and block the path of . . . with thorny wishes after the order of Balaam until . . . runs back to the Saviour, in the name of Jesus.

4. Let all strange lovers begin to avoid . . . as from today, in the name of Jesus.

5. Lord, ordain terrifying noises against all evil collaborators confusing . . . .

6. O Lord, build a wall of hindrance around . . . so that he will be unable to carry out any ungodly activity.

7. Let all the good things that . . . is enjoying thereby hardening his heart to the truth be withdrawn, in Jesus' name.

8. Let . . . become sick and restless on tasting any alcohol or using any addictive material, in the name of Jesus.

9. I break every curse of the vagabond upon the life of . . . ., in the mighty name of Jesus.

10. Let the angels of the living God begin to pursue all strange lovers caging . . . , in the name of Jesus.

11. Lord, walk back to the foundation of my marriage and carry out the necessary surgical operation.

12. I bind every strongman militating against my home, in Jesus' name.

13. Let every gadget of marriage destruction be frustrated in my home, in the name of Jesus.

14. Let every evil anti-marriage linkage with our parents be dashed to pieces, in the name of Jesus.

15. Every evil effect of external interferences in our marriage be completely neutralized, in the name of Jesus.

16. I paralyse every architect of conflict and hostility in my home, in the name of Jesus.

17. Let every evil power trying to redraw my marriage map be put to shame, in the name of Jesus.

18. Let all extra-marital relationship with other "partners" collapse and die, in the name of Jesus.

19. I paralyse the activities of the spirit of . . . (*pick from the under listed*), and I command you to loose your hold upon . . ., in the name of Jesus.

- criticism	- unreasonable behaviour	
- accusation	- arguing	- intimidation
- rejecting the truth	- pride	- self-importance
- self-centeredness	- self-exaltation	- selfishness
- stubbornness	- superiority	- intolerance
- cruelty	- retaliation	- impatience
- bitterness	- anger	- hatred
- fighting	- contention	- violence
- rebellion	- deception	- restlessness
- withdrawal	- confusion	- family molestation
- lust of the eyes	- lust of the flesh	- dishonesty
- disrespect	- personality disorders	
- cursing	- lying	- inherited curses
- occultic practices		

20. Thank God for answer to your prayer.

FOR MULTIPLE BREAKTHROUGHS

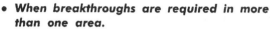

Psalm 143:7-9

- *When breakthroughs are required in more than one area.*
- *When there is evidence of multiple hindrances to breakthroughs.*
- *When a person experiences the all-doors-closed syndrome.*

God is unlimited and is interested in demonstrating to you His vast resources by plunging you into multiple break-throughs. As someone puts it, "God is a God of too much."

Revelation 3:7: *". . . these things saith He that is holy, he that is true, he that hath the key of David, he that openeth, and no man shutteth; and shutteth and no man openeth."*

Every time the windows of heaven open, the unprecedented happens. In Genesis 28:12-16, when Jacob was running away from the wrath of Esau, the windows of heaven opened and he saw angels ascending and descending upon him. This marked Jacob's first encounter with God and it brought promises, blessings and a reaffirmation of the Abrahamic covenant.

Also, when the Syrian army laid a siege on Samaria, and the famine in the land was severe, and everything was expensive, Elisha gave a prophecy of God's deliverance (2 Kings 7:1-20). One of the King's officers said, "Even if God opened the windows of heaven, the miracle could not happen." Elisha then replied that he would see it with his eyes but not taste it. God indeed opened the windows of heaven! The Syrians were scared by the heavenly noise and they fled. Overnight, there was divine provision.

Psalm 78:23-29 also records how God supernaturally fed the Israelites in the desert for 40 years, by opening the doors of heaven.

Paying your tithes will cause the windows of heaven to open. It will cause God to rebuke the devourers and every hindering power so that you can receive multiple breakthroughs (Malachi 3:10-12).

As you pray these prayers with faith in God, "He that openeth and no man can shut" will step into your situation and open the windows of heaven so that you can receive your multiple breakthroughs! He will also shut every door of poverty, failure and lack.

● MAKE THESE POWERFUL CONFESSIONS AND PERSONALISE THEM

Ps. 31:2: *Bow down thine ear to me; deliver me speedily: be thou my strong rock, for an house of defence to save me.*

Ps. 143:7: *Hear me speedily, O LORD: my spirit faileth: hide not thy face from me, lest I be like unto them that go down into the pit.*

Isa. 58:8: *Then shall thy light break forth as the morning, and thine health shall spring forth speedily: and thy righteousness shall go before thee; the glory of the LORD shall be thy rereward.*

Luke 18:8: *I tell you that he will avenge them speedily.*

Ps. 102:2: *Hide not thy face from me in the day when I am in trouble; incline thine ear unto me: in the day when I call answer me speedily.*

Jer. 1:12: *Then said the LORD unto me, Thou hast well seen: for I will hasten my word to perform it.*

Jer. 29:11: *For I know the thoughts that I think toward you, saith the LORD, thoughts of peace, and not of evil, to give you an expected end.*

● PRAISE WORSHIP

Praise Him from the bottom of your heart for answered prayers.

1. All boasting powers delegated against me, be silenced, in the name of Jesus.

2. I withdraw my benefits from the hands of the oppressors, in the name of Jesus.

3. Let all unprofitable marks in my life be erased with the blood of Jesus.

4. Let every power chasing away my blessings be paralyzed, in the name of Jesus.

5. Let every good thing eaten up by the enemy be vomited, in the name of Jesus.

6. Let heavenly fire ignite my prayer life, in the name of Jesus.

7. Let the anointing for spiritual breakthroughs fall mightily on me, in the name of Jesus.

8. O Lord, empower my prayer life.

9. O Lord, make me a prayer addict.

10. O Lord, revive and ignite my prayer life.

11. I reject every spiritual contamination, in the name of Jesus.

12. Let every negative plan and activity against my life be reversed to good, in the name of Jesus.

13. O Lord, let the second touch of Your power fall upon me now.

14. Lord, give me divine prescription to my problems today.

15. Lord, give me power to overcome obstacles to breakthroughs.

16. Lord, ignite in me the fire that will make me a weapon.

17. Let the word of God explode in me, in the name of Jesus.

18. I break all curses of leaking blessings, in the name of Jesus.

19. Let all spiritual holes in my life be closed with the blood of Jesus.

20. Lord, help me to locate the defect in the clay of my life.

21. I refuse to be used as a bad example, in the name of Jesus.

22. I bind the spirit of negative destiny in every area of my life, in the name of Jesus.

23. Lord, let me be at the right place at the right time throughout the days of my life.

24. Lord, purge the foundation of my life with Your fire.

25. O Lord, forgive me for operating below the spiritual level You planned for me.

26. Lord, purge my life with Your fire.

27. Lord, clear spiritual clogs from my life.

28. Lord, make me the voice of deliverance and blessings.

29. I clear my goods from the warehouse of the strongman, in the name of Jesus.

30. I seal my victory with the blood of Jesus.

31. Lord Jesus, I thank You for answers to my prayer.

DISSOLVING UNPROFITABLE GROWTH

Psalm 18:45

- *To expel and dissolve every unprofitable growth inside the womb or other parts of the body.*
- *Deliverance from satanic plantations inside the body.*
- *To completely dissolve evil stubborn growth.*

The power of prayer of faith, is capable of clearing away all the strange spirits constructing evil growth in your life and terminate their operations.

Psalm 97:5: *"The hills melted like wax at the presence of the Lord, at the presence of the Lord of the whole earth."*

Why do the hills melt like wax at His presence? Because, there is a fire that goes out before Him which burn up His enemies round about. (Psalm 97:3). It is written that our God is a consuming fire (Hebrews 12:29).

Hills here represent everything that is an enemy of God. Cancer, fibroid, satanic growths and deposits must melt and disappear at the presence of God.

"In His presence is fullness of joy and at His right hand are pleasures forever more" (Psalm 16:11). As you stand in the presence of your Maker, He will fill you with joy. Every unprofitable growth will be dissolved by the fire that goes before Him! It is His pleasure to heal you, to deliver you and to recreate all your body parts as He originally created them (Psalm 139:15-16).

These prayers will bring the presence and the fire of God into your situation! Rejoice, for your joy must be full. The enemy and his agents cannot stand in the presence of God.

- **MAKE THESE CONFESSIONS BOLDLY AND LOUDLY**

Ps. 56:9: *When I cry unto thee, then shall mine enemies turn back: this I know; for God is for me.*

Mal. 4:2: *But unto you that fear my name shall the Sun of righteousness arise with healing in his wings; and ye shall go forth, and grow up as calves of the stall.*

Gal. 3:13-14: *Christ hath redeemed us from the curse of the law, being made a curse for us: for it is written, Cursed is every one that hangeth on a tree: That the blessing of Abraham might come on the Gentiles through Jesus Christ; that we might receive the promise of the Spirit through faith.*

Col. 2:14-15: *Blotting out the handwriting of ordinances that was against us, which was contrary to us, and took it out of the way, nailing it to his cross; And having spoiled principalities and powers, he made a shew of them openly, triumphing over them in it.*

Matt. 8:17: *That it might be fulfilled which was spoken by Esaias the prophet, saying, Himself took our infirmities, and bare our sicknesses.*

Rom. 16:20: *And the God of peace shall bruise Satan under your feet shortly. The grace of our Lord Jesus Christ be with you. Amen.*

Matt. 3:10: *And now also the axe is laid unto the root of the trees: therefore every tree which bringeth not forth good fruit is hewn down, and cast into the fire.*

1 Jn. 3:8b: *For this purpose the Son of God was manifested, that he might destroy the works of the devil.*

2 Tim. 4:18: *And the Lord shall deliver me from every evil work, and will preserve me unto his heavenly kingdom: to whom be glory for ever and ever. Amen.*

Jesus is Lord over my spirit, soul and body for the word of God tells me that at the name of Jesus every knee shall bow. I can do all things through Christ who strengthens me. The Lord is my shepherd, I shall not want. Jesus has delivered me from the powers of darkness and has translated me into the kingdom of His dear Son. In Jesus I have redemption through His shed blood and also forgiveness of sins. Jesus has blotted out the handwriting of ordinances that was against me which was contrary to me, and took it out of the way nailing it to His cross. I am the body of Christ. I am redeemed from the curse because Jesus bore my physical and spiritual diseases in His body. I have the mind of Christ and hold the thoughts, feelings and purposes of His heart.

- **PRAISE WORSHIP**

1. Thank the Lord for His power to deliver from any form of bondage.
2. I apply the blood of Jesus to my spirit, soul, body and womb.
3. Let the fire of God saturate my womb, in the name of Jesus.
4. Let every design against my life be completely nullified, in the name of Jesus.
5. Let all evil labels fashioned by the camp of the enemy against my life be rubbed off with the blood of Jesus.

Sing the song HOLY GHOST FIRE, FIRE FALL ON ME with full concentration and in faith.

6. I vomit every satanic deposit in my life, in the mighty name of Jesus.

(Prime the expulsion of these things by coughing slightly. Refuse to swallow any saliva coming out from the mouth)

7. I break myself loose from the bondage of stagnancy, in the mighty name of Jesus.
8. Lord, destroy with Your fire anything that makes Your promise to fail in my life no matter the origin.

As you pray No 9, take 3-4 deep breaths determinedly expelling and flushing out spiritual contamination. Do so aggressively, in the mighty name of Jesus.

9. Let the blood, the fire and the living water of the Most High God wash my system clean from:
   - unprofitable growth in my womb
   - evil plantation
   - evil deposits from spirit husband
   - impurities acquired from parental contamination
   - evil spiritual consumption
   - hidden sicknesses
   - remote control mechanisms
   - physical and spiritual incisions

    - satanic poisons

    - evil stamps, labels and links.

10. Let every area of my life become too hot for any evil to inhabit, in the name of Jesus.

11. Evil growth in my life, be uprooted, in the name of Jesus.

12. Let my body reject every evil habitation, in the mighty name of our Lord Jesus Christ.

13. O Lord, reverse all evil arrangements attached consciously or unconsciously to my life.

14. I reject all evil manipulations and manipulators, in the mighty name of Jesus.

15. I break the power of the occult, witchcraft and familiar spirits over my life, in the name of Jesus.

Prime the expulsion of satanic deposits (Nos 16-18) by heaving up and applying little force upon the lower part of the abdomen.

16. I deliver and pass out any satanic deposit in my intestine, in the name of Jesus.

17. I deliver and pass out any satanic deposit in my reproductive organs, in the name of Jesus.

18. I deliver and pass out any satanic deposit in my womb, in the name of Jesus.

19. *In the name of Jesus, I declare before all the forces of darkness that "Jesus Christ is Lord over every department of my life."*

20. You foreign hand laid on my womb, release me, in Jesus' name.

21. In the name of Jesus, I renounce, break and loose myself from all

    - demonic holds   - psychic powers

    - bonds of physical illness   - bondage

22. In the name of Jesus, I break and loose myself from all evil curses, chains, spells, jinxes, bewitchments, witchcraft or sorcery which may have been put upon me.

23. Let a creative miracle take place in my womb and reproductive system, in the name of Jesus.

24. Father, I ask You, in the name of Jesus Christ, to send out Your angels and have them unearth and break all evil storage vessels fashioned against me.

25. I loose myself from every evil influence, dark spirit and satanic bondage, in the name of Jesus.

26. I confess and declare that my body is the temple of the Holy Spirit, redeemed, cleansed, and sanctified by the blood of Jesus Christ.

27. I bind, plunder and render to naught every strongman assigned to my womb, reproductive system and marital life, in Jesus' name.

28. God who quickens the dead, quicken my womb and reproductive system, in the name of Jesus.

29. I release myself from the hold of spirits of sterility, infertility and fear, in the name of Jesus.

30. All spirits rooted in fornication, come out of my womb with all your roots, in the mighty name of our Lord Jesus.

31. All spirits rooted in sexual perversion, come out of my womb with all your roots, in the mighty name of our Lord Jesus.

32. All spirits rooted in spirit husband, come out of my womb with all your roots, in the mighty name of our Lord Jesus.

33. All spirits rooted in masturbation, come out of my womb with all your roots, in the mighty name of our Lord Jesus.

34. All spirits rooted in guilt, come out of my womb with all your roots, in the mighty name of our Lord Jesus.

35. All spirits rooted in pornography, come out of my womb with all your roots, in the mighty name of our Lord Jesus.

36. Sing this song: *There is power mighty in the blood . . ..*

37. Thank the Lord for your healing and deliverance.

COME ALIVE

Ezek. 37: 1-11

• *For resurrection of dead organs or dead babies in the womb.*

The Father, the Son and the Holy Spirit are still in the business of raising the dead. But you have to get into action by resorting to aggressive prayer and violent faith against any of your dead organs or situations.

Romans 8:11: *"But if the Spirit of Him that raised up Jesus from the dead dwell in you, He that raised up Christ from the dead shall also quicken your mortal bodies by His Spirit that dwelleth in you."*

The Holy Spirit is the God's executive agent on earth. He is the creative power of God. Going back to Genesis 1 we see that the Holy Spirit played a crucial role in bringing order out of the chaos of Genesis 1:2.

It is this same Holy Spirit that dwells in you! Yes, He dwells in you. It was through the Holy Spirit that you got born again, He is the one that convicts you as a sinner (John 16:8-11). You house the Holy Spirit, that is why the Bible says, "Know ye not that ye art the temple of God, and that the Spirit of God dwelleth in your" (1 Cor. 3:16).

If the Holy Spirit, the power that raised Jesus from the dead, dwells in your body, then every dead organ in your body, or the baby in your womb, must receive life! These prayer points will cause life to flow into your mortal body!

• CONFESSIONS

John 5:21: *For as the Father raiseth up the dead, and quickeneth them; even so the Son quickeneth whom he will.*

John 6:63: *It is the spirit that quickeneth; the flesh profiteth nothing: the words that I speak unto you, they are spirit, and they are life.*

Rom. 4:17: *(As it is written, I have made thee a father of many nations,) before him whom he believed, even God, who quickeneth the dead, and calleth those things which be not as though they were.*

John 11:25: *Jesus said unto her, I am the resurrection, and the life: he that believeth in me, though he were dead, yet shall he live:*

- **PRAISE WORSHIP**

Slot in the name of the organ you are praying about into the dotted lines

1. Let Your resurrection power come upon my . . ., in the mighty name of Jesus.

2. I bind every spirit of death operating in my . . ., in the mighty name of Jesus.

3. I command every dead bone in my . . . to come alive, in the name of Jesus.

4. You evil hand laid on my . . ., receive the thunder and the fire of God and be roasted, in the name of Jesus.

5. I command every evil monitoring gadget fashioned against my . . . to be destroyed, in the name of Jesus.

6. I breathe in the life of God and I reject every spirit of death and hell, in the name of Jesus.

7. I recover every miracle that I have lost through unbelief, in the name of Jesus.

8. Father, let Your creative power operate afresh in . . . area of my life, in the name of Jesus.

9. Father, let the fire of the Holy Ghost enter into my blood stream and cleanse my system, in the name of Jesus.

10. I release my . . . from the cage of every household wickedness, in the name of Jesus.

11. Let every information about my . . . be erased from every satanic memory, in the name of Jesus.

12. I command every evil plantation in my life: **Come out with all your roots, in the name of Jesus!** (*Lay your hands on your stomach and*

keep repeating the emphasized area.)

13. Evil strangers in my body, come all the way out of your hiding places, in the name of Jesus.

14. I cough out and vomit any food eaten from the table of the devil, in the name of Jesus. *(Cough them out and vomit them in faith. Prime the expulsion.)*

15. Let all negative materials circulating in my blood stream be evacuated, in the name of Jesus.

16. I drink the blood of Jesus. *(Physically swallow and drink it in faith. Keep doing this for some time.)*

17. *Lay one hand on your head and the other on your stomach or navel and begin to pray like this:* Holy Ghost fire, burn from the top of my head to the sole of my feet. *Begin to mention every organ of your body; your kidney, liver, intestine, blood, etc. You must not rush at this level, because the fire will actually come and you may start feeling the heat.*

18. I cut myself off from every spirit of . . . *(mention the name of your place of birth)*, in the name of Jesus.

19. I cut myself off from every tribal spirit and curses, in Jesus' name.

20. I cut myself off from every territorial spirit and curses, in the name of Jesus.

21. Holy Ghost fire, purge my life.

22. I claim my complete deliverance, in the name of Jesus, from the spirit of . . . *(mention those things you do not desire in your life)*.

23. I break the hold of any evil power over my life, in Jesus' name.

24. I move from bondage into liberty, in the name of Jesus.

25. Thank God for answers to your prayer points.

EASE OF PASSAGE
Isa. 40:4

- *To ease procurement of travelling documents and approvals.*
- *To facilitate travels.*

Neither mountain nor valley, neither crooked path nor rough road - no obstruction can hinder a true heaven-bound pilgrimage. You have the right to order for heavenly bulldozer to clear hindrances to your breakthrough.

Isaiah 43:19: *"Behold, I will do a new thing; now it shall spring forth; shall ye not know it? I will even make a way in the wilderness, and rivers in the dessert."*

This trip you are going on, is it part of God's will for your life? Will it glorify God? What is God saying about it? Is God telling you to go? If the answers to these questions are Yes, then take this prayer points violently and see God remove every hindrance and stumbling block to your travelling.

When God says He will make a way, He simply means that He will handle every impossible situation and begin to fashion and recreate everything until there is a way for you.

The God that made an express way for the Israelites through the Red Sea, will grant you ease of passage as you pray these prayers in faith.

- **CONFESSIONS**

Rev. 12:11: *And they overcame him by the blood of the Lamb, and by the word of their testimony; and they loved not their lives unto the death.*

Rom. 8:37: *Nay, in all these things we are more than conquerors through him that loved us.*

Ps. 55:16: *As for me, I will call upon God; and the LORD shall save me.*

Ps. 118:10-14: *All nations compassed me about: but in the name of the LORD will I destroy them. They compassed me about; yea, they compassed me about: but in the name of the LORD I will destroy them. They compassed* *me about like bees; they are quenched as the fire of thorns: for in the name of the LORD I will destroy them. Thou hast thrust sore at me that I might fall: but the LORD helped me. The LORD is my strength and song, and is become my salvation.*

Mal. 3:6: *For I am the LORD, I change not; therefore ye sons of Jacob are not consumed.*

Acts 2:24: *Whom God hath raised up, having loosed the pains of death: because it was not possible that he should be holden of it.*

● **PRAISE WORSHIP**

1. Thank God because He is the only One who can advance you.

2. Let every hindrance and barrier to my journey be rolled away, in the name of Jesus.

3. Let every satanic network designed against my breakthroughs be shattered to pieces, in the name of Jesus.

4. Let the spirit of favour and goodwill come upon my life, in the name of Jesus.

5. Let every eye monitoring my breakthroughs receive the arrows of fire, in the name of Jesus.

6. I remove my name and address from the control of evil manipulators, in the name of Jesus.

7. Let the angels of the living God roll away the stone blocking my financial, physical and spiritual breakthroughs, in the name Jesus.

8. Let God arise and let all the enemies of my breakthroughs be scattered, in the name of Jesus.

9. All evil spirits masquerading to trouble me, be bound, in the name of Jesus.

10. O Lord, bring me into favour with all those who will decide on my advancement.

11. O Lord, cause a divine substitution to happen if this is what will move me ahead.

12. I reject the spirit of the tail and I claim the spirit of the head, in the name of Jesus.

13. I command all evil records planted by the devil in anyone's mind against my advancement to be shattered to pieces, in Jesus' name.

14. O Lord, transfer, remove or change all human agents who are bent on stopping my plan.

15. I receive the anointing to excel above my contemporaries, in the name of Jesus.

16. Lord, help me to identify and deal with any weakness in me that can hinder my progress.

17. I bind every strongman delegated to hinder my progress, in the name of Jesus.

18. I receive the mandate to put to flight every enemy of my breakthroughs, in the name of Jesus.

19. I bind and render to nought you spirit of . . . (pick from the under listed), in the mighty name of Jesus.

- demonic antagonism   - strife
- marginal success   - wrong words
- bad feet/bad luck   - confusion
- evil collaborators   - blank mind
- mind dullness   - memory failure
- demonic delays   - costly mistakes
- evil followers   - demonic opinions against me
- unprofitable questions - unprofitable controversies
- demonic logic and unprofitable interviews

20. Thank God for answering your prayers.

REVOKING EVIL DECREES
Col. 2:14,15

- *For those who are under the influence of curses, spells and evil covenants.*

The power to revoke or reverse any evil spell cast on you by evil people, has been made available to you through the sacrifice of Christ when He was hanged on the cross.

Job 22:28: *"Thou shall decree a thing and it shall be established unto you; and the light shall shine upon thy ways."*

God decreed the heavens and the earth into being. As He spoke, He laid down divine laws which up till today are still effective. He gave Adam that same power. Adam named all the animals.

God has given us that same power, the power to decree. Proverbs 8:15 says, "By me (wisdom) kings reign and princes decree justice." In the book of Esther, Haman wrote an evil decree against the Jews. By the law of the Medes and Persian once the king signed a decree, it could not be revoked even by the king. Queen Esther and the Jews went into three days fasting and prayers for deliverance from Haman-inspired evil decree.

God granted Esther favour with the king and after a few meetings with him, she and the Jews were given permission to offset this evil decree but not to cancel it (Esther 8:8-11). They were to gather together and fight.

God has given us more authority than King Ahasuerus gave the Jews. We have the power by the shed blood of Jesus to cancel and completely blot out every satanic decree and evil handwriting against our lives. Let us stand up and fight. Let us break the stronghold and revoke every satanic decree against our lives.

- ## CONFESSIONS

Isa. 8:8-10: *And he shall pass through Judah; he shall overflow and go over, he shall reach even to the neck; and the stretching out of his wings shall fill the breadth of thy land, O Immanuel. Associate yourselves, O ye people, and ye shall be broken in pieces; and give ear, all ye of far countries: gird yourselves, and ye shall be broken in pieces; gird yourselves, and ye shall be broken in pieces. Take counsel together, and it shall come to nought; speak the word, and it shall not stand: for God is with us.*

- **NOTE: Prayers for revoking evil decrees have to be said aggressively and violently. Pray like spiritual soldiers.**
- **Make these confessions out loud.**

Jesus Christ has purchased my freedom from the curse of the law and all its condemnations, by offering Himself as a curse for me. I can no longer labour under the burden of the law fro I have become a saint, a lively stone, a built-up spiritual stone and a holy priesthood, to offer up spiritual sacrifices acceptable to God by Christ. I am a chosen generation, a royal priesthood, a peculiar person; that I should show forth the praises of Him who has called me out of darkness into His marvelous light.

The Name of Jesus Christ is given unto me to exercise authority in three different worlds, the earth, the seas and beneath the earth. For the Bible says, "God has highly exalted him and has freely bestowed upon him the name that is above every name, so that when I pronounce that name it becomes a strong tower for me, it makes everything in the heavenlies that is against my prayers to bow, so also those in the earth and in the seas beneath the earth."

In Jesus' name, I take authority over the heavenlies, the earth, the seas and under the earth and the things in them. I destroy with the sword of the Spirit every body of darkness that is poised to stand against my prayer or to reinforce against me.

Jesus Christ is my personal Lord. He is my Saviour. He is my redeemer and my deliverer. His blood has done so much for me and it is the reason for my living today. The blood saved me from the wrath of God inspired by the consequences of my sins. Through the blood I have received forgiveness of my sins; through the blood God became merciful to my unrighteousness and He is no longer remembering my past. Now, I am justified by the blood of Jesus Christ; for faith in the blood of Jesus delivers me from every accusation that the devil makes against me.

It is written that if Jesus Christ sets me free, I am free indeed. I confess and receive freedom from every ancestral curse of untimely death, ancestral curse of marital destruction or frustration, ancestral curse of poverty or financial handicap, ancestral curse of infirmity, and ancestral curse of failure at the edge of breakthroughs.

By the blood of Jesus, there is no condemnation for me who is in Christ Jesus, for I walk not after the flesh, but after the spirit and the law of the spirit of life in Christ Jesus has made me free from the law of sin and death. I confess that every ancestral dedication of children in my family lineage to idols, gods sacred waters and trees is broken upon my life. For I shall not suffer for the sins of my forefathers, everyone shall dear his own iniquity. By the blood of Jesus every unconscious covenant with familiar spirits in my family be broken and release me.

By the power in the blood of Jesus I decree that every curse of sexual immorality over my life, as a result of incest, lesbianism, homosexuality, bestiality, fornication, adultery, oral sex. Abortion, the sexual sins of my father and the sexual iniquities of my mother, be broken now, in the name of Jesus. For Jesus was bruised for my transgressions.

Every curse affecting my dwelling place, my positions, my land and properties, as a result of any past rituals or sacrifices performed on them, be broken by the power in the blood of Jesus.

It is written, life and death are in the power of the tongue and by the words of our mouth we shall be condemned or justified. Every curse placed over my life and property through witchcraft curses, spells, jinx, enchantments and incantations, be broken by the blood of Jesus. Every curse I have personally attracted to my life through my actions, promises, vows, oaths and negative confessions, be broken by the blood of Jesus. The scripture says, whatsoever I bind here on earth shall be bound in heavens. I bind the activities of these curses and loose myself from their grip.

The Bible says, where I sold myself to without money the Lord will buy me back. Every curse resulting from my consultations with spirits, herbalists, oracles, mediums and palmists, I break you with the blood of Jesus and loose your grip over my life.

Every curse activated through my personal sins, be removed by the blood of Jesus I confess that I am now in the service of God. My body is the temple of God, as it is written that God will dwell in me and walk in me and be my God and I shall be His. I command all the demons operation these curses to vacate my life and property. Let their activities come to an end and the blessings of God begin to replace their curses.

In the place of any curse that ever affects me. I confess these scriptures: And I have peace through the blood of his cross, by him to reconcile all things unto himself, I confess that everything that pertains to me is reconciled to Christ.

The Lord will give me strength. He will bless me and my household with peace. The Lord God will bless me as He promised me and I shall lend unto many nations, I shall not borrow and I shall reign over many nations. The Lord shall open unto me His good treasure. The heaven shall give rain unto my land in its season and bless all the work of my hand. The Lord shall cause my enemies, who rise up against me, to be defeated before my face. They shall come out against me in one way, they shall be defeated before me in seven ways. The Lord will establish me as a person holy to himself as He has spoken.

I shall be head and not tail, and blessed shall be my land, my storehouse, my business place, my dwelling place, and the works of my hand. The Lord shall not suffer destruction and peril to come upon me all the days of my life. I seal my confession with the precious blood of the Lamb of God.

● PRAISE WORSHIP

1. I reject every evil manipulation in all areas of my life, in the name of Jesus.
2. I reject every deceptive family control mechanism, in Jesus' name.
3. Let the curse of impossibility issued against me bounce back on the enemy, in the mighty name of Jesus.
4. Let every agent of impossibility fashioned against me receive permanent failure, in the name of Jesus.

5. Let every plantation of impossibility in my life be roasted, in the name of Jesus.

6. I refuse to be diverted from the path of blessings, in Jesus' name.

7. Let every satanic agent deflecting my blessings stumble and fall to rise no more, in the name of Jesus.

8. I command every evil power drinking the milk of my life to begin to vomit them, in the name of Jesus.

9. Let every satanic prayer against my life be reversed, in the name of Jesus.

10. Let every access satan has to my life be withdrawn permanently, in the name of Jesus.

11. I curse every satanic mountain-problem in my life, in Jesus' name.

12. Let all fake friends be exposed and be disgraced, in Jesus' name.

13. Let all evil collaborators in disguise be exposed and be disgraced, in the name of Jesus.

14. Let all spiritual vultures in any area of my life be paralyzed, in the name of Jesus.

15. Evil family river, do not touch me, in the name of Jesus.

16. Holy Spirit, help me to really discover myself.

17. I release my hand from every bewitchment, in Jesus' name.

18. I forbid any re-grouping and reinforcement of any evil against me, in the name of Jesus.

19. Let every vow of the enemy against my life be nullified, in the name of Jesus.

20. O Lord, reverse all evil curses issued against me.

21. Let every satanic decision and judgement against me be rendered null and void, in the name of Jesus.

22. Thank God for answers to your prayers.

FOR STUBBORN SITUATIONS
Psalm 18

- *To disgrace iron-like and stubborn situations. Users may find it convinient to divide the prayer points into 10 sections for firm handling*

Stubborn and unpleasant situations sometimes do require stubborn measure of violent faith and prayer.

Obad. 1:3,4: *"The pride of thy heart hath deceived thee, thou that dwellest in the clefts of the rock, whose habitation is high; that saith in his heart, who shall bring me down to the ground? Though thou exalt thyself as the eagle, and though thou set thy nest among the stars, thence will I bring thee down, saith the LORD."*

More often than not, stubborn situations arise because of satanic embargoes. Rejoice, beloved, because no matter how powerful the stronghold of the enemy is; no matter how secure the enemy feels, the Lord will disgrace him.. The enemy has won long enough. He has been boasting long enough. The time to silence him has come. Pride goes before a fall. Goliath was the pride of the Philistines. He boasted against Israel for 40 days and 40 nights. Only one stone from David's sling killed him.

It doesn't matter how long the situation has been there, as you pray these prayers with spiritual violence, God will fight for you! (Exodus 14:14).

• CONFESSION

Job 5:12: *He disappointeth the devices of the crafty, so that their hands cannot perform their enterprise.*

Isa. 49:24-26: *Shall the prey be taken from the mighty, or the lawful captive delivered? But thus saith the LORD, Even the captives of the mighty shall be taken away, and the prey of the terrible shall be delivered: for I will contend with him that contendeth with thee, and I will save thy children. And I will feed them that oppress thee with their own flesh; and they shall* *be drunken with their own blood, as with sweet wine: and all flesh shall know that I the LORD am thy Saviour and thy Redeemer, the mighty One of Jacob.*

Isa. 54:17: *No weapon that is formed against thee shall prosper; and every tongue that shall rise against thee in judgment thou shalt condemn. This is the heritage of the servants of the LORD, and their righteousness is of me, saith the LORD.*

Rev. 13:10: *He that leadeth into captivity shall go into captivity: he that killeth with the sword must be killed with the sword. Here is the patience and the faith of the saints.*

Isa. 50:7-9: *For the Lord GOD will help me; therefore shall I not be confounded: therefore have I set my face like a flint, and I know that I shall not be ashamed. He is near that justifieth me; who will contend with me? let us stand together: who is mine adversary? let him come near to me. Behold, the Lord GOD will help me; who is he that shall condemn me? lo, they all shall wax old as a garment; the moth shall eat them up.*

Isa. 54:15: *Behold, they shall surely gather together, but not by me: whosoever shall gather together against thee shall fall for thy sake.*

Isa. 59:19: *So shall they fear the name of the LORD from the west, and his glory from the rising of the sun. When the enemy shall come in like a flood, the Spirit of the LORD shall lift up a standard against him.*

Isa. 8:9-10: *Associate yourselves, O ye people, and ye shall be broken in pieces; and give ear, all ye of far countries: gird yourselves, and ye shall be broken in pieces; gird yourselves, and ye shall be broken in pieces. Take counsel together, and it shall come to nought; speak the word, and it shall not stand: for God is with us.*

Jer. 1:8, 19: *Be not afraid of their faces: for I am with thee to deliver thee, saith the LORD. . . . And they shall fight against thee; but they shall not prevail against thee; for I am with thee, saith the LORD, to deliver thee.*

Deut. 33:25-27: *Thy shoes shall be iron and brass; and as thy days, so shall thy strength be. There is none like unto the God of Jeshurun, who rideth upon the heaven in thy help, and in his excellency on the sky. The* *eternal God is thy refuge, and underneath are the everlasting arms: and he shall thrust out the enemy from before thee; and shall say, Destroy them.*

Ps. 68:1-2: *Let God arise, let his enemies be scattered: let them also that hate him flee before him. As smoke is driven away, so drive them away: as wax melteth before the fire, so let the wicked perish at the presence of God.*

Obad. 1:3-4: *The pride of thine heart hath deceived thee, thou that dwellest in the clefts of the rock, whose habitation is high; that saith in his heart, Who shall bring me down to the ground? Though thou exalt thyself as the eagle, and though thou set thy nest among the stars, thence will I bring thee down, saith the LORD.*

Zech. 4:7: *Who art thou, O great mountain? before Zerubbabel thou shalt become a plain: and he shall bring forth the headstone thereof with shoutings, crying, Grace, grace unto it.*

Rom. 16:20: *And the God of peace shall bruise Satan under your feet shortly. The grace of our Lord Jesus Christ be with you. Amen.*

2 Tim. 4:18: *And the Lord shall deliver me from every evil work, and will preserve me unto his heavenly kingdom: to whom be glory for ever and ever. Amen.*

Matt. 18:18: *Verily I say unto you, Whatsoever ye shall bind on earth shall be bound in heaven: and whatsoever ye shall loose on earth shall be loosed in heaven.*

Luke 10:19: *Behold, I give unto you power to tread on serpents and scorpions, and over all the power of the enemy: and nothing shall by any means hurt you.*

Ps. 91:7,10,13 : *A thousand shall fall at thy side, and ten thousand at thy right hand; but it shall not come nigh thee. There shall no evil befall thee, neither shall any plague come nigh thy dwelling. Thou shalt tread upon the lion and adder: the young lion and the dragon shalt thou trample under feet.*

Josh. 1:5: *There shall not any man be able to stand before thee all the days of thy life: as I was with Moses, so I will be with thee: I will not fail thee, nor forsake thee.*

Num. 23:23: *Surely there is no enchantment against Jacob, neither is there any divination against Israel: according to this time it shall be said of Jacob and of Israel, What hath God wrought!*

Rev. 12:11: *And they overcame him by the blood of the Lamb, and by the word of their testimony; and they loved not their lives unto the death.*

3 Jn. 1:2: *Beloved, I wish above all things that thou mayest prosper and be in health, even as thy soul prospereth.*

● **NOTE***: Prayers are to be said violently and aggressively (10 days night vigil, 12:00 - 3:00 a.m. or three days dry fast). Schedule out the prayer points for each day.*

● **PRAISE WORSHIP**

1. Praise and worship the Most High for He reigns.
2. Let God arise in His anger and fight for me.
3. I refuse to allow my angels of blessings to depart, in Jesus' name.
4. I cancel every evil effect of names from evil origins in my life, in the name of Jesus.
5. I paralyse all aggression addressed at my star, in Jesus' name.
6. I neutralize all problems originating from the mistakes of my parents, in the name of Jesus.
7. Lord, bring honey out of the rock for me.
8. Lord, open up all the good doors of my life that household wickedness have shut.
9. Let all anti-breakthrough designs against my life be shattered to irreparable pieces, in the name of Jesus.
10. I paralyse all satanic antagonism from the womb, in Jesus' name.
11. I command open disgrace on the mask of the enemy, in the name of Jesus.

12. I paralyse all evil legs roaming about for my sake, in Jesus' name.

13. Let all evil blood that has mingled with my blood be drained out, in the name of Jesus.

14. I trample upon every enemy of my advancement and promotion, in the name of Jesus.

15. I break every evil collective unity organised against me, in the name of Jesus.

16. Let all evil counsellors against me follow the wrong programme, in the name of Jesus.

17. Let the backbone of the stubborn pursuer and strongman break, in the name of Jesus.

18. I destabilize the controller of any land of bondage in my life, in the name of Jesus.

19. O Lord, enlarge my coasts beyond my wildest dream.

20. Holy Ghost, seal all pockets that have demonic holes, in the name of Jesus.

21. Let the fire of disgrace fall upon demonic prophets assigned against my life, in the name of Jesus.

22. No dark meeting held on my behalf shall prosper, in Jesus' name.

23. I claim back my goods presently residing in wrong hands, in the name of Jesus.

24. Let the blood and strength of stubborn oppressors dry up, in the name of Jesus.

25. Let the head of every serpent power fashioned against me be broken, in the name of Jesus.

26. Let the head of every marine power fashioned against me be broken, in the name of Jesus.

27. Let every evil trend directing my affairs be reversed, in the name of Jesus.

28. O Lord, uproot evil things from my life.

29. O Lord, plant good things in my life.
30. I cancel every unconscious negative agreement, in Jesus' name.
31. Lord, make me Your sharp battle axe.
32. Let every spiritual weakness in my life receive termination, in the name of Jesus.
33. Let every financial failure in my life receive termination, in the name of Jesus.
34. Let every sickness in my life receive termination, in Jesus' name.
35. Let every architect of problems receive termination, in the name of Jesus.
36. I refuse to reap any satanic harvest in any area of my life, in the name of Jesus.
37. I paralyse all spiritual wolves working against my life, in the name of Jesus.
38. That which hinders me from greatness, begin to give way now, in the name of Jesus.
39. Every imprisoned and buried potentials, come forth now, in the name of Jesus.
40. I command all unfriendly helpers in every area of my life to depart, in the name of Jesus.
41. I render null and void the effect of any interaction with satanic agents moving around as men and women, in the name of Jesus.
42. I pull down the stronghold of evil strangers in every area of my life, in the name of Jesus.
43. Any negative transaction currently affecting my life negatively, be canceled, in the name of Jesus.
44. I command all the dark works done against me in secret to be exposed and nullified, in the name of Jesus.
45. I loose myself from any dark spirit, in the name of Jesus.
46. Let all incantations against me be cancelled, in Jesus' name.

47. I command all oppressors to retreat and flee in defeat this moment, in the name of Jesus.

48. I bind every strongman having my goods in his possessions, in the name of Jesus.

49. I break the curse of automatic failure working upon my life, in the name of Jesus.

50. Let the anointing to prosper fall mightily upon me now, in the name of Jesus.

51. Let every anti-progress altar fashioned against me be destroyed with the fire of God, in the name of Jesus.

52. I command my destiny to begin to change to the better, in the name of Jesus.

53. Let my hand become the sword of fire to cut down demonic trees, in the name of Jesus.

54. Let the stamping of my feet defeat the camp of the enemy, in the name of Jesus.

55. All boastful evil powers delegated against me, be silenced, in the name of Jesus.

56. I withdraw my benefits from the hands of the oppressors, in the name of Jesus.

57. Let all unprofitable marks in my life be erased, in Jesus' name.

58. Let every power chasing blessings away from me be paralysed, in the name of Jesus.

59. Let the enemy begin to vomit every good thing he has eaten up in my life, in the name of Jesus.

60. O Lord, give me the power to overcome every obstacle to my breakthroughs.

61. I break all curses of leaking blessings, in the name of Jesus.

62. I clear my goods from the warehouse of the strongman, in the name of Jesus.

63. Let all satanic kingdoms working against me fail, in Jesus' name.

64. Let all hidden arrows in my life be troubled in their hiding places, in the name of Jesus.

65. I frustrate and disappoint every instrument of the enemy fashioned against me, in the name of Jesus.

66. I disarm every household enemy today, in the name of Jesus.

67. Let all those who trouble my Israel be troubled to death, in the name of Jesus.

68. I scatter all evil counsellors and conspirators fashioned against me, in the name of Jesus.

69. I scatter all evil forces shedding blood on my behalf, in Jesus' name.

70. O Lord, sharpen my dull sword (not studying the Word) and repair my broken shield (doubt and unbelief).

71. I take authority over every satanic attack on my home, in the name of Jesus.

72. I withdraw the staff of office of the strongman delegated against me, in the name of Jesus.

73. Let every opposition to my breakthroughs crash into pieces, in the name of Jesus.

74. I stand against every faith destroyer in my life, in Jesus' name.

75. I stand against every unprofitable agreement and reconciliation, in the name of Jesus.

76. I refuse to assist my enemies to fight, in the name of Jesus.

77. I paralyse every one behind the extension and the expansion of my problems, in the name of Jesus.

78. Let every tree of sorrow be uprooted in my life, in Jesus' name.

79. Let the rain of fire fall on the camp of every hardened enemy, in the name of Jesus.

80. Let the angels of God take them back into the darkness where they belong, in the name of Jesus.

81. I bind every spirit of bondage fashioned against me, in Jesus' name.

82. I bind every spirit of heaviness, in the name of Jesus.

83. I bind every spirit of slumber, in the name of Jesus.

84. I bind every sprit of paralysis, in the name of Jesus.

85. I bind every sprit of death and hell, in the name of Jesus.

86. Break every unprofitable covenant from age one to your present age. Do each three times, in the name of Jesus.

87. I unseat all evil powers siting on my promotions, in Jesus' name.

88. I break any curse brought upon me by any past generation, in the name of Jesus.

89. I bind and paralyse the spirit and activities of the wasters in my life, in the name of Jesus.

90. I bind and paralyse the spirit and activities of the devourers in my life, in the name of Jesus.

91. I bind and paralyse the spirit and activities of the emptier in my life, in the name of Jesus.

92. I bulldoze my way into breakthroughs, in the name of Jesus.

93. I render all evil attacks against my life impotent sevenfold, in the name of Jesus.

94. Let every evil maintenance officer assigned against my life receive spiritual paralysis, in the name of Jesus.

95. I revoke every satanic decree upon my life, in the name of Jesus.

96. I revoke every satanic decree upon my family, in Jesus' name.

97. I revoke every satanic decree upon my name, in Jesus' name.

98. I revoke every satanic decree upon my prosperity, in Jesus' name.

99. I silence all evil utterances against my life, in the name of Jesus.

100. O Lord, arise and bring final solution to all my stubborn situations.

UNSEATING THE STRONGMAN
Deut. 33:27

- **Three days prayer and fasting programme to unseat the strongman in charge of marriage, work, house, family, finances, etc.**

Strive to engage the everlasting arms of the Almighty God that upholds the whole universe, to overthrow that strongman who has been terrorising your life all these years.

Isaiah 49:24-26: *"Shall the prey be taken from the mighty, or the lawful captive delivered? But thus saith the Lord, even the captives of the mighty shall be taken away, and the prey of the terrible shall be delivered: for I will contend with him that contendeth with thee, and I will save thy children. And I will feed them that oppress thee with their own flesh and they shall be drunken with their own blood, as with sweet wine. And all flesh shall know that I thy Lord am thy Saviour and thy Redeemer, the mighty One of Jacob."*

It doesn't matter what door you opened to the enemy to allow him get a foothold in your life. The important thing is to close every door you've opened to the enemy through sin. Even if he is there legally, the Scriptures say he has to go!

The first thing you have to do is to repent and ask for God's forgiveness. Once you are right with God, you are on the road to deliverance from the strongman. These prayer points are designed to destroy every strongman in any area of your life by fire!

DAY 1

• CONFESSIONS

Matt. 12:29: *Or else how can one enter into a strong man's house, and spoil his goods, except he first bind the strong man? and then he will spoil his house.*

Mark 3:27: *No man can enter into a strong man's house, and spoil his* *goods, except he will first bind the strong man; and then he will spoil his house.*

Luke 11:21: *When a strong man armed keepeth his palace, his goods are in peace:*

• PRAISE WORSHIP

1. Thank the Lord that the gate of hell shall not prevail against this establishment.

2. I order confusion and the scattering of tongues among all wicked associations militating against the peace of this establishment, in the name of Jesus.

3. Let the wisdom of all evil counselors in this establishment be rendered to nothing, in the name of Jesus.

4. O Lord, cause an explosion of Your power in this establishment.

5. Let my life be barricaded by the edge of fire and let me be soaked and covered with the blood of Jesus.

6. O Lord, smite all evil tongues rising up against me by the cheek bones and break the jaws of the evil.

7. Let every handwriting contrary to my peace receive intensive disgrace, in the name of Jesus.

DAY 2

• CONFESSIONS

Matt. 12:29: *Or else how can one enter into a strong man's house, and spoil his goods, except he first bind the strong man? and then he will spoil his house.*

Mark 3:27: *No man can enter into a strong man's house, and spoil his goods, except he will first bind the strong man; and then he will spoil his house.*

Luke 11:21: *When a strong man armed keepeth his palace, his goods are in peace:*

• PRAISE WORSHIP

1. Let every decision taken against me by the wicked be rendered null and void, in the name of Jesus.

2. I fire back every demonic arrow targeted at me and my family, in the name of Jesus.

3. I break every spiritual mirror and monitor fashioned against me, in the name of Jesus.

4. Pray in the spirit for 10 to 15 minutes.

5. I bind and I render powerless all the strongmen who are currently troubling this establishment, in the name of Jesus.

6. I unseat every stronghold delegated against me in this establishment, in the name of Jesus.

7. Let the strongman pursuing me drink his own blood and eat his own flesh, in the name of Jesus.

DAY 3

• CONFESSIONS

Matt. 12:29: *Or else how can one enter into a strong man's house, and spoil his goods, except he first bind the strong man? and then he will spoil his house.*

Mark 3:27: *No man can enter into a strong man's house, and spoil his goods, except he will first bind the strong man; and then he will spoil his house.*

Luke 11:21: *When a strong man armed keepeth his palace, his goods are in peace:*

• PRAISE WORSHIP

1. Let all evil devices that the strongman has fashioned against me be turned against him, in the name of Jesus.

2. I render null and void every ritual, incantation, spell and curse issued against me by any strongman, in the name of Jesus.

3. I disband any wicked meeting held in the spirit realm against me and my position, in the name of Jesus.

4. Lord, turn me into untouchable hot coals of fire.

5. Let my office, my car, my home and all my properties be too hot for this strongman to handle, in the name of Jesus.

6. Let the evil strongman delegated against me in this establishment make mistakes that will advance my course, in the name of Jesus.

7. Thank the Lord for answered prayers.

NEW OPENING
Isaiah 43:19

- *Seven days prayer and fasting programme forthose desiring that new doors should be opened for them and fresh opportunities should rush to their bossom.*

Your coming to trust in the word of the Lord God of Israel marks the end of your tears and sorrow, and a new opening to fulfillment of your life's aspiration and eternal life.

Ecclesiastes 9:11: *"I returned and saw under the sun that the race is not to the swift, nor the battle to the strong, neither yet bread to the wise, nor get riches to men of understanding, nor yet favour to men of skill; but time and chance happeneth to them all."*

Hard work is indeed very good. But securing profitable opening is only by divine direction. Opportunities are never lost because every opportunity one missed is picked up by someone else. Where you get to in life is not determined by how good or how qualified you are, it is based on your being in the right place at the right time. The only way we can be in the right place at the right time is to be led by the Spirit of God. This will only happen if we wait on the Lord. The Scripture says that God will reveal deep things to us by His Spirit (1 Cor. 2:9,10). If you don't wait on God, how will the Holy Spirit speak to you? If you want new openings, learn to wait on God for instructions. The instructions will lead you to fresh opportunities and new openings.

As you use these prayer points, your eyes will be opened to see your desired opportunities.

DAY 1

- CONFESSION

Ps. 24:7-10: *Lift up your heads, O ye gates; and be ye lift up, ye everlasting doors; and the King of glory shall come in. Who is this King of glory? The LORD strong and mighty, the LORD mighty in battle. Lift up your heads, O ye gates; even lift them up, ye everlasting doors; and the King of glory* *shall come in. Who is this King of glory? The LORD of hosts, he is the King of glory.*

● **PRAISE WORSHIP**

1. Thank the Lord for what He is going to use this prayer programme to do in your life.
2. O Lord, plant good things in my life.
3. O Lord, uproot evil things from my life.
4. I cancel every unconscious negative agreement, in Jesus' name.
5. Lord, make me Your battle axe.
6. Let every spiritual weakness in my life receive termination now, in the name of Jesus.
7. Let every financial failure in my life receive termination now, in the name of Jesus.

DAY 2

● **CONFESSION**

Ps. 24:7-10: *Lift up your heads, O ye gates; and be ye lift up, ye everlasting doors; and the King of glory shall come in. Who is this King of glory? The LORD strong and mighty, the LORD mighty in battle. Lift up your heads, O ye gates; even lift them up, ye everlasting doors; and the King of glory shall come in. Who is this King of glory? The LORD of hosts, he is the King of glory.*

● **PRAISE WORSHIP**

1. Let every sickness in my life receive termination now, in the name of Jesus.
2. Let every architect of problems receive termination now, in the name of Jesus.
3. I paralyze all spiritual wolves working against my life, in the name of Jesus.

4. Whatever is hindering me from attaining greatness begin to give way now, in the mighty name of Jesus.

5. Let every imprisoned and buried potentials begin to come forth now, in the name of Jesus.

6. You unfriendly helpers, I command you in the name of our Lord Jesus Christ, depart from me.

7. Let every negative transactions currently affecting my life negatively be canceled, in the name of Jesus.

DAY 3

• CONFESSION

Ps. 24:7-10: *Lift up your heads, O ye gates; and be ye lift up, ye everlasting doors; and the King of glory shall come in. Who is this King of glory? The LORD strong and mighty, the LORD mighty in battle. Lift up your heads, O ye gates; even lift them up, ye everlasting doors; and the King of glory shall come in. Who is this King of glory? The LORD of hosts, he is the King of glory.*

• PRAISE WORSHIP

1. I command all the dark works done against my life in the secret to be exposed and be nullified, in the name of Jesus.

2. I loose myself from any dark spirit, in the name of Jesus.

3. O Lord, if my life is on the wrong course, correct me.

4. Let every anti-progress altar fashioned against me be destroyed with the thunder fire of God, in the name of Jesus.

5. I command my destiny for change to the better, in Jesus' name.

6. Let my hand become a sword of fire to cut down demonic trees, in the name of Jesus.

7. All boastful powers delegated against me, be silenced permanently, in the name of Jesus.

DAY 4

● CONFESSION

Ps. 24:7-10: *Lift up your heads, O ye gates; and be ye lift up, ye everlasting doors; and the King of glory shall come in. Who is this King of glory? The LORD strong and mighty, the LORD mighty in battle. Lift up your heads, O ye gates; even lift them up, ye everlasting doors; and the King of glory shall come in. Who is this King of glory? The LORD of hosts, he is the King of glory.*

● PRAISE WORSHIP

1. I withdraw all my benefits from the hands of the oppressors, in the name of Jesus.

2. Let all unprofitable marks in my life be erased, in Jesus' name.

3. Let every power chasing away my blessings be paralyzed, in the name of Jesus.

4. Let every good thing eaten up by the enemy be vomited now, in the name of Jesus.

5. Let the anointing for spiritual breakthroughs fall upon me, in the name of Jesus.

6. O Lord, make me a prayer addict.

7. O Lord, ignite my prayer life with Your fire.

DAY 5

● CONFESSION

Ps. 24:7-10: *Lift up your heads, O ye gates; and be ye lift up, ye everlasting doors; and the King of glory shall come in. Who is this King of glory? The LORD strong and mighty, the LORD mighty in battle. Lift up your heads, O ye gates; even lift them up, ye everlasting doors; and the King of glory shall come in. Who is this King of glory? The LORD of hosts, he is the King of glory.*

• PRAISE WORSHIP

1. O Lord, empower my prayer altar.
2. I reject every spiritual contamination, in the name of Jesus.
3. O Lord, give me power to overcome all obstacles to my breakthroughs.
4. O Lord, give me divine prescription to my problems.
5. I break all curses of leaking blessings, in the name of Jesus.
6. Let all spiritual holes in my life be closed with the blood of Jesus, in the name of Jesus.
7. Lord, help me to locate the defect in the clay of my life.

DAY 6

• CONFESSION

Ps. 24:7-10: *Lift up your heads, O ye gates; and be ye lift up, ye everlasting doors; and the King of glory shall come in. Who is this King of glory? The LORD strong and mighty, the LORD mighty in battle. Lift up your heads, O ye gates; even lift them up, ye everlasting doors; and the King of glory shall come in. Who is this King of glory? The LORD of hosts, he is the King of glory.*

• PRAISE WORSHIP

1. Lord, let me be at the right place at the right time.
2. I disarm every household enemy today, in the name of Jesus.
3. Let my enemies pitch their tents against one another, in the name of Jesus.
4. I frustrate and disappoint every instrument of the enemy fashioned against me, in the name of Jesus.
5. I seal my victory with the blood of Jesus.
6. You God of new beginnings, open fresh door of prosperity for me, in the name of Jesus.
7. O Lord, open new doors of financial breakthroughs for me, in the name of Jesus.

DAY 7

• CONFESSION

Ps. 24:7-10: *Lift up your heads, O ye gates; and be ye lift up, ye everlasting doors; and the King of glory shall come in. Who is this King of glory? The LORD strong and mighty, the LORD mighty in battle. Lift up your heads, O ye gates; even lift them up, ye everlasting doors; and the King of glory shall come in. Who is this King of glory? The LORD of hosts, he is the King of glory.*

• PRAISE WORSHIP

1. I receive the mandate to paralyse all powers that swallow miracles, in the name of Jesus.

2. I claim the anointing for good success in every area of my life, in the name of Jesus.

3. I retrieve all my confiscated blessings from the prison yard of my financial enemies, in the name of Jesus.

4. O Lord, give me anointed ideas and lead me to the path of blessings.

5. I bind, plunder and render powerless every strongman working against my breakthroughs, in the name of Jesus.

6. Be Thou exalted O Lord, in all my financial dealings.

7. Thank the Lord for answered prayers.

AGAINST DEMON-INSPIRED SICKNESS

Deut. 7:15

- **For sicknesses not yielding to medication.**
- **Clear case of sicknesses that cannot be diagnosed effectively.**

Power to overcome satan and the sicknesses caused by him has been given to us by the Lord Jesus Christ.

Luke 13:16: *"And ought not this woman, being a daughter of Abraham, whom satan hath bound, lo, these eighteen years, be loosed from this bond on the Sabbath day?"*

This Scripture clearly states that this woman's problem was caused by satan. For 18 years she had been going about looking for a solution to this infirmity. Everything the doctors suggested failed. Her problem was spiritual and not physical. There are many today with similar problem. Satan has bound them with the spirit of infirmity and the spirit of death and hell are at work in their lives. They've spent so much for a cure but each specialist they visited could not help them. The result is the same: not responding to drugs and the statement: "There's nothing medically wrong with this patient." If you find yourself or your loved one in this situation, invite Jesus to take control by speaking such **WORD** of healing and deliverance as: "Woman thou art loosed." Every child of God has been healed by His stripes (1 Peter 2:24). Healing is the children's bread (Matthew 15:26). Jesus is waiting for you to ask for your daily bread.

- **CONFESSION**

Isa. 53:5: *But he was wounded for our transgressions, he was bruised for our iniquities: the chastisement of our peace was upon him; and with his stripes we are healed.*

- **PRAISE WORSHIP**

1. I confess all the sins of my forefathers that I know about.

2. Ask the Lord to forgive those you do not know about.

3. Ask the Lord do separate you completely from all the sins of your forefathers by the precious blood of Jesus.

4. Ask the Lord to remove the curse if it is from Him.

5. Command the curse of . . . to be broken, in Jesus' name.

6. Apply the oil and command all demons associated with the curse to leave at once, in the name of Jesus.

7. Command any demon afflicting the . . . or causing . . . to leave at once, in the name of Jesus.

8. Ask the Lord to heal all the damages done.

TO REVOKE EVIL DEDICATION
Gal. 3:13,14

- **For arresting parental dedication to evil spirits, idols, shrines, etc.**

It is your responsibility to appropriate the curse-breaking power of Christ to get rid of any effect of dedication to the power of darkness.

Numbers 6:27: *"And they shall put my name upon the children of Israel; and I will bless them."*

God can only bless those that have been dedicated to Him. He can only bless those that have His name upon their lives. There are many people that God cannot bless because of their evil dedication, those dedicated to evil spirits, family idols, family shrines, river spirits etc. Jabez cried out to God, "O that thou would bless me indeed, and enlarge my coast, and that thy hand might be with me and thou would keep me from evil that it will not grieve me! And the Lord granted his request" (1 Chron. 4:10).

His name which means 'born in sorrow' glorified the devil. When Jabez cried out, God heard him and granted his request. The Bible records that he was more honourable than his brethren.

Have you been dedicated to an idol, a shrine or evil spirits? Does your name glorify God? As you cry out to Him in prayers, He will revoke every evil dedication in your life.

- **CONFESSION**

Num. 23:23: *Surely there is no enchantment against Jacob, neither is there any divination against Israel: according to this time it shall be said of Jacob and of Israel, What hath God wrought!*

- **PRAISE WORSHIP**

1. I confess the sins of my ancestors (list them).
2. Ask the Lord for forgiveness.
3. Let the power in the blood of Jesus separate me from the sins of my ancestors, in the name of Jesus.

4. I renounce any evil dedication placed upon my life, in Jesus' name.

5. I break every evil edict and ordination, in the name of Jesus.

6. I renounce and loose myself from every negative dedication placed upon my life, in the name of Jesus.

7. I command all demons associated with the dedication to leave now, in the name of Jesus Christ.

8. I take authority over all the associated curses, in Jesus' name.

9. Lord, cancel the evil consequences of any broken demonic promise or dedication.

10. I take authority over all the curses emanating from broken dedication, in the name of Jesus.

11. I command all demons associated with any broken evil parental vow and dedication to depart from me now, in Jesus' name.

WAR AGAINST MARRIAGE BREAKERS

Isa. 14:27

- *To deliver your home from the hands of marriage manipulators.*
- *To silence satanic intruders into your marriage.*

The major problems facing the world today emanate from broken homes and the chief culprit behind these is Satan. Be a party to the total elimination of this terrible disease going on in the world today.

Hebrews 13:4: *"Marriage is honourable in all, and the bed undefiled; but whoremongers and adulterers God will judge."*

Marriage is an institution God holds in high esteem and He frowns at any power within or without that would want to break the home, more so, if the marriage has been instituted in accordance with the Bible.

For God to be on your side, and for Him to protect your marriage from powers that wreck marriages, you must not be an adulterer. You must uphold the sanctity of marriage (Heb. 13:14). If you have not been leading a scriptural life, you need to cry to God for forgiveness because you have opened the door for marriage breakers already.

Praying these prayer points whilst you keep the door effectively open is like pouring water into a basket. For example, if you are the second or third wife of your husband, you do not have a scriptural right to pray these prayer points.

But if you are properly married, be rest assured that God is very bitter against marriage breakers. Listen "What therefore God has joined together, let no man put asunder" (Matt. 19:6). You have power to take sides with God and destroy every power trying to break your marriage.

- ## CONFESSION

Matt. 19:6: *Wherefore they are no more twain, but one flesh. What therefore God hath joined together, let not man put asunder.*

● **PRAISE WORSHIP**

1. I paralyse every architect of conflict and hostility in my home, in the name of Jesus.

2. I withdraw my marriage from the hands of evil designers, in the name of Jesus.

3. Let every power trying to re-draw my marriage map be put to shame, in the name of Jesus.

4. Let all household wickedness release my home, in Jesus' name.

5. I receive deliverance from every evil plantation designed to bring me and my children under the bondage of the devil, in Jesus' name.

6. I paralyse every spirit of hatred and hostility militating against my home, in the name of Jesus.

7. I spoil and destabilise every satanic plan against my home, in the name of Jesus.

8. I deliver my marriage from the hands of home-wreckers, in the name of Jesus.

9. I pursue, overtake and recover my marriage from the hands of marriage breakers, in the name of Jesus.

10. Every evil effect of external interference in my marriage, be completely neutralized, in the name of Jesus.

11. Lord, dissolve and render to nought every evil counsel fashioned against my home.

12. Every power preventing me as a wife from accepting the headship of my husband, become paralysed, in the name of Jesus.

13. Let every imagination, thought, plan, decision, desire and expectation of divorce and separation against my home be nullified, in the name of Jesus.

14. Satan, hear the word of the Lord: You will not break my home, in the name of Jesus.

15. I bind all powers eating away the determination of my husband to stay

married to me, in the name of Jesus.

16. Let the satanic birds eating away my love from the heart of my husband vomit it, in the name of Jesus.

17. Pray in the spirit for at least ten (10) minutes.

18. Let all the extra-marital relationships with other "partners" collapse and die, in the name of Jesus.

19. I break every soul tie between my husband and . . . (*mention the name of the strange woman if you know it*), in Jesus' name.

20. I deliver my husband from the hand of evil seducers, in Jesus' name.

21. I break the hold of spirit wife and marriage upon my husband, in the name of Jesus.

22. I command failure, frustration and disappointment to come upon the strange relationship, in the name of Jesus.

23. I break the hold of the spirit of polygamy on my husband, in the name of Jesus.

24. Let the angels of the living God pursue the strange woman out of the life of my husband, in the name of Jesus.

25. I refuse to be second-hand wife or a single-parent, in Jesus' name.

26. I break the power of every evil manipulation fashioned against my home, in the name of Jesus.

27. I paralyse every vagabond spirit working in the life of my husband, in the name of Jesus.

28. I pull down (*pick from the under listed*) stronghold fashioned against my marriage, in the name of Jesus.

- evil association
- carelessness
- pride
- foolishness
- sour relationship

- being planless
- weak family altar
- unsaved partner or children
- unprofitable imitation
- communication gap

- suspicion   - evil counselors
- misplaced priority   - evil attachment to parents
- selfishness   - unprofitable comparison
- lack of knowledge of the word of God
- incomplete "leaving" and incomplete "cleaving" of couple

29. Begin to thank for everything He has done you.

DELIVERANCE OF
THE TONGUE

Prov. 21:23

- *For those whose mouths have not been purged by the fire of the Holy Ghost.*
- *When your tongue is putting you in trouble.*
- *When you find it difficult to speak with other tongues (inability to flow in the Holy Spirit).*

The tongue is noted as the most powerful generator of either the negative or the positive - good or evil occurrences', so, if any human organ needs deliverance at all, it is the tongue.

Proverbs 18:21: *"Death and life are in the power of the tongue and they that love it shall eat the fruit thereof."*

Almost all the powers God has given man can be traced to the spoken words Jesus said, "The WORDS that I speak unto you they are spirit, and they are life" (John 6:63). When we speak God's words, they carry spirit and life. When we speak satan's words they carry bondage and death.

Our lives are a product of our confession. You can use your tongue to hurt, destroy or even kill yourself or others. No wonder the Scripture says, "And the tongue is a fire, a world of iniquity" (James 3:6).

The challenge for your is to strive for the Holy Spirit to help you realise God's plan for your life. James 3:2 says for in many things we offend all if any man offend not in word; the same is a perfect man.

As you pray these prayer points with determination, the blood of Jesus will wash away all the satanic acid on your tongue.

● CONFESSIONS

Prov. 12:18: *There is that speaketh like the piercings of a sword: but the tongue of the wise is health.*

Prov. 21:23: *Whoso keepeth his mouth and his tongue keepeth his soul from troubles.*

Prov. 18:21: *Death and life are in the power of the tongue: and they that love it shall eat the fruit thereof.*

Prov. 15:4: *A wholesome tongue is a tree of life: but perverseness therein is a breach in the spirit.*

Isa. 50:4: *The Lord GOD hath given me the tongue of the learned, that I should know how to speak a word in season to him that is weary: he wakeneth morning by morning, he wakeneth mine ear to hear as the learned.*

• PRAISE WORSHIP

1. Thank the Lord for His faithfulness.
2. I cover myself with the blood of Jesus.
3. I command all the spiritual evil in my life to be destroyed, in the name of Jesus.
4. I paralyse and nullify the activities of jungle and vagabond spirits in my life, in the name of Jesus.

Decree aggressively and prime out the expulsion of the following:

5. I decree the exit of the following spirits from my life, in the name of Jesus.

    - lying   - exaggeration   - talkativeness   - cursing
    - speech perversion - stammering - nagging   - murmuring

6. Let the fire of God purge my tongue from the contamination of . . . (pick from the under listed), in the name of Jesus

    - evil consumption   - demonic incision   - oral sex   - evil kiss
    - evil vows   - evil marks and labels   - herbal concoction
    - sexual perversion

7. Lord, deliver me from the spirit of self-destruction.
8. I cut myself off from every spirit of tongue and venomous speech, in the name of Jesus.
9. I command every venomous and acidic trait in me, inherited or ac-

quired, to depart, in the name of Jesus.

10. Let every serpentine spirit and poison depart from my tongue, in the name of Jesus.

11. I command every agent of bondage and destruction in my tongue to depart, in the name of Jesus.

12. Lord, repair all damages done to my life as a result of the wrong use of my tongue.

13. I command the evil progress of the enemies in my life to be halted, in the name of Jesus.

14. Lord, deliver my tongue from becoming a cemetery of evil.

15. I withdraw all the evil words I have uttered against my life, home, etc., from the satanic bank, in the name of Jesus.

16. Lord, deliver my life from the hand of evil broadcasters, in the name of Jesus.

17. I refuse to turn back at the edge of my miracles, in Jesus' name.

18. Lord, heal me of all diseases of the tongue.

19. I loose myself from the grip of territorial and tribal spirits, in the name of Jesus.

20. Let every problem in my life that originated from

- evil tongue   - demonic prophecy
- witchcraft and familiar spirits curses
- medical and clinical prophecy   - all strange tongues

receive divine instant solution, in the name of Jesus.

21. Lord, give me a wholesome tongue.

22. Lord, make my voice the voice of deliverance, healing, power, solution and life.

23. Praise God for He has answered you.

FOR LOVED ONES WHO HATE THE GOSPEL

Acts 16:31

- *Regular prayers for relatives who are not born again.*

Jesus tells us to pray that our joy may be full. This can only materialize when you are able to pray through to salvation for your loved ones who are averse to the gospel.

2 Corinthians 4:4: *"In whom the god of this world has blinded the minds of them which believe not, lest the light of the glorious gospel of Christ, who is the image of God should shine unto them."*

Satan is the god of this world and has blinded the eyes of many with money, sex and position. His major weapon is deception. He would make a person feel that what he has to offer is better than what God is offering the person.

Unfortunately, many have fallen into this trap of the enemy. They have become blind to the love of God and the sacrifice of His only begotten Son. All they care about is what they want now, and what they can achieve here. The spirit of acquisition has taken over. They don't even believe in the living God.

As you truly use these prayer points to intercede for your loved ones, every blindfold of the enemy will be removed. All the lies he has told them shall be exposed. The Lord will dispel every darkness in their lives so that the light of the glorious gospel can shine into their lives.

- **CONFESSIONS**

Eph. 1:16-23: *Cease not to give thanks for you, making mention of you in my prayers; That the God of our Lord Jesus Christ, the Father of glory, may give unto you the spirit of wisdom and revelation in the knowledge of him: The eyes of your understanding being enlightened; that ye may know what is the hope of his calling, and what the riches of the glory of his inheritance in the saints, And what is the exceeding greatness of his power to us-ward who believe, according to the working of his mighty power,*

Which he wrought in Christ, when he raised him from the dead, and set him at his own right hand in the heavenly places, Far above all principality, and power, and might, and dominion, and every name that is named, not only in this world, but also in that which is to come: And hath put all things under his feet, and gave him to be the head over all things to the church, Which is his body, the fulness of him that filleth all in all.

Eph. 3:14-21: *For this cause I bow my knees unto the Father of our Lord Jesus Christ, Of whom the whole family in heaven and earth is named, That he would grant you, according to the riches of his glory, to be strengthened with might by his Spirit in the inner man; That Christ may dwell in your hearts by faith; that ye, being rooted and grounded in love, May be able to comprehend with all saints what is the breadth, and length, and depth, and height; And to know the love of Christ, which passeth knowledge, that ye might be filled with all the fulness of God. Now unto him that is able to do exceeding abundantly above all that we ask or think, according to the power that worketh in us, Unto him be glory in the church by Christ Jesus throughout all ages, world without end. Amen.*

Ps. 21:2: *Thou hast given him his heart's desire, and hast not withholden the request of his lips.*

Ps. 86:16: *O turn unto me, and have mercy upon me; give thy strength unto thy servant, and save the son of thine handmaid.*

Isa. 49:25: *But thus saith the LORD, Even the captives of the mighty shall be taken away, and the prey of the terrible shall be delivered: for I will contend with him that contendeth with thee, and I will save thy children.*

Isa. 54:13: *And all thy children shall be taught of the LORD; and great shall be the peace of thy children.*

Hosea 2:6-15: *Therefore, behold, I will hedge up thy way with thorns, and make a wall, that she shall not find her paths. And she shall follow after her lovers, but she shall not overtake them; and she shall seek them, but shall not find them: then shall she say, I will go and return to my first husband; for then was it better with me than now. For she did not know that I gave her corn, and wine, and oil, and multiplied her silver and gold, which they* *prepared for Baal. Therefore will I return, and take away my corn in the time thereof, and my wine in the season thereof, and will recover my wool and my flax given to cover her nakedness. And now will I discover her lewdness in the sight of her lovers, and none shall deliver her out of mine hand. I will also cause all her mirth to cease, her feast days, her new moons, and her sabbaths, and all her solemn feasts. And I will destroy her vines and her fig trees, whereof she hath said, These are my rewards that my lovers have given me: and I will make them a forest, and the beasts of the field shall eat them. And I will visit upon her the days of Baalim, wherein she burned incense to them, and she decked herself with her earrings and her jewels, and she went after her lovers, and forgat me, saith the LORD. Therefore, behold, I will allure her, and bring her into the wilderness, and speak comfortably unto her. And I will give her her vineyards from thence, and the valley of Achor for a door of hope: and she shall sing there, as in the days of her youth, and as in the day when she came up out of the land of Egypt.*

• PRAISE WORSHIP

1. Thank the Lord because it is not His will that anyone should perish.

2. Father, in the name of Jesus, give unto . . . labels *(mention the name of the person)* the spirits of wisdom and revelation in the knowledge of You.

3. Let every stronghold of the enemy barricading the mind of . . . *(mention the name of the person)* from receiving the Lord be pulled down, in the name of Jesus.

4. Let all hindrances coming between the heart of . . . *(mention the name of the person)* and the gospel be melted away by the Fire of the Holy Spirit, in the name of Jesus.

5. In the name of Jesus, I bind the strongman attached to the life of . . . *(mention the name of the person)*, for keeping him from receiving Jesus Christ as his Lord and Saviour.

6. Lord, build a hedge of thorns aroundlabelslabels*(mention the name*

of the person), so that he turns to the Lord.

7. All the children who have been dedicated to the Lord and have become bound, be loosed, in the name of Jesus.

8. In the name of Jesus, I break the curse placed on . . . *(mention the name of the person)*, binding him from receiving the Lord.

9. You spirit of death and hell, release . . . *(mention the name of the person)*, in the name of Jesus.

10. Every desire of the enemy on the soul of . . . *(mention the name of the person)* will not prosper, in the name of Jesus.

11. You spirit of destruction, release . . . *(mention the name of the person)*, in the name of Jesus.

12. I bind every spirit of mind blindness in the life of . . . *(mention the name of the person)*, in the name of Jesus.

13. Let there be no peace or rest in the mind of . . . *(mention the name of the person)* until he surrenders to the Lord Jesus Christ.

14. Spirit of bondage, lukewarmness and perdition, release . . . *(mention the name of the person)*, in the name of Jesus.

15. Lord, open the eyes of . . . *(mention the name of the person)* to his own spiritual condition, in the name of Jesus.

16. I bind the strongman shielding . . . *(mention the name of the person)* from receiving the gospel, in the name of Jesus.

17. Lord, send people across the path of . . . *(mention the name of the person)* who can share the gospel with him.

18. Father, let spiritual blindness be erased from the life of . . . *(mention the name of the person)*, in the name of Jesus.

19. Father, grant . . . *(mention the name of the person)* repentance leading to a personal relationship with Jesus.

20. I come against the powers of darkness blinding and holding . . . *(mention the name of the person)* back from receiving the gospel, in the name of Jesus.

21. I command you spirit of the power of the air to loose your hold on . . . *(mention the name of the person)* so that he will be free to accept Jesus as Lord and Saviour, in the name of Jesus.

22. I tear down and smash every stronghold of deception keeping . . . *(mention the name of the person)* in the enemy's camp, in the name of Jesus.

23. Holy Spirit, reveal to me other strongholds that need to be broken in the life of . . . *(mention the name of the person)*, in Jesus' name.

24. Let . . . *(mention the name of the person)* come from the kingdom of darkness into the kingdom of light, in the name of Jesus.

25. Lord, let Your plan and purpose for the life of . . . *(mention the name of the person)* prevail.

26. Lord, let Your mercy and Your grace overwhelm . . . *(mention the name of the person)* so that he may be saved.

27. Thank the Lord for answering your prayers.

FOR PARENTS DESIRING GODLY SPOUSE FOR THEIR CHILDREN

Gen 24:3-4

- *Prayers for parents who want their children to marry godly husbands and wives.*

A concerned parent like Abraham would not undermine the importance of seeking the face of the Lord to know the God-chosen life partner for his son. The person your child marries could determine his eternal destiny!

Genesis 18:19: *"For I know him that he will command his children and his household after him, and they shall keep the way of the Lord, to do justice and judgement; that the Lord may bring upon Abraham that which he hath spoken."*

In this passage God says that He chose Abraham because He knew that Abraham would bring up his children in the right way. He would train them in the way of the Lord. This would ensure that the promise of God to Abraham would be fulfilled, i.e. if his children had not walked in the ways of God, that would have been the end of the Abrahamic covenant since God cannot bless those that do not follow Him.

When it was time for Isaac to get married, Abraham sent his servant Eleazar to his country with strict instruction to get a wife for his son. He knew God hated unequal yoke of marriage with unbelievers. Till today, that is the stand of God.

These prayer points are designed for parents who love God and want His will for their children in marriage.

• CONFESSIONS

Matt. 7:7: *Ask, and it shall be given you; seek, and ye shall find; knock, and it shall be opened unto you:*

Josh. 24:15: *And if it seem evil unto you to serve the LORD, choose you this day whom ye will serve; whether the gods which your fathers served that were on the other side of the flood, or the gods of the Amorites, in whose land ye dwell: but as for me and my house, we will serve the LORD.*

Isa. 54:13: *And all thy children shall be taught of the LORD; and great shall be the peace of thy children.*

Isa. 54:17: *No weapon that is formed against thee shall prosper; and every tongue that shall rise against thee in judgment thou shalt condemn. This is the heritage of the servants of the LORD, and their righteousness is of me, saith the LORD.*

Isa. 49:25: *But thus saith the LORD, Even the captives of the mighty shall be taken away, and the prey of the terrible shall be delivered: for I will contend with him that contendeth with thee, and I will save thy children.*

• PRAISE WORSHIP

1. Thank God because He alone is the perfect matchmaker.
2. Lord, release the man/woman You have preordained as my daughter's/son's husband/wife.
3. Lord, cause it to happen that the divine match will come forth soon.
4. Lord, let it be a person who loves You wholeheartedly.
5. Lord, establish their home in accordance with the Scriptures (Read Eph. 5:20-28).
6. Father, let all satanic barriers keeping them from meeting be dissolved, in the name of Jesus.
7. Lord, send forth Your warring angels to battle on their behalf.
8. Lord, I believe You have created my daughter/son for a special man/woman of God. Bring it to pass, in Jesus' name.
9. I stand in the gap and call him/her out of obscurity into his/her life, in the name of Jesus.
10. I reject the provision of counterfeit spouse by the enemy, in the name of Jesus.
11. I cut off the flow of any inherited marital problems into the life of my children, in the name of Jesus.
12. Let patience reign in the life of . . . *(mention the name of the person)* until the right person comes, in the name of Jesus.

13. Father, in the name of Jesus, just as Abraham sent his servant to find his son, Isaac, a wife, send the Holy Spirit to bring my son's/daughter's future wife/husband to him/her.

14. Thank the Lord for the answer.

FOR DIVINE ELEVATION
Psalm 27:6

- *For those desiring spiritual elevation.*
- *For those who desire elevation in their career/ work/*

True, divine promotion cannot be derived from nepotism, favoritism, tribalism, kickbacks, clubs, occultism and all sorts of magical feats, but through patiently waiting on God and maintaining the Christian character of holiness, honesty and righteousness.

I Samuel 2: 7: *"The Lord maketh poor, and maketh rich: he bringeth low, and lifted up."*

God opened the book of remembrance for Hannah and put a song in her mouth. In her song of thanksgiving, she recognized the fact that God is the only one that has the power to bring low or lift high.

She had been taunted, and hurt with many evil words. "You can never amount to anything" "You are living a wasted life", "Look at you, what have you achieved in life?" The enemy had turned her glory to shame.

When there was no one and nowhere to turn to, Hannah entered into the house of God. She cried out to God from the bitterness of her soul. The Bible says, "The Lord remembered Hannah" (1 Samuel 1:19).

These prayer points are designed to bring 'the God that elevates' into your situation and, like Hannah, God will lift you above every reproach and taunt of your enemy.

- **CONFESSIONS**

Ps. 75:6-7: *For promotion cometh neither from the east, nor from the west, nor from the south. But God is the judge: he putteth down one, and setteth up another.*

Deut. 28:13: *And the LORD shall make thee the head, and not the tail; and thou shalt be above only, and thou shalt not be beneath; if that thou* *hearken unto the commandments of the LORD thy God, which I command thee this day, to observe and to do them:*

- **PRAISE WORSHIP**

1. Thank the Lord from the bottom of your heart for what He will use this prayer programme to do in your life.

2. I reject every backward journey, in the name of Jesus.

3. I paralyse every strongman assigned to this institution, in the name of Jesus.

4. Let every agent of shame working against me be paralysed, in the name of Jesus.

5. I paralyse the activities of household wickedness over my life, in the name of Jesus.

6. I quench every strange fire emanating from evil tongues against me, in the name of Jesus.

7. Lord, give me power for maximum achievement in this place, in the name of Jesus.

8. O Lord, give me the confronting authority to achieve effortless results.

9. Lord, fill me with wisdom like an angel.

10. I break every curse of unfruitfulness placed upon my life, in the name of Jesus.

11. I break every curse of untimely death, in the name of Jesus.

12. Lord, fortify me with Your power.

13. Let the counter-movement of the Holy Spirit frustrate every evil device against me, in the name of Jesus.

14. Father Lord, give me the tongue of the learned.

15. Lord, make my voice the voice of peace, deliverance, power and solution.

16. Lord, give me divine direction that will propel this institution to greatness through me.

17. Every power assigned, to use my family/job, etc to torment me, be paralysed, in the name of Jesus.

18. Lord Jesus, give me an excellent spirit.

19. Thank God for answered prayers.

FOR RESTORATION

Zec. 10:6

- When your debtors are refusing or are un able to pay.
- When you lose your job unrighteously.
- When your things have been stolen and you desire recovery and arrest of the thieves.
- When you desire a recovery of past financial losses.
- Whenever you want to 'possess your possession'.

No matter the spiritual height from which you have fallen, God is very much interested in restoring you, if only you can cry unto Him for mercy.

Job 42: 10: "And the Lord turned the captivity of Job, when he prayed for his friends; also the Lord gave Job twice as much as he had before."

It is the devil's job to steal, to kill and to destroy. (John 10:10). His greatest design is to destroy the image of God in man. He will use any method. The Bible says, "When the hedge is broken, the serpents will bite" (Ecclesiastes 10:8).

Many, through carelessness break the protective hedge God has placed around their lives and property. Thus they allow the enemy to destroy it. The good news is that what is killed, stolen or destroyed by the enemy can be restored by God. Jesus said, "I am come that you might have life and life more abundantly "(John 10:10). God has promised in Joel 2:25 to restore unto us our lost and wasted years. Everything lost to the devil will be restored by God.

Job lost all but in the end everything was restored to him even in multiple-fold.

As you pray these prayer points, power for restoration will be released into your life.

- CONFESSIONS

Joel 2:25-26: *And I will restore to you the years that the locust hath eaten, the cankerworm, and the caterpiller, and the palmerworm, my great army which I sent among you. And ye shall eat in plenty, and be satisfied, and praise the name of the LORD your God, that hath dealt wondrously with you: and my people shall never be ashamed.*

Isa. 41:18-20: *I will open rivers in high places, and fountains in the midst of the valleys: I will make the wilderness a pool of water, and the dry land springs of water. I will plant in the wilderness the cedar, the shittah tree, and the myrtle, and the oil tree; I will set in the desert the fir tree, and the pine, and the box tree together: That they may see, and know, and consider, and understand together, that the hand of the LORD hath done this, and the Holy One of Israel hath created it.*

• PRAISE WORSHIP

1. Thank God for the name of Jesus.

2. Lord, open doors of opportunity to me through this prayer, in the name of Jesus.

3. I command all evil unknown forces organised against my life to be scattered, in the name of Jesus.

4. I paralyse every activity of physical and spiritual parasites and de vourers in my life, in the name of Jesus.

5. Powers denying me my due miracles, receive the stones of fire, in the name of Jesus.

6. I recover all the ground that I had lost to the enemy, in Jesus' name.

7. I bind the spirit of depression, frustration and disillusionment in my life, in the name of Jesus.

8. Heavenly surgeons, perform the necessary surgical operations in all the areas of my life, in the name of Jesus.

9. Lord Jesus, carry out all the repairs that are necessary in my life.

Decree aggressively

10. I command all the damages done to my life by . . . (*pick from the under listed*) to be repaired, in the name of Jesus.

    - evil tongue   - demonic prophecies

- witchcraft spells and curses   - personal negative confessions

- household wickedness

11. Let all the parasites feeding on any area of my life be roasted, in the name of Jesus.

12. Fire of God, consume the evil clock of the enemy that is working against my life, in the name of Jesus.

13. My life is not a fertile ground for any evil to thrive in, Jesus' name.

14. I command all doors of good things, closed against me by the enemy to be opened, in the name of Jesus.

15. I reject the spirit of impossibility, I claim open doors, in the name of Jesus.

16. I decree restoration seven fold in . . . areas of my life, in the name of Jesus.

17. I refuse to wage war against myself, in the name of Jesus.

18. Lord, make my case a miracle. Shock my foes, friends, and even myself, in the name of Jesus.

19. Lord, give me the solution to any problem facing me, in the name of Jesus.

20. Trees of problems in my life, dry up to the roots, in Jesus' name.

21. Walls of physical and spiritual opposition, fall after the order of Jericho, in the name of Jesus.

22. Let my king Uzziah die, so that I can see Your face, O Lord, in the name of Jesus.

23. I posses the power to pursue, overtake and recover my goods from spiritual Egyptians, in the name of Jesus.

24. Let every spell, jinxes, and demonic incantations rendered against me be cancelled, in the name of Jesus.

25. I cancel every effect of any strange help received from Egypt regarding this problem, in the name of Jesus.

26. Lord, heal all wounds and spiritual bullets sustained from attacks of the enemy.

27. Let all hidden potentials and gifts that will make me great, stolen from me, be restored 21 fold, in the name of Jesus.

28. I reject the spirit of regret, woes and disappointment, in the name of Jesus.

29. Lord, give me power for a new beginning.

30. Lord, make my life a miracle and be glorified in every area of it, in the name of Jesus.

31. Lord Jesus, I thank You for answering my prayer.

POWER TO OBTAIN PROFITABLE EMPLOYMENT

Psalm 113:7-8

- *When you desire a new job.*
- *When you are to face an interview panel for a position.*
- *When your certificate has been cursed or is operating under satanic embargo.*
- *For those who are tired of joblessness.*

The provision of God for you as a born again and obedient child of God is to get the best things of this life and hereafter.

Haggai 1:6: *"Ye have sown much, and bring in little, ye eat, but ye have not enough; ye drink, but ye are not filled with drinks; ye clothe you, but there is none warm, and he that earneth wages earneth wages to put into a bag with holes."*

Not all employments are profitable. Many people work like elephants and eat like ants. They have nothing to show for all their labour. It is like, all they earn goes into a bag with holes.

God's desire is for His children to have enough for themselves and to be able to give others. We as children of God are blessed to be a blessing to other people. We are supposed to be able to provide for ourselves, our families, assist in the work of God and assist the needy. When our income is not able to meet these demands, something is wrong. We need to pray and ask God for a profitable employment.

God does not want his children to manage poverty. He desires to satisfy us with good things! He desires that our needs be met. "The blessings of God maketh rich and adds no sorrow" (Prov. 10:22).

As you pray these prayer points, every yoke of profitless hard work will be destroyed and God will give you a profitable employment.

- **INSTRUCTIONS**

1. *Repent from all KNOWN SINS.*

2. *Find out scriptures that promise you what you desire.*

3. *Memorize and meditate on these scriptures and feed constantly on them as they promise you victory.*

4. *Quote these scriptures against satan, worry, anxiety, fear and negative circumstances.*

5. *Ask the Father, in the name of Jesus, for the desire of your heart. Believe that you have already received.*

6. *Resolve not to allow doubt to enter your mind. Reject every thought of failure and doubt. REJECT every dream, vision, prophecy, that tells you that your prayers are not answered.*

7. *See yourself in the new position and keep confessing it.*

8. *Always give thanks to God for the answer to your prayers.*

● **CONFESSIONS**

Deut. 28:13: *And the LORD shall make thee the head, and not the tail; and thou shalt be above only, and thou shalt not be beneath; if that thou hearken unto the commandments of the LORD thy God, which I command thee this day, to observe and to do them.*

Prov. 21:1: *The king's heart is in the hand of the LORD, as the rivers of water: he turneth it whithersoever he will.*

Prov. 11:27: *He that diligently seeketh good procureth favour: but he that seeketh mischief, it shall come unto him.*

Zech. 12:10: *And I will pour upon the house of David, and upon the inhabitants of Jerusalem, the spirit of grace and of supplications: and they shall look upon me whom they have pierced, and they shall mourn for him, as one mourneth for his only son, and shall be in bitterness for him, as one that is in bitterness for his firstborn.*

Ps. 8:5: *For thou hast made him a little lower than the angels, and hast crowned him with glory and honour.*

Eph. 3:19-20: *And to know the love of Christ, which passeth knowledge, that ye might be filled with all the fulness of God. Now unto him that is able to do exceeding abundantly above all that we ask or think, according to the power that worketh in us.*

Ps. 30:5: *For his anger endureth but a moment; in his favour is life: weeping may endure for a night, but joy cometh in the morning.*

Dan. 1:9: *Now God had brought Daniel into favour and tender love with the prince of the eunuchs.*

Ps. 34:10: *The young lions do lack, and suffer hunger: but they that seek the LORD shall not want any good thing.*

Ps. 75:6: *For promotion cometh neither from the east, nor from the west, nor from the south.*

Ps. 113:5,7-8: *Who is like unto the LORD our God, who dwelleth on high, He raiseth up the poor out of the dust, and lifteth the needy out of the dunghill; That he may set him with princes, even with the princes of his people.*

Phil. 4:13,19: *I can do all things through Christ which strengtheneth me . . . . But my God shall supply all your need according to his riches in glory by Christ Jesus.*

Gal. 6:17: *From henceforth let no man trouble me: for I bear in my body the marks of the Lord Jesus.*

• PRAISE WORSHIP

1. Thank the Lord because He alone can advance you.

2. O Lord, bring me into favour with all those who will decide on my employment.

3. O Lord, cause a divine substitution to happen if this is what will move me ahead.

4. I reject the spirit of the tail and I claim the spirit of the head, in the name of Jesus.

5. I command all evil records planted by the devil in anyone's mind against my employment to be shattered to pieces, in Jesus' name.

6. O Lord, transfer, remove or change all human agents that are bent on stopping my employment.

7. I receive the anointing to excel above my contemporaries, in the name of Jesus.

8. Lord, catapult me into greatness as You did for Daniel in the land of Babylon.

9. I bind every strongman delegated to hinder my progress, in the name of Jesus.

10. O Lord, despatch Your angels to roll away every stumbling block to my employment.

11. I bind and render to naught the spirit of . . . (pick from the under listed), in the mighty name of Jesus.

- demonic antagonism   - unprofitable questions
- strife   - confusion
- marginal success   - mind blankness
- wrong words   - mind dullness
- bad feet/bad luck   - memory failure
- demonic opinions against me
- unprofitable controversies
- evil collaborators
- demonic logic and unprofitable interviews

12. I claim the position of . . . ., in the mighty name of Jesus (name the specific position being sought).

13. Lord, hammer my matter into the mind of those who will assist me so that they do not suffer from a demonic loss of memory.

14. I paralyse the handiwork of house hold enemies and envious agents in this matter, in the name of Jesus.

15. Let all the adversaries of my breakthroughs be put to shame, in the name of Jesus.

16. I claim the power to overcome and to excel amongst all competitors, in the name of Jesus.

17. Let any decision by any panel be favourable unto me, in the name of Jesus.

18. All competitors with me in this issue will find my defeat unattainable, in the name of Jesus.

19. Praise the Lord for answered prayers.

USING THE BLOOD OF JESUS AS A WEAPON
2 Cor. 10:3-5

- *Regular prayers to overcome the satanic on slaught.*
- *Deliverance prayers for stubborn cases.*

The blood of Jesus is one of the potent weapons against spiritual wickedness in high places and to demolish every stronghold of satanic forces. It cannot achieve less for you.

Revelation 12:11: *"And they overcame him by the blood of the Lamb and the Word of their testimony and they loved not their lives unto the death."*

The blood of Jesus can never lose its power because it is a divine blood. *"Jesus is the only begotten of the father"* (John 1:14). The blood of Jesus avails for everything imaginable. If we are going to experience the power in the blood of Jesus we have to personally apply it to our lives and our situations. We apply the blood of Jesus, by decrees, i.e. we confess it. *"The blood of Jesus speaks better things than the blood of Abel"* (Hebrews 12:24). The blood of Jesus can speak destruction upon your enemies, healing to your body, protection to your family, etc. The blood of Jesus brings life to you. The Bible says, *"The life of the flesh is in the blood. . ."* (Leviticus 17:11). The blood of Jesus contains the life of Jesus. Divine life!

The power for overcoming is in this blood. These prayer points will teach you how to pray, using the blood of Jesus as a weapon.

- ## CONFESSION

Rev. 12:11: *And they overcame him by the blood of the Lamb, and by the word of their testimony; and they loved not their lives unto the death.*

In the name of Jesus Christ, I am a beloved child of God. I believe in God, I believe in Jesus Christ and I believe in the blessed Holy Spirit Who is dwelling in the inside of me. I believe in the unshakeable and eternal power in the word of God. I believe that life and death are in my tongue. I believe that as I make this confession unto life with the power in my tongue, according to the words which the Lord has this day put in my mouth, I shall prosper.

It is written that Jesus Christ offered His blood as a drink, and His flesh as bread that whosoever drinks and eats it shall not die forever. Now, with strong faith in my heart I hold in my hand a cup containing the blood of Lamb of God and I drink it, that I may have life eternal.

I receive unto myself the virtues, strength, power, might and anointing in the blood. And I say, let the blood quicken all that is dead within me. Let all sucked sapped and paralysed spiritual milk and strength of my life be resurrected by the blood. Let the blood re-energise, revitalise, reactivate and revive all dead potentials and spiritual gifts within me.

Let the blood flush out of me all inherited or self-acquired evil deposits in my system. Let it purify my blood system. Let it make old things pass away in my life and transform everything to become new. Let the power in the blood clean my spiritual vision and wash my spiritual pipe that I may be receiving of the Lord unhindered.

I eat with the heart of faith the flesh of Jesus. For it is written, His flesh is bread indeed. I eat it now so that I can also eat with Him in His glory. I eat the flesh of Jesus to receive new spiritual strength and vigour, strength and vigour to put under subjection all works of the flesh, strength and vigour to paralyse the desires of my flesh, strength and vigour to paralyse the power of my flesh and make it obedient to the laws of the Lord.

As I eat and drink the flesh and blood of my Lord Jesus Christ, I renew my covenant with Him and I receive the life therein; for it is written, life is in the blood. Thus I possess the life and the Spirit of Christ in me. Amen.

Jeremiah found the word of God and did eat it, and it became the joy of his heart. I have found the word of God and now like vitamin pills I throw it into my mouth and chew and digest it. Let it produce within me the power to rejoice in the Holy Ghost, the power to be steadfast in following God, the power to walk circumspectly, the power of holy living and the power of unashamed faithfulness in all circumstances.

The word of God is spirit and it is life. It entered Ezekiel and he was put back on his feet. Let the word of God raise up in me every downtrodden area of mylife. Let the word like fire purify me and restore any parts stolen or destroyed by the enemy. Let the word build me up and give me inheritance amongst all sanctified brethren.

Let the joy of the Lord strengthen me. Let His right hand of righteousness uphold me. Let His countenance brighten up my life. Let the horn of His salvation lift me up out of the valley of life and let His living anointing oil fan on me like the dew of Hermon and fill my life.

Lord, make me drunken with the blood of Jesus and I shall be full of life eternity.

Father Lord, as it is written, that I should be strong in the Lord and in the power of His might, I ask that You be my might and strength all the days of my life. Gird me with Your strength and let me not fall into the pit of my enemies and I will praise You all the days of my life.

With my heart I believe the word of God. With my mouth I have confessed unto salvation and justification. Oh Lord, let it be performed unto me as I have prayed, in Jesus Christ's only mighty name. Amen.

• PRAISE WORSHIP

1. Thank You Father for the benefits and provision of the blood of Jesus.
2. I stand on the ground of the blood of Jesus to proclaim victory over sin, satan and his agents and the world.
3. I apply the blood of Jesus to every stubborn problem in my life.
4. I plead the blood of Jesus upon my body - from the top of my head to the sole of my feet.
5. I soak my life in the blood of Jesus.
6. I paralyse all satanic oppressors delegated against me with the blood of Jesus.
7. I hold the blood of Jesus as a shield against any power that is already poised to resist me, in the name of Jesus.

8. By the blood of Jesus, I stand against every device of distraction.

9. I stand upon the word of god and I declare myself unmoveable, in the name of Jesus.

10. Let every door that I have opened to the enemy be closed forever with the blood of Jesus.

11. Make each of the following powerful confessions 70 times.

   - Through the blood of Jesus, I have been redeemed out of the hands of the devil.

   - I walk in the light and the blood of Jesus cleanses me from all sins.

   - Through the blood of Jesus I am justified, sanctified and made holy with God's holiness.

   - Through the blood of Jesus, I have the life of God in me.

   - Through the blood of Jesus, I have access the presence of the Lord.

12. I paralyse and cut off the head of my Goliath with the blood of Jesus.

13. If there is anything in me that is not of God, I don't want it. Depart, in the mighty name of Jesus.

14. Let the blood of the Cross stand between me and any dark power delegated against me.

15. I curse every work of darkness in my life to dry to the roots by the blood of Jesus.

16. I defeat, paralyse and erase . . . (*pick from the under listed*) by the blood of Jesus.

   - spirit of demotion   - financial downgrading
   - failure at the edge of miracle   - inherited problems
   - vision killers   - dream attackers
   - marital problems

17. Let the power of the blood of Jesus be released on my behalf and let it speak against every dead bone in my life.

18. Let the power of the blood of Jesus be released on my behalf and let it speak against every stubborn mountain in my life.

19. In the name of Jesus, I plead the blood of Jesus.

20. In the name of Jesus, I apply the blood of Jesus over my house.

21. In the name of Jesus, I soak myself in the blood of Jesus.

22. In the name of Jesus, I apply the blood of Jesus. Demons, you cannot enter my house.

23. I draw a circle of the blood of Jesus around me.

24. I draw the blood line of protection around my property.

25. I overcome you satan by the blood of the Lamb.

26. You cannot put any sickness on me because I am redeemed by the blood of the Lamb.

27. Let the blood of Jesus speak confusion into the camp of the enemy.

28. Let the blood of Jesus speak destruction unto every evil growth in my life.

29. Let the blood of Jesus speak disappearance unto every infirmity in my life.

30. Let the blood of Jesus speak peace unto every broken marriage.

31. Mr. Devil, see the blood of Jesus. The One who shed the blood crushed your head and He is my Lord.

32. Let the blood of Jesus speak victory and prosperity unto my life.

33. I sprinkle the blood of Jesus on all my properties.

34. Let the blood of Jesus dry up every evil tree used against me.

35. You evil power, I bring to bear the power of the blood of Jesus to bind you.

36. I render every evil power militating against me impotent by the blood of Jesus.

37. I hold the blood against you and declare that you have been defeated.

38. Let the blood of Jesus minister defeat to every evil work in my life.

39. Let the blood of Jesus bring down to nothing any evil work in my life.
40. I minister death unto the enemy of progress in my life by the blood of Jesus.
41. I bind the staying power of any problem by the blood of Jesus.
42. I create a boundary against you devil by the blood of Jesus.
43. I hold the blood of Jesus against any evil spirit working against me.
44. I hold the blood of Jesus against you, you spirit of . . . (mention what is troubling you). You have to flee.
45. I enter the holy of holies by the blood of Jesus.
46. I hold the blood of Jesus against the spirit of stagnation in any area of my life.
47. I hold the blood of Jesus against demonic delay of my miracles.
48. I hold the blood of Jesus against failure at the edge of success.
49. I hold the blood of Jesus against lack of good helpers.
50. I hold the blood of Jesus against fruitless efforts in my life.
51. I hold the blood of Jesus against occupying wrong positions.
52. I hold the blood of Jesus against every delayed and denied promotion.
53. I hold the blood of Jesus against dead accounts.
54. I hold the blood of Jesus against evil diversion.
55. I hold the blood of Jesus against lost foreign benefits.
56. I hold the blood of Jesus against satanic prophecies.
57. I hold the blood of Jesus against vagabond anointing.
58. I hold the blood of Jesus against profit starvation.
59. I hold the blood of Jesus against tortoise and snail anointing.

RELEASE FROM COLLECTIVE CAPTIVITY

Obad. 1:17

- *For release from collective bondage or corporate curses.*
- *To remove yourself under any evil umbrella*
- *To break inherited yokes and evil family patterns.*
- To disgrace familiar spirits.

As you plunge into prayers, all those who gather against you to destroy you shall be scattered unto desolation. Biblical history of those who were delivered from collective captivity would repeat itself in your life, if you too follow the principles that made their deliverance possible.

John 8:32: *"And ye shall know the truth, and the truth shall make you free."*

You don't have to follow any evil family pattern, e.g. lateness in marriage, broken homes, poverty, lack of progress in life and failure. Christ has made provision for your freedom!

The mistake many believers make is that they think once they give their lives to Christ all their problems are over, without their doing anything. Many do not believe in the ministry of deliverance. Beloved, it is only the truth you know that will make you free. That is why the Scripture says, "Therefore my people have gone into captivity, because they have no knowledge" (Isa 5:13).

The story is told of a man who bought a ship ticket to America with all he had. At sea, he was very hungry. He watched people going in to the dinning room to eat, but since he did not have any money to pay, he did not go. The day before he arrived in America, he decided to eat and decided that whatever the staff of the ship wanted to do to him, they were free to do it. After his meal, he was expecting the waiter to bring the bill. He summoned up courage and asked how much he was to pay. The waiter said, "Nothing, because the cost of food has been included in the ticket you bought." This man suffered many days of hunger because he did not know his rights. Beloved, don't be ignorant of your rights as a child of God. The truth you know will make you free.

These prayer points are designed to deliver you from evil family rivers, evil family patterns, evil bondage, yokes, curses and covenants. Your case can be different from others. Jesus makes that difference!

• CONFESSIONS

Gal. 3:13-14: *Christ hath redeemed us from the curse of the law, being made a curse for us: for it is written, Cursed is every one that hangeth on a tree: That the blessing of Abraham might come on the Gentiles through Jesus Christ; that we might receive the promise of the Spirit through faith.*

Matt. 3:11: *I indeed baptize you with water unto repentance: but he that cometh after me is mightier than I, whose shoes I am not worthy to bear: he shall baptize you with the Holy Ghost, and with fire:*

Col. 1:13: *Who hath delivered us from the power of darkness, and hath translated us into the kingdom of his dear Son:*

Col. 2:15: *And having spoiled principalities and powers, he made a shew of them openly, triumphing over them in it.*

2 Tim. 4:18: *And the Lord shall deliver me from every evil work, and will preserve me unto his heavenly kingdom: to whom be glory for ever and ever. Amen.*

Ps. 27:2: *When the wicked, even mine enemies and my foes, came upon me to eat up my flesh, they stumbled and fell.*

• **NOTE:** *Prayer of release from collective captivity have to be said aggressively and violently. No stone should be left unturned. You must hate captivity with perfect hatred.*

• PRAISE WORSHIP

1. Thank God for making the provision for deliverance from any form of bondage.
2. Confess your sins and those of your ancestors, especially those sins linked to evil powers.
3. I cover myself with the blood of Jesus.
4. I release myself from any inherited bondage, in Jesus' name.
5. O Lord, send Your axe of fire to the foundation of my life and destroy every evil plantation.
6. Let the blood of Jesus flush out from my system every inherited sa-

tanic deposit, in the name of Jesus.

7. I release myself from the grip of any problem transferred to my life from the womb, in the name of Jesus.

8. Let the blood of Jesus and the fire of the Holy Ghost cleanse every organ in my body, in the name of Jesus.

9. I break and loose myself from every collective evil covenant, in the name of Jesus.

10. I break and loose myself from every collective curse, in the name of Jesus.

11. I vomit every evil consumption that I have been fed with as a child, in the name of Jesus.

12. I command all foundational strongmen attached to my life to be paralysed, in the name of Jesus.

13. Let any rod of the wicked rising up against my family line be rendered impotent for my sake, in the name of Jesus.

14. I cancel the consequences of any evil local name attached to my person, in the name of Jesus.

15. Pray aggressively against the following roots of collective captivity. Pray as follows: Every effect of . . . (*pick from the under listed one by one*), upon my life, come out with all your roots, in the name of Jesus.

- evil physical design
- parental curses
- envious rivalry
- demonic incisions
- dream pollution
- demonic initiations
- demonic blood transfusion
- demonic alteration of destiny
- fellowship with family idols

- evil dedication
- demonic marriage
- demonic sacrifice
- inherited infirmity
- evil laying on of hands
- wrong exposure to sex
- exposure to evil diviners
- fellowship with local idols

- destructive effect of polygamy
- fellowship with demonic consultants
- unscriptural manner of conception

16. Thank God for answering your prayer.

PARALYSING THE STRONGMAN
Psalm 118

- *The strongman is the principal or controlling demon over a family, place, person or thing. These are prayers to completely neutralise the activities of such agents*

Be strong and be courageous like Joshua and Caleb who stood their ground against the giants of Canaan. Be equally resolute in desperate prayer to confront and paralyse the strongman in your life.

Ephesians 6:2: *"For we wrestle not against flesh and blood, but against principalities, against powers, against the rulers of darkness of this world, against spiritual wickedness in high places."*

A strongman is the controller of a group of spirits or the chief over a group of spirits, what the Bible calls "rulers of darkness of this world" (Ephesians 6:12). He acts as the prison warden of the devil, confiscating the blessings of people. He is the wicked ruler over every nation, town and family. I am supposed to live under the dominion of the strongman. The power to overcome has been given to me because the greater one lives inside me (1 John 4:4). Every strongman in charge of my case has to bow to the Lordship of Jesus Christ in me. My faith in God will help me overcome because I am born of God. (1 John 5:4).

God has given us the weapons with which to fight. "The weapons of our warfare are not carnal but mighty through God to the pulling down of stronghold" (2 Corin.10:4). We have the ability to overcome the strongman.

As you pray, the strongman attacking you will be permanently paralysed.

- **CONFESSION**

Ps. 149:1-9: *Praise ye the LORD. Sing unto the LORD a new song, and his praise in the congregation of saints. Let Israel rejoice in him that made him: let the children of Zion be joyful in their King. Let them praise his name in the dance: let them sing praises unto him with the timbrel and harp. For the LORD taketh pleasure in his people: he will beautify the* *meek with salvation. Let the saints be joyful in glory: let them sing aloud upon their beds. Let the high praises of God be in their mouth, and a twoedged sword in their hand; To execute vengeance upon the heathen, and punishments upon the people; To bind their kings with chains, and their nobles with fetters of iron; To execute upon them the judgment written: this honour have all his saints. Praise ye the LORD.*

• PRAISE WORSHIP

1. I withdraw the control of my life from the hands and domination of household wickedness, in the name of Jesus.

2. I withdraw my future from the influence and control of household wickedness, in the name of Jesus.

3. I release myself from any unconscious satanic bondage, in the name of Jesus.

4. Let every demonic power controlling my town be paralysed, in the name of Jesus.

5. Let the joy of the enemy over my life turn to sorrow, in the name of Jesus.

6. Let the organisation of the hosts of hell against me break down, in the name of Jesus.

7. Let all spiritual vultures wishing for my death, begin to receive the stones of fire now, in the name of Jesus.

8. I cut off any problem with a link to my parents, in Jesus' name.

9. I break every placental bondage, in the name of Jesus.

10. Let every nature of failure in my life go and let the nature of success come to me, in the name of Jesus.

11. I disgrace the strongman delegated by satan over my life, in the name of Jesus.

12. Let the rejoicing of the wicked over my life vanish, in Jesus' name.

13. I break myself free from the bondage of inherited spirit, in the name of Jesus.

14. Evil family tree in my life, be uprooted, in the mighty name of our Lord Jesus.

15. Let every bondage of inherited sickness over my life break in my life, in the name of Jesus.

16. I recall every power that has ever done me wrong, in the name of Jesus, and I issue judgement on the camp of the enemy as written in Psalm 149.

17. Let all my oppressors fall by their own counsels, in Jesus' name.

18. Let every chained spirit and blessings be released, in Jesus' name.

19. Let every ordination of paralysis be canceled, in Jesus' name.

20. Every problem attached to my name, be revoked, in Jesus' name.

21. Lord, reveal unto me every secret about my life that I need to know.

22. Let every evil remote control and spiritual satellites set up against me receive the thunder fire of God and be burnt to ashes, in the name of Jesus.

23. I command every strange and wicked voice calling my name to be silenced, in the name of Jesus.

24. Lord, purge me from every spiritual and physical poison I have taken through food, in the name of Jesus.

25. Lord, let the blood of Jesus wash away every mark of witches, wizards and wicked men from my life, in the name of Jesus.

26. I stand against faith destroyers in my life, in the name of Jesus.

27. I stand against lack of knowledge in the affairs of my life, in the name of Jesus.

28. I stand against the spirit of envy and the spirit of strife in my life, in the name of Jesus.

29. I stand against the spirit that fails to work in love in my life, in the name of Jesus.

30. I call down God's fire, thunder, lightning and tempest upon evil observers of the progress of my life, in the name of Jesus.

31. Let every organ in my body that is not functioning well receive divine touch and begin to function well, in the name of Jesus.

32. Every problem attached to my name be nullified, in Jesus' name.

33. Let the veil hiding my evil strongman be torn to pieces, in the name of Jesus.

34. My breakthroughs, manifest powerfully now, in the name of Jesus.

35. Let all blocked ways to success be opened, in the name of Jesus.

36. Let favour be upon my life from all directions from today, in the name of Jesus.

37. I break every unprogressive attachment to my place of birth, in the name of Jesus.

38. Let the anointing for supernatural breakthroughs come upon me, in the name of Jesus.

39. Lord, give unto me this day the keys to unlock all doors to my blessings, in the name of Jesus.

40. Let the power to discern unprofitable associations fall upon me now, in the name of Jesus.

41. Thank God for answering your prayer.

DISGRACING SATANIC AGENTS

Obad. 1:3-4

- *To disgrace all satanic agents.*
- *To disgrace evil operations.*

The Lord made good His promise concerning the disgrace of Satan and all his cohorts by shedding His blood on the cross of Calvary. You too can receive the mantle of power from Him to carry on the operations.

2 Corinthians 11:13, 15: *"For such are false apostles, deceitful workers, transforming themselves into the apostles of Christ . . . whose end shall be according to their works."*

Satanic ministers can be found in every living church. Their job is simply to hinder and if possible destroy the work of God. Many of their women go after the men of God, seeking to destroy them through sex and money, because they know that "smite the shepherd, and the sheep shall be scattered" (Zechariah 13:7). Once the pastor can be attacked the congregation will scatter.

Satanic agents also attack individuals. They seek to deceive and discourage. They cause division among the brethren. Paul's advice is, "Mark them which cause division and offenses contrary to the doctrine which ye have learned; and avoid them" (Romans 16:17).

How do we recognize these satanic agents? By discernment. Physically, they dress like christians, talk like christians and even work miracles (Matt. 7:15-23; Matt. 24:24).

As you pray these prayer points, your life and ministry will become too hot for the devil to handle.

● CONFESSION

1 Sam. 17:45-46: *Then said David to the Philistine, Thou comest to me with a sword, and with a spear, and with a shield: but I come to thee in the name of the LORD of hosts, the God of the armies of Israel, whom thou hast defied. This day will the LORD deliver thee into mine hand; and I will smite thee, and take thine head from thee; and I will give the carcases of* *the host of the Philistines this day unto the fowls of the air, and to the wild beasts of the earth; that all the earth may know that there is a God in Israel.*

● **PRAISE WORSHIP**

1. Thank God for all the benefits you have received from Him.

2. Say prayers of genuine repentance and forgiveness.

3. I command all demonic activities against my calling to receive disgrace and commotion, in the name of Jesus.

4. Father Lord, let my life, my ministry and my prayer life be extremely dangerous for the kingdom of darkness, in Jesus' name.

5. Father Lord, let all the motionless spiritual gifts and talents in my life begin to function for Your glory, in the name of Jesus.

6. I reject all uncontrollable crying, heaviness and regrets, in the name of Jesus.

7. I command all organised forces of darkness against my life to receive commotion, lightning and thunder, in the name of Jesus.

8. All demonic organised network against my spiritual and physical progress, be put to shame, in the name of Jesus.

9. I command all demonic mirrors and monitoring gadgets against my life to crack to pieces, in the name of Jesus.

10. I command every agent of frustration to loose its hold over my life, in the name of Jesus.

11. I command every agent of poverty to loose its hold over my life, in the name of Jesus.

12. I command every agent of debt to loose its hold over my life, in the name of Jesus.

13. I command every agent of defeat to loose its hold over my life, in the name of Jesus.

14. I command every agent of spiritual rags to loose its hold over my life, in the name of Jesus.

15. I command every agent of infirmity to loose its hold over my life, in the name of Jesus.

16. I command every agent of demonic delays to loose its hold over my life, in the name of Jesus.

17. I command every agent of demotion to loose its hold over my life, in the name of Jesus.

18. I command every agent of confusion to loose its hold over my life, in the name of Jesus.

19. I command every agent of backward movement to loose its hold over my life, in the name of Jesus.

20. I command every wicked oppressor to stumble and fall in every area of my life, in the name of Jesus.

21. I command the teeth of the ungodly gathered against me to break into pieces, in the name of Jesus.

22. I command all the instruments of failure fashioned against me to receive the fire of God and be roasted, in the name of Jesus.

23. I command all satanic weapons of attack fashioned against me and my family to receive the fire of God and be roasted, in Jesus' name

24. Thank God for answering your prayer.

BAPTISM OF FIRE
Acts 2

- *To get filled with fresh fire from heaven.*

The reason many undergo deliverance almost everyday is lack of fire of the Holy Ghost in their lives. The moment you possess fire, it marks an end to the harassment of evil forces in your life and your life would constitute a danger to the powers of darkness.

Acts 2:3: *"And there appeared unto them cloven tongues like as of fire, and it sat upon each of them."*

Fire is the symbol of the power and presence of God. It is the only thing that will convince the world of the awesome power of God. The unbelieving world wants to see the demonstration of the power of God.

Paul said, "And my speech and my preaching was not in enticing words of man's wisdom, but in demonstration of the Spirit and of power; that your faith should not stand in the wisdom of men but in the power of God" (2 Cor. 2:4,5). This is a powerful statement. Paul had received the fire of God. He was immersed in fire.

To do the work of God effectively and to be His witness, we need to be immersed in fire. It is possible to be baptized with the Holy Spirit, speak in tongues and not have fire. It is possible to be baptized in water and not have fire.

As believers we have talked enough. We have held seminars and conferences that have not affected the world. What we need now is to get fresh fire and demonstrate the power of God to a dying world. The Church was born with fire on the day of Pentecost and it must live and grow with this fire!

As ministers of God, we must to pray to become flames of fire (Hebrews 1:7), so that we can give light to the world. We need to be consumed with the zeal to do God's work. His words have to be like fire shut up in our bones. (Jeremiah 20:9) In this end times the only way the evil stronghold in many lives will be destroyed is by fire. The enemy has to be disgraced.

O Lord, send Your fire into our lives!

● **CONFESSION**

Matt. 3:11-12: *I indeed baptize you with water unto repentance: but he that cometh after me is mightier than I, whose shoes I am not worthy to bear: he shall baptize you with the Holy Ghost, and with fire: Whose fan is in his hand, and he will throughly purge his floor, and gather his wheat into the garner; but he will burn up the chaff with unquenchable fire.*

● **PRAISE WORSHIP**

1. Thank the Lord for the power of the Holy Spirit.
2. Confession of sins and repentance.
3. Father, let the Holy Spirit fill me afresh.
4. Father, let every unbroken area in my life be broken, in the name of Jesus.
5. Father, incubate me with fire of the Holy Spirit, in Jesus' name.
6. Let every anti-power bondage break in my life, in Jesus' name.
7. Let all strangers flee from my spirit and let the Holy Spirit take control, in the name of Jesus.
8. Lord, catapult my spiritual life to the mountain top.
9. Father, let heavens open and let the glory of God fall upon me, in the name of Jesus.
10. Father, let signs and wonders be my lot, in the name of Jesus.
11. I decree the joy of the oppressors upon my life to be turned into sorrow, in the name of Jesus.
12. Let all multiple strongmen operating against me be paralysed, in the name of Jesus.
13. Lord, open my eyes and ears to receive wondrous things from You.
14. Lord, grant me victory over temptation and satanic device.
15. Lord, ignite my spiritual life so that I will stop fishing in unprofitable waters.
16. Lord, release Your tongue of fire upon my life and burn away all spir-

itual filthiness present within me.

17. Father, make me to hunger and thirst for righteousness, in the name of Jesus.

18. Lord, help me to be ready to do your work without expecting any recognition from others.

19. Lord, give me victory over emphasizing the weaknesses and sins of other people while ignoring my own.

20. O Lord, give me depth and root in my faith.

21. O Lord, heal every area of backsliding in my spiritual life.

22. Lord, help me to be willing to serve others rather than wanting to exercise authority.

23. Lord, open my understanding concerning the Scriptures.

24. Lord, help me to live each day recognizing that the day will come when You will judge secret lives and innermost thoughts.

25. Lord, let me be willing to be the clay in Your hands, ready to be molded as You desire.

26. Lord, wake me up from any form of spiritual sleep and help me to put on the armour of light.

27. Lord, give me victory over all carnality and help me to be in the centre of Your will.

28. I stand against anything in my life that will cause others to stumble, in the name of Jesus.

29. Lord, help me to put away childish things and put on maturity.

30. Lord, empower me to stand firm against all the schemes and techniques of the devil.

31. Lord, give me a big appetite for the pure milk and solid food in the word.

32. Lord, empower me to stay away from anything or anybody who might take God's place in my heart.

33. O Lord, I thank You for the testimonies that will follow.

GREAT DELIVERANCE
Psalm 18:50

- *Warfare prayers during deliverance exercises.*
- *For personal deliverance exercises.*

Great deliverance is a function of freedom from sin, self and Satan. It also includes having authority and dominion over all things. This would be your lot as you draw a battle line with anti-deliverance forces.

Psalm 18:50: *"Great deliverance giveth he to his king; and sheweth mercy to his anointed, to David, and to his seed for evermore."*

Deliverance is the act of setting free from every form of bondage. The bondage can be in the form of yokes, covenants, curses, spiritual chains, addictions, etc.

Great deliverance can only be said to have taken place when you are genuinely delivered from sin and translated into the light of His dear Son (Col. 1:13), when flesh has no dominion over you. Great deliverance is when your body, soul and spirit are free from all forms of demonic manipulation.

As you give yourself to the study of the word of God, live a holy life and maintain an aggressive prayer life, victory is sure.

- **CONFESSIONS**

Judg. 15:7-9: *And Samson said unto them, Though ye have done this, yet will I be avenged of you, and after that I will cease. And he smote them hip and thigh with a great slaughter: and he went down and dwelt in the top of the rock Etam. Then the Philistines went up, and pitched in Judah, and spread themselves in Lehi.*

Gen. 45:7: *And God sent me before you to preserve you a posterity in the earth, and to save your lives by a great deliverance.*

1 Chr. 11:14: *And they set themselves in the midst of that parcel, and delivered it, and slew the Philistines; and the LORD saved them by a great deliverance.*

● INSTRUCTIONS

1. Sit comfortably.

2. Focus your attention on the Lord Jesus Christ.

3. Avoid distractions. If they come, do not concentrate on them.

4. Confess any known sin to the Lord.

5. Ask the Lord to bring to your memory the legal ground or the open doors that forces of spiritual wickedness are using to gain entrance into your life.

6. Enter into this period with aggressive prayer. All prayer points are to be said with holy anger, violently and with determined aggression.

● PRAISE WORSHIP

1. I release myself from every ancestral pollution, in Jesus' name.

2. I release myself from every spiritual pollution emanating from my parents' religion, in the name of Jesus.

3. I break and loose myself from every idol and related association, in the name of Jesus.

4. I release myself from every dream pollution, in Jesus' name.

5. Let all the rivers, trees, forests, evil companions, evil pursuers, pictures of dead relatives, snakes, spirit husbands, spirit wives, masquerades manipulated against me in the dream be completely destroyed by the power in the blood of the Lord Jesus.

6. I command every evil plantation in my life: **Come out with all your roots, in the name of Jesus!** (*Lay your hands on your stomach and keep repeating the emphasized area.*)

7. Evil strangers in my body, come all the way out of your hiding places, in the mighty name of Jesus.

8. Let all avenues of eating or drinking spiritual poisons be closed, in the name of Jesus.

9. I cough out and vomit any food eaten from the table of the devil, in the

name of Jesus. (*Cough them out and vomit them in faith. Prime the expulsion.*)

10. Let all negative materials circulating in my blood stream be evacuated, in the name of Jesus.

11. I drink the blood of Jesus. (*Physically swallow and drink it in faith. Keep doing this for some time.*)

12. *Lay one hand on your head and the other on your stomach or navel and begin to pray like this:* Holy Ghost fire, burn from the top of my head to the sole of my feet. *Begin to mention every organ of your body: your kidney, liver, intestine, blood, etc. You must not rush at this level, because the fire will actually come.*

13. I cut myself off from every spirit of . . . (*mention the name of your place of birth*), in the name of Jesus.

14. I cut myself off from every tribal spirit and curses, in Jesus' name.

15. I cut myself off from every territorial spirit and curses, in the name of Jesus.

16. Holy Ghost fire, purge my life completely.

17. I claim my complete deliverance in the name of Jesus from the spirit of . . . (*mention those things you do not desire in your life*).

18. I break the hold of any evil power over my life, in Jesus' name.

19. I move from bondage into liberty in every area of my life, in the name of Jesus.

20. Thank God for answers to your prayer.

REVERSING HIDDEN CURSES

2 Kings 2:18-22

- *Warfare prayers for breaking known and un known curses.*
- *Appropriate for use during deliverance min istrations or breaking of curses.*

The original situation of your life may be gene-rating bitter and unpleasant water, but as you go to the Lord in earnest prayer, the Lord would definitely apply His healing salt to sweeten the source of your life.

2 Samuel 22: 45 & 46: *"Strangers shall submit themselves unto me: as soon as they hear, they shall be obedient unto me. Strangers shall fade away, and they shall be afraid out of their close places."*

Many people are labouring under unexplainable burdens. To move forward there is an invisible barrier. The heaven has be-come as brass and the earth beneath like iron. When everything seems not to be working in spite of numerous efforts, there may be a hidden curse in place.

Proverbs 26:2 says, "Curse careless shall not come." This means there must be a reason for the curse. Curses are evil words backed up by supernatural powers. If a curse is not broken, it will con-tinue its evil operation.

We thank God that Christ has redeemed us from the curse of the law. These prayer points are designed to break hidden curses.

- CONFESSIONS

Gal. 3:13-14: *Christ hath redeemed us from the curse of the law, being made a curse for us: for it is written, Cursed is every one that hangeth on a tree: That the blessing of Abraham might come on the Gentiles through Jesus Christ; that we might receive the promise of the Spirit through faith.*

Num. 23:23: *Surely there is no enchantment against Jacob, neither is there any divination against Israel: according to this time it shall be said of Jacob and of Israel, What hath God wrought!*

● PRAISE WORSHIP

1. Praise the Lord for the redemptive power in the blood of Jesus.
2. Praise the Lord for redeeming us from the curse of the law.
3. Confess all sins that has given the enemy legal right to place any curse on you or your household.
4. Repent and ask God for forgiveness and cleansing.
5. I take authority over every curse upon my life, in Jesus' name.
6. I command all curses issued against me to be broken, in the name of Jesus.
7. I command all evil spirits associated with any curse to leave me now, in the name of Jesus.
8. I take authority over inherited curses and command them to be broken now, in the name of Jesus.
9. I take authority over curses emanating from . . . *(pick from the under listed)* and command them to be broken now, in Jesus' name.

   - evil dedication   - ancestral sins
   - handling cursed objects   - witchcraft curses
   - satanic agents   - spiritual ignorance
   - living in cursed land or housing
   - being born in a satanic altar
   - strange money or cursed gifts
   - partaking of food sacrificed to idols
   - conscious or unconscious honouring of demon idols
   - conscious or unconscious performance of demonic rituals

10. In the name of Jesus, I break any curse which may be in my parents' families back to ten generations.
11. I renounce and break all curses put on my family line and my descendants, in the name of Jesus.
12. I command every bad spirit of any curse to release me and go now, in

the name of Jesus (*spend time on this*).

13. I break every curse of automatic failure working in my family, in the name of Jesus.

14. I take authority over every curse of . . . *(pick from the under listed)* in my family, in the name of Jesus.

- sickness, infirmity and deformity
- financial destruction
- physical and spiritual destruction
- family destruction
- marital destruction

15. I cancel the consequences and evil effects of all curses, in the name of Jesus.

16. I take authority over every unconscious or playful curse issued on me, in the name of Jesus.

17. Let the root of my life be purged by the fire of the Holy Spirit, in the name of Jesus.

18. Let the root of my life be washed in the blood of Jesus.

19. I break and cancel every curse placed on children to punish their parents in my life, in the name of Jesus.

20. I break and cancel every curse placed on me out of jealousy, in the name of Jesus.

21. I break and cancel every clinical and medical curse, in Jesus' name.

22. I break and cancel every curse issued by satanic ministers, in the name of Jesus.

23. I break and cancel every curse emanating from evil prophecies, in the name of Jesus.

24. I release myself from any curse emanating from . . . *(pick from the under listed)*, in the name of Jesus.

- past heresies or blasphemies
- breaking a person's heart
- self-imposed curses
- past involvement in false religion
- tithe failures
- deliberate sinning
- negative words

- misappropriation of God's glory
- trying to purify the unclean
- past involvement in immorality and sexual perversion
- conscious and unconscious demonic sacrifice
- conscious or unconscious unrighteous denial of another person's right

25. I reverse all the curses, in the name of Jesus. There shall be no more . . . *(mention what you do not desire in your life - e.g., poverty, sickness, etc)*, in the name of Jesus. *(Pray out loud, aggressively.)*

26. Begin to bless the name of the Lord for the wonders He has done.

ANOINTING TO EXCEL
Psalm 8

- *For success in interviews, appointments, promotions, examinations and employments.*
- *When you want to excel and be favoured above others.*
- *When you want God to be glorified in your career.*

God wants you to excel. If you are not experiencing this at present, pray these prayers and defy anything keeping you from excelling.

Proverbs 4:7: *"Wisdom is the principal thing; therefore get wisdom: and with all thy getting get understanding."*

To excel in life you must know what to do at all times. You must know God's desire for your life. Wisdom is the mind of Christ revealed to those who seek to know God.

Joseph was a remarkable man. He knew where God was taking him. He knew that his father, mother and brothers would bow to him. As a slave he excelled. Potiphar made him 'overseer over his house' (Genesis 39:2-6). As a prisoner Joseph also excelled. The Bible says, "And the keeper of the prison committed to Joseph's hand all the prisoners that were in the prison, and whatsoever they did there, he was the doer of it" (Genesis 39:21). After his training Joseph was promoted to the Palace. "Pharaoh said unto Joseph, ASee, I have set thee over all the land of Egypt" (Genesis 41:41).

It is said of Daniel that excellent wisdom was in him (Daniel 5:14) and an excellent spirit was found in him (Daniel 6:3). No wonder, as a slave in a foreign land Daniel was the first of the three presidents that ruled 120 princes (Daniel 6:1,2). Because of the anointing to excel that was in Daniel's life, he served four heathen kings, Nebuchadnezzar, Belshazzar, Darius and Cyrus.

Solomon, the wise king asked for wisdom and God gave him riches and honour also (1 Kings 3:9-14). His reign was the most peaceful in Israel, the richest kings and queens came to pay him homage. Proverbs 4: 8 & 4 says wisdom: (i) will promote us: (ii) bring us honour (iii) give us an ornament of grace (iv) give us a crown of glory.

If you desire to excel in whatever situation or circumstance you find yourself, ask God for the anointing of excellent wisdom (James 1:5).

These prayer points have been specially vomited by the Lord to cause you to excel in all you set out to do!

• CONFESSION

Deut. 28:13: *And the LORD shall make thee the head, and not the tail; and thou shalt be above only, and thou shalt not be beneath; if that thou hearken unto the commandments of the LORD thy God, which I command thee this day, to observe and to do them:*

• PRAISE WORSHIP

1. I refuse to allow my angel of blessings to depart, in Jesus' name.
2. I paralyse all aggression addressed to my star, in Jesus' name.
3. Let God arise in His anger and fight my war for me, in Jesus' name.
4. I neutralise all problems originating from the mistakes of my parents, in the name of Jesus.
5. I neutralise all problems originating from my past mistakes, in the name of Jesus.
6. Lord, bring honey out of the rock for me this month.
7. Lord, open all the good doors of my life that household wickedness have shut.
8. Let all anti-breakthrough designs against my life be shattered to irreparable pieces, in the name of Jesus.
9. I paralyse all satanic antagonism against my destiny right from the womb, in the name of Jesus.
10. I trample upon every enemy of my advancement and I unseat all evil powers siting on my promotions, in the name of Jesus.
11. O Lord, enlarge my coast beyond my wildest dream.
12. I claim back all my goods presently residing in wrong hands, in the name of Jesus.
13. O Lord, uproot evil things that are against my advancement from my life.
14. O Lord, plant into my life good things that will advance my cause.
15. Let every spiritual weakness in my life receive permanent termination, in the name of Jesus.

16. Let every financial failure in my life receive permanent termination, in the name of Jesus.

17. Let every sickness fashioned to pull my advancement down receive permanent termination, in the name of Jesus.

18. Let every architect of problems against my advancement receive permanent termination, in the name of Jesus.

19. I refuse to reap any satanic harvest in any area of my life, in the name of Jesus.

20. I paralyse all spiritual wolves working against my life, in the name of Jesus.

21. Whatever hinders me from greatness, begin to give way now, in the mighty name of Jesus.

22. Every imprisoned and buried potentials, come forth now, in the name of Jesus.

23. I command all unfriendly helpers in every area of my life to depart, in the name of Jesus.

24. I render null and void the effect of any interaction with satanic agents moving around as men or women, in the name of Jesus.

25. I bind every strongman having my goods in his possessions, in the name of Jesus.

26. I break the curse of automatic failure working in any department of my life, in the name of Jesus.

27. Let the anointing to excel and prosper fall mightily upon every department of my life, in the name of Jesus.

28. Let every anti-progress altar fashioned against me be destroyed with the fire of God, in the name of Jesus.

29. I withdraw my benefits from the hands of the oppressors, in the name of Jesus.

30. Let every power chasing blessings away from me be paralysed, in the name of Jesus.

31. Let the enemy begin to vomit every good thing he has eaten up in my life, in the name of Jesus.

32. O Lord, give me the power to overcome every obstacle to my breakthroughs.

33. I break all curses of leaking blessings, in the name of Jesus.

34. I clear my goods from the warehouse of the strongman, in the name of Jesus.

35. I frustrate and disappoint every instrument of the enemy fashioned against my advancement, in the name of Jesus.

36. I take authority over every satanic attack on my advancement, in the name of Jesus.

37. Let every opposition to my breakthroughs crash into pieces, in the name of Jesus.

38. I render all evil attacks against my advancements impotent, in the name of Jesus.

39. I stand against every faith destroyer in my life, in Jesus' name.

40. I bulldoze my way into breakthroughs this month, in Jesus' name.

41. Thank God for answering your prayers.

CRUSHING THE HEAD OF THE OPPRESSOR

Psalm 68

- *For the oppressed.*
- *For those who feel caged-in by life situations.*
- *When a group of people are being oppressed by another.*

Liaise with the Lord, who is great in battle, to crush the head of your oppressor today.

Romans 16:20: *"And the God of peace shall bruise Satan under your feet shortly. The grace of our Lord Jesus Christ be with you Amen."*

The devil is the oppressor; he is the one who oppress people with sickness, disease, poverty and death. But the Bible says . . . "How God anointed Jesus of Nazareth with the Holy Ghost and with power who went about doing good and healing all those that were oppressed of the devil for God was with Him" (Acts 10:38).

The first Bible prophecy is found in Genesis 3:15 which says, ... "The seed of the woman will bruise his head." That is why Col. 2:15 says, "Having spoiled principalities and powers, He made a show of them openly triumphing over them in it." Jesus has crushed the head of the oppressor. He openly stripped him of his powers and authority on the resurrection morning.

Grace is unmerited favour, "We are saved by grace through faith . . . Not of works lest any man should boast" (Ephesians 2:8-9). We've been saved by grace and the only way we can live our christian lives and overcome is by grace!

The grace of God upon your life will cause you to crush the head of the oppressor as you use these prayer points.

- ## CONFESSION

Isa. 54:10: *For the mountains shall depart, and the hills be removed; but my kindness shall not depart from thee, neither shall the covenant of my peace be removed, saith the LORD that hath mercy on thee.*

● PRAISE WORSHIP

1. Help me, O Lord, to recognise Your voice.
2. Lord, where I am blind, give me sight.
3. I throw off every burden of worry in my life, in Jesus' name.
4. I refuse to be entangled with any evil friend, in the name of Jesus.
5. I paralyse every evil hand pointing at my blessings, in Jesus' name.
6. I withdraw every satanic instruction against me from the memory of the evil messenger, in the name of Jesus.
7. O Lord, enough is enough. Let hidden infirmity in my life depart by fire, in the name of Jesus.
8. Let all evil rivers and shrines working against me receive the fire of God, in the mighty name of Jesus.
9. O Lord, give me a miracle that would dumbfound the world.
10. I cast down every roadblock hiding my progress, in Jesus' name.
11. Let my spiritual temperature send terror to the camp of the enemy, in the name of Jesus.
12. O Lord, release me from every evil word and evil silence.
13. I refuse to be made a spiritual rag, in the name of Jesus.
14. Let every spiritual handicap to breakthroughs in my life be melted by the fire of God, in the name of Jesus.
15. I recover any organ of my body stored in the bank of the enemy, in the name of Jesus.
16. O Lord, reorganise my body system to reject all satanic arrows.
17. I command every evil growth in my life to come out with all its roots, in the name of Jesus.
18. I drink the divine worm-expeller, in the name of Jesus.
19. I refuse to be glued to any problem in any department of my life, in the name of Jesus.
20. Let any power storing my blessings in the air begin to release them unto me now, in the name of Jesus.

21. Let any power storing my blessings inside any body of water begin to release them unto me now, in the name of Jesus.

22. Let any power storing my blessings inside any inanimate object begin to release them unto me now, in the name of Jesus.

23. Let any power storing my blessings in any tree begin to release them unto me now, in the name of Jesus.

24. Let not my enemies triumph over me O Lord.

25. I clear my goods out of every satanic warehouse, in Jesus' name.

26. Let the angels conveying my blessings receive overcoming divine assistance, in the name of Jesus.

27. I paralyse the power of the prince of the air upon my prayers, in the name of Jesus.

28. All satanic laughter at my life, be turned to sorrow, in Jesus' name

29. Let every mountain of hindrance to my prayers be melted by the divine fire, in the name of Jesus.

30. Let the displacing power of the Holy Spirit displace any darkness in my life and replace it with light.

31. O Lord, convert every failure in my life to success.

32. O Lord, convert every frustration in my life to fulfilment.

33. O Lord, convert every rejection in my life to acceptance.

34. O Lord, convert every pain in my life to pleasure.

35. O Lord, convert every poverty in my life to blessing.

36. O Lord, convert every mistake in my life to perfection.

37. O Lord, convert every sickness in my life to health.

38. I crush the head of every problem-serpent, in the name of Jesus.

39. I trample upon every problem-serpent and scorpion, in Jesus' name

40. I bind and paralyse the spirit and activities of the wasters upon my life, in the name of Jesus.

41. I bind and paralyse the spirit and activities of the devourers upon my life, in the name of Jesus.

42. I bind and paralyse the spirit and activities of the 'emptier' upon my life, in the name of Jesus.

43. Begin to thank God for answers to prayer.

YOUR FIRST PRAYER MEETING IN THE NEW YEAR

Psalm 24:7-10

● *For the first day of the year.*

To start every new year with the Lord in prayer is a wise step into victory and breakthroughs, not only through the new year but to eternity.

Job 36:11: *"If they obey and serve him, they shall spend their days in prosperity and their years in pleasure."*

The birth of a new child, the dawn of a new day, the start of a new year, all bring feelings of excitement, joy, hope and promise. There is an air of great expectations when we put God first at the beginning of everything we do. We can be rest assured that the end will be good, He is the Alpha and the Omega (Revelations 1:5).

How do we put God first? (i) By praying to Him to know His will. Once we know His will then we can obey Him. If He has given an instruction that we haven't followed, He won't say anything else till we go back and obey His instruction. (ii) By committing our ways, our plans and desires into His hands. When we desire to serve Him, He will work in us both to will and to do of His good pleasure (Phillipians 2:13). Our will will become bound to His will. When we do these two things the Bible says we will spend our days in prosperity and our years in pleasure.

As we start the new year, make sure you put God first, make God number one. "Seek ye first the kingdom of God and His right-eousness and all these things shall be added unto you" (Matthew 6:33).

● **CONFESSION**

Isa. **43:19**: *Behold, I will do a new thing; now it shall spring forth; shall ye not know it? I will even make a way in the wilderness, and rivers in the desert.*

● **PRAISE WORSHIP**

1. Thank the Lord for His goodness and wonderful works in your life.

2. O Lord, perfect all good things concerning me this year.

3. Let God be God in my life this year, in the name of Jesus.

4. Let God arise and disgrace every power challenging my God, in the name of Jesus.

5. Let all my disappointments become divine appointments, in the name of Jesus.

6. Let all satanic winds and storms be silenced, in the name of Jesus.

7. You God of new beginnings, begin a new dimension of wonders in my life this year, in the name of Jesus.

8. Let that which hinders me from greatness be smashed to pieces, in the name of Jesus.

9. Let every anti-breakthrough altar fashioned against me be destroyed, in the name of Jesus.

10. Let the anointing for spiritual breakthroughs fall upon me, in the name of Jesus.

11. Lord, let me be at the right place at the right time.

12. You God of new beginnings, open fresh doors of prosperity to me, in the name of Jesus.

13. O Lord, give me anointed ideas and lead me to new paths of blessings, in the name of Jesus.

14. Let all my wasted years and efforts be converted to multiple blessings, in the name of Jesus.

15. My finances will not enter into the clutches of financial hunger this year, in the name of Jesus.

16. I reject every spirit of financial embarrassment, in Jesus' name.

17. O Lord, bring honey out of the rock for me and let me find the way where men say there is no way.

18. I withdraw all the evil words I have spoken against my life, home, work, etc., from satanic records, in the name of Jesus.

19. This year, I will not turn back at the edge of my miracles, in the name of Jesus.

20. Let every architect of hatred, hostility and conflict in the home be paralysed, in the name of Jesus.

21. I command every satanic limitation to my health and finances to be removed, in the name of Jesus.

22. Let all inherited limitations to obtaining good things depart, in the name of Jesus.

23. O Lord, arise and disgrace every power challenging my God.

24. At the name of Jesus, let every knee of satanic embarrassment bow.

25. I refuse to eat the bread of sorrow this year, in Jesus' name.

26. I cast all problem-serpents and scorpions into the fire of judgement, in the name of Jesus.

27. Let the East wind paralyze and disgrace all my spiritual Pharaohs and Egyptians, in the name of Jesus.

28. Do something in my life in this prayer session that will change my life for good, in the name of Jesus.

29. Lord, give unto me the divine mantle to cross my problem-Jordan.

30. I will not dance to any unprofitable music this year, in Jesus' name.

31. My God shall supply all my needs according to His riches in glory, in the name of Jesus.

32. I shall not die but live to declare the works of God, in Jesus' name.

33. My shoes shall be as iron to trample upon serpents and scorpions this year, in the name of Jesus.

34. I claim explosive miracles for every department of my life this year, in the name of Jesus.

35. Let my life experience revival fire this year, in the name of Jesus.

36. Begin to thank God for everything.

THE AGGRESSIVE PRAYER OF THE PSALMIST

Psalm 144:1

● Use the prayer points of the Psalmist when things look stubborn; unyielding and defiant. The Psalmist understood spiritual warfare. His prayer points may appear to be too hot for junior students in the school of spiritual warfare, because they contain dreadful pronouncements against the enemies of God. The Psalms are a handbook on the warfare of the righteous against demonic forces. Many Christians claim that the prayers of the Psalmist contradict Our Lord's injunction to love our enemies. True, it is a sin to hate any human being. But it is also a sin to love demons and hard-core satanic agents. The Psalmist refused to kill King Saul, his human enemy, even when he found the opportunities.

You must pray against spiritual enemies and not human foes who are mere instruments. Always remember, the only language understood by the enemies of our souls is VIOLENCE and RESOUNDING DEFEAT. Spiritual warfare prayers are to be directed against the powers of darkness and not human beings.

The challenge posed by increased strategies of the power of darkness, most especially against Christianity, calls for an aggressive and violent warfare prayer to counter such satanic revival.

Matthew 11:12: "And from the days of John the Baptist until now the Kingdom of God suffereth Violence, and the violent take it by force."

God recognises spiritual violence. David, the man after God's heart wrote some shocking Psalms. These Psalms are generally referred to as imperator cursing psalms. They are Psalms 10, 28, 35,59.69, 109. 137 and 140. In these psalms, David asks God to do terrible things to his enemies: their teeth should break, they should be as chaff before the wind, their wives should become widows and their children fatherless. Let their way be dark and slippery, let the angel of God chase them, let the angel of God persecute them, let their habitation be desolate, let that which will be for their welfare become a trap. All these are cries of what David wanted God to do to his enemies.

These prayer points will attack the spirits warring against your life.

• PRAISE WORSHIP

1. Let the powers of the wicked be blown away as the chaff which the wind is driving away, in the name of Jesus.

2. Let the way of the wicked powers assigned to any department of my life perish, in the name of Jesus.

3. O Lord, laugh all evil counsellors that are against me to scorn.

4. O Lord, have in derision all the evil kings that are gathered for my sake.

5. O Lord, break them with a rod of iron.

6. O Lord, dash them to pieces like a potter's vessel.

7. O Lord, smite all my enemies upon the cheek bone.

8. O Lord, break the teeth of the wicked.

9. O Lord, destroy the enemies using poisonous tongues and sepulchral throat against my life.

10. Let the enemies fall by their own counsels, in the name of Jesus.

11. Let the wicked be cast out in the multitude of their transgression, in the name of Jesus.

12. O Lord, let all my enemies be ashamed and be troubled.

13. O Lord, let all my enemies receive sudden shame and take their arrows back.

14. Arise, O Lord, in Your anger and lift up Yourself because of the rage of my enemies.

15. O Lord, let the wickedness of the wicked come to an end.

16. O Lord, prepare the instruments of death against my persecutors.

17. O Lord, ordain Your arrows against my persecutors.

18. O Lord, let the enemies of my soul fall into the pit which they dug.

19. O Lord, let the mischief of the oppressors come upon their own heads.

20. O Lord, let the violent dealing of the enemy come down upon his own path.

21. Lord, let my enemies fall and perish at Your presence.

22. Lord, let the net of the enemy catch his own feet.

23. Let the wicked be taken in devices that they have imagined, in the name of Jesus.

24. Lord, break the arm of the wicked.

25. Let the sorrows of my enemies be multiplied.

26. Arise, Lord, disappoint the enemy and deliver my soul from the wicked.

27. Let the thunder, hailstones, coals of fire, lightning and arrows from the Lord scatter the forces of the enemy, in the name of Jesus.

28. Lord, give unto me the necks of mine enemies.

29. Let all oppressors be beaten small as the dust before the wind, in the name of Jesus.

30. Let them be cast out as the dirt in the streets, in Jesus' name.

31. O Lord, swallow the oppressors and persecutors in Your wrath.

32. Lord, let the fire devour the wicked and their seeds.

33. Lord, deliver my soul from the power of the dog and from the mouth of the lion.

34. Lord, let all the mischievous devices of the enemy refuse to perform.

35. Let all the eaters of flesh and drinkers of blood stumble and fall, in the name of Jesus.

36. Lord, render to my enemies their desert.

37. Let all lips speaking grievous things proudly and contemptuously against me be silenced, in the name of Jesus.

38. Lord, send Your angels to sow terror and panic in the hearts of all witch-doctors gathered for my sake.

39. Evil shall slay the wicked; and they that hate the righteous shall be desolate, in the name of Jesus.

40. O Lord, fight against them that fight against me.

41. Let them be confounded and put to shame that seek after my soul, in the name of Jesus.

42. Let them be turned back and brought to confusion that devise my hurt, in the name of Jesus.

43. Let the angels of the Lord chase and persecute the enemies of my soul, in the name of Jesus.

44. Let the way of my enemies be dark and slippery, in Jesus' name.

45. Let destruction come upon my enemies unawares, in Jesus' name.

46. Lord, let not them that are mine enemies wrongfully rejoice over me, neither let them wink the eye that hate me without a cause.

47. Let them be ashamed and brought to confusion together that rejoice at my hurt, in the name of Jesus.

48. Let them be clothed with shame and dishonour that magnify themselves against me, in the name of Jesus.

49. Let the sword of the wicked enter into their own heart and let their bows be broken, in the name of Jesus.

50. All the enemies of the Lord shall be as the fat of lamb, in smoke shall they be consumed, in the name of Jesus.

51. Let all my enemies be laid in the grave like a sheep and let death feed on them, in the name of Jesus.

52. O Lord, destroy and divide the tongues of the enemy.

53. O God, break the teeth of the enemy in their mouth, in Jesus' name

54. Let them melt away as waters which run continually, in the name of Jesus.

55. When the enemy bends his bow to shoot his arrows, let him be cut in pieces, in the name of Jesus.

56. Let every one of the oppressors pass away like the untimely birth of a woman that they may not see the sun, in the name of Jesus.

57. Let them wander up and down for meat and grudge if they be not satisfied, in the name of Jesus.

58. Let the wicked fall by the sword and become a portion for foxes, in the name of Jesus.

59. God shall wound the head of the enemy and the hairy scalp of the wicked, in the name of Jesus.

60. Let their table become a snare before them, in the name of Jesus.

61. Let that which should have been for their welfare become a trap, in the name of Jesus.

62. Let the extortioner catch all that the enemy has, and let the strangers spoil his labour, in the name of Jesus.

63. As he loved cursing, so let it come unto him; as he delighted not in blessing, so let it be far from him, in the name of Jesus.

64. Let them be as grass upon the house tops which withers before it grows up, in the name of Jesus.

65. Lord, stretch forth Your hand against my enemies.

66. Let the mischief of their own lips cover them, in the name of Jesus.

67. Grant not, O Lord, the desires of the wicked and further not his wicked device, in the name of Jesus.

68. Let burning coals fall upon them, in the name of Jesus.

69. Let them be cut into fire and the deep pit and rise not up again, in the name of Jesus.

70. Let their eyes be darkened that they see not, in the name of Jesus.

71. Make their loins shake continuously, in the name of Jesus.

72. Let their habitations become desolate, let there be no one to dwell in them, in the name of Jesus.

73. Add iniquity unto their iniquity, in the name of Jesus.

74. Let them be covered with reproach and dishonour that seek my hurt, in the name of Jesus.

75. Persecute them with tempest and make them afraid with Thy storm, in the name of Jesus.

76. Mine eyes also shall see my desire on my enemies and mine ears shall hear my desire of the wicked that rise up against me, in Jesus' name.

77. Let his children be continually vagabonds and beggars, let them seek their bread out of desolate places, in the name of Jesus.

78. Let evil hunt the violent enemy to overthrow him, in Jesus' name.

79. O Lord, cast forth lightning and scatter them.

80. Let God arise and let all His enemies be scattered, in Jesus' name.

81. Let the lifter and the glory of my head be exalted above all gods, in the name of Jesus.

TO ARREST UNPROFITABLE LATENESS IN MARRIAGE

Hab. 2:3

- **For spinsters and bachelors who feel that obtaining the right partner is getting rather late.** The best way to arrest delay in marriage is to engage in constant wrestling bouts with the enemy and to call back all the benefits you would have gained if you had gotten married earlier. God is waiting for you to fight it out with your enemy.

Isaiah 34:16: *"Seek ye out of the book of the LORD, and read: no one of these shall fail, none shall want her mate: for my mouth it hath commanded, and his spirit it hath gathered them."*

No word of God shall lack power of fulfillment! God's words are always backed by His authority and we know His words cannot return to Him void. We serve a God that cannot lie. His dreams, vision and words concerning our lives will surely come to pass. God is the one that instituted marriage and He performed the first wedding ceremony in Genesis chapter 2. God has a man for every woman and if you feel that you have lost God's perfect will for your life, don't forget that for every Vashti there is an Esther.

Lateness in marriage can come as a result of collective captivity, manipulations of household wickedness, spirit husband/wife and other anti-marriage forces. "In His time God makes all things beautiful" (Ecclesiastes 3:11). The God that makes all things beautiful, will step into your situation, break down every wall of partition between you and your God-ordained partner (Ephesians 2:14) and gather you together by His Spirit (Isaiah 34:16; Ephesians 2:13). Our God is faithful! He never comes late. He will hasten His words (concerning your marriage) to perform it. (Jeremiah 1:12).

- **CONFESSIONS**

Phil. 2:9-10: *Wherefore God also hath highly exalted him, and given him a name which is above every name: That at the name of Jesus every knee should bow, of things in heaven, and things in earth, and things under the earth;*

Col. 2:13: *And you, being dead in your sins and the uncircumcision of your flesh, hath he quickened together with him, having forgiven you all trespasses;*

Rev. 12:11: *And they overcame him by the blood of the Lamb, and by the word of their testimony; and they loved not their lives unto the death.*

Luke 1:37: *For with God nothing shall be impossible.*

● **PRAISE WORSHIP**

1. Thank the Lord because your miracle has come.

2. Ask the Lord to forgive you any sin that would hinder answers to your prayers.

3. Lord, make known to me the secrets of my inner life.

4. Help me Lord, to discover my real self.

5. Let every imagination of the enemy against my marital life be rendered impotent, in the name of Jesus.

6. I refuse to co-operate with any anti-marriage spells and curses, in the name of Jesus.

7. I cancel every bewitchment fashioned against my settling down in marriage, in the name of Jesus.

8. Let every force magnetising the wrong people to me be paralysed, in the name of Jesus.

9. I break every covenant of marital failure and late marriage, in the name of Jesus.

10. I cancel every spiritual wedding conducted consciously or unconsciously on my behalf, in the name of Jesus.

11. I remove the hand of household wickedness from my marital life, in the name of Jesus.

12. Let every incantation, incisions, hexes and other spiritually harmful

activities working against me, be completely neutralized, in the name of Jesus.

13. I command all forces of evil manipulating, delaying or hindering my marriage to be completely paralysed, in the name of Jesus.

14. Let all evil anti-marriage marks be removed, in Jesus' name.

15. Lord, restore me to the perfect way in which You created me if I have been altered.

16. Father, let Your fire destroy every satanic weapon fashioned against my marriage, in the name of Jesus.

17. Lord, expose all the schemes and plans of satan ever devised against me through any source and at any time.

18. I forsake any personal sin that has given ground to the enemy, in the name of Jesus.

19. I reclaim all the ground I have lost to the enemy, in Jesus' name.

20. I apply the power in the name and blood of Jesus to my marital situation.

21. I apply the blood of Jesus to remove all consequences of evil operations and oppression, in the name of Jesus.

22. I break the binding effect of anything of evil ever put upon me from any source, in the name of Jesus.

23. Let all the enemies of Jesus Christ operating against my life be exposed, in the name of Jesus.

24. I sever myself from any satanic linkage and any strange power, in the name of Jesus.

25. I remove the right of the enemy to afflict my plan to get married, in the name of Jesus.

26. I break every bondage of inherited marital confusion, in the name of Jesus.

27. I bind and plunder the goods of every strongman attached to my marriage, in the name of Jesus.

28. Let the angels of the living God roll away the stone blocking my marital breakthrough, in the name of Jesus.
29. I remove my name from the book of seers of goodness without manifestation, in the name of Jesus.
30. Let God arise and let all the enemies of my marital breakthrough be scattered, in the name of Jesus.
31. Let the fire of God melt away the stones hindering my marital blessings, in the mighty name of Jesus.
32. Let the cloud blocking the sunlight of my glory and breakthrough be dispersed, in the name of Jesus.
33. Let all evil spirits masquerading to trouble my marital life be bound, in the name of Jesus.
34. The pregnancy of good things within me will not be aborted by any contrary power, in the name of Jesus.
35. Lord, let wonderful changes begin to be my lot from this week.
36. I reject every spirit of the tail in all areas of my life, in Jesus' name.
37. I receive my right match, in the name of Jesus.
38. I stand against every spirit of discouragement, fear, worry and frustration, in the name of Jesus.
39. Lord, turn away all that would jilt, disappoint or fail me.
40. Thank God for the victory.

I SHALL BE THE CROWN OF GLORY

Psalm 8

- *When dumbfounding breakthroughs are desired.*
- *When others are laughing you to scorn.*

God has destined mankind to show forth His glory, but man's archenemy came to dismantle it by introducing sin to mankind. But the good news is that God has visited man again through Christ to restore the lost glory. Rise up now and claim back your own share of the glory.

Psalm 3:3: *"But thou O Lord, art a shield for me; my glory and the lifter up of mine head."*

The room became silent as Mary entered. They had been talking about her gain. She immediately rushed out in embarrassment. The shame and reproach of being barren was becoming more than she could bear. Peter hung his head down. There was no money anywhere to feed his family. The shame of having to beg for money to feed, filled him with despair.

Whatever is causing you to weep and your head to be bowed will be destroyed as you pray these prayer points. God is your glory, He is the lifter up of your head.

When the enemy says 'there is no way', when the enemy says, 'it is finished'. When the enemy says, 'just give up' - beloved, begin to rejoice, because God will make a way for you! The garment of heaviness, shame and reproach is going to be torn off your body by the Lord of glory!

God is saying to you today, "O thou afflicted, tossed with tempest and not comforted, behold I will lay thy stones with fair colours, and lay thy foundations with sapphires. And I will make thy windows of agates, and thy gates of carbuncles, and all thy borders of pleasant stones" (Isaiah 54:11-12).

God will build you up! He will make you a precious jewel in His hands! Truly you will be a crown of glory in the hands of God.

• CONFESSION

Isa. 62:3: *Thou shalt also be a crown of glory in the hand of the LORD, and a royal diadem in the hand of thy God.*

• PRAISE WORSHIP

1. I break every hold of witchcraft working against my life, in the name of Jesus.

2. I command a change in all unprofitable situations in my life, in the name of Jesus.

3. I command my battle to change to blessings, in Jesus' name.

4. Let every mountain of satanic confrontation be disgraced, in the name of Jesus.

5. Let every mountain of impossibility be dashed to pieces, in the name of Jesus.

6. Let new wells spring up in my desert, in the name of Jesus.

7. O Lord, bear me up on Eagle's wings before my enemies.

8. O Lord, anoint my eyes to see my divine opportunities.

9. I refuse to allow my past to influence my future negatively, in the name of Jesus.

10. Let every satanic battle confronting me fall apart, in Jesus' name.

11. I bind the strongman of financial embarrassment, in Jesus' name.

12. I declare myself free from the plagues of spiritual Egypt, in the name of Jesus.

13. I command all crooked and difficult areas of my life to begin to yield testimonies, in the name of Jesus.

14. Let the spirit of excellence manifest in every area of my life, in the name of Jesus.

15. Let the fear of me fill the minds of the enemy and let them panic, in the name of Jesus.

16. My years shall not be in struggle but in prosperity, in Jesus' name.

17. Let the oppressors drown in their own Red Sea, in Jesus' name.
18. I receive power to leap over every wall that the enemy has built, in the name of Jesus.
19. Let the enemy fall into his own trap, in the name of Jesus.
20. O Lord, make my miracle invisible to my enemies.
21. O Lord, re-organise my system to confuse evil observers.
22. I resist all spiritual sabotage and cunning attacks, in Jesus' name.
23. Let the fire of God protect my miracle, in the name of Jesus.
24. Let the root of every night terror dry up, in the name of Jesus.
25. Let all the weapons of the enemy work against them, in the name of Jesus.
26. The mockery of my enemies shall result in my advancement, in the name of Jesus.
27. O Lord, turn my mourning to dancing and my tears to joy.
28. Let the sword and pit of the enemy turn against him, in the name of Jesus.
29. Let attacks by household wickedness melt away, in Jesus' name.
30. Every Goliath defying my prayers, be impotent, in Jesus' name.
31. O Lord, display Your power against every unrepentant opposition in my life.
32. Let evil intention of mockers turn against them, in Jesus' name.
33. O Lord, convert my opposition to promotion.
34. I uproot every evil testimony, in the name of Jesus.
35. I thank O Lord, for the deliverance.

DISGRACING STUBBORN AND UNREPENTANT OPPOSITION

Exodus 14

- *When Pharaoh-like pursuers are after you.*
- *When you are being openly threatened and harassed by wicked forces.*
- *When oppressive forces appear glued to you or some situations.*

God is willing to repeat what He did to the stubborn pursuer and unrepentant Pharaoh, to the enemies of your life who are victimizing you, provided you do not turn your back on Canaan and face Egypt.

Isaiah 41:11 & 12: "Behold, all they that were incensed against me shall be ashamed and confounded: they shall be as nothing; and they that strive with me shall perish. I will seek them, and I will not find them, even them that contend with me; they that war with me shall be as nothing and as a thing of nought."

The spirit of Egypt is a stubborn spirit that seeks to destroy a person. After God gave the Egyptians 10 blows, they still pursued the Israelites into the Red Sea. "And the Lord hardened the heart of Pharaoh King of Egypt, and he pursued the children of Israel; and the children of Israel went out with a high hand" (Exodus 14:8). The spirit of Egypt represents demonic powers while Pharaoh represents the spirit of the unrepentant stubborn pursuer.

Are you tired of constant satanic harassment? You've been going from one problem to another without rest? Then these prayers are for you. God will thrust out your enemies before you and say 'destroy them'. They will be as chaff before the wind, they will become as nothing. Pharaoh and all his chariots drowned in the Red Sea. There was no trace of them. So shall be the end of the stubborn and unrepentant opposition attacking you.

- **CONFESSION**

Deut. 33:27: *The eternal God is thy refuge, and underneath are the everlasting arms: and he shall thrust out the enemy from before thee; and shall say, Destroy them.*

• PRAISE WORSHIP

1. O Lord, I will not leave You unless You bless me in this prayer session.

2. Every evil preparation against me, be frustrated, in Jesus' name.

3. O Lord, multiply my joy, peace and blessings.

4. I reject every spirit that fails at the edge of breakthroughs, in the name of Jesus.

5. I refuse to reap any evil harvest, in the name of Jesus.

6. Divine favour of God, overshadow my life from now, in Jesus' name.

7. I renounce every inherited poverty in my life, in the name of Jesus.

8. Let the foundation of my life be repaired and begin to carry divine prosperity, in the name of Jesus.

9. Let every evil bird flying for my sake receive the arrow of fire, in the name of Jesus.

10. Lord, begin to restore me to the perfect way in which You created me.

11. All my past defeats, be converted to victory, in the name of Jesus.

12. O Lord, make my life a terror to the enemy.

13. Let my hands begin to break every citadel of the enemy in every department of my life, in the name of Jesus.

14. Devil, I declare you publicly disgraced in my life, in Jesus' name.

15. Let the fire of God begin to destroy every evil imagination against any department of my life, in the name of Jesus.

16. Let all evil imaginations fashioned against my life fail woefully, in the name of Jesus.

17. Lord, expose and disgrace all the schemes of satan ever devised against me through any source and at any time.

18. I forsake all personal sin that has given ground to the enemy in my life, in the name of Jesus.

19. I reclaim all the ground I have lost to the enemy, in Jesus' name.

20. I apply the power in the name and the blood of Jesus to my situation now, in the name of Jesus.

21. I apply the blood and the name of Jesus to remove all consequences of evil oppression in my life, in the name of Jesus.

22. In Your authority O Lord, I break the binding effect of anything evil ever put upon me from any source, in the name of Jesus.

23. I bind all enemy spirits that oppress me and remove them from my life, in the name of Jesus.

24. I command the power of the enemy working against my progress to take flight now, in the name of Jesus.

25. O Lord, let my hands be trained for battle and assign me my place in Your army.

26. I expose all enemies of Jesus Christ operating against my life, in the name of Jesus.

27. I sever myself from satan and any strange power, in Jesus' name.

28. I remove the right of any strange powers to afflict me and I proclaim their judgement under the hand of God, in Jesus' name.

29. I weaken the power of any strange power fashioned against me with the blood of Jesus shed on the cross at calvary, in the name of Jesus.

30. I break every bondage of inherited sickness in my life, in the name of Jesus.

31. Spirit of infirmity in my life, come out now, in the name of Jesus.

32. O Lord, confuse every issue of my life before the eyes of the enemy.

33. O Lord, soak me and my family in the blood of Jesus.

34. I declare that death and sickness have no hold on me and my family, in the name of Jesus.

35. O Lord, help me to fulfil the programme of my life.

36. All stubborn covenants in my life, be broken now, in Jesus' name.

37. Lord Jesus, convert my body to Holy Ghost fire.

38. O Lord, ignite the fire of revival in my soul.

39. Let all flesh eaters assigned against my life stumble and fall whenever they want to carry out their operation, in Jesus' name.

40. Let all my blessings that the enemy have swallowed be vomited now, in the name of Jesus.

41. The good things that are at the point of death in my life, receive life now, in the name of Jesus.

42. Begin to prophesy unto your problems, in the name of Jesus.

43. All the pregnancies of the devil upon my life, be aborted, in the name of Jesus.

44. I command all the hands that cover my blessings to be lifted, in the name of Jesus.

45. I command the eggs laid by the enemy against my life to break before hatching, in the name of Jesus.

46. O Lord, clothe me with untouchable fire.

47. O Lord, make me Your battle axe.

48. Lord, reveal to me the secrets of all the strangers hiding in my life.

49. All anti-progressive forces, I summon you together and I issue the judgement of the fire of God upon you, in the name of Jesus.

50. Jesus, I invite You to be Lord over every department of my life.

51. Father Lord, I confess my sins and ask that You will forgive and cleanse me, in the name of Jesus.

52. I forgive all those who have hurt or offended me, in Jesus' name.

53. I claim my freedom from the consequences of all curses, in the name of Jesus.

54. I claim my freedom from the consequences of evil pronouncements, in the name of Jesus.

55. I claim my freedom from the consequences of hereditary diseases, in the name of Jesus.

56. I claim my freedom from the consequences of attitudinal problems, in the name of Jesus.

57. I claim my freedom from the consequences of idolatry, in the name of Jesus.

58. I claim my freedom from the consequences of sins and misfortunes, in the name of Jesus.

59. Let no evil power trouble me any more, in the name of Jesus.

60. Every demonic transference into the affairs of my life, be broken, in the name of Jesus.

61. Every demonic communication into the affairs of my life, be broken, in the name of Jesus.

62. Every demonic resistance to my prayers, be broken, in Jesus' name.

63. Every demonic reinforcement against my life, be broken, in the name of Jesus.

64. Power of God, be released into my body now, in Jesus' name.

65. Let the power of God be released upon my body from the crown of my head to the sole of my feet, in the name of Jesus.

66. Every afflicting force, be consumed by fire, in the name of Jesus.

67. Evil strangers, come out of your hiding place in any area of my life, in the name of Jesus.

68. I cast out the spirit of evil inheritance, in the name of Jesus.

69. I stand against every addictive desire in my life, in Jesus' name.

70. Let the healing power of God flow into every damaged part of my body, in the name of Jesus.

71. I release the creative miracle of God into every department of my life, in the name of Jesus.

72. O Lord, begin to restore me to full abundant life.

73. O Lord, empower my life with Your authority over every demonic force that set themselves against my life.

74. O Lord, let all the impossible begin to become possible for me in every department of my life.

75. O Lord, take me from where I am to where You want me to be.

76. O Lord, make a way for me where there is no way.
77. O Lord, grant me the power to be fulfilled, successful and prosperous in life.
78. O Lord, break me up in every department of my life.
79. O Lord, make me to move from breakthrough into dumbfounding miracles in all areas of my life.
80. O Lord, make me to break out of every obstacle on my way to progress in life.
81. O Lord, establish me in truth, Godliness and faithfulness.
82. O Lord, add flavour to my work.
83. O Lord, add increase to my work.
84. O Lord, add profitability to my work.
85. O Lord, promote and preserve my life.
86. I reject the plans and agenda of the enemies against my life, in the name of Jesus.
87. I reject the assignments and weapons of the enemy against my life, in the name of Jesus.
88. Let every weapon and evil design against me fail totally, in the name of Jesus.
89. I reject premature death, in the name of Jesus.
90. I reject nightmares and sudden destruction, in the name of Jesus.
91. I reject dryness in my walk with God, in the name of Jesus.
92. I reject financial debt, in the name of Jesus.
93. I reject lack and famine in my life, in the name of Jesus.
94. I reject physical and spiritual accident in my going in and coming out, in the name of Jesus.
95. I reject sickness in my spirit, soul and body, in the name of Jesus.
96. I stand against every evil work in my life, in the name of Jesus.
97. I overcome powerlessness, confusion and every attack of the enemy, in the name of Jesus.

98. I command spiritual divorce between me and every power of darkness, in the name of Jesus.

99. Let every poison and arrow of the enemy be neutralized, in the name of Jesus.

100. I break every yoke of unfruitfulness in my life, in Jesus' name.

101. I cancel the plans and the mark of the enemy upon my life, in the name of Jesus.

102. Lord Jesus, break all harmful genetic ties in my life.

103. Lord Jesus, set me free from any negative thing that came against me before I was born, in the name of Jesus.

104. Lord Jesus, use Your blood to clean all my spiritual wounds.

105. From now on, I bulldoze my way into supernatural breakthroughs in every department of my life, in the name of Jesus.

106. I render all evil attacks against my potentials and destiny impotent, in the name of Jesus.

107. I command every evil maintenance officer on assignment in my life to stumble and fall, in the name of Jesus.

108. I revoke every satanic decree upon that which God has purposed to make me great, in the name of Jesus.

109. I revoke every satanic decree upon my life, in the name of Jesus.

110. I revoke every satanic decree upon my family, in Jesus' name.

111. I revoke every satanic decree upon my prosperity, in Jesus' name.

112. I silence all evil utterances against me, in the name of Jesus.

113. I revoke every evil law being used against my life, in Jesus' name.

114. I decree that my house will not be pulled down by contrary wind, in the name of Jesus.

115. O Lord, let me trade with You and make me profit in it.

116. O Lord, that which will make Your blessings to jump over me, begin to roast them with the fire of God.

117. O Lord, remove from every department of my life that which will hinder

the purpose of God for my life, in the name of Jesus.

118. Let every root of evil desires in me be roasted with the fire of God, in the name of Jesus.

119. Lord, charge my spiritual battery with Your fire.

120. O Lord, reveal to me any area of my body being used as an instrument of unrighteousness.

121. O Lord, let me for ever be a good pillar in the house of God.

122. O Lord, increase in me the divine power to pursue, overtake and recover.

123. Let the fire of God destroy every stubborn foundational problem in my life, in the name of Jesus.

124. Let every link, label and stamp of the oppressors in any department of my life be destroyed by the blood of Jesus.

125. I command every evil spiritual pregnancy to be aborted now, in the name of Jesus.

126. Let every dirty hand be removed from all the affairs of my life, in the name of Jesus.

127. Let every effect of evil access to my blood be reversed, in the name of Jesus.

128. All the enemies of holiness in my life, flee, in the name of Jesus.

129. Holy Spirit, incubate me with Your fire, in the name of Jesus.

130. Let every thing done against me under the devil's anointing be neutralised, in the name of Jesus.

131. I command all evil vessels despatched against me to crash into irreparable pieces, in the name of Jesus.

132. I command my possessions being kept in satanic banks to be released, in the name of Jesus.

133. I remove my name from the book of untimely death, in the name of Jesus.

134. I remove my name from the book of tragedy, in Jesus' name.

135. All evil umbrellas preventing heavenly showers from falling upon me, be roasted, in the name of Jesus.

136. Let all the evil associations summoned for my sake be scattered to pieces, in the name of Jesus.

137. Father, crucify anything in me that would remove my name from the book of life, in the name of Jesus.

138. Father, help me to crucify my flesh, in the name of Jesus.

139. If my name has been removed from the book of life, Father, re-write it, in the name of Jesus.

140. Lord, give me power to overcome myself.

RECOVERY OF GLORY
Esther 7 & 8

- *When you want to shine.*
- *When you desire to recover your lost glory.*

Have you been written off by people because of a recent tragedy that befell you? You are as sured that like Esther, Mordecai and the entire Jews of the reign of Ahasuerus were restored to their glory. So the Lord will do for you.

John 17:22: *"And the glory which thou gavest me, I have given them . . ."*

Sin destroys the image and the glory of God in our lives. "For all have sinned and fallen short of the glory of God" (Romans 3: 23). When you do not know who you are, you will allow the devil to steal your glory by sinning against God.

Adam and Eve were created in the image and after the likeness of God. (Genesis 1:27). The devil in his evil wisdom told them to eat the forbidden fruit so they could be like gods (Genesis 3:3). Note the difference; God created them in His image, the devil wanted them to become gods with a small 'g'. Because they did not know who they were, they were deceived, they sinned against God and the privilege God gave them was last. Their glory was stolen.

Every time we sin, we open the door for the enemy to attack the image of God in us and to steal our glory.

Jesus died so we can recover the glory Adam and Eve lost to the devil. He has given us His glory. He has crowned us with glory and honour (Hebrews 2:7). As you pray these prayers with faith, God will cause your light to rise from obscurity, and you darkness will be as noon day (Isaiah 58:10).

- **CONFESSION**

Isa. 62:2-3: *And the Gentiles shall see thy righteousness, and all kings thy glory: and thou shalt be called by a new name, which the mouth of the LORD shall name. Thou shalt also be a crown of glory in the hand of the LORD, and a royal diadem in the hand of thy God.*

● PRAISE WORSHIP

1. Let every problem connected to polygamy in my life be nullified by the blood of Jesus.

2. All satanic deposits in my life, be roasted, in the name of Jesus.

3. I command every satanic reinforcement against me to scatter into pieces, in the name of Jesus.

4. Every power of any family idol affecting my life, my home and my work be broken, in the name of Jesus.

5. I cancel all evil vows that are affecting me negatively, in the name of Jesus.

6. Let the clock and the time-table of the enemy for my life be destroyed, in the name of Jesus.

7. O Lord, let my enemies be rescheduled to useless and harmless assignments.

8. Let every good thing that is dead in my life begin to receive life now, in the name of Jesus.

9. Every evil device against me, be disappointed, in the name of Jesus

10. Let the mighty healing power of God overshadow me now, in the name of Jesus.

11. I bind every spirit working against answers to my prayers, in the name of Jesus.

12. I disarm any power that has made a covenant with the ground, water and wind about me, in the name of Jesus.

13. O Lord, make my life invisible to demonic observers.

14. I bind all remote control spirits fashioned against me, in the name of Jesus.

15. I withdraw all the bullets and ammunition made available to the enemy, in the name of Jesus.

16. I revoke any conscious or unconscious covenant with the spirit of death, in the name of Jesus.

17. O Lord, I submit my tongue to You, take absolute control of it.

18. Let the heavenly Surgeon come down and perform surgical operations where necessary in my life, in the name of Jesus.

19. I refuse to be spiritually amputated, in the name of Jesus.

20. I refuse to wage war against myself, in the name of Jesus.

21. O Lord, wake me up from any form of spiritual sleep.

22. All evil seeds planted by fear into my life, be uprooted by the axe of God, in the name of Jesus.

23. Let Your kingdom be established in every area of my life, O Lord.

24. I cancel all former negotiations with the devil, in the name of Jesus.

25. I renounce any signature of my name in satanic possession, in the name of Jesus.

26. I renounce any ceremony linking me to any evil power, in the name of Jesus.

27. I renounce and cancel every evil spiritual marriage, in Jesus' name.

28. I release myself from any covenant made with satan, in the name of Jesus.

29. All satanic assignments for my life, be frustrated, in Jesus' name.

30. I paralyse all evil spirit-guides assigned to me, in Jesus' name.

31. I release myself from every blood donation to the devil, in the name of Jesus.

32. I release myself from any eating or drinking from satanic table, in the name of Jesus.

33. I cancel any evil attachment from satanic worship, in Jesus' name.

34. I paralyse and disband all satanic parents assigned to me, in the name of Jesus.

35. I paralyse and disband all satanic mothers assigned to me, in the name of Jesus.

36. I paralyse and disband all satanic fathers assigned to me, in the name of Jesus.

37. I renounce any satanic baptism, in the name of Jesus.

38. I release myself from every urine manipulation, in Jesus' name.

39. I nullify the consequences of any conscious or unconscious offer of satanic sacrifices, in the name of Jesus.

40. I rebuke all deceiving spirits by the blood and resurrection of the Lord Jesus Christ.

41. I renounce every satanic claim of ownership to any department of my life, in the name of Jesus.

42. I release my foundations from the grip of household wickedness, in the name of Jesus.

43. I release my foundation from the grip of satanic manipulations, in the name of Jesus.

44. I release myself from any satanic brake applied to any department of my life, in the name of Jesus.

45. I break every foundational curse, in the name of Jesus.

46. Let the angel of the living God begin to roll away every evil stone blocking my pathway, in the name of Jesus.

47. Let the fire of God destroy all evil registers containing information about my life, in the name of Jesus.

48. Holy Ghost fire, begin to melt away every satanic deposit in my life, in the name of Jesus.

49. Let my oppressors come against each other, in the name of Jesus.

50. Every placental-mediated problem, receive solution now, in the name of Jesus.

51. I break every evil control over my life, in the name of Jesus.

52. I close every tap of sorrow in my life, in the name of Jesus.

53. Let the powers stealing the honey of my life be paralysed, in the name of Jesus.

54. I nullify all spiritual poisons, in the name of Jesus.

55. Let evil satanic worm die, in the name of Jesus.

56. Holy Ghost fire, destroy all satanic poisons in my body, in the name of Jesus.

57. I declare holy rebellion against the forces of oppression working against my life, in the name of Jesus.

58. I possess divine hatred against local wickedness, in Jesus' name.

59. I refuse to follow satanic road map for my life, in Jesus' name.

60. I defy every satanic army and I command them to bow, in the name of Jesus.

61. I destroy the pride of the enemy over my life, in the name of Jesus.

62. Let my God answer all my evil challengers by fire, in Jesus' name.

63. I break up every satanic concrete caging my potentials, in the name of Jesus.

64. I refuse to be part and parcel of my problems, in Jesus' name.

65. I take authority over all the powers of darkness operating in the air, land and sea against my life, in the name of Jesus.

66. Let all weapons of captivity fashioned against me be disgraced, in the name of Jesus.

67. I decree healing and restoration to my soul, body and spirit, in the name of Jesus.

68. I decree success, breakthroughs and progress into my handiwork, in the name of Jesus.

69. I decree happiness, peace and harmony into my handiwork, in the name of Jesus.

70. I destablise and paralyse all territorial spirits delegated against me, in the name of Jesus.

71. Let thunder and fire of God destroy every satanic monitoring device, in the name of Jesus.

72. I paralyse and destroy all satanic embargoes placed on my progress, in the name of Jesus.

73. Let all evil powers seeking my destruction begin to turn against each

other, in the name of Jesus.

74. Let all the havoc created by lack of patience in my life be repaired, in the name of Jesus.

75. Let all goodness withdrawn as a result of my being impatient be returned seven-fold, in the name of Jesus.

76. O Lord, remove every bitterness from my heart.

77. Spirit of the living God, fall afresh on me now, in Jesus' name.

78. I command every part of my body to receive spiritual correction, in the name of Jesus.

79. I nullify all spiritual weapons being used to slow down my progress, in the name of Jesus.

80. I cancel all strongholds that the spirit of fear has built in me, in the name of Jesus.

81. O Lord, begin to baptize every area of my life with Your dumbfounding miracles.

82. I nullify every evil effect of fear in my life, in the name of Jesus.

83. O Lord, give me the spirit of boldness.

84. Let all the powers that shake off God's blessings in my life be removed and be destroyed, in the name of Jesus.

85. I place myself now under the cross of Jesus.

86. I cover myself with the precious blood of Jesus.

87. I surround myself with the light of Christ.

88. The devil will not interfere with the Lord's work in my life, in the name of Jesus.

89. I put on God's armour to resist the devil's tactics, in Jesus' name.

90. O Lord, reveal to me any way that satan has a hold on my life.

91. I claim back any territory of my life handed over to satan, in the name of Jesus.

92. I bind all forces of evil in the air, fire, water and ground being set in motion against my life, in the name of Jesus.

93. I forbid any spirit from any source from harming me in any way, in the name of Jesus.

94. I reject every spirit of seduction, in the name of Jesus.

95. I refuse to let sin have dominion over me, in the name of Jesus.

96. I reject every satanic promise on any department of my life, in the name of Jesus.

97. Let the powers setting themselves up in opposition to me be paralysed, in the name of Jesus.

98. I cancel the effect of all former satanic benefits in my life, in the name of Jesus.

99. I bind you spirit of anger in my life, in the name of Jesus.

100. O Lord, fill me with strength to replace weakness.

101. Let all spiritual contamination be washed away by the blood of Jesus.

102. Let the cleansing and healing waters of the Lord flow into my life now, in the name of Jesus.

103. Father, I surrender to You today, with all my heart and soul, in the name of Jesus.

104. Lord, come into my heart in a deeper way.

105. I say yes to You today, O Lord.

106. I open all the secret places of my heart to You. Come in, Lord Jesus.

107. I surrender every department of my life to You, O Lord, in the name of Jesus

108. I surrender my past, present and future to You, O Lord.

109. Come Holy Spirit and baptize me with the fire of Your love, in the name of Jesus.

110. Holy Spirit, melt me, mold me, fill me and use me, in Jesus' name.

111. Holy Spirit, expand my capacity, in the name of Jesus.

112. Holy Spirit, work in me in a powerful way, in the name of Jesus.

113. Lord, let Your purpose for my life be fulfilled.

114. Electric love of the Lord, flow into my being, in Jesus' name.

115. O Lord, wash and cleanse me from past wounds and scars.

116. O Lord, bring light into the shadows of my life.

117. O Lord, bring light into all the dark rooms in my soul.

118. O Lord, uproot the root cause of any chronic failure in my life, in the name of Jesus.

119. Let all good things buried come alive, in the name of Jesus.

120. I reject every evil manipulation, in the name of Jesus.

121. I reject every deceptive family control, in the name of Jesus.

122. Let the curse of impossibility issued against me bounce back on the enemy, in the name of Jesus.

123. Let the agents of impossibility working against my desired miracles be completely paralysed, in the name of Jesus.

124. Let the plantations of impossibility in any department of my life receive fire and be roasted, in the name of Jesus.

125. I refuse to be diverted from the path of my blessings, in the name of Jesus.

126. Let every satanic angel deflecting blessings on my way stumble and fall, in the name of Jesus.

127. I command the powers drinking the milk of my life to begin to vomit it now, in the name of Jesus.

128. Let every satan-inspired prayers against my life be reversed and turn to blessings, in the name of Jesus.

129. Let satanic access to my life be withdrawn completely, in the name of Jesus.

130. I curse every satanic mountain-problem in my life, in Jesus' name.

131. Let every fake friend in the camp of my life be exposed and disgraced, in the name of Jesus.

132. Let every evil collaborator in disguise be exposed and disgraced, in the name of Jesus.

133. Let all spiritual vultures wishing my spiritual death be paralysed, in the name of Jesus.

134. Let no evil family river touch any area of my life, in Jesus' name.

135. Holy Spirit, help me to discover my very self, in Jesus' name.

136. I release my hand from every bewitchment, in the name of Jesus.

137. I forbid regrouping and reinforcement of any evil against my life, in the name of Jesus.

138. Let every vow of the enemy against my life be totally nullified, in the name of Jesus.

139. Lord, reverse all curses issued against me to good.

140. Let every satanic decision and judgement against my life become null and void, in the name of Jesus.

CONFRONT AND CONQUER
1 Samuel 17

- *For deliverance.*
- *To declare war and engage in the ministry of conflict.*

The aggressive attitude of young David to Goliath confirms that attack is the best form of defence. Therefore equip yourself with unfailing amour of the Lord and launch an attack against every Goliath harassing your life.

Romans 8:31, 37: *"What shall we then say to these things? If God be for us, who can be against us?... Nay, in all these things we are more than conquerors through Him that loved us."*

When two opposing camps meet, the result is a confrontation! And it is the stronger party that will conquer. We thank God for I John 5:4 that says, "Whosoever is born of God overcometh the world; and this is the victory that overcometh the world, even our faith." God does not expect us to run from our enemies. He expects us to stand and face them. That is why Paul says, "Having done all to stand, stand therefore. . ." (Ephesians 6:13,14).

We should learn to use the spiritual weapons that God has provided for us. This is the only way we can conquer. AFor though we walk in the flesh we do not war after the flesh: (for the weapons of our warfare are not carnal, but mighty through God to the pulling down of strongholds).

This prayer programme is designed to storm the places of safety (strongholds) of the enemy. As you start this prayer programme, every stronghold the enemy has erected against your life will be pulled down.

- **CONFESSION**

Num. 23:24: *Behold, the people shall rise up as a great lion, and lift up himself as a young lion: he shall not lie down until he eat of the prey, and drink the blood of the slain.*

● **PRAISE WORSHIP**

1. I command all serpentine and scorpion spirits to depart and go now, in the name of Jesus.

2. The spirit of self-destruction will not prosper in my life, in the name of Jesus.

3. The spirit of self-termination will not prosper in my life, in the name of Jesus.

4. Every evil inner voices, be silenced in my life, in Jesus' name.

5. Let the concrete constructed by the enemy to stop the germination of my miracles be broken to pieces, in the name of Jesus.

6. Let the blood of Jesus erase the legal ground the enemy has against me, in the name of Jesus.

7. I close all the doors opened to the enemy forever with the blood of Jesus.

8. Let all the footholds and seat of the enemy in my life be abolished, in the name of Jesus.

9. I command all words contrary to God's word spoken against me to fall dead to the ground and bear no fruit, in the name of Jesus.

10. Let the tongue of the enemy of my soul be divided and be destroyed, in the name of Jesus.

11. I withdraw every personal invitation I have given to the enemy for my destruction, in the name of Jesus.

12. I vomit every satanic poison in my life, in the name of Jesus.

13. Let all evil hosts gathered against me begin to scatter and never regroup again, in the name of Jesus.

14. Let all anti-testimony forces fashioned against my life be scattered by the thunder of God and never regroup against me again, in the name of Jesus.

15. I reject partial or temporary freedom, in the name of Jesus.

16. I break the power of any demonic spell issued against my life, in the name of Jesus.

17. I paralyse all evil powers delaying my miracles, in Jesus' name.

18. Let the anointing of the overcomer fall mightily upon my life, in the name of Jesus.

19. Let my tongue become an instrument of the glory of God, in the name of Jesus.

20. Let my hands become an instrument of divine prosperity, in the name of Jesus.

21. Let my eyes become an instrument of divine revelation, in the name of Jesus.

22. Let all my oppressors receive the leprosy of divine judgement, in the name of Jesus.

23. I withdraw my name from the list of untimely death, in Jesus' name.

24. Let every evil consumption be flushed out of my system, in the name of Jesus.

25. You agents of frustration, I command you in the name of our Lord Jesus Christ, loose your hold over my life.

26. You agents of poverty, I command you in the name of our Lord Jesus Christ, loose your hold over my life.

27. You agents of debt, I command you in the name of our Lord Jesus Christ, loose your hold over my life.

28. You agents of spiritual rags, I command you in the name of our Lord Jesus Christ, loose your hold over my life.

29. You agents of defeat, I command you in the name of our Lord Jesus Christ, loose your hold over my life.

30. You agents of infirmity, I command you in the name of our Lord Jesus Christ, loose your hold over my life.

31. You agents of demotion, I command you in the name of our Lord Jesus Christ, loose your hold over my life.

32. You agents of demonic delays, I command you in the name of our Lord Jesus Christ, loose your hold over my life.

33. You agents of confusion, I command you in the name of our Lord Jesus Christ, loose your hold over my life.

34. You agents of backwardness, I command you, in the name of our Lord Jesus Christ, loose your hold over my life.

35. Every instrument of failure fashioned against me, be destroyed, in the name of Jesus.

36. Every instrument of satanic weapons fashioned against me, be destroyed, in the name of Jesus.

37. Every instrument of satanic computers fashioned against me, be destroyed, in the name of Jesus.

38. Every instrument of satanic satellites and cameras fashioned against me, be destroyed, in the name of Jesus.

39. Every instrument of satanic remote control fashioned against me, be destroyed, in the name of Jesus.

40. Every instrument of satanic labels and marks against me, be destroyed, in the name of Jesus.

41. Let the fire of the Holy Ghost begin to flow into my blood stream, in the name of Jesus.

42. Let every deposit that is against my benefits flow out now, in the name of Jesus.

43. I release every internal organ in my body from every evil covenant, in the name of Jesus.

44. I release my life from the hands of any former occultic friend, in the name of Jesus.

45. Let all satanic deposits acquired from evil consumption flow out of my body system now, in the name of Jesus.

46. O Lord, quicken Your word to perform it this month in my life.

47. I decree termination to all leaking blessings in my life, in the name of Jesus.

48. I release myself from any evil soul-tie operated against me by any

demonic human agent, in the name of Jesus.

49. I release my life from any bondage emanating from past sins, in the name of Jesus.

50. Let all the evil effects of seeking help from Egypt be totally nullified, in the name of Jesus.

51. Let the effect of all evil attachments to my life be nullified, in the name of Jesus.

52. Let all hormones in my body receive divine touch and function perfectly, in the name of Jesus.

53. I reject every spirit of hormonal imbalance, in the name of Jesus.

54. I release myself from the bondage of evil attachment, in the name of Jesus.

55. O Lord, re-organise my life to receive multiple blessings.

56. O Lord, open my life to accommodate Your glory.

57. Anything in my life, conscious or unconscious, delaying my desired breakthroughs, be taken out now, in the name of Jesus.

58. Let my life be released from every evil touch, in the name of Jesus.

59. Lord, make my life super-fertile and increase my fruits.

60. Let my body system confuse the enemies, in the name of Jesus.

61. I reject every spirit of financial embarrassment, in Jesus' name.

62. Let power begin to change hands in my finances, in Jesus' name.

63. I release myself from any family curse reinforcing financial problems, in the name of Jesus.

64. I nullify the evil effect of manipulation of my finances, in the name of Jesus.

65. Let all powers in possession of my finances release them now, in the name of Jesus.

66. I release my finances from the cage of any evil altar, in the name of Jesus.

67. I release myself from any evil transfer of spirits by giving and taking money, in the name of Jesus.

68. Let every demonic programme for my financial life be nullified, in the name of Jesus.

69. Holy Spirit, quicken my finances, in the name of Jesus.

70. Holy Spirit, overshadow my finances, in the name of Jesus.

71. Let all evil consumption be evacuated from my head, stomach and entire body, in the name of Jesus.

72. I dissociate myself from any Invitation by demonic friends, in the name of Jesus.

73. I charge my finances with the fire of the Holy Ghost, in the name of Jesus.

74. O Lord, let me have favour in Your sight.

75. Lord, give unto me spiritual revelation that would advance my life.

76. O Lord, rend the heavens open and reveal hidden treasures to me.

77. O Lord, rend the heavens open and bring helpers to me in Your own way.

78. I cast every masquerading problem into the Red Sea, in the name of Jesus.

79. O Lord, refresh and energize me.

80. Let the anointing for holiness fall upon me, in the name of Jesus.

81. I possess the gate of the enemy today, in the name of Jesus.

82. I claim increased vision, in the name of Jesus.

83. I claim increased wisdom, in the name of Jesus.

84. My spirit, soul and body, be complete in every way, in Jesus' name.

85. Lord, make a hedge to protect my family, property and possession.

86. Lord, send Your angels to battle on my behalf.

87. All attacks and traps of the enemy, be frustrated, in Jesus' name.

88. I walk in divine safety and I refuse to enter into the net of the enemy, in the name of Jesus.

89. O God, be my hiding place and preserve me from evil in all areas of life, in the name of Jesus.

90. God, surround me with songs of deliverance, in the name of Jesus.

91. I conquer evil with good in my life and in my environment, in the name of Jesus.

92. I conquer fear with faith in my life, in the name of Jesus.

93. I render all evil challenges over my life powerless, in Jesus' name.

94. Let Your fire destroy and damage my spiritual ignorance, in the name of Jesus.

95. I fire back all the arrows of the enemy, in the name of Jesus.

96. O Lord, provide a way of escape from spiritual traps for me.

97. O Lord, surprise my adversaries by making my life a miracle in all areas.

98. O Lord, deliver my shoulder from evil burdens.

99. O Lord, remove spiritual baskets from me.

100. I reverse all the problems I have caused with my mouth, in the name of Jesus.

101. I command all spiritual vehicles fashioned against me to crash, in the name of Jesus.

102. O Lord, let all strange fires being prepared by the enemy whether in the second heaven, on earth or underneath the earth be quenched, in the name of Jesus.

103. Let every evil tongue issuing destruction against my life be condemned, in the name of Jesus.

104. Let all those who trouble my Israel be disbanded and confused, in the name of Jesus.

105. Let the blood of Jesus begin to cleanse off all unprofitable marks in my life, in the name of Jesus.

106. Let all strange hands that have touched my blood for evil manipulation be nuetralized by the blood of Jesus.

107. I reject every spirit that abandons blessings in my life, in the name of Jesus.

108. I receive divine victory over the host of wickedness surrounding me, in the name of Jesus.

109. I bind every spirit of deception working against me, in the name of Jesus.

110. I stand against every dream of defeat, in the name of Jesus.

111. Let every spirit that has ever attacked me or that is attacking me in the form of a cat receive the fire of God and be burnt to ashes, in the name of Jesus.

112. Let every spirit that has ever attacked me or that is attacking me in the form of spider receive the fire of God and be burnt to ashes, in the name of Jesus.

113. Let every spirit that has ever attacked me or that is attacking me in the form of snakes receive the fire of God and be burnt to ashes, in the name of Jesus.

114. Let every spirit that has ever attacked me or that is attacking me in the form of dogs receive the fire of God and burn to ashes, in the name of Jesus.

115. I refuse to follow any evil design for my life, in the name of Jesus.

116. Let the assignments and activities of satan in my life be frustrated, in the name of Jesus.

117. O Lord, cleanse my mind of every painful and destructive memory, in the name of Jesus.

118. I break the stronghold of witchcraft upon my life, in Jesus' name.

119. I loose myself from the bondage of ungodly covenants and dedication, in the name of Jesus.

120. I release myself from every serpentine bites and poisons, in the name of Jesus.

121. I cut myself off from the curse of eating meat sacrificed unto idols, in the name of Jesus.

122. I release myself from any satanic diagnosis, in the name of Jesus.

123. I release myself from the domination and control of every family idol, in the name of Jesus.

124. I bind and cast out the spirit which executes the fear of revenge by former idol master, in the name of Jesus.

125. I break the power of every evil ritual aimed at me, in the name of Jesus.

126. I drink the blood of Jesus.

127. Holy Ghost fire, purge my life completely now, in Jesus' name.

128. I claim my complete deliverance, in the name of Jesus, from every spirit of the valley.

129. I break the hold of any evil power over my life, in Jesus' name.

130. I move from bondage into liberty, in the name of Jesus.

131. I receive deliverance from every demonic inhibition, in the name of Jesus.

132. I claim complete liberty, in the name of Jesus.

133. I release myself from every demonic inhibition, in Jesus' name.

134. I pull down every stubborn stronghold of satan in any department of my life, in the name of Jesus.

135. I release myself from all demonic subjection to my parents, in the name of Jesus.

136. I break every demonic bondage to any fetish priest, in the name of Jesus.

137. I release myself from the curse of eating meat sacrificed to idols, in the name of Jesus.

138. I pull down any evil stronghold built into my life by any person in charge of me as an infant, in the name of Jesus.

139. I pull down the stronghold of evil dedication, in Jesus' name.

140. I release myself from the spirit of my town and village, in the name of Jesus.

DUMBFOUNDING PROMOTIONS

Mark 10:46-52

- *When you desire divine promotions.*
- *When you desire dumbfounding promotions and elevations.*

If you too can adopt the attitude of the blind Bartimeaus as he desperately cried out and arrested the attention of the Lord, you can be sure that your promotion will become a dream come true.

Psalm 113:7,8: *"He raiseth up the poor out of the dust, and lifteth the needy out of the dunghill; That He may set him with Princes, even with the princes of his people."*

Jehovah EL Roi, is one of the covenant names of God I love very much. It is a name that gives me great comfort and hope. This name was given to an Egyptian slave named Hagar. You can read the story in Genesis 16.

Jehovah EL Roi means, "Thou God seest me" (Genesis 16:13). God cares so much about us that He has numbered the hairs on our head. He knows every little detail about us.

Rahab is another undeserved candidate for God's blessing. Jehovah EL Roi sought her out. She was the prostitute who received the two spies that were sent to Jericho (Joshua 2:4; 6:17). She was to become the second woman in the genealogy of Christ and the great-great grandmother of King David.

Ruth was a Moabite. A tribe despised by the Israelites. She clung to the God of the Jews, and became the third woman in the genealogy of Christ and the great grandmother of King David.

God is still in the business of raising reprobates out of the dunghill to set among the princes of His people. Invite Jehovah EL Roi into your situation and He will set you among the princes of His people.

- CONFESSION

Ps. 92:10: *But my horn shalt thou exalt like the horn of an unicorn: I shall be anointed with fresh oil.*

● PRAISE WORSHIP

1. Let all pronouncements uttered against me by poisonous tongues be nullified, in the name of Jesus.

2. I cut myself off from every territorial spirit, in the name of Jesus.

3. I rebuke the devourer in my life, in the name of Jesus.

4. Heal in me, O Lord, whatever needs to be healed.

5. Replace in me O Lord, whatever needs to be replaced.

6. Transform in me O Lord, whatever needs to be transformed.

7. Let the fire of the Lord consume every darkness in my life, in the name of Jesus.

8. I loose myself from the bondage of profitless hard-work, in the name of Jesus.

9. Let all evil enquiries about my life be rendered null and void, in the name of Jesus.

10. I loose myself from any power of witchcraft and bewitchment, in the name of Jesus.

11. I loose myself from every satanic bondage, in the name of Jesus.

12. I cancel the power of all curses upon my head, in Jesus' name.

13. Satan, I close any door which I have opened to you through ignorance, in the name of Jesus.

14. I bind the strongman over myself, in the name of Jesus.

15. I bind the strongman over my family, in the name of Jesus.

16. I bind the strongman over my blessings, in the name of Jesus.

17. I bind the strongman over my business, in the name of Jesus.

18. I command the armour of the strongman to be roasted completely, in the name of Jesus.

19. I command all curses issued against me to be smashed and broken, in the name of Jesus.

20. I command total restoration and healing to take place in my body now, in the name of Jesus.

21. I loose myself from all inherited bondage, in the name of Jesus.

22. I vomit every satanic poison that I have swallowed, in Jesus' name.

23. Evil hands, release me now, in the name of Jesus.

24. I remove myself from satanic bus stops, in the name of Jesus.

25. Let every owner of evil loads in my life begin to carry their evil loads, in the name of Jesus.

26. I destroy evil remote controlling power working over my life, in the name of Jesus.

27. Holy Ghost fire, incubate me, in the name of Jesus.

28. I reverse every evil design that is against my life, in Jesus' name.

29. You evil strongman over my progress in life, be bound, in the name of Jesus.

30. I command all evil authorities over my life to break, in Jesus' name.

31. I remove my name from the book of backwardness, in Jesus' name.

32. O Lord, make me a channel of blessings to others.

33. Holy Spirit, take total control of my ability to frame words, in the name of Jesus.

34. Let every scorpion set in motion against me be rendered sting-less, in the name of Jesus.

35. Let every serpent set in motion against my spiritual progress be rendered venom-less, in the name of Jesus.

36. Let the camp of the enemy of my soul be put in total disarray, in the name of Jesus.

37. Let all my Herod that are still alive begin to receive spiritual decay now, in the name of Jesus.

38. Evil worms in any part of my body, hidden or open, die and be ejected, in the name of Jesus.

39. All evil handwriting against me, be paralysed, in the name of Jesus.

40. All those circulating my name for evil, be disgraced, in Jesus' name.

41. Let all evil friends make mistakes that would expose them, in the name of Jesus.

42. Let the strongmen from both sides of my family begin to fight and destroy themselves, in the name of Jesus.

43. O Lord, let not Your perfect peace depart from me.

44. I refuse to put on the garment of tribulation prepared by my enemies, in the name of Jesus.

45. O Lord, give unto me the spirit that flees from sin.

46. Let the secrets of hidden and open enemies be revealed, in the name of Jesus.

47. Let every satanic net fashioned against me receive destruction, in the name of Jesus.

48. I embrace the divine fire from above, in the name of Jesus.

49. Father, in the name of Jesus, I remove my name and my life from any book of failure.

50. Father Lord, re-organise my life according to Your own will, in the name of Jesus.

51. Father Lord, begin to repair those things in my life that I have destroyed with my own hands, in the name of Jesus.

52. Let shame be poured out upon all the powers struggling to put me to shame, in the name of Jesus.

53. O Lord, begin to set me free from any physical and spiritual bondage.

54. Let the ground open up now, and begin to swallow every problem in my life now, in the name of Jesus.

55. O Lord, walk back through every second of my life and begin to make me whole.

56. O Lord, go back into my third and fourth generations and break all unprofitable family ties.

57. Set me free, O Lord, from any negative force transmitted to me in my mother's womb.

58. Let the spiritual eraser begin to wipe away every painful and unprofitable stubborn memories from my mind, in Jesus' name.

59. Lord, repair any damage done to my spirit by satanic agents.

60. Let all covenants of failure break, in the name of Jesus.

61. I break all covenant bondage, in the name of Jesus.

62. Let the fire of God begin to consume every darkness in my family, in the name of Jesus.

63. O Lord, cause a new heart to be created in me by Your power.

64. Lord, let the right spirit be renewed within me.

65. Let the root of irritation that keeps anger alive in my life be removed now, in the name of Jesus.

66. I reject every thought that I will never change, in Jesus' name.

67. Let Your Spirit cleanse and control anger in my life, in Jesus' name.

68. Lord, produce the power of self-control and gentleness in me.

69. I reject all that robs me of the joy of my inheritance in the kingdom of God, in the name of Jesus.

70. All evil mountains, break your powers over my life, in Jesus' name.

71. O Lord, give me the enablement to always hear Your voice.

72. Lord, enable me to always know Your heart on any issue in my life.

73. O Lord, by the power of the blood of Jesus, remove from my life any hindrance of the enemy.

74. Let all darkness be driven away from my life, in the name of Jesus.

75. Let me be shielded away from all deception, in the name of Jesus.

76. O Lord, illuminate Your truth in my understanding.

77. O Lord, with the eyes of my heart let me begin to see You clearly in all areas.

78. O Lord, take every power that is not of You away from my life.

79. I separate myself from satan and his kingdom, in Jesus' name.

80. I renounce the kingdom of darkness and embrace the kingdom of our Lord Jesus Christ.

81. Lord Jesus, deliver me from evil.

82. I apply the blood of our Lord Jesus Christ now to break all evil curses upon my life, in the name of Jesus.

83. I shall be anointed with fresh oil from heaven, in the name of Jesus.

84. O Lord, reveal the strongholds that hinder revival and give satan advantage in my life.

85. O Lord, begin to carry out a deep work in my heart now.

86. I kill all strange animals sent against me with the sword of the Lord, in the name of Jesus.

87. I divorce every satanic husband / wife, in the name of Jesus.

88. Fire of God, be released on every demonic child, in Jesus' name.

89. Let evil spiritual homes be burnt down, in the name of Jesus.

90. I reject the spirit of slavery and hardship in my life, in Jesus' name.

91. I dissolve every anti-breakthrough strategy fashioned against me, in the name of Jesus.

92. Let the hands of evil refuse to perform their enterprise in my life, in the name of Jesus.

93. There shall be no compromise or dialogue with any stubborn problem in my life, in the name of Jesus.

94. O Lord, close the gap between where I am and where You want me to be.

95. Let all demonic jailers be roasted, in the name of Jesus.

96. Let the blood of Jesus erase the legal ground the enemy has against me, in the name of Jesus.

97. Let the power to overcome obstacles of failure in my life fall upon me now, in the name of Jesus.

98. Lord, send the axe of fire to the root of my problem.

99. O Lord, revive my prayer life with Your hand of fire.

100. Let all my buried virtues be exhumed, in the name of Jesus.

101. I command evil progress in my life to cease, in Jesus' name.

102. I declare the enemy to be the grasshopper, I am the giant, in the name of Jesus.

103. Those constructing coffins for me and my household, I command you to enter into your coffins, in the name of Jesus.

104. I bind the spirit of death and hell upon my life, in Jesus' name.

105. O Lord, remove totally from my mind, every image of jealousy, lust and evil intention.

106. I stand against all confusing forces within me, in Jesus' name.

107. Lord, order my inner life so that I can hear You clearly.

108. Let me see what You see in me, O Lord.

109. I ask You, Lord Jesus, to make me uncomfortable till I get on the right track for Your.

110. O Lord, wash my brain with Your blood and remove bad habits which are physically engraved there.

111. Lord, heal any hormonal imbalance or other secretions in my body.

112. Let Your healing power take firm root within me, O Lord.

113. I cut down the powers of witches working against any department of my life, in the name of Jesus.

114. I cut down the powers of wizards working against any department of my life, in the name of Jesus.

115. I cut down the powers of spiritual properties working against any department of my life, in the name of Jesus.

116. I cut down the powers of territorial forces working against any department of my life, in the name of Jesus.

117. I cut down the powers of ancestral and familiar spirits working against any department of my life, in the name of Jesus.

118. I cut down the powers of mermaid spirits working against any department of my life, in the name of Jesus.

119. I cut down the powers of evil manipulation working against any department of my life, in the name of Jesus.

120. I cut down the powers of evil monitors working against any depart ment of my life, in the name of Jesus.

121. I cut down the powers of evil arrows working against any department of my life, in the name of Jesus.

122. I cut down the powers of evil decisions working against any department of my life, in the name of Jesus.

123. O Lord, add more fire to my fire.

124. O Lord, begin to raise your seven-fold standard against all my enemies.

125. O Lord, use me as Your battle axe.

126. Let the angels of war be released in a mighty number on my behalf now, in the name of Jesus.

127. I destroy every power of darkness in the air, on the land, in the sea and in the forest delegated against my progress, in the name of Jesus.

128. I bind all anti-deliverance demons reinforcing evil against me, in the name of Jesus.

129. I bind all anti-miracle demons striving to steal my miracles, in the name of Jesus.

130. I destroy every satanic cage fashioned against any department of my life, in the name of Jesus.

131. I destroy every satanic chain fashioned against any department of my life, in the name of Jesus.

132. Let every satanic instruments against any department of my life be neutralized now, in the name of Jesus.

133. I destroy all the web of satan against any department of my life, in the name of Jesus.

134. I disconnect any satanic linkage to anyone dead or alive, in the name of Jesus.

135. Let every spiritual equipment set against my health be broken into

pieces, in the name of Jesus.

136. Let all spiritual rumours being used against me be dashed to pieces, in the name of Jesus.

137. Let all evil terrestrial and celestial spirits working against my progress be paralysed, in the name of Jesus.

138. I destroy all protective coverings of the enemy protecting them against Holy Ghost fire, in the name of Jesus.

139. I cancel every careless word which I have spoken and which satan is using against any department of my life, in the name of Jesus.

140. I destroy any satanic attachment to any of my properties, in the name of Jesus.

LET THE GOD OF SUDDENLY ARISE

Judges 6

- *When you arrive at a Red-Sea situation and you desire that Jehovah should arise and surprise your enemies.*

One of the reasons we are counselled by the word of God to be vigilant and sober is that when the Lord God of suddenly arises, you would not miss His benefits.

Psalm 102:2: *"Hide not thy face from me in the day when I am in trouble; incline thine ear unto me; in the day when I call answer me speadily."*

We serve the God of the suddenly. "The Lord whom you seek, shall suddenly come to His temple" (Malachi 3:10). Our God is the God who does things unexpectedly, speedily and quickly. He does them at a time we do not expect, in a way we cannot imagine, so that He and only He can take all the glory.

Certain phrases are used in Scripture to discuss the events of the last days. e.g. like a thief in the night (1 Thessalonians 5:2; 2 Peter 3:10) and in the twinkling of an eye (1 Corinthians 15:52). These describe the suddenness and the unexpected way the day of the Lord will come. They also describe how fast God works when He wants to deal with the one who troubles our Israel. God said in Isaiah 48:3 that, I have declared the former things from the beginning; and they went forth out of my mouth, and I shewed them; I did them suddenly, and they came to pass.

The Red Sea is that which stands between you and your promised land, it is also that which the Lord will use to destroy your enemies after the order of Pharaoh. God of the suddenly will arise and execute vengeance on all your enemies.

• CONFESSION

Micah 7:8: *Rejoice not against me, O mine enemy: when I fall, I shall arise; when I sit in darkness, the LORD shall be a light unto me.*

• PRAISE WORSHIP

1. I separate my life from all evil idols present in my place of birth, in the name of Jesus.

2. I separate my life from all evil streams present in my place of birth, in the name of Jesus.

3. I separate my life from all evil shrines present in my place of birth, in the name of Jesus.

4. All agents banking my blessings, release them now, in Jesus' name.

5. I destroy all the evil peace, evil agreement, evil unit, evil love, evil happiness, evil understanding, evil communication and evil gathering fashioned against my life, in the name of Jesus.

6. Begin to bless yourself with all kind of blessings.

7. Let every power of the oppressors rise up against them, in the name of Jesus.

8. Let my affairs become too hot for the enemy to handle, in the name of Jesus.

9. I retrieve my blessings from the camp of evil confiscators, in the name of Jesus.

10. Let my promotion manifest powerfully, in the name of Jesus.

11. I disband all evil hosts gathered against my progress, in the name of Jesus.

12. Let all anti-testimony forces working against my life scatter into irreparable pieces, in the name of Jesus.

13. Let the joy of the enemy upon the progress of my life be turned into sorrow, in the name of Jesus.

14. I paralyse every pocket with evil holes in my life, in Jesus' name.

15. Let the power, glory and the kingdom of the living God come upon every department of my life, in the name of Jesus.

16. Let all drinkers of blood and eaters of flesh hunting for my life begin to stumble and fall, in the name of Jesus.

17. I break the power of any demonic spell issued against my life, in the name of Jesus.
18. Let all bitter water flow out of my handiwork, in the name of Jesus.
19. I paralyse all powers that expand problems, in the name of Jesus.
20. I paralyse all powers that delay miracles, in the name of Jesus.
21. I paralyse all marriage destroyers, in the name of Jesus.
22. I paralyse all anti-miracle agents, in the name of Jesus.
23. I paralyse all financial destroyers, in the name of Jesus.
24. O Lord, make me a channel of Your blessings.
25. Let my hand be stronger than all opposing hands, in Jesus' name.
26. Every stone of hindrance, be rolled out of my way, in Jesus' name.
27. Let my tongue become an instrument of the glory of God, in the name of Jesus.
28. Let my hands become an instrument of divine prosperity, in the name of Jesus.
29. Let my eyes become an instrument of divine revelation, in the name of Jesus.
30. Let my ears become an instrument of divine revelation, in the name of Jesus.
31. The anointing of the overcomer, fall upon my life, in Jesus' name.
32. I command every agent of wickedness to loose his hold over my life now, in the name of Jesus.
33. I command every agent of discouragement to loose its hold over my life now, in the name of Jesus.
34. I command every agent of frustration to loose its hold over my life now, in the name of Jesus.
35. I command every agent of poverty to loose its hold over my life now, in the name of Jesus.
36. I command every agent of debt to loose its hold over my life now, in the name of Jesus.

37. I command every agent of spiritual rags to loose its hold over my life now, in the name of Jesus.

38. I command every agent of defeat to loose its hold over my life now, in the name of Jesus.

39. I command every agent of infirmity to loose its hold over my life now, in the name of Jesus.

40. I command every agent of demotion to loose its hold over my life now, in the name of Jesus.

41. I command every agent of demonic delays to loose its hold over my life now, in the name of Jesus.

42. I command every agent of confusion to loose its hold over my life now, in the name of Jesus.

43. I command every agent of backwardness to loose its hold over my life now, in the name of Jesus.

44. Let all wicked oppressors against me begin to stumble and fall, in the name of Jesus.

45. Let God break the teeth of the ungodly gathered against me, in the name of Jesus.

46. All the instruments of failure, be roasted in my life, in Jesus' name.

47. Let all satanic weapons of attack against my life be roasted, in the name of Jesus.

48. Let all satanic computers set in motion to monitor my life be roasted, in the name of Jesus.

49. Let all satanic records keeping the steps of my progress be roasted, in the name of Jesus.

50. Let all satanic satellites and cameras being used to observe my spiritual life be roasted, in the name of Jesus.

51. Let all remote control equipment being used against me in the second heaven be roasted, in the name of Jesus.

52. Let all satanic labels and marks be completely wiped off from my life, in the name of Jesus.

53. O Lord, let not Your death for me be in vain.

54. O Lord, remove worldly bondage from my spirit.

55. O Lord, revive my spiritual life.

56. Let the thunder fire of God begin to destroy any part of my body in the evil world, in the name of Jesus.

57. I set myself loose from every worldly entanglement that has hindered me from serving the Lord, in the name of Jesus.

58. O Lord, make me Your battle axe.

59. O Lord, begin to speak unto my soul.

60. I will not perish with the world, in the name of Jesus.

61. Let the fire of God come down and drown all the fires of the enemy set against my life, in the name of Jesus.

62. I damage the resistance of prayer resistant demons, in the name of Jesus.

63. Let every environmental-sickness depart from my life by the blood of Jesus.

64. I paralyse all powers blocking my vision and quenching my fire, in the name of Jesus.

65. I pull down all evil kingdoms working against me, in Jesus' name.

66. I destroy the kingdom of the strongman, in the name of Jesus.

67. I destroy the armour and weapon of the strongman, in Jesus' name.

68. O Lord, release Your angels to police my surroundings.

69. Let every impurity in my life be flushed out by the blood of Jesus, in the name of Jesus.

70. All evil angels on guard against me, be paralysed, in Jesus' name.

71. All satanic traffic wardens diverting good things away from me, be paralysed, in the name of Jesus.

72. I demolish and destroy my personal Jericho, in the name of Jesus.

73. Let satanic serpents dispatched against me, receive madness, in the name of Jesus.

74. Let satanic serpents dispatched against my family, be paralysed and be roasted, in the name of Jesus.

75. I retrieve all the breakthrough keys the enemy has stolen from me, in the name of Jesus.

76. I break down the stronghold of witchcraft in my family, in the name of Jesus.

77. Let all satanic parasites die, in the name of Jesus.

78. Let all bewitched properties in my possession receive deliverance now, in the name of Jesus.

79. Let the secrets of strange children in my family be revealed, in the name of Jesus.

80. Let the tongue raining incantations on me dry up, in Jesus' name.

81. I break every satanic connection in the air, water and soil against my life, in the name of Jesus.

82. Let the hunters of my soul shoot themselves, in the name of Jesus.

83. My heart will not be a stony ground for the word of God, in the name of Jesus.

84. My heart will not be a way side place for the word of God, in the name of Jesus.

85. My heart will not be a ground of thorns for the word of God, in the name of Jesus.

86. Let the handwriting of the enemy turn against them, in the name of Jesus.

87. Every evil king installed against me, be paralysed, in Jesus' name.

88. I paralyse all satanic agents struggling against my life, in the name of Jesus.

89. All strongholds of debt, be dashed to pieces, in the name of Jesus.

90. All strongholds of oppression, be dashed to pieces, in Jesus' name.

91. All strongholds of infirmity, be dashed to pieces, in Jesus' name.

92. All strongholds of curses and covenants, be dashed to pieces, in the name of Jesus.

93. All strongholds of unprofitable load, be dashed to pieces, in the name of Jesus.

94. Let any area of my life that is obeying any demonic instruction, come back to itself now, in the name of Jesus.

95. Let all the forces of affliction and oppression fashioned against me be paralysed, in the name of Jesus.

96. All chronic diseases, go back to their senders, in the name of Jesus

97. I stand against the operations of the spirit of death and hell in my life, in the name of Jesus.

98. Let the counsel of the devil to destroy my home be frustrated, in the name of Jesus.

99. I bind the spirit of doubt in my life, in the name of Jesus.

100. I bind the spirit of unbelief in my life, in the name of Jesus.

101. I bind the spirit of fear in my life, in the name of Jesus.

102. I bind the spirit of tradition in my life, in the name of Jesus.

103. I destroy every stronghold of the power of darkness in my family, in the name of Jesus.

104. Let all the evil effects of ritual killings upon my life by my ancestors be neutralised, in the name of Jesus.

105. My case will not be impossible, in the name of Jesus.

106. Agents of hindrance to breakthroughs in my life, begin to depart, in the name of Jesus.

107. O Lord, let my will be lost in Your will.

108. I bind the strength, power and activities of the wasters upon the progress of my life, in the name of Jesus.

109. I bind the strength, power and activities of the emptier upon the progress of my life, in the name of Jesus.

110. I bind the strength, power and activities of the devourers upon the progress of my life, in the name of Jesus.

111. I cancel all ungodly parental designs upon my life, in the name of Jesus.

112. Let all satanic agents camping around me be roasted by the fire of God, in the name of Jesus.

113. Let all the evil powers militating against my physical and spiritual peace be roasted, in the name of Jesus.

114. Let every territorial power hindering answers to my prayer be brought down to the pit, in the name of Jesus.

115. I will not run ahead of God on every issue of my life, in the name of Jesus.

116. I will not ask in contrary to God's will for my life, in Jesus' name.

117. Let everything that is harbouring 'prayer killers' in my life receive the thunder fire of God and be roasted, in the name of Jesus.

118. Every bondage renovator, be totally paralysed, in Jesus' name.

119. Let the evil power siphoning my blessings be paralysed, in the name of Jesus.

120. Let the army of the living God pour down liquid fire on all the oppressors of my life, in the name of Jesus.

121. Let every oracle working against my life turn against its master, in the name of Jesus.

122. Let there be an outpouring of unrest on all the hunters of my soul, in the name of Jesus.

123. Lord, promote and advance me to a dumbfounding state.

124. Every evil war fashioned against me, collapse and fail, in the name of Jesus.

125. I paralyse any power trying to unseat me from my place of blessings, in the name of Jesus.

126. I arrest every demonic conspiracy against me, in Jesus' name.

127. Let all satanic assignments against my life be disgraced, in the name of Jesus.

128. I smash and pull down every satanic stronghold working against the progress of my life, in the name of Jesus.

129. Let all evil strategies to divert my goodness and miracles be frustrated, in the name of Jesus.

130. I recover all grounds that I have yielded to the powers of darkness, in the name of Jesus.

131. I reverse all satanic programmes on my life, in the name of Jesus.

132. I command all evil societies working against me to scatter into pieces, in the name of Jesus.

133. I bind every spirit working against answers to my prayers, in the name of Jesus.

134. The forces of wasters will not have any hold upon my life, in the name of Jesus.

135. The forces of wasters will not have hold upon my marriage, in the name of Jesus.

136. The forces of wasters will not have any hold upon my destiny, in the name of Jesus.

137. The forces of wasters will not have any hold upon my progress in life, in the name of Jesus.

138. I tear up every spiritual application written to the school of poverty, in the name of Jesus.

139. O Lord, transport me from minimum to maximum.

140. Lord, touch me with Your unchanging hand of miracles.

TREADING UPON SERPENTS AND SCORPIONS

Acts 28

- *When you are aware that you have been surrounded by forces of darkness.*
- *When your enemies are challenging the power of God in your life.*
- *When you desire to disgrace serpentine and scorpion-like enemies.*

When you are soaked with power and fire of God's anointing, you would be totally immune from poisonous bite of any form of venomous beast and fiery darts of spiritual wickedness.

Luke 10:19: *"Behold, I give unto you power to tread on serpents and scorpions, and over all the power of the enemy; and nothing shall by any means hurt you."*

The devil is referred to as the serpent. Serpents are satanic powers that seek to deceive through evil wisdom, while scorpions represent powers that poison and pollute. God has given us power over *all* the powers of the enemy. It doesn't matter what name they are called, it doesn't matter where they reside in heaven on earth or under the earth, it doesn't matter what their hierarchy is in the satanic kingdom or how they carry out their activities. All these are irrelevant. God has given us power - delegated authority - to destroy satan's work. We have absolute mastery over serpents, scorpions and all the power of the enemy - spiritually and physically - they cannot harm us.

"Wherefore God also has highly exalted Him, and given Him a name which is above every name; That at the name of Jesus every knee should bow, of things in heaven, and things in earth, and things under the earth; And that every tongue should confess that Jesus Christ is Lord, to the glory of God the Father" (Phil. 2: 9-11).

The ultimate authority of the believer is in the name of JESUS!

- CONFESSION

Luke 10:19: *Behold, I give unto you power to tread on serpents and scor-*

*pions, and over all the power of the enemy: and nothing shall by any means
hurt you.*

- **PRAISE WORSHIP**

1. Lord, convert my negative to positive.

2. Let all the dead branches in the growing tree of my life be cut off and be replaced, in the name of Jesus.

3. I destroy any oath or vow made secretly against me, in the name of Jesus.

4. I command all closed doors of goodness to begin to open unto me, in the name of Jesus.

5. Let all my goodness swimming in the sea of life enter the net spread by God's angel, in the name of Jesus.

6. I will arise from fear to faith, in the name of Jesus.

7. I receive restoration of what I lost through unbelief, in Jesus' name.

8. I reject every leadership into the wrong roads of life, in the name of Jesus.

9. Lord, make me a source of supernatural blessings to others.

10. Lord, begin to do that which is necessary to bring revival to my life.

11. Lord, remove the stumbling block in my walk with you.

12. Let me be swift to hear and slow to speak, O Lord.

13. Let me always commit my ways unto you, O Lord.

14. I will not be sorrowful; for the joy of the Lord is my strength, in the name of Jesus.

15. Let the power to mount up with wings as Eagles fall upon me, in the name of Jesus.

16. O Lord, remove all confusion from me.

17. I will trust in the Lord with all my heart. I will not lean on my own understanding, in the name of Jesus.

18. Lord, instruct me and teach me in the way that I should go.

19. Let me always cast my burdens upon You, O Lord.

20. I shall not be disgraced in any area of my life, in the name of Jesus.

21. I refuse to be dismayed, in the name of Jesus.

22. I shall not die but live and declare the works of the living God, in the name of Jesus.

23. I shall obtain joy and gladness; sorrow and sighing shall flee from my life, in the name of Jesus.

24. I receive deliverance from all spirits of adversity and afflictions, in the name of Jesus.

25. Let every ladder of the enemy in my life be broken into pieces, in the name of Jesus.

26. I command the angels of the Lord to execute judgement on evil forces against my family, in the name of Jesus.

27. I invite the spirit of confusion and division to come upon the forces of the enemy, in the name of Jesus.

28. I send the arrow of God upon every power challenging my peace, joy and prosperity, in the name of Jesus.

29. I command the wind, sun and moon to run contrary to every demonic presence in my family, in the name of Jesus.

30. I cancel all curses, known or unknown to me by the blood of Jesus, in the name of Jesus.

31. Let the consequences of the enemy's defeat upon my life be nullified, in the name of Jesus.

32. O Lord, give me power to face all the challenges of the enemy, in the name of Jesus.

33. I loose myself from the bondage of fear, in the name of Jesus.

34. I cancel all enchantments, curses and spells that are against my life, in the name of Jesus.

35. Let every tree planted by fear in my life dry to the roots, in the name of Jesus.

36. I claim my divine promotion today, in the name of Jesus.

37. Lord, make me succeed and bring me into prosperity.

38. Promotion, progress and success are mine today, in Jesus' name.

39. Eaters of flesh and drinkers of blood, begin to stumble and fall before me, in the name of Jesus.

40. I command stubborn pursuers to pursue themselves, in the name of Jesus.

41. Spirit of sleeplessness, mother of sickness, be bound, in the name of Jesus.

42. Let the spirit of fear and storms that leads to a panic depart from my life, in the name of Jesus.

43. Let the blood of Jesus cleanse me, from head to the toe, of every evil mark, in the name of Jesus.

44. You devourers, vanish from my labours, in the name of Jesus.

45. You windows of heaven, open for me now, in the name of Jesus.

46. I trample on scorpions and serpents, in the name of Jesus.

47. Let the power to pray above my normal level fall upon me, in the name of Jesus.

48. My body, begin to reject all evil strangers in you, in Jesus' name.

49. Let the air and earth run contrary to all antagonistic forces in my life, in the name of Jesus.

50. I break every family curse upon my life, in the name of Jesus.

51. Everything that needs replacement in my life, receive replacement, in the name of Jesus.

52. O Lord, pump Your blood into my blood.

53. Let impossibilities in my life become possible, in the name of Jesus.

54. I refuse to be shaken by the enemy, in the name of Jesus.

55. I regain my balance today, in the name of Jesus.

56. I claim abundance in every area of my life, in the name of Jesus.

57. Let all evil marks in my life go, in the name of Jesus.

58. I reverse every damage done to my life from the womb, in the name of Jesus.

59. Let the evil curse placed upon my family be removed by the blood of Jesus.

60. I bind and render to nought, all evil counsels and imaginations against my life, in the name of Jesus.

61. Let the entrance doors to poverty and exit doors of blessings in my life be closed, in the name of Jesus.

62. Let my enemies bow before me and congratulate me, in the name of Jesus.

63. O Lord, remove from my life every garment of suffering as You did for Joseph.

64. O Lord, remove from my life every garment of sickness as You did for Hezekiah.

65. O Lord, remove from my life every garment of debt as You did for the widow and Elisha.

66. O Lord, remove from my life every garment of reproach as You did for Hannah.

67. O Lord, remove from my life every garment of death as You did for the three Hebrew men.

68. My test, be miraculously converted to testimonies, in Jesus' name.

69. My burdens, be miraculously converted to blessings, in the name of Jesus.

70. My trials, be miraculously converted to triumph, in Jesus' name.

71. I run into the tower of divine power, in the name of Jesus.

72. I run into the city of divine solution to problems, in Jesus' name.

73. Let my breakthroughs begin to locate me and glue themselves to me, in the name of Jesus.

74. I paralyse every agent of shame in any area of my life, in the name of Jesus.

75. I drink the tonic and vitamin of the Holy Ghost, in Jesus' name.

76. All satanic desires upon my life, be frustrated, in Jesus' name.

77. My oppressors, begin to oppress yourselves, in the name of Jesus.

78. I renounce every unconscious evil membership, in Jesus' name.

79. I eject every illegal occupants from my life, in the name of Jesus.

80. Every chained spirit and blessing, be released, in Jesus' name.

81. I cancel every ordination of paralysis and death, in Jesus' name.

82. Let evil problems attached to my names be neutralised by the blood of Jesus.

83. Let the thunder fire of God break all strange meetings held for my sake, in the name of Jesus.

84. I stand against faith destroyers, in the name of Jesus.

85. I confuse the camp of the enemy with the blood of Jesus.

86. O Lord, deliver me from any stronghold satan may have in my life because of my sins and those of my ancestors.

87. I break all bondage in any area of my life, in the name of Jesus.

88. I break all ungodly soul ties with all past sex partners, in the name of Jesus.

89. Spirit of bondage, release my life, in the name of Jesus.

90. Spirit of heaviness, depart from my spirit, in the name of Jesus.

91. Spirit of slumber, depart from my spirit, in the name of Jesus.

92. Spirit of paralysis, depart from my life, in the name of Jesus.

93. I break every curse of death upon my life, in the name of Jesus.

94. You strangers, begin to flee from the house of my life, in the name of Jesus.

95. Let the rain of fire fall on every camp of the enemy of my breakthroughs, in the name of Jesus.

96. O Lord, give me strength to begin to do that which seems impossible to me.

97. Anointing that destroys every yoke, fall on me, in Jesus' name.

98. Let the East wind blow away all the evil hosts around me, in the name of Jesus.

99. Let the Holy Ghost fire dry up all sicknesses in my body, in the name of Jesus.

100. Let the secret of any Judas in my camp be revealed, in the name of Jesus.

101. All you that seek my life, turn away, in the name of Jesus.

102. Woe unto the evil vessel that the enemy is using to do me harm, in the name of Jesus.

103. O Lord, give me hunger and thirst for you.

104. O Lord, break the power of old habits in my life with Your rod.

105. O Lord, enable me to dwell in safety all the days of my life.

106. O Lord, protect me from the snares of the fowler.

107. O Lord, enable me to forsake negative thoughts.

108. Let the God who answers by fire answer me now, in Jesus' name.

109. Let every evil tongue rising against me be put to shame, in the name of Jesus.

110. I reject every unprofitable reconciliation, in the name of Jesus.

111. My prayers shall bring abundant blessings to me, in Jesus' name.

112. My prayers shall bring transformation and testimony to me, in the name of Jesus.

113. My prayers shall bring dumbfounding success to me, in the name of Jesus.

114. My prayers shall bring abundant prosperity to me, in the name of Jesus.

115. My prayers shall bring explosive spiritual revival to me, in the name of Jesus.

116. My prayers shall bring dumbfounding miracles to me, in the name of Jesus.

117. Every anti-miracle force in my life, perish now, in Jesus' name.

118. Blood of Jesus, blot out all hindrances to my miracles.

119. Failure in receiving miracles shall not be my lot.

120. O Lord, ordain dumbfounding miracles into my life now.

121. O God, envelope me in your miracles and wonder.

122. O God, order my steps, perfectly into outstanding miracles and wonders.

123. In this programme, I receive financial dumbfounding miracles, in the name of Jesus.

124. In this programme, I receive marital dumbfounding miracles, in the name of Jesus.

125. In this programme, I receive spiritual dumbfounding miracles, in the name of Jesus.

126. Dumbfounding miracles, begin to locate me in every area of my life, in the name of Jesus.

127. I cast down every road block hiding my breakthrough, in the name of Jesus.

128. I command every hindrance to my breakthrough to melt in the fire of God, in the name of Jesus.

129. I command every cloak of hindrance to my breakthrough to be burnt to ashes, in the name of Jesus.

130. Every flame of stagnation in my life, be put out by the blood of Jesus, in the name of Jesus.

131. Let the crushing hammer of God, crush every force opposing my breakthrough, in the name of Jesus.

132. Lord dumbfound the world with my breakthrough, in Jesus' name.

133. Let the whirlwind of God fall grievously upon those sitting on my breakthrough, in the name of Jesus.

134. Every stubborn evil tree, hiding my breakthrough, be uprooted, in the name of Jesus.

135. I receive power for dumbfounding breakthroughs, in Jesus' name.

136. Let the anointing for a mighty breakthrough fall upon me, in the name of Jesus.

137. Father Lord, build a wall of fire round me and my family, in the name of Jesus.

138. Fire of God, be my guide in every area of my life, in Jesus' name.

139. I protect my life and that of my family with the fire of God, in the name of Jesus.

140. I destroy the ammunition of my enemy, in the name of Jesus.

I KNOW THAT MY REDEEMER LIVETH

Job 42

- *When you face a Job-like situation and you desire that God should manifest His power.* The trials, temptations and adversities of Job and his ultimate triumph and the restoration of all his losses, establishes the fact that the great Redeemer lives. This is sufficient to allay any fear you may have concerning any bitter experience you are undergoing at present.

Job 19:25: *"For I know that my Redeemer liveth, and that He shall stand at the latter day upon the earth:"*

Our redeemer is God or the Messiah. The word redeem means to buy back. The laws of the redemption of property are recorded in Leviticus 25. Property can be returned to the owner or his next of kin at any time or in the Year of Jubilee.

Jesus is our Redeemer. He is the 'Firstborn of every creature' (Col. 1:15). He is our Big Brother and He has come to redeem us from the clutches of satan, sin, sickness, death and poverty (Gal. 3:13). By His death on the cross, He purchased us with His precious blood so that we can be His own (1 Peter 1:18,19).

Jesus is alive, making intercession for the saints. As our Redeemer He:

- teaches us how to profit, i.e. gives us divine prosperity and increase (Isaiah 48:17).
- teaches us the way we should go, i.e. gives us divine direction (Isaiah 48:1).
- gives us divine security (Psalm 78:35).
- helps us, i.e. divine assistance (Isaiah 41:14).
- blots out our sins, i.e. divine forgiveness (Isaiah 44:22).
- chooses us for greatness, i.e. divine election (Isaiah 49:7).
- shows us mercy, i.e. divine favour (Isaiah 54:8).
- transfers the wealth of the gentiles to you, i.e. divine elevation (Isa. 60:16).
- pleads your cause (Jer. 50:34).
- redeems our lives from destruction, i.e. divine deliverance (Psalm 103:4).

• CONFESSION

Jer. 1:12: *Then said the LORD unto me, Thou hast well seen: for I will hasten my word to perform it.*

• PRAISE WORSHIP

1. I cancel my name and that of my family from the death register, with the fire of God, in the name of Jesus.

2. Every weapon of destruction fashioned against me, be destroyed by the fire of God, in the name of Jesus.

3. Fire of God, fight for me in every area of my life, in Jesus' name.

4. Every hindrance to my protection, be melted by the fire of God, in the name of Jesus.

5. Every evil gathering against me, be scattered by the thunder fire of God, in the name of Jesus.

6. O Lord, let Your fire destroy every evil list containing my name, in the name of Jesus.

7. All failures of the past, be converted to success, in Jesus' name.

8. O Lord, let the former rain, the latter rain and Your blessing pour down on me now.

9. O Lord, let all the failure mechanism of the enemy designed against my success, be frustrated, in the name of Jesus.

10. I receive power from on high and I paralyze all the powers of darkness that are diverting my blessings, in the name of Jesus.

11. Beginning from this day, I employ the services of the angels of God to open unto me every door of opportunity and breakthroughs, in the name of Jesus.

12. I will not go around in circles again, I will make progress, in the name of Jesus.

13. I shall not build for another to inhabit and I shall not plant for another to eat, in the name of Jesus.

14. I paralyze the powers of the emptier concerning my handiwork, in the name of Jesus.

15. O Lord, let every locust, caterpillar and palmer-worm assigned to eat the fruit of my labour be roasted by the fire of God.

16. The enemy shall not spoil my testimony in this programme, in the name of Jesus.

17. I reject every backward journey, in the name of Jesus.

18. I paralyze every strongman attached to any area of my life, in the name of Jesus.

19. Let every agent of shame fashioned to work against my life be paralyzed, in the name of Jesus.

20. I paralyze the activities of household wickedness over my life, in the name of Jesus.

21. I quench every strange fire emanating from evil tongues against me, in the name of Jesus.

22. Lord, give me power for maximum achievement.

23. O Lord, give me comforting authority to achieve my goal.

24. Lord, fortify me with Your power.

25. (Lay your right hand on your head while praying this prayer point.) Every curse of profitless hard work, break, in the name of Jesus.

26. (Lay your right hand on your head while praying this prayer point.) Every curse of non-achievement, break, in the name of Jesus.

27. Lay your right hand on your head and pray like this: Every curse of backwardness, break, in the name of Jesus.

28. I paralyze every spirit of disobedience in my life, in Jesus' name.

29. I refuse to disobey the voice of God, in the name of Jesus.

30. Every root of rebellion in my life, be uprooted, in Jesus' name.

31. Fountain of rebellion in my life, dry up, in the name of Jesus.

32. Contrary powers fueling rebellion in my life, die, in Jesus' name.

33. Every inspiration of witchcraft in my family, be destroyed, in the name of Jesus.

34. Blood of Jesus, blot out every evil mark of witchcraft in my life, in the name of Jesus.

35. Every garment put upon me by witchcraft, be torn to pieces, in the name of Jesus.

36. Angels of God, begin to pursue my household enemies, let their ways be dark and slippery, in the name of Jesus.

37. Lord, confuse them and turn them against themselves.

38. I break every evil unconscious agreement with household enemies concerning my miracles, in the name of Jesus.

39. Household witchcraft, fall down and die, in the name of Jesus.

40. O Lord, drag all the household wickedness to the dead sea and bury them there.

41. O Lord, I refuse to follow the evil pattern of my household enemies.

42. My life, jump out from the cage of household wickedness, in the name of Jesus.

43. I command all my blessings and potentials buried by wicked household enemies to be exhumed, in the name of Jesus.

44. I will see the goodness of the Lord in the land of the living, in the name of Jesus.

45. Everything done against me to spoil my joy, receive destruction, in the name of Jesus.

46. O Lord, as Abraham received favour in Your eyes, let me receive Your favour, so that I can excel in every area of my life.

47. Lord Jesus, deal bountifully with me in this programme.

48. It does not matter, whether I deserve it or not, I receive immeasurable favour from the Lord, in the name of Jesus.

49. Every blessing God has attributed to me in this programme will not pass me by, in the name of Jesus.

50. My blessing will not be transferred to my neighbor in this programme, in the name of Jesus.

51. Father Lord, disgrace every power that is out to thwart Your programme for my life, in the name of Jesus.

52. Every step I take shall lead to outstanding success, in Jesus' name.

53. I shall prevail with man and with God in every area of my life, in the name of Jesus.

54. Every habitation of infirmity in my life, break to pieces, in the name of Jesus.

55. My body, soul and spirit, reject every evil load, in Jesus' name.

56. Evil foundation in my life, I pull you down today, in the mighty name of Jesus.

57. Every inherited sickness in my life, depart from me now, in the name of Jesus.

58. Every evil water in my body, get out, in the name of Jesus.

59. I cancel the effect of every evil dedication in my life, in the name of Jesus.

60. Holy Ghost fire, immunize my blood against satanic poisoning, in the name of Jesus.

61. Father Lord, put self control in my mouth, in the name of Jesus.

62. I refuse to get used to ill health, in the name of Jesus.

63. Every door open to infirmity in my life, be permanently closed today, in the name of Jesus.

64. Every power contenting with God in my life, be roasted, in the name of Jesus.

65. Every power preventing God's glory from manifesting in my life, be paralysed, in the name of Jesus.

66. I loose myself from the spirit of desolation, in the name of Jesus.

67. Let God be God in my home, in the name of Jesus.

68. Let God be God in my health, in the name of Jesus.

69. Let God be God in my career, in the name of Jesus.

70. Let God be God in my economy, in the name of Jesus.

71. Glory of God, envelope every department of my life, in the name of Jesus.

72. The Lord that answereth by fire, be my God, in the name of Jesus.

73. In this programme, all my enemies shall scatter to rise no more, in the name of Jesus.

74. Blood of Jesus, cry against all evil gatherings arranged for my sake, in the name of Jesus.

75. Father Lord, convert all my past failures to unlimited victories, in the name of Jesus.

76. Lord Jesus, create room for my advancement in every area of my life.

77. All evil thoughts against me, Lord turn them to be good for me.

78. Father Lord, give evil men for my life where evil decisions have been taken against me, in the name of Jesus.

79. O Lord, advertise Your dumbfounding prosperity in my life.

80. Let the showers of dumbfounding prosperity fall in every department of my life, in the name of Jesus.

81. I claim all my prosperity in this programme, in the name of Jesus.

82. Every door of my prosperity that has been shut, be opened now, in the name of Jesus.

83. O Lord, convert my poverty to prosperity, in the name of Jesus.

84. O Lord, convert my mistake to perfection, in the name of Jesus.

85. O Lord, convert my frustration to fulfillment, in the name of Jesus.

86. O Lord, bring honey out of the rock for me, in the name of Jesus.

87. I stand against every evil covenant of sudden death, in the name of Jesus.

88. I break every conscious and unconscious evil covenant of untimely death, in the name of Jesus.

89. You spirit of death and hell, you have no document in my life, in the name of Jesus.

90. You stones of death, depart from my ways, in the name of Jesus.

91. O Lord, make me a voice of deliverance and blessing.

92. I tread upon the high places of the enemies, in the name of Jesus.

93. I bind and render useless, every blood sucking demon, in the name of Jesus.

94. You evil current of death, loose your grip over my life, in the name of Jesus.

95. I frustrate the decisions of the evil openers in my family, in the name of Jesus.

96. Fire of protection, cover my family, in the name of Jesus.

97. O Lord, make my way perfect, in the name of Jesus.

98. Throughout the days of my life, I shall not be put to shame, in the name of Jesus.

99. I reject every garment of shame, in the name of Jesus.

100. I reject every shoe of shame, in the name of Jesus.

101. I reject every head-gear and cap of shame, in the name of Jesus.

102. Shamefulness shall not be my lot, in the name of Jesus.

103. Every demonic limitation of my progress as a result of shame, be removed, in the name of Jesus.

104. Every network of shame around me, be paralysed, in the name of Jesus.

105. Those who seek for my shame shall die for my sake, in the name of Jesus.

106. As far as shame is concerned, I shall not record any point for satan, in the name of Jesus.

107. In the name of Jesus, I shall not eat the bread of sorrow, I shall not eat the bread of shame and I shall not eat the bread of defeat.

108. No evil will touch me throughout my life, in the name of Jesus.

109. In this programme, I shall reach my goal, in the name of Jesus.

110. In every area of my life, my enemies will not catch me, in the name of Jesus.

111. In every area of my life, I shall run and not grow weary, I shall walk and shall not faint.

112. O Lord, in every area of my life, let not my life disgrace You.

113. I will not be a victim of failure and I shall not bite my finger for any reason, in the name of Jesus.

114. Help me O Lord, to meet up with God's standard for my life.

115. I refuse to be a candidate to the spirit of amputation, in the name of Jesus.

116. With each day of my life, I shall move to higher ground, in the name of Jesus.

117. Every spirit of shame set in motion against my life, I bind you, in the name of Jesus.

118. Every spirit competing with my breakthroughs, be chained, in the name of Jesus.

119. I bind every spirit of slavery, in the name of Jesus.

120. In every day of my life, I disgrace all my stubborn pursuers, in the name of Jesus.

121. I bind, every spirit of Herod, in the name of Jesus.

122. Every spirit challenging my God, be disgraced, in Jesus' name.

123. Every Red Sea before me, be parted, in the name of Jesus.

124. I command every spirit of bad ending to be bound in every area of my life, in the name of Jesus.

125. Every spirit of Saul, be disgraced in my life, in the name of Jesus.

126. Every spirit of Pharaoh, be disgraced in my life, in Jesus' name.

127. I reject every evil invitation to backwardness, in Jesus' name.

128. I command every stone of hindrance in my life to be rolled away, in the name of Jesus.

129. Father Lord, roll away every stone o f poverty from my life, in the name Jesus.

130. Let every stone of infertility in my marriage be rolled away, in the name of Jesus.

131. Let every stone of non-achievement in my life be rolled away, in the name of Jesus.

132. My God, roll away every stone of hardship and slavery from my life, in the name of Jesus.

133. My God, roll away every stone of failure planted in my life, my home and in my business, in the name of Jesus.

134. You stones of hindrance, planted at the edge of my breakthroughs, be rolled away, in the name of Jesus.

135. You stones of stagnancy, stationed at the border of my life, be rolled away, in the name of Jesus.

136. My God, let every stone of the 'amputator' planted at the beginning of my life, at the middle of my life and at the end of my life, be rolled away, in the name of Jesus.

137. Father Lord, I thank You for all the stones You have rolled away, I forbid their return, in the name of Jesus.

138. Let the power from above come upon me, in the name of Jesus.

139. Father Lord, advertise Your power in every area of my life, in the name of Jesus.

140. Father Lord, make me a power generator, throughout the days of my life, in the name of Jesus.

141. Let the power to live a holy life throughout the days of my life fall upon me, in the name of Jesus.

142. Let the power to live a victorious life throughout the days of my life fall upon me, in the name of Jesus.

143. Let the power to prosper throughout the days of my life fall upon me, in the name of Jesus.

144. Let the power to be in good health throughout the days of my life fall upon me, in the name of Jesus.

145. Let the power to disgrace my enemies throughout the days of my life fall upon me, in the name of Jesus.

146. Let the power of Christ rest upon me now, in the name of Jesus.

147. Let the power to bind and loose fall upon me now, in the name of Jesus.

148. Father Lord, let Your key of revival unlock every department of my life for Your revival fire, in the name of Jesus.

149. Every area of my life that is at the point of death, receive the touch of revival, in the name of Jesus.

150. Father Lord, send down Your fire and anointing into my life, in the name of Jesus.

151. Every uncrucified area in my life, receive the touch of fire and be crucified, in the name of Jesus.

152. Let the fire fall and consume all hindrances to my advancement, in the name of Jesus.

153. You stubborn problems in my life, receive the Holy Ghost dynamite, in the name of Jesus.

154. You carry-over miracle from my past fasting and prayer programmes, receive the touch of fire and be materialised, in the name of Jesus.

155. Holy Ghost fire, baptize me with prayer miracle, in Jesus' name.

156. Every area of my life that needs deliverance, receive the touch of fire and be delivered, in the name of Jesus.

157. Let my angels of blessing locate me now, in the name of Jesus.

158. Every satanic programme of impossibility, I cancel you now, in the name of Jesus.

159. Every household wickedness and its programme of impossibility, be paralysed, in the name of Jesus.

160. No curse will land on my head, in the name of Jesus.

161. Throughout the days of my life, I will not waste money on my health: the Lord shall be my healer, in the name of Jesus.

162. Throughout the days of my life, I will be in the right place at the right time.

163. Throughout the days of my life, I will not depart from the fire of God's protection, in the name of Jesus.

164. Throughout the days of my life, I will not be a candidate for incurable disease, in the name of Jesus.

165. Every weapon of captivity, be disgraced, in the name of Jesus.

166. Lord, before I finish this programme, I need an outstanding miracle in every area of my life.

167. Let every attack planned against the progress of my life be frustrated, in the name of Jesus.

168. I command the spirits of harassment and torment to leave me, in the name of Jesus.

169. Lord, begin to speak soundness into my mind and being.

170. I reverse every witchcraft curse issued against my progress, in the name of Jesus.

171. I condemn all the spirits condemning me, in the name of Jesus.

172. Let divine accuracy come into my life and operations, in the name of Jesus.

173. No evil directive will manifest in my life, in the name of Jesus.

174. Let the plans and purposes of heaven be fulfilled in my life, in the name of Jesus.

175. O Lord, bring to me friends that reverence Your name and keep all others away.

176. Let divine strength come into my life, in the name of Jesus.

177. O Lord, cause Yourself to be real in my life.

178. O Lord, show Yourself in my life today.

179. Let every stronghold working against my peace be destroyed, in the name of Jesus.

180. Let the power to destroy every decree of darkness operating in my life fall upon me now, in the name of Jesus.

181. Lord, deliver my tongue from evil silence.

182. Lord, let my tongue tell others of Your life.

183. Lord, loose my tongue and use it for Your glory.

184. Lord, let my tongue bring straying sheep back to the fold.

185. Lord, let my tongue strengthen those who are discouraged.

186. Lord, let my tongue guide the sad and the lonely.

187. Lord, baptise my tongue with love and fire.

188. Let every unrepentant and stubborn pursuers be disgraced in my life, in the name of Jesus.

189. Let every iron-like curse working against my life b e broken by the blood of Jesus, in the name of Jesus.

190. Let every problem designed to disgrace me receive open shame, in the name of Jesus.

191. Let every problem anchor in my life be uprooted, in Jesus' name.

192. Multiple evil covenants, be broken by the blood of Jesus, in the name of Jesus.

193. Multiple curses, be broken by the blood of Jesus, in Jesus' name.

194. Everything done against me with evil padlocks, be nullified by the blood of Jesus, in the name of Jesus.

195. Everything done against me at any cross-roads, be nullified by the blood of Jesus, in the name of Jesus.

196. Let every stubborn and prayer resisting demon receive stones of fire and thunder, in the name of Jesus.

197. Every stubborn and prayer resisting sickness, loose your evil hold upon my life, in the name of Jesus.

198. Every problem associated with the dead, be smashed by the blood of Jesus, in the name of Jesus.

199. I recover my stolen property seven fold, in the name of Jesus.

200. Let every evil memory about me be erased by the blood of Jesus, in the name of Jesus.

201. I disallow my breakthroughs from being caged, in Jesus' name.

202. Let the sun of my prosperity arise and scatter every cloud of poverty, in the name of Jesus.

203. I decree unstoppable advancement upon my life, in Jesus' name.

204. I soak every day of my life in the blood of J esus and in signs and wonders, in the name of Jesus.

205. I break every stronghold of oppression in my life, in Jesus' name.

206. Let every satanic joy about my life be terminated, in the name of Jesus.

207. I paralyse every household wickedness, in the name of Jesus.

208. Let every satanic spreading river dry up by the blood of Jesus, in the name of Jesus.

209. I bind every ancestral spirit and command them to loose their hold over my life, in the name of Jesus.

210. Ancestral spirits, pack your loads and go out of my life, in the name of Jesus.

DELIVERANCE FROM FOUNDATIONAL POLLUTION

Gal. 3:13,14; Col. 2:14,15

- *This is recommended as the first series of prayer to be said during deliverance sessions.*
- *To obtain deliverance from foundational contamination and bondage.*
- *To release yourself from ancestral yokes and burdens.*
- *To clean up unprofitable spiritual background militating against physical and spiritual progress.*

There is no gainsaying that the background of many people is saturated with satanic pollution, and as such, the earlier you understand this, the better.

Ps. 11:3: *"If the foundations be destroyed, what can the righteous do?"*

The righteous should run to Christ. "But of Him are ye in Christ Jesus, who of God is made unto us wisdom, and righteousness and sanctification and redemption" (I Corinthians 1:30).

Our foundation refers to our background and the experiences we've passed through that have brought us where we are today. At birth some were dedicated to idols, or given satanic names. Some had their placenta manipulated or eaten. There could be ancestral curses and covenants working in their lives. They could have had terrible experiences which opened the door for demons to enter their lives, e.g. rape; armed robbery attacks or accident.

All these things are pollutants which will hinder spiritual progress. It will stop you from reaching your goal in Christ. Jesus seeks a deep fellowship with you, but as long as these things remain in your life you cannot go higher. When we run to Christ:

- we receive wisdom. We obtain favour and life. Proverbs 8;35.

- we receive righteousness: we become the righteousness of God in Christ Jesus (1 Corn.5:21). We are established by His righteousness (Isaiah 54:14).

- we receive sanctification: we are made holy, we are purified, body, spirit and soul (1 Thess. 5:23).

- we receive redemption: we are redeemed from the curse of the law, sickness, sin, disease, death and poverty.

As you embark on this prayer programme, you will receive wisdom, righteousness, sanctification, redemption and complete deliverance.

• CONFESSION

Obad. 1:17 : *But upon mount Zion shall be deliverance, and there shall be holiness; and the house of Jacob shall possess their possessions.*

• **NOTE: *Prayers of release from foundational bondage have to be said aggressively and violently. No stone should be left un-turned. You must hate the foundational bondage with perfect hatred.***

1. Thank God for making provision for deliverance from any form of bondage.
2. Confess your sins and those of your ancestors, especially those sins linked to evil powers.
3. I cover myself with the blood of Jesus.
4. I release myself from any inherited bondage, in the name of Jesus.
5. O Lord, send Your axe of fire to the foundation of my life and destroy every evil plantation.
6. Let the blood of Jesus flush out from my system every inherited satanic deposit, in the name of Jesus.
7. I release myself from the grip of any problem transferred into my life from the womb, in the name of Jesus.
8. Let the blood of Jesus and the fire of the Holy Ghost cleanse every organ in my body, in the name of Jesus.
9. I break and loose myself from every inherited evil covenant, in the name of Jesus.
10. I break and loose myself from every inherited evil curse, in the name of Jesus.
11. I vomit every evil consumption that I have been fed with as a child, in the name of Jesus.
12. I command all foundational strongmen attached to my life to be paralysed, in the name of Jesus.
13. Let any rod of the wicked rising up against my family line be rendered impotent for my sake, in the name of Jesus.

14. I cancel the consequences of any evil local name attached to my person, in the name of Jesus.

15. Pray aggressively against the following evil foundations. Pray as follows: You (*pick the under listed one by one*), loose your hold over my life and be purged out of my foundation, in Jesus' name.

- destructive effect of polygamy   - evil physical design
- parental Curses   - envious rivalry
- evil dedication   - fellowship with local idols
- demonic incisions   - demonic marriage
- dream pollution   - evil laying on of hands
- demonic sacrifice   - fellowship with family idols
- demonic initiations   - inherited infirmity
- wrong exposure to sex   - exposure to evil diviner
- demonic blood transfusion   - demonic alteration of destiny
- fellowship with demonic consultants
- unscriptural manner of conception

16. You evil foundational plantation, come out of my life with all your roots, in the name of Jesus.

17. I break and loose myself from every form of demonic bewitching, in the name of Jesus.

18. I release myself from every evil domination and control, in the name of Jesus.

19. Let the blood of Jesus be transfused into my blood vessel, in the name of Jesus.

20. Let every gate opened to the enemy by my foundation be closed for ever with the blood of Jesus.

21. Lord Jesus, walk back into every second of my life and deliver me where I need deliverance, heal me where I need healing, transform me where I need transformation.

22. I reject, revoke and renounce my membership with any evil association, in the name of Jesus.

23. I withdraw and cancel my name from any evil register with the blood of Jesus, in the name of Jesus.

24. I reject and renounce any evil name given to me consciously or unconsciously, in any evil association, in the name of Jesus.

25. I purge myself with the blood of Jesus of all evil foods I have eaten consciously or unconsciously in any evil association, in the name of Jesus.

26. I withdraw any part of my body and blood in custody of any evil altar, in the name of Jesus.

27. I withdraw my pictures, image and inner-man from any evil altar and coffers of evil associations, in the name of Jesus.

28. I return any of the things of evil associations I am consciously or unconsciously connected with, the instruments and any other properties at my disposal, in the name of Jesus.

29. I hereby confess total separation from any evil association, in the name of Jesus.

30. Holy Spirit, build a wall of fire round me that will completely make it impossible for any evil spirit to come to me again.

31. I break any covenant binding me with any evil association, in the name of Jesus.

32. I break all inherited covenants I have entered into consciously or unconsciously, in the name of Jesus.

33. I bind the demons attached to these covenants and cast them into the deep, in the name of Jesus.

34. I resist every attempt to return me back to any evil association with the blood of Jesus, fire, brimstone and thunder of God, in the name of Jesus.

35. I renounce and revoke all the oaths I took consciously or unconsciously while entering any evil association, in Jesus' name.

36. I break and cancel every evil mark, incision, writing placed in my spirit and body as a result of my membership of any evil association with the blood of Jesus and purify my body, soul and spirit with the Holy Ghost fire, in the name of Jesus.

37. I break all covenants inherited from my ancestors on the father's and mother's sides, in the name of Jesus.

38. Lord, break down every evil foundation of my life and rebuild a new one on Christ the Rock.

39. I command the fire of God to roast and burn to ashes every evil bird, snake, or any other animal attached to my life by any evil association, in the name of Jesus.

40. I dismantle every hindrance, obstacle or blockage put in my way of progress by any evil association, in the name of Jesus.

41. All the doors of blessings and breakthrough shut against me by any evil association, I command you to be opened, in Jesus' name.

42. I break and cancel every inherited curse, in the name of Jesus.

43. Lord, remove from me all the curses placed upon my ancestral families as a result of their involvement in evil associations, in the name of Jesus.

44. I break and cancel every curse placed upon me by my parents, in the name of Jesus.

45. I break and cancel every curse, spell, hex, enchantment, bewitching, incantation placed upon me by any satanic agent, in the name of Jesus.

46. I break and revoke every blood and soul-tie covenant and yokes attached to any satanic agent, in the name of Jesus.

47. I purge myself of all the evil foods I have eaten consciously or unconsciously with the blood of Jesus and purify myself with the fire of the Holy Ghost, in the name of Jesus.

48. All demonic spirits attached to any covenant and curses in every de-

partment of my life, be roasted with the fire of God, in the name of Jesus.

49. I declare my body, soul and spirit a no-go-area for all evil spirits, in the name of Jesus.

50. Lord, let every area of my life experience Your wonder-working power.

51. I refuse to enter into any trap set by any evil association against my life, in the name of Jesus.

52. I break and loose myself from every collective covenant, in the name of Jesus.

53. I break and loose myself from every collective curse, in the name of Jesus.

54. I break and cancel every covenant with any idol and the yoke attached to it, in the name of Jesus.

55. I break and cancel any evil covenant entered into by my parents on my behalf and all the yoke attached to it, in the name of Jesus.

56. I command the fire of God to roast the forces of hindrance and obstacles and paralyse their powers, in the name of Jesus.

57. Lord, let the Holy Ghost effect immediate breakthrough in every area of my life, in the name of Jesus.

58. I confess that my deliverance shall remain permanent never to be reversed again, in the name of Jesus.

59. Let all evil competitors stumble and fall, in the name of Jesus.

60. Let all my adversaries make mistakes that will advance my cause, in the name of Jesus.

61. I send confusion into the camp of all evil counselors planing against my progress, in the name of Jesus.

62. I command darkness into the camp of the enemy, in Jesus' name.

63. I remove my name from the book of failure and demonic sidetracking, in the name of Jesus.

64. Lord, give me power to
   - make use of divine opportunity presented to me
   - possess more wisdom than my competitor
   - drink from the well of salvation
   - make my paths confusing to the enemy
   - always be ahead of my competitors in terms of favour and independent assessment, in the name of Jesus.

65. Let all the adversaries of my breakthroughs be put to shame, in the name of Jesus.

66. In the movement of Your power throughout this programme, Lord, do not pass me by.

67. I command all the scorpion spirits sent against me to become stingless, in the name of Jesus.

68. Let all my Herod receive spiritual decay, in the name of Jesus.

69. Let every power circulating my name for evil receive disgrace, in the name of Jesus.

70. Thank the Lord for answers to your prayer.

DEFEATING SATANIC REINFORCEMENT

2 Samuel 15:1-31

- *To paralyse evil reinforcement and dissolve satanic network.*

The advice of the Christian song-writer, "Christian seek not yet repose" holds true for any serious heaven-bound believer, because such person is a target of continuous bombardment of forces of hell. Hence you must wake up to confront every assault of satanic reinforcement against you.

Daniel 7:25: *"And he shall speak great words against the Most High, and shall wear out the saints of the Most High . . .."*

You can call the devil many names, but you cannot call him a fool. His kingdom is highly organized (Ephesians 6:12). The devil is a good strategist who doesn't give up easily. He is very persistent and consistent in attacking the children of God. The major strategy he wants to use in the last days is to wear out the saints. This means a constant bombardment with trials, tribulation, afflictions, infirmities, etc. When he tries and fails, he will "depart for a season", like he did after tempting Jesus (Luke 4:13).

His departing for a season is only to go and regroup, reinforce and get ready for another attack. Beloved, this is the time for you to fortify yourself with fire. It is not the time to take things easy with dark powers. We thank God for His promise in Isaiah 54:15, "Behold, they shall surely gather together, but not by me: whosoever shall gather together against thee shall fall for thy sake." Let us watch and pray.

These prayer points will defeat every satanic reinforcement and destroy satanic networks.

- **CONFESSION**

Romans 9:33 : *As it is written, Behold, I lay in Zion a stumbling stone and rock of offence: and whosoever believeth on him shall not be ashamed.*

• PRAISE WORSHIP

1. Let every organised strategy of the hosts of demonic world against my life be rendered to nothing, in the name of Jesus.

2. I command all demonic spirits transferred into my life through demonic contact to be withdrawn and be cast into fire, in the name of Jesus.

3. Every demonic influence targeted at destroying my vision, dream and ministry, receive total disappointment, in the name of Jesus.

4. Let every demonic trap set against my life be shattered to pieces, in the name of Jesus.

5. I command all demonic activities against my calling to receive disgrace and commotion, in the name of Jesus.

6. All partners in demonic businesses militating against my life should receive commotion and be dis organised, in the name of Jesus.

7. Father Lord, let my life, ministry and prayer life be extremely dangerous for the kingdom of darkness, in the name of Jesus.

8. All demonic-organised seductive appearances to pull me down should be rendered null and void, in the name of Jesus.

9. Father Lord, show me an immeasurable forgiveness daily in my life, in the name of Jesus.

10. Father Lord, don't terminate my divine spiritual assignments on earth but help me to accomplish them, in the name of Jesus.

11. My Lord and my God, raise up intercessors to stand in the gap for me always, in the name of Jesus.

12. Father Lord, let all the motionless spiritual gifts and talents in my life begin to function for Your glory, in the name of Jesus.

13. I reject all uncontrollable crying, heaviness and regrets, in the name of Jesus.

14. Father Lord, help me so that my divine spiritual assignments shall not be transferred to another person, in the name of Jesus.

15. I command all organised forces of darkness against my life to receive

commotion, lightning and thunder, in the name of Jesus.

16. All demonic organised network against my spiritual and physical ambition, be put to shame, in the name of Jesus.

17. I command all demonic mirrors and monitoring gadgets against my spiritual life to crack to pieces, in the name of Jesus.

18. Let the demonic computers and the operators militating against my life receive destruction, in the name of Jesus.

19. Father, don't render me unfit for Your work, in Jesus' name.

20. Father, don't take my life before I fulfil my ministry, in Jesus' name.

21. Every spiritual spider webbing problems into my life, die, in the name of Jesus.

22. I disconnect my household from every satanic network, in the name of Jesus.

23. All the satanic gadgets being used to monitor my progress, be destroyed by the thunder fire of God, in the name of Jesus.

24. I command every evil cycle in my life to break, in Jesus' name.

25. Every local representative of satanic network in my life, be paralysed, in the name of Jesus.

26. Every satanic network working in contact with household enemy, be brought to shame, in the name of Jesus.

27. All satanic network obstructing my blessings, fire of God melt them away, in the name of Jesus.

28. All the sources of power of every evil work, be quenched in my life, in the name of Jesus.

29. I paralyse every evil network set against my life, in Jesus' name.

30. All satanic network arranged against me for the rest of my life, I command you to fail woefully, in the name of Jesus.

31. All the vehicles of evil counsellors that carry them for evil counsel, be destroyed, in the name of Jesus.

32. Let the spirit of madness fall upon all evil counsellors of my life, in the name of Jesus.

33. Let all those walking ignorantly with evil counsellors receive the spirit of poverty, in the name of Jesus.

34. Let all powers working with evil counsellors concerning issues of my life receive total failure, in the name of Jesus.

35. Lord, turn evil counsellors and their counsels over my life to nought today.

36. Let the spirit of disorganisation fall upon every evil counsellor taking evil counsel over my life and family, in the name of Jesus.

37. You rebellious spirit, go into the midst of all evil counsellors now and scatter them, in the name of Jesus.

38. Lord, let the spirit of confusion fall into the midst of the evil counsellors, in the name of Jesus.

39. You evil counsellors, begin to eat the bread of sorrow and drink bitter water from today henceforth, in the name of Jesus.

40. Every good thing that any evil counsellor has destroyed in my life, be repaired from today, in the name of Jesus.

41. Let the wicked assigned to my life bow and let their lives be shortened, in the mighty name of Jesus.

42. The wickedness of the wicked shall swallow them up, in the name of Jesus.

43. I decree that the habitation of my household wickedness shall be totally desolate, in the name of Jesus.

44. I command the East wind to sweep away the wicked, in the name of Jesus.

45. O Lord, let the wicked bow and be slain by evil, in Jesus' name.

46. You wicked forces troubling the church of God, receive the sharp sword of God and be silent in the grave, in Jesus' name.

47. O Lord, rain Your fire of anger upon the wicked, in Jesus' name.

48. Let all the wicked struggling with me bow and perish, in the name of Jesus.

49. O Lord, release Your anger upon the wicked and consume them.

50. Any disease agent living in my body now, die, in Jesus' name.

51. I will not partake in wearing satanic uniform, in the name of Jesus.

52. Let every bad effect of any evil thing that I have eaten be cancelled, in the name of Jesus.

53. Nobody will transfer any disease into my life, in Jesus' name.

54. O Lord, give me Your own immunization, in the name of Jesus.

55. I refuse to harbour any genetic disease, in the name of Jesus.

56. O Lord, transfuse me with the blood of Jesus.

57. I refuse to be bewitched, in the name of Jesus.

58. Let all satanic worms in my body die, in the name of Jesus.

59. My health will not waste my money, in the name of Jesus.

60. I break the backbone of all my family idols, in the name of Jesus.

61. I paralyse every strongman enforcing demonic power against my life, in the name of Jesus.

62. Special announcement: I refuse to be your candidate, you family idol, in the name of Jesus.

63. I refuse every demonic transfer from my family shrine, in the name of Jesus.

64. I refuse to be remotely controlled from my village, in Jesus' name.

65. Let all my family idols be buried in the Red Sea, in Jesus' name.

66. Another special announcement: As from today, I become too hot to be handled by any negative power, in the name of Jesus.

67. Let lightning discomfit the source of power of my village idols, in the name of Jesus.

68. Every unprofitable covenant that has prospered so far in my life, break today, in the name of Jesus.

69. I move to the level the Lord wants me to be, in Jesus' name.

70. Thank the Lord for answered prayer.

BRINGING THE STRONGMAN TO OPEN SHAME

Col. 2; Samuel 17

- *To put to shame the strongman, who is the principal or controlling demon over a family, place, person or thing.*

Jesus, your Lord and master, gave the chief strongman a technical knockout and open shame; David too put Goliath to unprecedented shame in the history of Philistine's warfare. With aggression, do the same to your strongman.

Luke 11:21: *"When a strong man armed keepeth his palace, his goods are in peace. But when a stronger than he shall come upon him, and overcome him, he taketh from him all his armour wherein he trusted, and divideth his spoils."*

The strongman is the controller of a group of spirits or a chief over a group of spirits. The Bible calls strongmen "rulers of darkness of this world" (Eph. 6:12). They act as the prison wardens of the devil, confiscating the blessings of people. They are the wicked rulers over every nation, town and family.

A strongman can be attached to someone's career, business, ministerial calling or marriage: To bring the strongman to open shame:

- the person must be a stronger man. We thank God that Jesus has made us the stronger man. He has given us power over all the power of the enemy so we can subdue them and have control over them (Luke 10:19).

- we must bind the strong man (Matthew 12:29; Mark 3:27). To bind means to overcome and have power over, to make powerless, to render impotent, to fasten or tie so as to be unable to move or do anything.

- Then we can go in, collect our goods and spoil the strong-man. We are told in Colossians 2:15, "And having spoiled principalities and powers, Jesus made a show of them openly triumphing over them in it." We have the power to do this.

The anointing of a warrior will fall upon your life as you pray, and the strongman attached to your life will be brought to an open shame!

• CONFESSION

Col. 2:15 : *And having spoiled principalities and powers, he made a shew of them openly, triumphing over them in it.*

• PRAISE WORSHIP

1. Fire of God, minister destruction to the ministry of destruction in my family, in the name of Jesus.

2. I consume the shrine of the strongman in my family with the fire of God, in the name of Jesus.

3. Let stones of fire pursue and dominate all the strongmen in my life, in the name of Jesus.

4. I receive strength and power to be a warrior and not to worry, in the name of Jesus.

5. I smash the head of the strongman on the wall of fire, in the name of Jesus.

6. Let hell open its mouth without measure and swallow all suckers of peace in my life, in the name of Jesus.

7. No regrouping, no reinforcement against me by the strongmen in my family, in the name of Jesus.

8. Let the angel of God roll the stones of fire to hinder the strongman on my ways, in the name of Jesus.

9. I cause open disgrace to all strongmen in my family, in Jesus' name.

10. Let all the enemy of my soul start their days with confusion and end it in destruction, in the name of Jesus.

11. O Lord, release from my mind any image of jealousy, lust and evil intentions.

12. I stand against all confusing forces within me, in Jesus' name.

13. O Lord, order my inner life so that I can hear You.

14. Let me see what You see in me.

15. I ask You to make me uncomfortable till I get to the right track.

16. O Lord, wash my brain with the blood of Jesus and remove bad habits which are physically engraved there.

17. Lord, heal any hormonal imbalance or other secretions in my body.

18. O Lord, heal in me whatever needs to be healed.

19. O Lord, replace in me whatever needs to be replaced.

20. O Lord, transform in me whatever needs to be transformed.

21. O Lord, let Your healing power take firm root within me.

22. Let the strongmen from both sides of my family begin to destroy themselves now, in the name of Jesus.

23. The strongman from my father's side, the strongman from my mother's side, begin to destroy yourselves, in the name of Jesus.

24. I refuse to wear the garment of sorrow, in the name of Jesus.

25. All stubborn pursuers in my life, I command you to die, in the name of Jesus.

26. All satanic arrows presently in my life, lose your power, in the name of Jesus.

27. Let every organised evil arrow against my life be paralysed, in the name of Jesus.

28. I fire back all satanic arrows of depression at the edge of my breakthroughs, in the name of Jesus.

29. I fire back all satanic arrows of spiritual and physical sicknesses, in the name of Jesus.

30. I fire back all satanic arrows of weakness in prayer and Bible reading, in the name of Jesus.

31. I fire back all satanic arrows of business failure, in Jesus' name.

32. I fire back all evil arrows from the household enemy, in the name of Jesus.

33. I fire back all evil arrows from my unfriendly friends, in Jesus' name

34. Power of God, bring to life all my good benefits that satanic arrows have paralysed, in the name of Jesus.

35. I cover my life and all my belongings from satanic arrows by the blood of Jesus Christ.

36. Thank the Lord that the gate of hell shall not prevail against your life.

37. I order confusion and scattering of tongues amongst all wicked associations militating against the peace of my life, in Jesus' name.

38. Let the wisdom of all evil counsellors in my life be rendered to nothing, in the name of Jesus.

39. O Lord, cause an explosion of Your power in my handiwork.

40. Let my life be barricaded by the edge of fire and let me be soaked and covered with the blood of Jesus.

41. O Lord, smite all evil tongues rising against me by the cheek bones and break the jaw of the evil.

42. Let every handwriting contrary to my peace receive intensive disgrace, in the name of Jesus.

43. Let every decision taken against me by the wicked be rendered null and void, in the name of Jesus.

44. I fire back every demonic arrow targeted at me and my family, in the name of Jesus.

45. I break every spiritual mirror and monitors fashioned against me, in the name of Jesus.

46. Pray in the spirit 10 to 15 minutes.

47. I bind and I render to nothing all the strongmen that are currently troubling my life, in the name of Jesus.

48. I disgrace . . . (pick from the under listed), in the name of Jesus
    - delegated satanic agents
    - water spirits
    - satanic prophets
    - occultic consultants
    - the original possessors of our family (like crocodiles, shrines, human sacrifices, etc.)
    - drinkers of blood
    - spirit of sexual perversion

- demonic food sellers
- selling polluted foods & bread of sorrow

49. Thank the Lord for answered prayers.

50. Let every power of the oppressors rise up against them, in the name of Jesus.

51. Let my affairs become too hot for the enemy to handle, in the name of Jesus.

52. I retrieve my blessings from the camp of evil confiscators, in the name of Jesus.

53. I vomit every satanic poison, in the name of Jesus.

54. Let my promotion manifest powerfully, in the name of Jesus.

55. I disband all evil hosts gathered against me, in the name of Jesus.

56. Let all anti-testimony forces scatter, in the name of Jesus.

57. Let the joy of the enemy upon my life be turned to sorrow, in the name of Jesus.

58. I paralyse every pocket with holes, in the name of Jesus.

59. Let Your power, Your glory and kingdom come upon my life, in the name of Jesus.

60. Let all drinkers of blood and eaters of flesh begin to eat their own flesh and drink their own blood to satisfaction, in Jesus' name.

61. I reject temporary freedom in every area of my life, in Jesus' name.

62. I reject partial freedom in every area of my life, in Jesus' name.

63. I claim total victory and freedom in all areas of my life, in the name of Jesus.

64. I break the power of any demonic spell issued against my life, in the name of Jesus.

65. Let all bitter water flow out of my handiwork, in Jesus' name.

66. I withdraw all the bullets and ammunition made available to the enemy, in the name of Jesus.

67. I bind the spirit of death and hell over my life, in Jesus' name.

68. My name, become thunder, fire and lightening in the hands of those calling you for evil purposes, in the name of Jesus.

69. I decree that there shall be no reinforcement, no re-grouping of any strongmen against me, in the name of Jesus.

70. Thank the Lord for answered prayer.

OPEN HEAVENS
Genesis 28:1-17
- *To blast the heavens open*
- *To paralyse satanic angels contending with our angels of blessing*

The tenacity of your prayer must be capable of causing the heavens to open for your sake.

Isaiah 64:1: *"Oh that thou wouldest rent the heavens, that thou wouldest come down, that the mountain might flow down at thy presence."*

Open heavens will enable us to obtain the breakthroughs we need for our lives. When the heavens open the angels of God will begin to ascend and descend bringing multiple blessings for the saints. These blessings include favour, power, promotion, breakthrough, finances, good health, sound mind, peace, etc.

One of the curses in Deuteronomy 28:23 says, "And the heaven over thy head shall be brass, and the earth that is under thy feet shall be iron." This shows that it is possible for someone's heaven to be closed. These prayer points are targeted at blasting the heavens open.

When the heavens become brass, your angels cannot reach you. Daniel fasted for 21 days. When his angel of blessing came he said: "Fear not Daniel: for from the *first day* that thou did set thine heart to understand, and to chasten thyself before thy God, thy words were heard, and I am come for thy words. But the prince of the kingdom of Persia withstood me one and twenty days: but, lo Michael, one of the chief prince, came to help me; and I remained there with the prince of Persia" (Daniel 10: 12, 13). The heaven was closed because of satanic obstacles. Daniel faithfully continued praying till his answer came. We need to continue praying; prayer is the key that turns God's promises into reality.

As you use these prayer points, "God will rend the heavens", the angels of God will begin to ascend and descend upon your life (John 1:51).

• CONFESSION

Psalm 113:5,7,8: *Who is like unto the LORD our God, who dwelleth on high, He raiseth up the poor out of the dust, and lifteth the needy out of the dunghill; That he may set him with princes, even with the princes of his people.*

Make these confessions out loud.

God is not a man that He should lie nor the son of man that He should repent of any of His pronouncements. Once has God spoken twice have I heard this that all power belongs to God. Therefore, I believe every word of god, because the word is God Himself and if God cannot lie, every promise of God for my life will come to pass.

As I make this confession, I declare to the devil that I am not ignorant of who I am in Christ; I am born again, I have been crucified with Christ. Now I am seated with Him in heavenly places, I am a saint, I belong to God. Jesus bought me with His own precious and blameless blood and has translated my life from the kingdom of darkness into His kingdom of light, peace and abundance of life.

I stand on the victory of Jesus over satan and over death and hell, for it is written, that Jesus first of all descended into the lower parts of the earth and stripped the devil off all his powers and ascended on high, leading captivity captive, and gave gifts unto men. By this victory let any gathering of the powers of darkness that is against my prayers be defeated by the blood of Jesus.

The day I wholeheartedly gave my life to Christ, I submitted myself to God. Therefore, satan, I have the authority to resist you and your attacks against my sound relationship with my Maker, Jehovah God.

Through my faith in Jesus Christ, I have become a seed of Abraham. The blessings of Abraham are mine. The Scripture says I am blessed with faithful Abraham. I am a partaker of all God's heavenly blessings. It is written, that God has blessed all His children with all spiritual blessings in the heavenly places. The Lord God is a sun and shield, the Lord will give grace and glory. No good thing will He withhold from them that walk uprightly.

The Scripture says if I ask I will receive. I ask and by faith I receive grace and glory from God. Jehovah God is all sufficient. The Bible says He is more than sufficient. I ask for God's divine abundance in every area of my life and I receive it.

I confess and receive it, that my prayer is a sweet smelling savour in the nostrils of God. I ask and receive His grace and glory to incubate me and my prayers. As it is written, I shall be a crown of glory in the hand of God, a royal diadem in the hand of my Maker; I begin to shine as a shinning light. The light of God is in me, darkness cannot abide in me and cannot overshadow me. The light of the glory of God shall be seen over me and all eyes shall see it together. Anywhere I go I shall always stand off. Even when darkness shall cover the earth and dense darkness over all people, the Lord shall arise upon me and His glory shall be seen upon me. I shall see and be radiant. My heart shall thrill and tremble with joy and be enlarged; because the abundance of the sea shall be turned to me. Unto me shall the nations come with their treasures. Foreigners shall build up my walls, and their kings shall minister to me. In God's wrath He smote me, but in His favour, pleasure and good will He has had mercy and love for me.

The sons of those who afflicted me shall come bending low to me, and all those who despised me shall bow down at me feet, and they shall call me the city of the Lord, the Zion of the Holy One of Israel. Whereas I have been forsaken and hated so that no good thing passed through me, God will make me an eternal glory, a joy from age to age. I shall eat the riches of the gentiles, and in their glory I shall boast myself and all shall see and shall acknowledge that I am the seed which the Lord has blessed.

God has spoken to my life, I believe it and I begin to manifest it. I am not a failure, I shall operate at the head only and not beneath. I shall dwell on the mountain always and not in the valley, I shall no longer experience the activities of the spirit of Pisgah. I shall no longer be disappointed of fail at the edge of my desired miracles, success and victory, for the blood of Jesus has cleansed from my life every mark of witchcraft of hatred, jealousy and envy.

I trample under my feet every serpent of treachery, evil reports, accusations, machinations and criticism. No counsel of the wicked shall stand against me. If God be for me who can be against me. No weapon that is fashioned against me shall prosper, and every tongue that rises up against me is already condemned. Therefore, I tear down in faith every spiritual wall of partition between me and my divinely appointed helpers and benefactors.

Right now, I stand in my position as a true child of Jehovah God, ordained to reign as a king on earth and I decree the flavour of divine favour of God to fill me. God has put His word in my mouth as a weapon of destruction and restoration. I use that power to speak destruction upon all devil's agents assigned to hinder me and divert my blessings. I use the same weapon to decree restoration upon my life. It is written that I should not consider the former things, God shall do a new thing in my life and it shall speedily spring forth. Now I ask that new things begin to spring forth in my marriage, new things shall begin to spring forth in my business and finances, new things shall begin to spring forth in my spiritual life.

The Lord will make His face to shine upon me always and shall be gracious unto me. His light will shine on my path and His favour will encompass me all the days of my life.

I cover my confessions with the precious blood of the Lamb of God. Amen.

• PRAISE WORSHIP

1. Thank the Lord because He is the only One who cannot be stopped when He makes up His mind to advance you.
2. O Lord, bring me into favour with all those that will decide on my advancement.
3. O Lord, cause a divine substitution to happen if this is what will move me ahead.
4. I reject the spirit of the tail and I claim the spirit of the head.
5. I command all evil records planted by the devil in anyone's mind against my advancement to be shattered to pieces, in Jesus' name.

6. Oh Lord, transfer, remove or change all human agents that are bent on stopping my advancement.

7. O Lord, smooth out my path to the top by the hand of fire.

8. I receive the anointing to excel above my contemporaries, in the name of Jesus.

9. Lord, catapult me into greatness as You did for Daniel in the land of Babylon.

10. Lord, help me to identify and deal with any weaknesses in me that can hinder my progress.

11. I bind every strongman delegated to hinder my progress, in the name of Jesus.

12. O Lord, despatch Your angels to roll away every stumbling block to my promotion, advancement and elevation.

13. Let power change hands in my place of work to the hands of the Holy Spirit, in the name of Jesus.

14. I receive the mandate to put to flight every enemy of my breakthroughs, in the name of Jesus.

15. I bind and render to naught . . . (pick from the under listed), in the mighty name of Jesus.

- demonic antagonism
- strife
- marginal success
- wrong words
- bad feet/bad luck
- demonic opinions against me
- evil collaborators
- demonic logic and unprofitable interviews
- unprofitable controversies
- unprofitable questions
- confusion
- mind blankness
- mind dullness
- memory failure

16. I claim the position of . . . , in the mighty name of Jesus.

17. Let the mark of the blood of Jesus, of divine favour and protection be upon my life, in the name of Jesus.

18. Lord, prepare me as a living sanctuary for You.

19. Father Lord, rend the heavens and come down at my cry.

20. Let every evil terrestrial and celestial spirit working against me be paralysed, in the name of Jesus.

21. Let power from above fall on me to do the impossible, in the name of Jesus.

22. Let every good and perfect gift from above locate me today, in the name of Jesus.

23. I prophecy unto every imperfect gift in my life, become perfect, in the name of Jesus.

24. I command the rain of abundance, goodness, favour and mercy to fall on every department of my life, in the name of Jesus.

25. Let divine glory from above overshadow my life now, in the name of Jesus.

26. I paralyse all the enemies that are against my open heavens, in the name of Jesus.

27. I paralyse all powers that expands problems, in the name of Jesus.

28. I paralyse all powers that delay miracle, in the name of Jesus.

29. I paralyse all marriage destroyers, in the name of Jesus.

30. I paralyse all anti-miracle agents in every area of my life, in the name of Jesus.

31. O Lord, make me a channel of Your blessings in all areas of life.

32. Let my hand be stronger than all opposing hands, in Jesus' name.

33. Every stone of hindrance, be rolled out of my way, in Jesus' name.

34. My tongue, become an instrument of Your glory, in Jesus' name.

35. My hands, become an instrument of divine prosperity, in the name of Jesus.

36. My eyes, become an instrument of divine revelation, in the name of Jesus.

37. My ears, become an instrument of divine revelation, in Jesus' name.

38. Anointing of the overcomer, fall upon my life, in Jesus' name.

39. I withdraw my name from the list of untimely death, in Jesus' name.

40. Let every evil consumption be flushed out of my system, in the name of Jesus.

41. Let agents of wickedness begin to loose their holds over my life, in the name of Jesus.

42. Let agents of discouragement begin to loose their holds over my life, in the name of Jesus.

43. I send the arrows or any gun shot in the dream back to the senders, in the name of Jesus.

44. I receive back all my stolen properties, in the name of Jesus.

45. Here I am O Lord, soak me in Your abundance.

46. I don't want to make the mistake of my past life again. I don't want to experience the failure of the past in future, in the name of Jesus.

47. I paralyse every enemy of my breakthroughs, they will not function in my life any longer, in the name of Jesus.

48. Every mountain of evil, be cast into the Red Sea, in Jesus' name.

49. I paralyse every evil record working against me, in Jesus' name.

50. Let every secret of hidden and open enemy be revealed to me, in the name of Jesus.

51. All the owners of evil luggage of infirmities, carry your load now, in the name of Jesus.

52. All you spirits of infirmity, hear the word of the Lord: Depart from my life now, in the name of Jesus.

53. I remove my name from the book of untimely death, in the name of Jesus.

54. My peace is too hot for the enemy to touch, in the name of Jesus.

55. I command all satanic net to be roasted, in the name of Jesus.

56. Throughout the days of my life, my enemy shall receive double disgrace, in the name of Jesus.

57. All enemies of my blessings, stumble and fall, in Jesus' name.

58. From the north, south, east and west, let all my blessings begin to locate me, in the name of Jesus.

59. Let the songs of joy fill my tabernacle all the days of my life, in the name of Jesus.

60. Anywhere I go, I will find favour, in the name of Jesus.

61. Anywhere I face or turn to, the enemy will run without stopping, in the name of Jesus.

62. O Lord, make me Your good vessel.

63. Lord, convert me from spiritual dwarf to spiritual giant.

64. Lord, ordain me to do exploits in every area of my life.

65. I break to pieces all spiritual weapons of warfare that have been formed against me, in the name of Jesus.

66. I release the bomb of fire into the camp of the enemies of my life, in the name of Jesus.

67. No contrary power and demon shall be able to stand before me all the days of my life, in Jesus' name.

68. Lord, let my prayers avail much with God and arouse disasters in the kingdom of darkness.

69. The affairs of my life will be too hot for the enemy to handle, in the name of Jesus.

70. Through the power of the Lord, I shall break through all manners of opposition, in the name of Jesus.

71. Let each second, minute and hour of my life deliver good things unto me, in the name of Jesus.

LIVING THE MOUNTAIN TOP LIFE

1 Cor. 13

- *For those who are tired of being candidates of the valley*
- *Who want to mount up with wings as eagles*

It was because Elijah was on the top of the mountain that he was able to see the enemies who came three times to capture him. In the same vein, except you climb the mountain of fire and miracles, victory may continue to elude you.

Isaiah 40:31: *"But they that wait upon the Lord shall renew their strength; they shall mount up with wings as eagles; they shall run, and not be weary; and they shall walk and not faint."*

God expects His children to be eagle believers. "As an eagle stirreth up her nest, fluttereth over her young, and spreadeth abroad her wings, so the Lord alone did lead them and there was no strange god with him" (Deut. 32:11,12). To live the mountain top life we need to be able to mount up like the eagle. (i)The eagle is a very strong and powerful bird. It weighs 4 kilograms and it can carry a weight of 20 kilograms. Where God is taking us to has nothing to do with our physical make up. (ii) The average life span of an eagle is 120 years. God will surely satisfy us with long life (Ps. 91:16). (iii) The eagle can fly 30,000ft. above sea level. When we are lifted up spiritually and on fire for God, there is no witch or wizard that can harm us. (iv) The eagle is the only bird that can look towards the sun. So when it is being chased, it flies towards the sun and his enemies turn back. As believers, while we run to Christ when being pursued, our enemies will turn back. "When I cry unto thee, then shall mine enemies turn back; thus I know; for God is for me" (Ps. 56:9). (v) The eagle has sharp eyes. We must pray that every cataract blinding our spiritual eyes should be dissolved by fire. Our spiritual capacity must be fully developed. (vi) The Mother eagle always takes time to train her children.

We have to mount up, before we can live the mountain top life. Every hindrance to our mounting up will be destroyed as we wait upon the Lord and pray violently.

● **CONFESSION**

Romans 14:17: *For the kingdom of God is not meat and drink; but right-eousness, and peace, and joy in the Holy Ghost.*

● **PRAISE WORSHIP**

1. I command every spiritual contamination in my life to receive healing, in the name of Jesus.
2. Brush of the Lord, begin to scrub out every dirt in my spiritual pipe.
3. Every rusted pipe in my life, receive a change, in Jesus' name.
4. I command every power eating up my spiritual pipe to be roasted, in the name of Jesus.
5. I command every blockage in my spiritual pipe to be removed, in the name of Jesus.
6. I command the hole in my spiritual pipe to be closed, in the name of Jesus.
7. Let the heavenly plumber, repair my spiritual pipe, in Jesus' name.
8. Let my spiritual pipe receive the strength of God against any contamination, in the name of Jesus.
9. I receive heavenly flushing in my spiritual pipe, in Jesus' name.
10. I confess that my spiritual pipe shall be effective throughout my life, in the name of Jesus.
11. Every evil padlock and every evil chain, go back to the senders, in the name of Jesus.
12. I rebuke every spirit of deafness and blindness in my life, in the name of Jesus.
13. I bind the strongman behind my spiritual blindness and deafness and paralyse his operations in my life, in Jesus' name.
14. I anoint my eyes and my ears with the blood of Jesus.
15. O Lord, restore my spiritual eyes and ears, in the name of Jesus.
16. Lord, anoint my eyes and my ears that they may see and hear.

17. I send the fire of God to my eyes and ears to melt away any satanic deposits, in the name of Jesus.

18. Spiritual eyes and ears, I command you in the name of Jesus, be opened.

19. In the name of Jesus, I capture every power behind my spiritual blindness and deafness.

20. Let every spiritual screen and ear drum receive healing, in the name of Jesus.

21. You blind and deaf spirit, loose your hold over my life, in the name of Jesus.

22. I will not throw away my gift of salvation, in the name of Jesus.

23. Let water of life flush out every unwanted strangers in my life, in the name of Jesus.

24. You haters of God's salvation in my life, I command you to be fried, in the name of Jesus.

25. You pollutants of life, I pollute you, in the name of Jesus.

26. Lord, put into my hand the gift that will elevate my life.

27. Holy Spirit fire, cook me to the glory of God, in the name of Jesus.

28. O Lord, let the anointing of the Holy Spirit break every yoke of backward movement in my life, in the name of Jesus.

29. Let the blood of Jesus remove any unprogressive label from every aspect of my life, in the name of Jesus.

30. I reject the spirit of the tail, I choose the spirit of the head, in the name of Jesus.

31. I paralyse the ability of any demonic power limiting my progress, in the name of Jesus.

32. O Lord, give unto me the key to good success, so that anywhere I go the doors of good success will be opened unto me.

33. O Lord, establish me as a holy person unto You , in Jesus' name.

34. O Lord, let the anointing to excel in my spiritual and physical life fall on me, in the name of Jesus.

35. I declare with my mouth that nothing shall be impossible with me, in the name of Jesus.

36. I reject the anointing of non-achievement in my handiwork, in the name of Jesus.

37. O Lord, let Your favour and that of men encompass me this year, in the name of Jesus.

38. Holy Spirit, control my ability to frame my words.

39. Let scorpions be rendered stingless in every area of my life, in the name of Jesus.

40. Let serpents be rendered harmless in every area of my life, in the name of Jesus.

41. Let the camp of the enemy be put in disarray, in Jesus' name.

42. Let all my Herod receive spiritual decay, in the name of Jesus.

43. Let evil worms in any area of my life die, in the name of Jesus.

44. Let all evil handwritings against me be paralysed, in Jesus' name.

45. All those circulating my name for evil, be disgraced, in Jesus' name.

46. Let evil friends make mistakes that would expose them, in the name of Jesus.

47. Let the strongmen from both sides of my family destroy themselves, in the name of Jesus.

48. Let not my peace depart from me, O Lord.

49. I refuse to wear the garment of tribulation and sorrow, in the name of Jesus.

50. O Lord, let the spirit that flees from sin incubate my life.

51. Let the secrets of hidden and open enemies be revealed, in the name of Jesus.

52. I command every satanic net to receive destruction, in the name of Jesus.

53. O Lord, create in me a clean heart by Your power.
54. O Lord, renew a right spirit within me.
55. I renounce my rights to my anger, in the name of Jesus.
56. O Lord, remove from me the root of irritation that keeps anger alive in me.
57. I reject all thoughts that I will never change, in the name of Jesus.
58. Spirit of God, cleanse and control anger in my life, in Jesus' name.
59. O Lord, produce in me the power of self-control and gentleness.
60. I reject all that rob me of the joy of my inheritance in Your kingdom.
61. I speak to all evil mountains and break their powers over my life, in the name of Jesus.
62. Lord, enable me to hear Your voice.
63. Lord, let me know Your mind.
64. Lord, by the power of the blood, remove from my life any hindrance of the enemy.
65. Every evil garment of shame, be roasted, in the name of Jesus.
66. Every evil garment of filthiness, be roasted, in the name of Jesus.
67. Every evil garment of spiritual laziness, be roasted, in Jesus' name.
68. Every evil garment of dishonour, be roasted, in Jesus' name.
69. Every evil garment of physical and spiritual depression, be roasted, in the name of Jesus.
70. Every evil garment of evil confessions, be roasted, in Jesus' name.

POWER TO PROSPER
Psalm 34

- *For all-round prosperity and turn-around breakthroughs.*

The power to obtain genuine prosperity re-sides only in the gospel of Christ. Power from any other source is a counterfeit. It leads back-wards and results in a bleak eternity.

3 John 2: *"Beloved, I wish above all things that thou mayest prosper and be in health even as thy soul prospereth."*

God desires all-round prosperity for His children. We are to prosper spiritually, physically and materially. Our material and physical blessings are proportional to our spiritual blessings. The more we increase spiritually the more we will increase physically and materially. The more of God we have in our lives the more we will prosper and be in health. That is why we are told, "Seek ye first the kingdom of God and His righteousness: all these things shall be added unto you" (Matthew 6:33). It is God that gives us the power to get wealth (Deut. 8:18) and teaches us to profit (Isa. 48:17). According to Psalm 1:3, when we trust in the Lord and put *all* our hope on Him: "We will be like a tree planted by the rivers of water." This means we will not lack anything. All our needs will be met. The Lord, our Shepherd, will supply all our needs (Psalm 23:1).

Jeremiah continues: "That spreadeth her roots by the river." We have all the food we need to grow physically and spiritually. We are rooted and built up in Him. In the secular world we are successful in whatever we lay our hands to do.

"And shall not see when heat cometh, but her leaf shall be green." This means that if there is a plague or any disease killing people, we will still remain healthy. What happens to the world does not affect us. Our finances, health and life remain buoyant.

"And shall not be careful in the year of drought, neither shall cease from yielding fruit." This backs up the Scripture that says, "In times of famine my people shall be satisfied." No matter what happens to the world, as long as we are growing spiritually and prospering spiritually all other areas of our lives will prosper and bear fruit. As you pray, you will prosper, and be in health even as your soul prospers!

● **CONFESSION**

Psalm 34:10 :*The young lions do lack, and suffer hunger: but they that seek the LORD shall not want any good thing.*

● **PRAISE WORSHIP**

1. Thank God for His provision so far.

2. Let all security-men in charge of satanic banks that are harbouring my blessings be paralysed, in the name of Jesus.

3. I terminate the appointment of all satanic bankers and managers, in the name of Jesus.

4. I command the thunder of God to break to pieces all the satanic strong-rooms harbouring my properties, in Jesus' name.

5. I possess all my properties, in the name of Jesus.

6. Let all satanic instruments (the legal tenders and the cheque) used against me be completely destroyed, in Jesus' name.

7. I command all satanic clearing houses and agents to be roasted, in the name of Jesus.

8. I paralyse completely all satanic transactions and contracts against my life, in the name of Jesus.

9. Let all satanic network and computers fashioned against me be disorganized, in the name of Jesus.

10. Heavenly Father, let all blood that has been stored up in satanic bank come forth, in the name of Jesus.

11. I refuse to be an object for satanic transaction, in Jesus' name.

12. I refuse to do profitless work, in the name of Jesus.

13. Every evil force against my handiwork, be paralysed, in the name of Jesus.

14. I send back to the sender every arrow of spiritual deposit and advance payment against my handiwork, in the name of Jesus.

15. You my handiwork, receive divine profit, in the name of Jesus.

16. I cover my handiwork with the fire of God, in the name of Jesus.

17. I cover my handiwork with hot coals of fire, untouchable for evil forces, in the name of Jesus.

18. O Lord, put to shame every evil force that is against my handiwork.

19. My handiwork, receive the touch of the Lord, in Jesus' name.

20. Every tree of profitless hard work, be uprooted, in Jesus' name.

21. Profitless hard-work, pack your load and go out of my life, in the name of Jesus.

22. I will not carry any evil load forward in my life, in Jesus' name.

23. O Lord, drain out satanic deposits from my business and handiwork.

24. Let all the strange hands and legs walk out of my business and handiwork, in the name of Jesus.

25. Let the spirit of favour fall upon me now, in the name of Jesus.

26. O Lord, enlarge my coast.

27. I rebuke every devourer in my handiwork, in the name of Jesus.

28. O Lord, cause ministering angels to bring in customers and money into my business.

29. I bind every spirit of error, in the name of Jesus.

30. Let every trouble emanating from envious business partners be rendered null and void, in the name of Jesus.

31. O Lord, surprise me with abundance in every area of my life.

32. I command a quit notice to . . ., in the name of Jesus.

    - evil legs on finances

    - evil powers keeping the copy of my registration certificates

    - every operational curses

33. Let the anointing for money-yielding ideas fall upon my life, in the name of Jesus.

34. I bind every spirit of fake and useless investment , in Jesus' name.

35. I command every effect of strange money on my business to be neu-

tralized, in the name of Jesus.

36. Father Lord, let all satanic hosts against my prosperity receive blindness and commotion, in the name of Jesus.

37. All hindrances to my prosperity, be electrocuted, in Jesus' name.

38. Let all my mistakes be converted to miracles and testimonies, in the name of Jesus.

39. I command all those who vow to hinder my prosperity to somersault, become naked and confess to death, in Jesus' name.

40. I command all my buried blessings to be exhumed, in Jesus' name.

41. Father Lord, use both white and black men to bless me, in the name of Jesus.

42. I command all my pounds sterling and dollars' miracles to locate me, in the name of Jesus.

43. All my blessings attached to my place of birth, be released, in the name of Jesus.

44. Father Lord, use all the people in my environment to bless me and let anointing of prosperity fall on me, in the name of Jesus.

45. Lord, by the power of the blood, remove from my life any hindrance of the enemy.

46. O Lord, drive away all darkness in every area of my life.

47. O Lord, shield me from all forms of deception.

48. O Lord, illuminate Your truth to my understanding.

49. Lord, let me, with the eyes of my heart, see You clearly.

50. Lord, take away from me all powers do not originate from You.

51. I separate myself from satan and his kingdom, in Jesus' name.

52. I renounce the kingdom of darkness and embrace the kingdom of Jesus Christ, in the name of Jesus.

53. Lord Jesus, deliver me from evil.

54. I apply the blood of Jesus Christ to break all evil curses.

55. I shall be anointed with fresh oil from heaven, in Jesus' name.

56. Lord, reveal strongholds that hinder revival and give satan advantage to me.

57. Lord Jesus, let a deep work begin in my heart.

58. I kill all strange animals sent against me with the sword of the Lord, in the name of Jesus.

59. I divorce every satanic husband, in the name of Jesus.

60. Let the fire of God be released on every demonic child in my family, in the name of Jesus.

61. Let all evil spiritual homes be burnt down, in the name of Jesus.

62. I reject the spirit of slavery and hardship in every area of my life, in the name of Jesus.

63. Let the spirit of delay and hindrance be cast out of my life, in the name of Jesus.

64. I dissolve every anti-breakthrough strategies, in Jesus' name.

65. Let the hands of evil refuse to perform their enterprise in any area of my life, in the name of Jesus.

66. I decree that there shall not be compromise and dialogue between me and my enemies, in the name of Jesus.

67. I pull down all strongholds of evil over my life and the lives of members of my family, in the name of Jesus.

68. Lord, close the gap between where I am and where You want me to be.

69. Let all demonic jailers be roasted, in the name of Jesus.

70. Thank the Lord for answered prayers.

ENOUGH IS ENOUGH
Hebrews 11

- *When you are tired of being 'red'.*
- *When you are fed-up with being fed-up.*
- *When you have had enough of satanic attacks.*

The display of violent faith and stubborn aggression against all negative forces operating in your life is the only means by which you can put the enemy to flight.

Genesis 27:40: *"And by the sword shalt thou live, and shalt serve thy brother; and it shall come to pass when thou shalt have dominion, that thou shalt break his yoke from off thy neck."*

The situation you are in right now may be of your own making. You may have opened some doors to the enemy to keep attacking you. It may be through anger, over-indulgence in food, fornication, adultery or debts. You should have known by now that if you give the devil an inch, he will take a foot. The day you get dissatisfied with your present situation is the day you will begin to move forward.

Jacob stole Esau's birthright, then he stole his blessings. When Esau cried out to his father, Isaac, by the spirit of God Isaac said, "When thou shalt have dominion, thou shalt break his yoke from off thy neck." This simply means the day you get tired of satanic attacks, that is the day of your freedom.

Beloved, until we get to the point where we can say 'Enough is Enough' there will be no change. When we become divinely dissatisfied, and become spiritually restless, then we will begin to stir ourselves up. We will begin to shake off every spirit of slumber and laziness, then and only then will every yoke of the oppressor be broken in our lives. Then we will receive liberty in every area of our lives. Beloved, this is a divine principle. The day Jabez cried to God, He was heard. The day Hannah cried to God, the book of remembrance was opened for her sake. The day Jacob wrestled with God's angel he got his breakthrough. The moment the fire of God stirs up holy anger in you over your situation and you pray with spiritual violence, every yoke will be broken.

• CONFESSION

Isaiah 49:25,26 : *But thus saith the LORD, Even the captives of the mighty shall be taken away, and the prey of the terrible shall be delivered: for I will contend with him that contendeth with thee, and I will save thy children. And I will feed them that oppress thee with their own flesh; and they shall be drunken with their own blood, as with sweet wine: and all flesh shall know that I the LORD am thy Saviour and thy Redeemer, the mighty one of Jacob.*

• PRAISE WORSHIP

1. Thank God for what you have received in this programme so far.

2. I paralyse all the night caterers and I forbid their food in my dream, in the name of Jesus.

3. All pursuers in my dreams, begin to pursue yourself, in the name of Jesus.

4. I command my picture in the demonic kingdom, being used as a remote control against my life to burn into ashes, in Jesus' name.

5. I paralyse all the demonic delegates assigned to my life, in the name of Jesus.

6. I command total destruction of all satanic technology against my life, in the name of Jesus.

7. Every power of darkness hunting for my life, be roasted, in the name of Jesus.

8. Let all the contamination in my life through dreams be cleansed by the blood of Jesus.

9. Let the path of the enemy into my life be permanently closed, in the name of Jesus.

10. Father Lord, fill my life with the Holy Ghost fire, I want to vomit fire, in the name of Jesus.

11. I refuse to follow evil prescription, in the name of Jesus.

12. Let every evil thing done against me between the hours of 12 and 1 a.m. be nullified, in the name of Jesus.

13. Let every evil thing done against me between the hours of 1 and 2 a.m. be nullified, in the name of Jesus.

14. Let every evil thing done against me between the hours of 2 and 3 a.m. be nullified, in the name of Jesus.

15. Let every evil thing done against me between the hours of 3 and 4 a.m. be nullified, in the name of Jesus.

16. I loose myself from all inherited bondage, in the name of Jesus.

17. I vomit every satanic poison that I have swallowed, in Jesus' name.

18. Evil bands, release me, in the name of Jesus.

19. I remove myself from every satanic bus stop, in Jesus' name.

20. I drink the blood of Jesus.

21. Let every owner of evil load in my life begin to carry their loads, in the name of Jesus.

22. I destroy every evil remote controlling power fashioned against me, in the name of Jesus.

23. Holy Ghost fire, incubate my life.

24. I reverse every evil design fashioned against my life, in the name of Jesus.

25. Every hidden or open spirit of infirmity, depart from my life, in the name of Jesus.

26. You evil strongman, be bound, in the name of Jesus.

27. All evil authorities upon my life, I command you to break, in the name of Jesus.

28. I remove my name from the book of backward steps, in the name of Jesus.

29. O Lord, make me a channel of blessing.

30. I take as my weapon, the two edged-sword of the spirit and I cut down the powers of

   - witches   - familiar spirit

   - wizards   - ancestral/familiar spirits

- spirit wives
- spirit husbands
- spirit children
- evil spiritual properties

- mermaid spirits
- manipulators
- evil monitors
- evil arrows   - evil decisions

31. In the name of Jesus, I nullify every satanic embarrassment.

32. Lord, add more fire of the Holy Ghost to the fire that is burning my enemy.

33. Let the seven-fold standard be raised against all my enemies, in the name of Jesus.

34. O Lord, use me as Your battle axe.

35. Let the angels of war be released on my behalf, in Jesus' name.

36. In the mighty name of Jesus, I send the fire, thunder and stones of fire to destroy the powers of darkness in the air, land and sea.

37. In the name of Jesus, I bind all anti-deliverance demons in every area of my life.

38. In the name of Jesus, I bind all anti-miracle demons in every area of my life.

39. I destroy every satanic cage fashioned against my goodness, in the name of Jesus.

40. I destroy every satanic chain fashioned against my life, in the name of Jesus.

41. Let every satanic instrument that is against me be neutralized, in the name of Jesus.

42. I destroy all the web of satan against my life, in the name of Jesus.

43. I disconnect any satanic linkage to anyone dead or alive, in the name of Jesus.

44. Let every spiritual equipment set against me be broken to pieces, in the name of Jesus.

45. Let all spiritual mirrors used against me be dashed to pieces, in the name of Jesus.

46. I destroy all the protective coverings of the enemy protecting them against the Holy Ghost fire, in the name of Jesus.

47. I cancel every careless word which I have spoken and which satan is using against me, in the name of Jesus.

48. I destroy any satanic attachment to any of my properties, in the name of Jesus.

49. I destroy any of my properties *(pick from the list below)* at the evil altar in the evil world, in the name of Jesus.

   - image   - money   - pictures
   - any part of my body   - clothes   - finger nails
   - name

50. I come against all the curses issued against my future and progress, in the name of Jesus.

51. I separate myself from all evil rivers, evil idols, evil streams and evil shrines present in my place of birth, in the name of Jesus.

52. Let all agents banking my blessings release them unto me, in the name of Jesus.

53. I destroy all the evil peace, evil agreement, evil unity, evil love, evil happiness, evil understanding, evil communication and evil gathering that are fashioned against me, in the name of Jesus.

54. Begin to bless yourself with all manner of blessings.

55. Let agents of frustration begin to loose their hold over my life, in the name of Jesus.

56. Let agents of poverty begin to loose their hold over my life, in the name of Jesus.

57. Let agents of debt begin to loose their hold over my life, in the name of Jesus.

58. Let agents of spiritual rags begin to loose their hold over my life, in the name of Jesus.

59. Let agents of defeat begin to loose their hold over my life, in the name of Jesus.

60. Let agents of infirmity begin to loose their hold over my life, in the name of Jesus.

61. Let agents of demotion begin to loose their hold over my life, in the name of Jesus.

62. Let agents of demonic delay begin to loose their hold over my life, in the name of Jesus.

63. Let agents of confusion begin to loose their hold over my life, in the name of Jesus.

64. Let agents of backward movement begin to loose their hold over my life, in the name of Jesus.

65. Let all wicked oppressors stumble and fall in every area of my life, in the name of Jesus.

66. Let God break the teeth of the ungodly gathered against me, in the name of Jesus.

67. Let all the instruments of failure fashioned against my life receive the fire of God and be roasted, in the name of Jesus.

68. Let all satanic weapons of attack fashioned against me and my family receive the fire of God and be roasted, in Jesus' name.

69. Let all satanic computers fashioned against my life receive the fire of God and be roasted, in the name of Jesus.

70. Let all satanic records that are against my life receive the fire of God and be roasted, in the name of Jesus.

71. Let all satanic satellites and cameras used to monitor and manipulate my life receive the fire of God and be roasted, in the name of Jesus.

72. Let all satanic remote control fashioned against my life receive the fire of God and be roasted, in the name of Jesus.

73. Let all satanic labels and marks placed on my life be rubbed off by the blood of Jesus.

74. Let all anti-testimony forces gathered against me scatter, in the name of Jesus.

75. Let all oppressors in every area of my life receive the leprosy of divine judgement, in the name of Jesus.

76. Make me a pillar in Your house, O God.

77. Lord, give me power to pursue, overtake and recover.

78. Let Your fire destroy every foundational problem in my life, in the name of Jesus.

79. Let every evil link, label and stamp of the oppressors be destroyed by the blood of Jesus.

80. Every evil spiritual pregnancy, be aborted over my life, in the name of Jesus.

81. Let every dirty hand be removed from the affairs of my life, in the name of Jesus.

82. I remove my name from the book of untimely death, in the name of Jesus.

83 I remove my name from the book of tragedy, in Jesus' name.

84. All evil umbrellas preventing heavenly showers from falling upon me, be roasted, in the name of Jesus.

85. Let all evil associations summoned for my sake be scattered, in the name of Jesus.

86. Father Lord, crucify anything in me that would remove my name from the book of life.

87. Father Lord, help me to crucify my flesh.

88. If my name has been removed from the book of life, Father Lord, re-write it.

89. Lord, give me power to overcome myself.

90. Every problem connected with polygamy in my life, be nullified, in the name of Jesus.

91. Every curse issued by my husband/wife, be nullified, in the name of Jesus.

92. All satanic deposits in my life, be roasted, in the name of Jesus.

93. I command every satanic reinforcement against me to scatter, in the name of Jesus.

94. Every power of any family idol affecting my life and home, be broken now, in the name of Jesus.

95. I cancel all evil vows that are affecting me negatively, in the name of Jesus.

96. I destroy the clock and the time-table of the enemy for my life, in the name of Jesus.

97. Lord, reschedule my enemies to useless and harmless assignments.

98. Let every good thing that is dead in my life come alive now, in the name of Jesus.

99. Let every evil device against me be disappointed, in Jesus' name.

100. Healing power of God, overshadow me now, in Jesus' name.

101. I bind every spirit working against answers to my prayers, in the name of Jesus.

102. I disarm any power that has made a covenant with the ground, water and wind about me, in the name of Jesus.

103. Let my life be invisible to demonic observers , in Jesus' name.

104. I bind all remote control spirits, in the name of Jesus.

105. I withdraw all the ammunition made available to the enemy, in the name of Jesus.

106. I revoke all conscious or unconscious covenants with the spirit of death, in the name of Jesus.

107. Lord, I submit my tongue to You, take control.

108. Let the heavenly surgeons begin to perform all necessary surgical operations in every area of my life where necessary, in the name of Jesus.

109. I refuse to be spiritually amputated, in the name of Jesus.

110. I refuse to wage war against myself, in the name of Jesus.

111. O Lord, wake me up from any form of spiritual sleep.

112. All evil seeds planted by fear into my life, be uprooted, in the name of Jesus.

113. Let Your kingdom be established in every area of my life, in the name of Jesus.

114. Armies of heaven, disgrace my oppressors , in Jesus' name.

115. You emptier and wasters, release me now, in the name of Jesus.

116. Let my blood reject every poison, in the name of Jesus.

117. Let the enemy fall into the pit dug for my sake, in Jesus' name.

118. Let my life experience divine favour in all areas, in Jesus' name.

119. Woe unto the vessel sent by the enemy to do me any harm, in the name of Jesus.

120. I command all my blessings swallowed by satanic powers to be vomited now, in the name of Jesus.

121. All powers that are bent on doing me harm, receive paralysis, in the name of Jesus.

122. Every arrow of destruction fired at me, go back to the sender, in the name of Jesus.

123. The enemy will not convert my right hand to the left hand, in the name of Jesus.

124. Let all satanic letters against me be burnt, in the name of Jesus.

125. O Lord, let the tongues of my enemy be divided and be confused.

126. Let all the counsels of the wicked be broken, in Jesus' name.

127. I withdraw any personal invitation given to the enemy to harm me, in the name of Jesus.

128. O Lord. give me a miracle that would dumbfound the world .

129. I command every opposing knees to bow, in the name of Jesus.

130. I command my enemies to become my footstool, in Jesus' name.

131. O Lord, let me experience victory in every area of my life.

132. Let all my l ocked-up blessings rebel and come out of the prison, in the name of Jesus.

133. Let all attackers hiding within the tower of the enemy be revealed, in the name of Jesus.

134. Let every evil association against me be severely distabilized, in the name of Jesus.

135. I bind every activity and operations of the devil in my environment, in the name of Jesus.

136. I challenge my body with the fire of the Holy Ghost and command strangers to flee, in the name of Jesus.

137. All physical and spiritual sicknesses, flee, in the name of Jesus.

138. Let all the wicked spirits around me fall by their own wickedness, in the name of Jesus.

139. Any good thing that the enemy has removed in my life, be returned immediately, in the name of Jesus.

140. Let my name become thunder, fire and lightning in the hands of those calling it for evil purposes, in the name of Jesus.

HONEY OUT OF THE ROCK
Isaiah 43:19

- **For Christian businessmen seeking for contracts.**
- **For those who desire to find favour in academic, business, and other proposals.**

Taking honey out of the rock literally means doing the impossible. This is the exclusive preserve of the Almighty God, when He is called upon in prayer to deal with a seemingly impossible situation in your life.

Deut. 32:12,13: *"So the Lord alone did lead him, and there was no strange god with him. He made him ride on the high places of the earth, that he might eat the increase of the field; and he made them to suck honey out of the rock, and oil out of the flinty rock."*

God's ultimate desire is to bless His children. He desires our fellowship and obedience so that he can bless us. The Bible says, "The blessings of the Lord, maketh rich, and He addeth no sorrow with it." Many times, our disobedience cuts us off from God's blessing. Job 36:11 says, "If they obey and serve him, they will spend their days in prosperity and their years in pleasure." This means if they disobey Him and do not serve Him, they will spend their days in poverty and their years in sorrow and struggles. Beloved, it is better to obey Him. Let us make a quality decision now that we will obey Him always, when it is convenient and when it is not.

Honey out of the rock simply means that God will bring out blessings, favour and wealth for you out of impossible, barren and unlikely places. He will surprise you with His awesomeness! He will make a way for you where there is no way. If you want something that is not available God will create it for you out of nothing. All God requires from you is complete and total obedience.

- CONFESSIONS

Deut. 28:13: *And the LORD shall make thee the head, and not the tail; and thou shalt be above only, and thou shalt not be beneath; if that thou* *hearken unto the commandments of the LORD thy God, which I command thee this day, to observe and to do them:*

Job 22:28: *Thou shalt also decree a thing, and it shall be established unto thee: and the light shall shine upon thy ways.*

Ps. 8:5: *For thou hast made him a little lower than the angels, and hast crowned him with glory and honour.*

Ps. 30:5: *For his anger endureth but a moment; in his favour is life: weeping may endure for a night, but joy cometh in the morning.*

Ps. 73:24: *Thou shalt guide me with thy counsel, and afterward receive me to glory.*

Ps. 118:24: *This is the day which the LORD hath made; we will rejoice and be glad in it.*

Prov. 21:1: *The king's heart is in the hand of the LORD, as the rivers of water: he turneth it whithersoever he will.*

Prov. 11:27: *He that diligently seeketh good procureth favour: but he that seeketh mischief, it shall come unto him.*

Dan. 1:9: *Now God had brought Daniel into favour and tender love with the prince of the eunuchs.*

Zech. 12:10: *And I will pour upon the house of David, and upon the inhabitants of Jerusalem, the spirit of grace and of supplications: and they shall look upon me whom they have pierced, and they shall mourn for him, as one mourneth for his only son, and shall be in bitterness for him, as one that is in bitterness for his firstborn.*

John 10:27: *My sheep hear my voice, and I know them, and they follow me:*

Eph. 3:19-20: *And to know the love of Christ, which passeth knowledge, that ye might be filled with all the fulness of God. Now unto him that is able to do exceeding abundantly above all that we ask or think, according to the power that worketh in us,*

Eph. 5:17: *Wherefore be ye not unwise, but understanding what the will of the Lord is.*

2 Tim. 1:7: *For God hath not given us the spirit of fear; but of power, and of love, and of a sound mind.*

● **PRAISE WORSHIP**

1. Father, make all my proposals to find favour in the sight of .   .   ., in the name of Jesus.

2. Lord, let me find favour ,compassion and loving-kindness with .   .   . concerning this business.

3. All demonic obstacles that have been established in the heart of .   .   . against my prosperity, be destroyed, in the name of Jesus.

4. Lord, show .   .   . dreams, visions and restlessness that would advance my cause.

5. I command my money being caged by the enemy to be completely released, in the name of Jesus.

6. Lord, give me supernatural breakthroughs in all my present business proposals.

7. I bind and put to flight all the spirits of fear, anxiety and discourage-ment, in the name of Jesus.

8. Lord, let divine wisdom fall upon all who are supporting me in these matters.

9. I break the backbone of any further spirit of conspiracy and treachery, in the name of Jesus.

10. Lord, hammer my matter into the mind of those who will assist me so that they do not suffer from demonic loss of memory.

11. I paralyse the handiwork of house hold enemies and envious agents in this matter, in the name of Jesus.

12. You devil take your legs away from the top of my finances, in the mighty name of Jesus.

13. Let the fire of the Holy Spirit purge my finances from any evil mark put upon me, in the name of Jesus.

14. Father, guide and direct me to rectify any problem I have with my business.

15. Lord, forgive me for any wrong decision or wrong action or thought I engaged in.

16. Father, help me to see my mistakes and faults and to do all in my power to overcome and correct them, in the name of Jesus.

17. Father, show me what to do so that business crisis would not arise again in my business, in the name of Jesus.

18. Lord, give unto me the eagle eye and eyes of Elisha to foresee market situations.

19. Lord, give me wisdom to walk out of any unfavorable business situations.

20. Father, help me to formulate a plan of recovery to keep me at the top, in the name of Jesus.

21. Lord, send me divine counsellors who can help me with my business.

22. Lord, always help me to identify evil business traps.

23. Lord, help me to erect safeguards to prevent business failure.

24. Let Your seal and divine stamp fall upon all my business proposals, in the name of Jesus.

25. My proposals, be too hot for the enemy to sit upon, in Jesus' name.

26. Father, give us the anointing to get the job done above and beyond our own strength, abilities, gifts and talents.

27. Lord, help us to be on the look-out for ways to provide better products and services.

28. Lord, help me to yield to the Holy Spirit whenever I encounter circumstances beyond my knowledge.

29. In the mighty name of Jesus, I claim the following:
    - good reputation
    - favour with clients and customers
    - abundant prosperity

- divine wisdom for those who occupy important decision-making positions
- increased sales and services and expanded markets
- new product ideas and new servicing concepts

30. Lord, help me to do my very best at all times.
31. Father Lord, I dedicate and consecrate my business to You, in Jesus' name.
32. Thank the Lord for answered prayer.

PARALYSING EVIL HANDS
Jer. 17:18
- *For those who feel that they are being suppressed by hosts of darkness*

You can nip in the bud the growth of evil powers which may lead to a major disaster in your life. Rise against all evil hands through your fervent and importunate prayers.

Psalms 140:4; 9:16: *"Keep me O Lord from the hands of the wicked; preserve me from the violent man; who has purposed to overthrow my goings. . . . "The wicked is snared by the work of his hands."*

As you embark on this prayer programme all evil hands in your life will be paralysed and all the works they have used their hands to do against you, will begin to work against them.

The Bible talks of hands full of mischief (Psalm 26:10); hands swift to shed innocent blood (Proverbs 6:17) and hands engaged in adultery (Psalm 115:4). Whatever they are, evil hands seek to suppress and overthrow people"s progress.

It is these evil hands that form evil weapons against God's children. We thank God that all their weapons cannot prosper in our lives but they will begin to work in the lives of those who made them. God has promised to disappoint all their devices so that their hands cannot perform their enterprise. All the satanic handwriting against our lives have been destroyed by the blood of Jesus. As you begin to apply these truths to your life, all evil hands working against you will be paralysed.

- CONFESSIONS

Gal. 3:13-14: *Christ hath redeemed us from the curse of the law, being made a curse for us: for it is written, Cursed is every one that hangeth on a tree: That the blessing of Abraham might come on the Gentiles through Jesus Christ; that we might receive the promise of the Spirit through faith.*

Gal. 6:17: *From henceforth let no man trouble me: for I bear in my body the marks of the Lord Jesus.*

Col. 2:14-15: *Blotting out the handwriting of ordinances that was against us, which was contrary to us, and took it out of the way, nailing it to his cross; And having spoiled principalities and powers, he made a shew of them openly, triumphing over them in it.*

3 Jn. 1:2: *Beloved, I wish above all things that thou mayest prosper and be in health, even as thy soul prospereth.*

● **PRAISE WORSHIP**

1. Let the time-table of the enemy for my life be destroyed, in the name of Jesus.

2. I break every unprofitable covenant, curse and associated problems over my life, in the name of Jesus.

3. Every evil assignment of the enemy for my life, business, etc., I terminate you , in the name of Jesus.

4. All the trees of non-achievement in my life, receive the axe of fire of God and be uprooted, in the name of Jesus.

5. Every evil spiritual vehicle assigned to war against me by the devil, receive the fire of God and crash, in the name of Jesus.

6. Lord, send Your fire to the root of my life, destroy and purge everything that has been affecting my life negatively.

7. I recover all my stolen blessings now, in the name of Jesus.

8. Every demonic deposit in my body, soul and spirit, receive the fire of God and melt away, in the name of Jesus.

9. Every evil horse and the rider, militating against me, be thrown down and drawn in the sea, in the name of Jesus.

10. I remove myself from every evil domination or control, in the name of Jesus.

11. All inherited spirits in my life, go now, in the name of Jesus.

12. O Lord, I command every strongman/strong woman attached to my life to receive the finger of God and release me now.

13. Lord, let Your counter-movement work against every deeply rooted problem in my life.

14. O Lord, dismantle all horses of the unknown forces in my life.

15. Lord, reveal every deepened seed, known and unknown, behind all the problems that I have.

16. Multiple strongmen attached to my life, be paralysed and die, in the name of Jesus.

17. Every problem originated from evil tongues, be cancelled, in the name of Jesus.

18. I break the hand of problematic powers upon my life, in the name of Jesus.

19. I break myself loose from the stronghold of Jezebel spirits, water spirits and spirit husband/wife, in the name of Jesus.

20. Every completed work of the enemy over my life, be destroyed and all the evil effects, return to the senders, in the name of Jesus.

21. Begin to thank God for answers to your prayer.

SUCCESS IN COMPETITION

Daniel 1:17-20; Exod. 31:2,3,6

- *Success in any competitive venture.*
- *Breakthroughs in selective processes.*

The record of Daniel's success story in the strange idolatrous land of Babylon should pose a challenge to you as a believer in Christ. You stand a better chance of succeeding more than Daniel, owing to the availability of grace now which was absent at his time. Why not ask God for an outstanding success in all your endeavours.

Joshua 4:14: *"On that day the Lord magnified Joshua in the sight of all Israel; and they feared him, as they feared Moses all the days of his life."*

For you to win you need the Lord's favour. Once the Lord is on your side and He is with you, He will magnify you before the panel of judges, just as He magnified Joshua before the Israelites.

You need to spend time preparing, physically and spiritually. Your spiritual preparation includes handling these prayer points violently and fervently.

"The race is not to the swift, nor the battle to the strong, neither yet bread to the weak, nor yet riches to men of understanding, nor yet favour to men of skill; but time and chance happeneth to them all." Relax! According to this Scripture, your success does not depend how good you are. God is in control and if you are faithful to His laws, He will honour you before the panel of judges.

You also need to prepare physically. Before you face the panel make sure you are well-dressed, neat and tidy. When Pharaoh, sent for Joseph from the prison, before Joseph came to Pharaoh, the Bible records, "he shaved himself, and changed his raiment, and came unto Pharaoh" (Genesis 41:14). You have to look good! Also you need to have all the relevant facts and information at your finger tips!

As you prayerfully prepare, God will magnify you before the panel of judges, favour you and give you victory.

• CONFESSION

Ps. 119:99: *I have more understanding than all my teachers: for thy testimonies are my meditation.*

1 Kings 3:12: *Behold, I have done according to thy words: lo, I have given thee a wise and an understanding heart; so that there was none like thee before thee, neither after thee shall any arise like unto thee.*

Exod. 11:3: *And the LORD gave the people favour in the sight of the Egyptians. Moreover the man Moses was very great in the land of Egypt, in the sight of Pharaoh's servants, and in the sight of the people.*

Ps. 34:7: *The angel of the LORD encampeth round about them that fear him, and delivereth them.*

Ps. 138:8: *The LORD will perfect that which concerneth me: thy mercy, O LORD, endureth for ever: forsake not the works of thine own hands.*

Acts 2:47: *Praising God, and having favour with all the people. And the Lord added to the church daily such as should be saved.*

Acts 4:13: *Now when they saw the boldness of Peter and John, and perceived that they were unlearned and ignorant men, they marvelled; and they took knowledge of them, that they had been with Jesus.*

• NOTE:

1. *Repent from all known sins.*

2. *Find out scriptures that promise you what you desire:*

   Romans 8:32, Deut. 28:13, Isa. 41:11,12; 62:4, Psalm 91:13, Phil. 4:13, Joshua 1:5, Jer. 1:8,9, Prov. 16:7

3. *Memorize and meditate on these scriptures and feed constantly on them. Visualise your promised victory.*

4. *Quote these scriptures against satan, worry, anxiety, fear and negative circumstances.*

5. *Ask the Father in the name of Jesus for the desire of your heart. Believe that you have already received.*

6. *Resolve not to allow doubt to enter your mind. Reject every*

thought of failure and doubt. REJECT every dream, vision and prophecy that tells you that your prayers are not answered.

7. *See yourself in the new position and keep confessing it.*
8. *Always give thanks to God for the answer to your prayer.*

• PRAISE WORSHIP

1. I have more understanding than my teachers because God's testimonies are my meditations, in the name of Jesus.
2. Lord, give me understanding and wisdom.
3. I receive wisdom, knowledge and understanding for my preparation.
4. Angels of the living God, encamp round about me now and go before me to the competition, in the name of Jesus.
5. Father Lord, anoint my handiwork for success, in Jesus' name.
6. I claim divine wisdom to answer any questions directed at me in the competition, in the name of Jesus.
7. I excel my colleagues ten times like Daniel, in Jesus' name.
8. I will find favour before all the panel, in the name of Jesus.
9. O Lord, perfect everything concerning my preparation for the competition.
10. I bind and render to nothing every spirit of fear, in Jesus' name.
11. I release myself from every spirit of confusion and error, in the name of Jesus..
12. Father Lord, lay Your hand of fire upon my memory and give me retentive memory, in the name of Jesus.
13. Lord, keep me diligent in my private preparations.
14. Father, I dedicate all my faculties to You, in the name of Jesus.
15. Let all satanic mechanisms aimed at changing my destiny be frustrated, in the name of Jesus.
16. Let all unprofitable broadcasters of my goodness be silenced, in the name of Jesus.

17. Let every blessing confiscated by witchcraft spirits be released, in the name of Jesus.

18. Let every blessing confiscated by familiar spirits be released, in the name of Jesus.

19. Let every blessing confiscated by ancestral spirits be released, in the name of Jesus.

20. Let every blessing confiscated by envious enemies be released, in the name of Jesus.

21. Let every blessing confiscated by satanic agents be released, in the name of Jesus.

22. Let every blessing confiscated by principalities be released, in the name of Jesus.

23. Let every blessing confiscated by rulers of darkness be released, in the name of Jesus.

24. Let every blessing confiscated by evil powers be released, in the name of Jesus.

25. Let all the blessings confiscated by spiritual wickedness in the heavenly places be released, in the name of Jesus.

26. Let all demonic reverse gears installed to hinder my progress be roasted, in the name of Jesus.

27. Anointing of the overcomer, fall upon me, in the name of Jesus.

28. I claim my divine promotion today, in the name of Jesus.

29. Thank God for answers to your prayer.

POWER TO RETAIN
Isa. 65:23

- *For those suffering from miscarriages.*
- *For those who face spiritual attacks during pregnancy.*

Not only does God want you to possess your possessions, but He also wants you to retain all the blessings He has bestowed upon you. The only way to make your blessing to be permanent is to continue to be unrelenting in prayer.

Psalm 147:13: "For he has strengthened the bars of thy gates; he has blessed thy children within thee."

One of the blessings of serving God is that there will be no miscarriage or barrenness in the land. "And ye shall serve the Lord your God, and He shall bless thy bread, and thy water; and I will take sickness away from the midst of thee. There shall nothing cast their young, nor be barren, in thy land: the number of thy days will I fulfil" (Exodus 23:25,26).

God has many blessings for His children but practically all of them are hinged on obedience and service. God says He will strengthen the bars of your gate. This means that the Lord Himself will strengthen the entrance, the door of your womb. God will fortify your womb so that you can carry your baby nine months and be delivered safely. God says, "Apart from fortifying your womb, I will bless your children within you." This means that the baby you are carrying in your womb will not die but live to declare the works of God. To bless means to prosper. God will cause the baby in your womb to prosper, to live.

Our God is faithful! Psalm 34:5 says, "They looked unto Him and were lightened: and their faces were not ashamed" Who are you looking unto? The doctor, the specialist or your pastor? Change your focus today. Look unto Jesus, the author and the finisher of your faith (Hebrews 12:2). You will not be ashamed, He will lighten your face with joy. At the appointed time He will give you your Isaac. You will indeed laugh!

• CONFESSIONS

Ps. 31:2: *Bow down thine ear to me; deliver me speedily: be thou my strong rock, for an house of defence to save me.*

Ps. 143:7: *Hear me speedily, O LORD: my spirit faileth: hide not thy face from me, lest I be like unto them that go down into the pit.*

Isa. 58:8: *Then shall thy light break forth as the morning, and thine health shall spring forth speedily: and thy righteousness shall go before thee; the glory of the LORD shall be thy rereward.*

Luke 18:8: *I tell you that he will avenge them speedily.*

Ps. 102:2: *Hide not thy face from me in the day when I am in trouble; incline thine ear unto me: in the day when I call answer me speedily.*

Jer. 1:12: *Then said the LORD unto me, Thou hast well seen: for I will hasten my word to perform it.*

Jer. 29:11: *For I know the thoughts that I think toward you, saith the LORD, thoughts of peace, and not of evil, to give you an expected end.*

Ps. 56:9: *When I cry unto thee, then shall mine enemies turn back: this I know; for God is for me.*

Mal. 4:2: *But unto you that fear my name shall the Sun of righteousness arise with healing in his wings; and ye shall go forth, and grow up as calves of the stall.*

Gal. 3:13-14: *Christ hath redeemed us from the curse of the law, being made a curse for us: for it is written, Cursed is every one that hangeth on a tree: That the blessing of Abraham might come on the Gentiles through Jesus Christ; that we might receive the promise of the Spirit through faith.*

Col. 2:14-15: *Blotting out the handwriting of ordinances that was against us, which was contrary to us, and took it out of the way, nailing it to his cross; And having spoiled principalities and powers, he made a shew of them openly, triumphing over them in it.*

Matt. 8:17: *That it might be fulfilled which was spoken by Esaias the prophet, saying, Himself took our infirmities, and bare our sicknesses.*

Rom. 16:20: *And the God of peace shall bruise Satan under your feet* *shortly. The grace of our Lord Jesus Christ be with you. Amen.*

Matt. 3:10: *And now also the axe is laid unto the root of the trees: therefore every tree which bringeth not forth good fruit is hewn down, and cast into the fire. Every tree that bringeth not forth good fruit is hewn down, and cast into the fire.*

1 Jn. 3:8b: *. . . For this purpose the Son of God was manifested, that he might destroy the works of the devil.*

2 Tim. 4:18: *And the Lord shall deliver me from every evil work, and will preserve me unto his heavenly kingdom: to whom be glory for ever and ever. Amen.*

Jesus is Lord over my spirit, soul and body for the word of God tells me that at the name of Jesus every knee shall bow. I can do all things through Christ who strengthens me. The Lord is my shepherd, I shall not want. Jesus has delivered me from the powers of darkness and has translated me into the kingdom of His Dear Son. In Jesus I have redemption through His shed blood and also forgiveness of sins. Jesus has blotted out the handwriting of ordinances that was against me which was contrary to me, and took it out of the way nailing it to His cross. I am the body of Christ. I am redeemed from the curse because Jesus bore my physical and spiritual diseases in His body. I have the mind of Christ and hold the thoughts, feelings and purposes of His heart.

• PRAISE WORSHIP

1. Thank the Lord for His power to deliver from any form of bondage.
2. I confess the sins of my ancestors (list them).
3. Ask the Lord for forgiveness.
4. Ask the Lord to forgive those you do not know about.
5. Let the power in the blood of Jesus separate me from the sins of my ancestors, in the name of Jesus.
6. I renounce any evil dedication placed upon my life, in Jesus' name.

7. I break every evil edict and ordination, in the name of Jesus.

8. I renounce and loose myself from every negative dedication placed upon my life, in the name of Jesus.

9. I command all demons associated with the dedication to leave now, in the name of Jesus Christ.

10. I take authority over all the associated curses, in Jesus' name.

11. Lord, cancel the evil consequences of any broken demonic promise or dedication.

12. I take authority over all the curses emanating from broken dedication, in the name of Jesus.

13. I command all demons associated with any evil parental vow and dedication to depart from me now, in the name of Jesus.

14. Ask the Lord do separate you completely from all the sins of your forefathers by the precious blood of Jesus.

15. Ask the Lord to remove the curse if it was from Him.

16. Command the curse of . . . to be broken, in the name of Jesus.

17. Apply the oil and command all demons associated with the curse to leave at once, in the name of Jesus.

18. Command any demon afflicting the . . . or causing . . . to leave at once, in the name of Jesus.

19. Ask the Lord to heal all the damages done.

20. I dismiss and disband from my heart every thought, image or picture of failure in these matters, in Jesus' name.

21. I reject every spirit of doubt, fear and discouragement, in the name of Jesus.

22. I cancel all ungodly delays to the manifestations of my miracles, in the name of Jesus.

23. Let the angels of the living God roll away every stone of hindrance to the manifestation of my breakthroughs, in the name of Jesus.

24. O Lord, hasten Your word to perform it in every department of my life.

25. O Lord, avenge me of my adversaries speedily.

26. I refuse to agree with the enemies of my progress, in the mighty name of Jesus.

(Pray the next four prayer points according to the level of your faith)

27. O Lord, I desire breakthroughs concerning . . . today, in the name of Jesus.

28. O Lord, I desire breakthroughs concerning . . . this week, in the name of Jesus.

29. O Lord, I desire breakthroughs concerning . . . this month, in the name of Jesus.

30. O Lord, I desire breakthroughs concerning . . . this year, in the name of Jesus.

31. Let there be turbulence, re-arrangement, revision, re-organisation and re-routing of situations and circumstances in order to give path to my desired miracles, in the name of Jesus.

32. Let every hole present in the container of my life be mended, in the name of Jesus.

33. I bind, plunder and render to nothing every anti-testimony, anti-miracle and anti-prosperity forces, in Jesus' name.

34. The God who answered by fire and the God of Elijah, answer me by fire, in the name of Jesus.

35. The God who answered Moses speedily at the Red Sea, answer me by fire, in the name of Jesus.

36. The God who changed the lot of Jabez, answer me by fire, in the name of Jesus.

37. The God who quickeneth and calleth those things that be not as if they are, answer me by fire, in the name of Jesus.

38. I apply the blood of Jesus on my spirit, soul, body and my womb.

39. Let the fire of God saturate my womb, in the name of Jesus.

40. Let every evil design against my life be completely nullified, in the name of Jesus.

41. Let all evil labels fashioned by the camp of the enemy against my life be rubbed off by the blood of Jesus.

Sing this song: "Holy Ghost fire, fire fall on me {2x}, like the day of Pentecost, fire fall on me" with full concentration and in faith.

42. I release myself from every curse issued against my child-bearing, in the name of Jesus.

43. I renounce and release myself from every covenant of unprofitable lateness in child-bearing, in the name of Jesus.

44. I break myself loose from every soul-tie contrary to child-bearing, in the name of Jesus.

45. I cast out every spirit of death from my womb, in Jesus' name.

46. Let every power attracting attackers to me during pregnancy be exposed and be destroyed, in the name of Jesus.

47. I break myself loose from every spirit of *lateness*, in Jesus' name.

48. O Lord, perfect Your good works in my life.

49. I reject every curse of miscarriage and pre-mature birth in my family, in the name of Jesus.

50. I declare that there shall be no barrenness in my life, in Jesus' name.

51. Lord, remove the evil effect of anything that is unclean or destructive that has entered into my reproductive organs, in the name of Jesus.

52. I break any curse contrary to child-bearing transferred to me by any boyfriend, in the name of Jesus.

53. I arrest every hormonal problem, in the name of Jesus.

54. Let the walls of my womb be purged by divine fire , in Jesus' name.

55. Let all evil forces speaking defeat against my marriage be silenced, in the name of Jesus.

I SHALL NOT BE MOVED
Psalm 62:2

- When enemies plan to move you away from a place of blessing.
- When you feel the effect of satanic bombardment upon your life.
- When you are being pressurized by the enemy to flee from your resting place.

One with God is majority. One with God would chase thousands, he shall remain impregnable to the storms and tempests of life. Your coming to the side of the Lord means you shall never be moved and you shall stand against every odd situation.

Psalm 125:1: *"They that trust in the Lord shall be as Mount Zion, which cannot be removed but abideth forever."*

Trusting in God brings divine stability. When we trust God we become stable and it will be impossible for the devil to gain the upper hand in our lives.

King Hezekiah trusted God and he was not moved by the boasting and threats of the King of Assyria. II Kings 18: 5-7 has this to say about Hezekiah: "He trusted in the Lord God of Israel; so that after him was none like him among the Kings of Judah, nor any that were before him. For he clave to the Lord and departed not from following Him, but kept His commandments, which the Lord commanded Moses. And the Lord was with him; and he prospered withersoever he went forth:"

The three ingredients of divine trust as seen in the life of King Hezekiah are: (i) To cleave to God; to hold firm (ii) Not to backslide; Hezekiah did not stop following God. He did not depart from the faith. (iii) He kept the commandments of God.

Three blessings followed: (i) God was with Him. When God is with us, the enemy cannot overcome us. (ii) The Lord prospered Him in all areas of his life. (iii) The Lord gave him victory over the Assyrians just as He will give you victory over every satanic bombardment and boasting.

Hezekiah did not remove his focus from God. With each threat He went to the house of the Lord and sought God. Eventually one angel destroyed the whole Assyrian army.

God will give us peace (Isaiah 26:3). This peace will keep us standing and unmoved by satanic bombardment. "In returning and rest shall ye be saved; in quietness and in confidence shall be your strength" (Isaiah 30:15).

Let us return to the Lord, let us be still in His presence and know that He is God (Psalm 46:10). Then we will be like Mount Zion which cannot be removed.

• CONFESSIONS

Ps. 125:1: *They that trust in the LORD shall be as mount Zion, which cannot be removed, but abideth for ever.*

Rom. 9:33: *As it is written, Behold, I lay in Sion a stumbling stone and rock of offence: and whosoever believeth on him shall not be ashamed.*

Rev. 13:10: *He that leadeth into captivity shall go into captivity: he that killeth with the sword must be killed with the sword. Here is the patience and the faith of the saints.*

Isa. 50:7: *For the Lord GOD will help me; therefore shall I not be confounded: therefore have I set my face like a flint, and I know that I shall not be ashamed.*

• PRAISE WORSHIP

1. Holy Spirit, do not leave my house desolate, in the name of Jesus.
2. O Lord, renew my mind in Your word.
3. O Lord, give me the power to embarrass my enemies.
4. Every spiritual coffin I have constructed for my self, be destroyed by the fire of God, in the name of Jesus.
5. O Lord Jesus, choose me for miracle every day of my life.
6. O Lord, speak Your word of power into my situation.
7. O Lord, deliver me from the mouth of the lion.
8. O Lord, forgive me for bringing problems into my life.
9. O Lord, empower me to dwell in Noah's Ark.
10. O Lord, empower me to prosper.
11. O Lord, remove from my life anything that will make me to miss the rapture.
12. Let the blood of Jesus and the fire of the Holy Ghost, purge out of my life, every sin that will take me to hell fire, in the name of Jesus.
13. O Lord, empower me to dwell in safety.
14. I vomit every food of sin in my life, in the name of Jesus.

15. O Lord, speak life and fire into my life today.

16. I swallow the pill of aggressive resistance against sin and unrighteousness, in the name of Jesus.

17. Lord Jesus, pray for me so that I will not be winnowed like the chaff of wheat by the devil.

18. O Lord, bring help me from above and disgrace my oppressors.

19. I move from minimum to maximum for the glory of God, in the name of Jesus.

20. I paralyse every satanic opposition to my progress, in Jesus' name.

21. All my dragons shall be disgraced, in the name of Jesus.

22. I destroy the works of the destroyer upon my life, in Jesus' name.

23. Every wicked tree growing in my foundation, be uprooted now, in the name of Jesus.

24. I break every egg that the serpent has laid in any department of my life, in the name of Jesus.

25. Every serpentine and scorpion power militating against my life, be disgraced, in the name of Jesus.

26. O Lord, let all the serpents and scorpions assigned against me begin to fight themselves, in the name of Jesus.

27. Every serpent sent to destroy me, return to your sender, in the name of Jesus.

28. Every dumb and deaf spirit, begin to loose your hold upon my life now, in the name of Jesus.

29. My spiritual strength sapped by the serpent, receive divine touch of God and be restored, in the name of Jesus.

30. You serpent, loose your grip upon my spiritual strength, in the name of Jesus.

31. Every pollution done to my spiritual life and health by the serpent, be cleansed by the blood of Jesus, in the name of Jesus.

32. Every serpentine manipulation of my health, be frustrated and be rendered impotent, in the name of Jesus.

33. All you serpents, I command you to vomit my prosperity, health, marriage, finances and spiritual strength that you have swallowed, in the mighty name of Jesus.

BRINGING FORTH
Isa. 66:9

- *For miraculous conception.*
- *For defeating anti-pregnancy spirits.*

As a woman would experience pain before she brings forth, so you will undergo travails and pains in the form of prayer and fasting with violent faith before your miracles can materialise.

Isaiah 54:1: *"Sing, O barren, thou that didst not bear, break forth into singing, and cry aloud, thou that didst not travail with child: for more are the children of the desolate than the children of the married wife, saith the Lord."*

The question we need to ask is what kind of songs the barren should sing and not why the barren should sing. I believe God wants the barren to sing two songs.

1. The high praises of God: Ps. 149: 6-9:
- to execute vengeance on the heathen
- punishments on the people
- bind the kings (strongmen) with chains
- bind their nobles with iron
- to execute the written judgement, i.e.: "There shall not be male or female barren among you" (Deut. 7:14).

2. Songs of deliverance: Ps. 32;7: "Thou shalt preserve me from trouble; thou shalt compass me about with songs of deliverance."

Singing is a very important weapon in spiritual warfare. Jehosaphat (2 Chron. 20), overcame three armies by singing praise songs to God. All his people were singing was, "Praise the Lord for his mercy endureth forever." The mercy they desired was shown unto them. God gave them the victory. He will show you the mercy you desire. He will cause you to conceive and bring forth children.

Acts 16 records that Paul and Silas sang to God when they were in prison. All of a sudden there was a great earthquake and all their chains and bands fell off. As you begin to sing to God sincerely, all the yoke and bondage on your life will fall off.

The second principle demonstrated in our working Scripture is to cry aloud to God. Jabez cried out and God heard him. Hannah cried out and God opened His book of remembrance and Hannah had six children, four sons and two daughters (1 Samuel 1;2).

With high praises of God and songs of deliverance in your mouth, cry aloud to God using these prayer points. God will meet you at your point of need. He will give you godly male and female children.

● CONFESSIONS

Deut. 7:14-15: *Thou shalt be blessed above all people: there shall not be male or female barren among you, or among your cattle. And the LORD will take away from thee all sickness, and will put none of the evil diseases of Egypt, which thou knowest, upon thee; but will lay them upon all them that hate thee.*

Deut. 28:4, 11: *Blessed shall be the fruit of thy body, and the fruit of thy ground, and the fruit of thy cattle, the increase of thy kine, and the flocks of thy sheep. And the LORD shall make thee plenteous in goods, in the fruit of thy body, and in the fruit of thy cattle, and in the fruit of thy ground, in the land which the LORD sware unto thy fathers to give thee.*

Exod. 23:26: *There shall nothing cast their young, nor be barren, in thy land: the number of thy days I will fulfil.*

Ps. 115:14: *The LORD shall increase you more and more, you and your children.*

Ps. 128:3: *Thy wife shall be as a fruitful vine by the sides of thine house: thy children like olive plants round about thy table.*

1 Tim. 2:15: *Notwithstanding she shall be saved in childbearing, if they continue in faith and charity and holiness with sobriety.*

I Jn. 4:4: *Ye are of God, little children, and have overcome them: because greater is he that is in you, than he that is in the world.*

Col. 2:14-15: *Blotting out the handwriting of ordinances that was against us, which was contrary to us, and took it out of the way, nailing it to his cross; And having spoiled principalities and powers, he made a shew of them openly, triumphing over them in it.*

Phil. 4:19: *But my God shall supply all your need according to his riches in glory by Christ Jesus.*

Gal. 3:13-14: *Christ hath redeemed us from the curse of the law, being made a curse for us: for it is written, Cursed is every one that hangeth on a tree: That the blessing of Abraham might come on the Gentiles through Jesus Christ; that we might receive the promise of the Spirit through faith.*

Ps. 4:1-8: *Hear me when I call, O God of my righteousness: thou hast enlarged me when I was in distress; have mercy upon me, and hear my prayer. O ye sons of men, how long will ye turn my glory into shame? how long will ye love vanity, and seek after leasing? But know that the LORD hath set apart him that is godly for himself: the LORD will hear when I call unto him. Stand in awe, and sin not: commune with your own heart upon your bed, and be still. Offer the sacrifices of righteousness, and put your trust in the LORD. There be many that say, Who will shew us any good? LORD, lift thou up the light of thy countenance upon us. Thou hast put gladness in my heart, more than in the time that their corn and their wine increased. I will both lay me down in peace, and sleep: for thou, LORD, only makest me dwell in safety.*

● **PRAISE WORSHIP**

Worship God with the song: "How great Thou art".

Ask the Lord to forgive you any sin that would stand against your prayers.

While laying your hands on your womb and breasts, say the following prayers aggressively.

1. I withdraw everything the enemy has stolen from my life, in the name of Jesus.

2. I cancel all visions, dreams, words, curses contrary to conception and child bearing in my life, in the name of Jesus.

3. I command every negative imagination against my child-bearing to be cast down, in the name of Jesus.

4. Lord, let Your healing power flow into every area of my body relevant to conception and child bearing.

5. God who quickeneth the dead, quicken everything concerning my conception and child bearing, in the name of Jesus.

6. I bind, plunder and render to naught, every spiritual activity contrary to the peace of my home, in the name of Jesus.

7. I chase back all stubborn pursuers and cut off every unprofitable family covenant, in the name of Jesus.

8. O Lord, let this month be our month of miracle.

9. Let my womb be purged by the fire of the Holy Spirit, in the name of Jesus.

10. Let all evil hands be removed from the affairs of my life, in the name of Jesus.

11. I cover myself with the blood of Jesus.

12. I break every covenant with any sexual demon, in Jesus' name.

13. I rebuke the spirit of the dog and cast it out of my ways, in the name of Jesus.

14. Place a wall of fire around yourself.

15. Pray that ministering angels will surround you.

16. I render myself impenetrable to any occasional or regular anti-pregnancy spirit, in the name of Jesus. (Put one hand on your head, the other one on your womb.)

17. Let the fire of God purge the whole of my body system and remove impurities, in the name of Jesus.

18. I break every covenant of late child-bearing with the fire of God and blood of Jesus.

19. I renounce and denounce every bad spirit using my imaginations against me, in the name of Jesus.

20. Breathe in the fire of God and breathe out negative things.

CUTTING OFF EVIL LINKAGE
2Chr. 20:35-37

- *To break evil linkage and satanic bands.*

You cannot tell whether or not your problem results from your ancestral linkage with evil powers. This is why you must not leave any stone unturned if you don't want to miss your breakthrough.

2 Corinthians 6:17: *"Wherefore come out from among them and be ye separate, saith the Lord, and touch not the unclean thing and I will receive you."*

Many of us had been wrongly programmed before we knew the Lord. All those negative things that had been programmed into our lives have to go. The Bible says in Romans 12:2, "Be not conformed to the world but be transformed by the renewing of your mind." Some people have incisions and satanic labels on their bodies - linking them to evil family altars and rivers. These satanic linkages have to be cut off before the Lord can accept you. There is no fellowship between light and darkness.

When a baby is born it is separated from its mother when the placenta is cut off. In the same way when you get born again you have to severe yourself from every evil linkage with the world and with your past life. These include family traditions, customs, evil streams and altars that are contrary to the teachings of God.

- **CONFESSION**

Isa. 49:24-26: Shall the prey be taken from the mighty, or the lawful captive delivered? But thus saith the LORD, Even the captives of the mighty shall be taken away, and the prey of the terrible shall be delivered: for I will contend with him that contendeth with thee, and I will save thy children. And I will feed them that oppress thee with their own flesh; and they shall be drunken with their own blood, as with sweet wine: and all flesh shall know that I the LORD am thy Saviour and thy Redeemer, the mighty One of Jacob.

• PRAISE WORSHIP

1. I cut off every link and label of demonic oppression, in Jesus' name.

2. Let my God arise and put to flight every mind-control spirit, in the name of Jesus.

3. I command the spirit of death and hell to loose its hold upon my life, in the name of Jesus.

4. Let every material containing my inscription be spiritually withdrawn and their negative effects cancelled, in Jesus' name.

5. I command every organ of my body to receive the fire of the Holy Ghost and the blood of Jesus.

6. Every 'imagination-corrupter', be bound and loose your hold upon my life, in the name of Jesus.

7. Let all the rejecters of goodness, past, present and future, be bound and let them release me, in the name of Jesus.

8. I reject every garment of confusion, in the name of Jesus.

9. Ask for the anointing for spiritual knowledge, in Jesus' name.

10. The devil will not replace me in my service for the Lord, in the name of Jesus.

11. I reject and renounce every evil ordination of 'lateness in goodness', in the name of Jesus.

12. I break every demonic circle in my life, in the name of Jesus.

13. I command every evil spiritual clock to be destroyed with Holy Ghost fire, in the name of Jesus.

14. Anoint your eyelids and command every link attaching you to any evil clock or circle to be destroyed, in the name of Jesus.

15. Command spiritual label and stamp to be cleaned off with the blood of Jesus.

16. Every curse of bad circle in my life, break, in the name of Jesus.

17. Thank God for answers to your prayer.

DELIVERANCE FROM SPIRIT OF RELIGION

2 Cor. 11:3-4

- *To break free from spirits or religion.*
- *Release from the bondage of Babylon.*
- *Breaking the bondage of Roman Catholicism.*

Religion is the brainchild of the devil. It is aimed at confusing mankind concerning God's original plan and purpose to save, through our Lord Jesus Christ, from eternal perdition. Therefore shun this terrible spirit of doom today.

Matthew 7:21: *"Not everyone that saith unto me, Lord Lord, shall enter into the kingdom of heaven; but he that doeth the will of my father which is in heaven."*

God created the world and said that everyone that would come into it must be born of a woman. In the same way God has decreed the way man will enter the kingdom of heaven. Jesus is the only way to God. *"Jesus saith unto him, I am the way the truth and the life: no man cometh unto the father but by me"* (John 14:6).

Man has tried many other things but there is no way there. These prayer points are for those under the bondage and control of religious spirits.

If, for instance, I want to go to Ibadan and I get on to the road leading to Badagry, all I will end up doing is to get farther and farther away from my destination. Before I can get to Ibadan, I need to do a 'U-turn' and get on the right road.

Many seek to know God, but are going through ways He has not prescribed. Before you can really see God, you must repent and accept the sacrifice of Jesus. Pray these prayer points for deliverance from religious spirits or to deliver others.

● CONFESSION

Isa. 52:2: *Shake thyself from the dust; arise, and sit down, O Jerusalem: loose thyself from the bands of thy neck, O captive daughter of Zion.*

● PRAISE WORSHIP

1. Father, I confess that, in the past, I held unforgiveness, and sometimes bitterness and resentment in my heart against certain people who hurt or disappointed me.

   I now recognise this as a sin and confess it as sin, for You have said in Your word that if we confess our sin, You are faithful and just to forgive us our sin and to cleanse us of all unrighteousness (1 John 1:9).

   I do now forgive the following people I can remember, who have hurt or disappointed me. (Mention names of those who come to your mind.) I now freely forgive all these people and ask You to bless them if they are living. I also forgive myself for all my many faults and failures, for You have freely forgiven me.

   Thank You Father for freedom from the load of unforgiveness, bitterness and resentment, in the name of Jesus.

2. Father, I confess to You, that in the past, through ignorance, through curiosity or wilfully, I came into contact with certain religious activities. I now recognise this as sin and confess it as sin. I claim forgiveness, in the name of Jesus.

   Specifically, I do confess as sin and renounce all contacts which I have had with the following religious spirits. (Here, mention any thing in this category with which you have dabbled into or become involved with e.g. Babylonian spirits from Roman Catholic system, Catholic baptism, etc.)

3. I also renounce and confess as sin any oath which I have taken by any false god and any idolatrous practices in which I have been involved.

4. Satan, I rebuke you, in the name of Jesus, and I am closing any door which I or my ancestors may have opened to you and your demons, in the name of Jesus.

5. I renounce satan and all his demons, I declare them my enemies and

I command them to get out of my life completely, in the name of Jesus.

6. In the name of Jesus Christ, I now claim deliverance from any and all evil spirits which may be in me (Joel 2:28). Once and for all, I close the door in my life to all occult practices and command all related spirits to leave me now, in the name of Jesus.

7. I break every curse of family destruction, in the name of Jesus.

8. I release myself from the hold of any religious spirit strongman, in the name of Jesus.

9. I command all spirits of religion to loose their hold upon my life, in the name of Jesus.

10. Call the spirit you do not desire in your life by name. Then issue the command firmly and repeatedly that the spirits must come out, in the name of the Lord Jesus.

   Pray as follows: You spirit of . . .,

   1) Legalism
   2) Externalism
   3) Religious murder
   4) Lust and ambition for recognition
   5) Condemnation
   6) St. Ann
   7) St. Elizabeth
   8) Lust and ambition for position
   9) Lust and ambition for power and control in religious matters
   10) False love
   11) False gifts
   12) False tongues
   13) False compassion
   14) False prophecy
   15) False word of wisdom
   16) Religious dominance
   17) Self-serving
   18) Selfishness
   19) Greed
   20) No love
   21) No compassion
   22) Pretense
   23) Robbing
   24) Cheating
   25) Religious coldness
   26) False oaths
   27) Blockages
   28) Rigid Theology Construction
   29) Nimrod
   30) Semiramis

31) Tammuz
32) Hatred of the truth
33) Idolatry
34) Catholic baptism
35) Prayer to the saints
36) One True Church
37) One holy priesthood
38) Mass
39) Holy Eucharist
40) Adoration of the Most
41) Sorrowful mysteries of the Rosary
42) Joyful mysteries of the Rosary
43) Glorious mysteries of the Rosary
44) Holy Mother Church
45) Authority of the Pope
46) Infallibility of the Pope
47) Fear of the priest and nun
48) Confession to priest
49) Holy water
50) Sacred Heart of Jesus
51) Holy family
52) Stations of the Cross
53) Rosary
54) Crucifix
55) Candles
56) Blessings of the throat
57) St. Blaise
58) Fear of hell
59) Fear of purgatory
60) Guilt
61) Condemnation
62) Unworthiness
63) Good works
64) Mind control
65) Holy orders
66) Extreme unction
67) Confirmation
68) Sacraments
69) Benedictions
70) Human bone relics on the altars
71) Genuflecting
72) Feast days of the saints
73) Votive candles
74) Witchcraft control
75) Forced celibacy
76) Poverty
77) Religious medals
78) Sacrifice of the mass
79) Angel of good counsel
80) Sign of the cross
81) Spiritual adultery
82) Indulgence
83) Infant of plague
84) Religious hatred
85) Worship and veneration of Mary
86) Immaculate conception of Mary
87) Sacred heart of Mary
88) Immaculate heart of Mary
89) Mary Queen of Heaven
90) Mariolatry

91) May altars in honour of Mary

92) Our Lady of Lourdes

93) Our Lady of the Snows

94) Our Lady of Merodes

95) Our Lady of Fatima

96) Our Lady of Quadalupe

97) Queen of Martyrs

98) Queen of Peace

99) Mary

100) Star of the sea

101) Novenas

102) Scapulars

103) Moloch

104) Spiritual blindness

105) Spiritual deafness

106) Feast of Peace (Christmas)

107) Feast of Life (Easter)

108) Lent

109) Destruction of the family priesthood

110) Passion spirits of agony and ecstasy

111) Passing children through the fire

112) Babylonian spirits from the Roman Catholic system

113) Dedication to the priesthood or to be a nun

114) Joseph, guardian and protector of Mary and Jesus

115) Ashes on ash Wednesday

116) St. Therese

117) Little flower

118) St. Christopher

119) St. Jude

120) St. Catherine, etc.

Come out of my body, soul, spirit, memory and mind, in the name of Jesus. (Each of these things is backed by specific demon spirit. Do not lump everything together. Command each one to go out at a time. You must be specific if you have to be free.)

11. I loose myself from you, in the name of Jesus, and I command you to leave me right now, in the name of Jesus.

FOR SUPERNATURAL BREAKTHROUGHS

Isa. 64:1

- *For the salvation of relatives who are resisting the gospel.*
- *To break anti-gospel bondage.*
- *Personal, for purity and deliverance.*

Praying to achieve divine and supernatural breakthrough is not a child's play; you should do it with all the stamina you have and with a readiness to surrender all to God.

John 3:16: *"For God so loved the world, that He gave his only begotten son, that whosoever believeth on him should not perish but have everlasting life."*

The greatest miracle that can happen in anyone's life is the salvation of that soul. The day a person is translated from the kingdom of darkness into the kingdom of God' dear Son, we need to rejoice with that person. Indeed that is the greatest break-through anyone can receive.

Hebrews 9:27 "And as it is appointed unto men once to die, but after this judgement." Many live as if after this life there is nothing else. Beloved, after this life we are living, we will enter into eternity. We will spend eternity in either heaven or in hell. My question to you is, "Where will you spend eternity, in heaven or in hell?"

If you accept Jesus into your life to be your Lord and personal Saviour and you live a holy life, you will go to heaven. If you reject Christ, you will go to hell. Call on the Lord and let Him save your soul. Perhaps you have loved ones who are not saved; you need to begin to intercede for them fervently. If you don't have a burden to pray for lost souls, ask God to give you a burden for the unsaved. You need to break the hold of the powers of darkness that is preventing your family members and friends to accept Christ. As you stand in the gap, God will cause them to turn unto Him and break every stronghold of the enemy in their lives.

• CONFESSION

Ezek. 33:11: *Say unto them, As I live, saith the Lord GOD, I have no pleasure in the death of the wicked; but that the wicked turn from his way and live: turn ye, turn ye from your evil ways; for why will ye die, O house of Israel?*

• PRAISE WORSHIP

1. Thank the Lord because it is not His will that any should perish.

2. Father, in the name of Jesus, give unto . . ., the spirits of wisdom and revelation in the knowledge of You.

3. Let every stronghold of the enemy barricading the mind of . . ., from receiving the Lord be pulled down, in the name of Jesus.

4. Let all hindrances coming between the heart of . . . and the gospel be melted away by the fire of the Holy Spirit.

5. In Jesus' name, I bind the strongman attached to the life of . . ., keeping him from receiving Jesus Christ as his Lord and Saviour.

6. Lord, build a hedge of thorns around . . ., so that he turns to the Lord.

7. In the name of Jesus, I break the curse placed on . . ., binding him from receiving the Lord.

8. You spirit of death and hell, release . . ., in the name of Jesus.

9. Every desire of the enemy on the soul of . . ., will not prosper, in the name of Jesus.

10. I bind every spirit of mind blindness in the life of . . ., in the name of Jesus.

11. Spirit of bondage, lukewarmness and perdition, release . . ., in the name of Jesus.

12. I bind the strongman shielding . . ., from receiving the gospel, in the name of Jesus.

13. Father, let spiritual blindness be erased from the life of . . ., in the name of Jesus.

14. I come against the powers of darkness blinding and holding . . ., back from receiving the gospel, in the name of Jesus.

15. I command you spirit of the power of the air to loose your hold on . . . so that he will be free to accept Jesus as Lord and Saviour, in the name of Jesus.

16. I tear down and smash every stronghold of deception keeping . . ., in the enemy's camp, in the name of Jesus.

17. Let . . . come from the kingdom of darkness and into the kingdom of light, in the name of Jesus.

18. Lord, let Your plan and purpose for the life of . . . prevail.

19. Let every evil imagination against me wither from the source, in the name of Jesus.

20. Those laughing me to scorn shall witness my testimony, in the name of Jesus.

21. Let my point of ridicule be converted to a source of miracle, in the name of Jesus.

22. Let all powers sponsoring evil decisions against me be disgraced, in the name of Jesus.

23. Let the stronghold of every spirit of Korah, Dathan and Abiram militating against me be smashed to pieces, in the name of Jesus.

24. Let every spirit of Balaam hired to curse me fall after the order of Balaam, in the name of Jesus.

25. Let every spirit of Sanballat and Tobiah planning evil against me receive the stones of fire, in the name of Jesus.

26. Let every spirit of Egypt fall after the order of Pharaoh, in the name of Jesus.

27. Let every spirit of Herod be disgraced, in the name of Jesus.

28. Let every spirit of Goliath receive the stones of fire, in the name of Jesus.

29. Let every spirit of Pharaoh fall into the Red Sea of their own making, in the name of Jesus.

30. Let all satanic manipulations aimed at changing my destiny be frustrated, in the name of Jesus.

31. Let all unprofitable broadcasters of my goodness be silenced, in the name of Jesus.

32. Let all leaking bags and pockets be sealed up, in Jesus' name.

33. Let all evil monitoring eyes fashioned against me be blind, in the name of Jesus.

34. I command all demonic reverse gears installed to hinder my progress to be roasted, in the name of Jesus.

35. Let all evil advice given against my favour crash and disintegrate, in the name of Jesus.

36. You devourers, vanish from my labour, in the name of Jesus.

37. I loose myself from every satanic bondage, in the name of Jesus.

38. I cancel the power of all curses upon my head, in Jesus' name.

39. I command every spiritual contamination in my life to receive cleansing by the blood of Jesus, in the name of Jesus.

40. Let the brush of the Lord scrub out every dirt in my spiritual pipe, in the name of Jesus.

41. Every rusted spiritual pipe in my life, receive wholeness, in the name of Jesus.

42. I command every power eating up my spiritual pipe to be roasted, in the name of Jesus.

43. I command every blockage in my spiritual pipe to be removed, in the name of Jesus.

44. I command the hole in my spiritual pipe to be closed, in the name of Jesus.

45. Lord, ignite my calling with Your fire.

46. I receive heavenly flushing in my spiritual pipe, in Jesus' name.

47. Every evil spiritual padlock and evil chain hindering my spiritual growth, be roasted, in the name of Jesus.

48. I rebuke every spirit of spiritual deafness and blindness in my life, in the name of Jesus.

49. I bind the strongman behind my spiritual blindness and deafness and paralyze his operations in my life, in the name of Jesus.

50. I anoint my eyes and my ears with the blood of Jesus.

51. O Lord, restore my spiritual eyes and ears, in the name of Jesus.

52. Lord, anoint my eyes and my ears that they may see and hear wondrous things from heaven.

53. I send the fire of God to my eyes and ears to melt away satanic deposit, in the name of Jesus.

54. In the name of Jesus, I capture every power behind my spiritual blindness and deafness.

55. Let my spiritual sight and ear drum receive healing, in Jesus' name.

56. I will not loose my calling, in the name of Jesus.

57. You the enemies of the gospel in my life, be paralyzed, in the name of Jesus.

58. I reject every spiritual pollution, in the name of Jesus.

59. Lord, put into my hand the gift that will elevate my calling, in the name of Jesus.

60. O Lord, let the anointing of the Holy Spirit break every yoke of backward movements in my life, in the name of Jesus.

61. I reject the spirit of the tail, I choose the spirit of the head, in the name of Jesus.

62. I reject any demonic limitation to my progress, in Jesus' name.

63. Lord, give unto me, the key to good success, so that anywhere I go, the doors of good success will be opened unto me.

64. O Lord, let the anointing to excel in my spiritual and physical life fall on me, in the name of Jesus.

65. I reject the anointing of non-achievement in my handy work, in the name of Jesus.

66. Let all those circulating my name for evil, be disgraced, in the name of Jesus.

67. Let all evil friends make mistakes that would expose them, in the name of Jesus.

68. I refuse to wear the garment of tribulation and sorrow, in the name of Jesus.

69. O Lord, let the spirit that flees from sin incubate my life.

70. O Lord, produce in me the power of self-control and gentleness.

71. I loose . . . from the bondage the powers of darkness are putting on him / her by the blood of the Lord Jesus Christ.

72. By the blood of Jesus, I cancel and render null and void all commands issued by the powers of darkness in . . .'s life.

73. I bind the god of this age and declare he can longer blind . . . in darkness, in the name of Jesus.

74. Father Lord, let Your power draw . . . out of every trap, in the name of Jesus.

75. Let the powers of darkness be confounded and put to shame that seek after . . ., in the name of Jesus.

76. Father Lord, grant . . . opened eyes and ears, understanding heart and grace to be converted and healed, in the name of Jesus.

77. Lord, bring all of . . .'s thoughts captive to the obedience of Christ.

78. Let the hedge of thorns be built around . . . and let the hedge repel all the workers of darkness in his / her life, in Jesus' name.

79 Lord, grant . . . conviction of sin with Godly sorrow to repentance.

80. Thank God for answers to your prayer.

MAKE YOUR WAY PLAIN BEFORE MY FACE

Isa. 30:21

- *To enable you take the right decision on any issue.*
- *To make you know the mind of God on a particular issue.*

There is nothing as beautiful as walking according to the Lord's directives in all areas of your life. Understanding and following the will of God amounts to living a life of heaven on earth.

Colossians 1:9: *"For this cause we also, since the day heard it, do not cease to pray for you, and to desire that ye might be filled with the knowledge of His will in all wisdom and spiritual understanding."*

These prayer points are important for anyone who wants to do exploits in the kingdom of God. It is only the people that know God who will be strong and do exploits (Dan. 11:32). Moses saw God and knew Him intimately. God talked to him like a friend. The Bible says, "God has made known His ways unto Moses, His acts unto the children of Israel" (Ps. 103:7). If we want to know the ways of God, we must seek to know God intimately. Paul says, "That I may know Him, and the power of His resurrection, and the fellowship of His sufferings, being made conformable unto His death" (Phil. 3:10).

When we know God, then His will is revealed to us. When we receive the knowledge of His will we will also need: (i) wisdom which will show us the way we should build (ii) His will to be established.

Prov. 24:3 says: "Through wisdom is an house built, and by understanding it is established." And Paul encourages us not only to ask for His will but to pray for the wisdom to build and the understanding to establish it (Col. 1:9).

As you start this, God will make His way plain before you and give you the wisdom and understanding needed. "And thine ears shall hear a word behind thee, saying, This is the way, walk ye in it, when ye turn to the right hand, and when ye turn to the left" (Isa. 30:21).

● CONFESSIONS

Deut. 29:29: *The secret things belong unto the LORD our God: but those things which are revealed belong unto us and to our children for ever, that we may do all the words of this law.*

Ps. 5:8: *Lead me, O LORD, in thy righteousness because of mine enemies; make thy way straight before my face.*

Ps. 25:14: *The secret of the LORD is with them that fear him; and he will shew them his covenant.*

Dan. 2:22: *He revealeth the deep and secret things: he knoweth what is in the darkness, and the light dwelleth with him.*

Eph. 1:17: *That the God of our Lord Jesus Christ, the Father of glory, may give unto you the spirit of wisdom and revelation in the knowledge of him.*

● PRAISE WORSHIP

1. Thank God for the revelation power of the Holy Spirit.
2. O Lord, give unto me the Spirit of revelation and wisdom in the knowledge of Yourself.
3. O Lord, make Your way plain before my face on this issue.
4. O Lord, remove spiritual cataract from my eyes.
5. O Lord, forgive me for every false motive or thought that has ever been formed in my heart since the day I was born.
6. O Lord, forgive me for any lie that I have ever told against any person, system or organisation.
7. O Lord, deliver me from the bondage and sin of spiritual laziness.
8. O Lord, open up my eyes to see all I should on this issue.
9. O Lord, teach me deep and secret things.
10. O Lord, reveal to me every secret behind any problem that I have.
11. O Lord, bring to light every thing planned against me in darkness.
12. O Lord, ignite and revive my beneficial potentials.
13. O Lord, give me divine wisdom to operate my life.

14. O Lord, let every veil preventing me from having plain spiritual vision be removed.

15. O Lord, give unto me the spirit of revelation and wisdom in the knowledge of You.

16. O Lord, open my spiritual understanding.

17. O Lord, let me know all I should know about this issue.

18. O Lord, reveal to me every secret behind the particular issue, whether beneficial or not.

19. O Lord, remove from me any persistent buried grudges, half-acknowledged enmity against anyone and every other thing that can block my spiritual vision.

20. O Lord, teach me to know that which is worth knowing and love that which is worth loving and to dislike whatsoever is not pleasing to Your eyes.

21. O Lord, make me a vessel capable of knowing Your secret things.

22. Father, in the name of Jesus, I ask to know Your mind about . . . (*slot in the appropriate situation*) situation.

23. Let the spirit of prophesy and revelation fall upon the totality of my being, in the name of Jesus.

24. Holy Spirit, reveal deep and secret things to me about . . ., in the name of Jesus.

25. I bind every demon that pollutes spiritual vision and dreams, in the name of Jesus.

26. Let every dirt blocking my communication pipe with the living God be washed clean with the blood of Jesus, in Jesus' name.

27. I receive power to operate with sharp spiritual eyes that cannot be deceived, in the name of Jesus.

28. Let the glory and the power of the Almighty God, fall upon my life in a mighty way, in the name of Jesus.

29. I remove my name from the book of those who grope and stumble in darkness, in the name of Jesus.

30. Divine revelations, spiritual visions, dreams and information will not become scarce commodities in my life, in the name of Jesus.

31. I drink to the full in the well of salvation and anointing, in the name of Jesus.

32. O God, to whom no secret is hidden, make known unto me whether . . . (mention the name of the thing) is Your choice for me, in the name of Jesus.

33. Let every idol present consciously or unconsciously, in my heart concerning this issue be melted away by the fire of the Holy Spirit, in the name of Jesus.

34. I refuse to fall under the manipulation of the spirits of confusion, in the name of Jesus.

35. I refuse to make foundational mistakes in my decision, in the name of Jesus.

36. Father Lord, guide and direct me in knowing Your mind on this particular issue, in the name of Jesus.

37. I stand against all satanic attachments that may seek to confuse my decision, in the name of Jesus.

38. If . . . (mention the name of the thing) is not for me, O Lord, redirect my steps.

39. I bind the activities of . . . (pick from the list below) in my life, in the name of Jesus.

   - lust
   - ungodly family pressure
   - attachment to the wrong choice
   - spiritual blindness and deafness
   - ungodly impatience
   - ungodly infatuation
   - demonic manipulation in dreams and visions
   - confusing revelations
   - unprofitable advice

40. O God, You who reveals secret things, make known unto me Your choice for me in this issue, in the name of Jesus.

41. Holy Spirit, open my eyes and help me to make the right decision, in the name of Jesus.

42. Thank You Jesus for Your presence and the good testimonies that will follow.

43. Pray in the spirit for at least 15 minutes.

BREAKING THE EVIL FLOW
Numbers 23

- *To cut off every evil hereditary river flowing down from ancestors.*
- *Deliverance from territorial spirits and hereditary bondage.*
- *Cutting off evil bands of family bondage and co-operative curses.*

Israel was able to contain the evil flow of curses determined on them in the wilderness by Baalam, because she was in good relationship with her God. When you are living right with God according to the gospel, your prayer will be powerful enough to prevent any flow of evil into your life.

Romans 8:15: *"For ye have not received the spirit of bondage again to fear; but ye have received the spirit of adoption, whereby we cry Abba Father."*

The day you get born again is the day you receive the power to break every evil yoke and cut off every evil flow. "But as many as received Him, to them gave He power to become sons of God, even to them that believe on His name" (John 1:12). God has given us POWER to become His sons. That means that every satanic flow in your life has to be cut off and destroyed by this power so that you can flow in the Spirit of God and take on the nature of God. Every negative ancestral covenant and inherited bondage has to break. We have a new Father! God is our father (Matthew 23:9).

Have you been told that your genotype is SS? Then ask for divine flow of blood to transfuse your blood so that the evil flow will be broken. God can change your genotype from SS to AA. The adopted son has the same rights and privileges as the son born into the home. He becomes a co-heir to his new father's estate. We are heirs to God and joint-heirs with Christ. We are no longer slaves bound by sin. Let us wake up to who we are in Christ. Let us wake up to our rights and privileges. We belong to a new family. We have a new Father. We have a new covenant. We have a new inheritance!

• CONFESSION

Gal. 3:13-14: *Christ hath redeemed us from the curse of the law, being made a curse for us: for it is written, Cursed is every one that hangeth on a tree: That the blessing of Abraham might come on the Gentiles through Jesus Christ; that we might receive the promise of the Spirit through faith.*

• PRAISE WORSHIP

1. Thank God for making provision for deliverance from any form of bondage.
2. I release myself from any inherited bondage, in the name of Jesus.
3. I release myself from the grip of any problem transferred into my life from the womb, in the name of Jesus.
4. I break and loose myself from every inherited evil covenant, in the name of Jesus.
5. I break and loose myself from every inherited evil curse, in the name of Jesus.
6. I release myself from every inherited disease, in the name of Jesus.
7. Let the blood of Jesus correct any inherited defect in my body, in the name of Jesus.
8. In the name of Jesus, I break any curse of rejection from the womb or illegitimacy which may be in my family back to ten generations on both sides of the family.
9. I break all the curses of deformity, infirmity and sickness in my family back to ten generations on both sides of my family, in the name of Jesus.
10. Let my God arise and put to flight every mind-controlling spirit, in the name of Jesus.
11. I command the spirit of death and hell to loose its hold upon my life, in the name of Jesus.
12. I reject and renounce every ordination of 'lateness in goodness', in the name of Jesus.

13. I break every demonic circle in my life, in the name of Jesus.

14. I command every evil spiritual clock to be destroyed by the Holy Ghost fire, in the name of Jesus.

15. I command spiritual label and stamp to be cleaned off with the blood of Jesus.

16. O Lord, send Your axe of fire to the foundation of my life and destroy every evil plantation.

17. Father, let the fire of the Holy Ghost enter into my blood stream and cleanse my system, in the name of Jesus.

18. I renounce and break all evil demonic holds, strange powers, bondage and curses and loose myself and all my descendants from them, in the name of Jesus.

19. I renounce and break all evil curses, charms and bewitching put upon my family line and loose myself and all my descendants from them, in the name of Jesus.

20. I take authority over and order the binding of every strongman in every department of my life, in the name of Jesus.

21. I break every curse of automatic failure mechanism working in my family back to ten generations on both sides of my family, in the name of Jesus.

22. Pray aggressively against the following evil foundations. Pray as follows: You (*pick the under listed one by one*), loose your hold over my life and be purged out of my foundation, in Jesus' name.

- destructive effect of polygamy	- evil physical design
- unscriptural manners of conception	- parental curses
- demonic blood transfusion	- evil dedication
- demonic incisions	- demonic marriage
- dream pollution	- demonic sacrifice
- fellowship with family idols	- demonic initiations
- inherited infirmity	

RECEIVING FRESH FIRE FROM ABOVE

Acts 2

- *For receiving fresh fire from the Holy Ghost.*
- *To get on fire from above.*

A wise believer doesn't rely on the experience of yesterday's victory to fight today's battle, but rather he makes sure he receives fresh fire from above for each day's task. For your Christian life and ministry, you need to receive fresh fire from above.

Acts 2:3: *"And there appeared unto them cloven tongues like as of fire, and it sat upon each one of them."*

The church was born by fire on the day of Pentecost. Every Christian must receive the baptism of fire if he will do anything meaningful for the Lord. The fire of God in the life of a believer is the sign of divine approval that indeed he has been called, anointed and appointed by the Almighty God for the work of the ministry. It is impossible to do the work of God without fire. It is like trying to swim without water. When we have the fire of God, we will not be able to keep quiet, we will not be able to sit still. Jeremiah said, "Then I said, I will not make mention of Him, nor speak any more in His name. But His word was in mine heart as a burning fire shut up in my bones, and I was weary with forbearing, and I could not stay."

"God's word was like fire in His bones" (Jeremiah 20:9). It was such a powerful and compelling force that he could not hold it in. When you receive the fire of God, people will know. It is not something you can hide. The burning desire and the zeal for the kingdom of God will consume you. We need this fire daily. It is not something we need once. We need to be continually filled with the Holy Spirit and fire (Ephesians 5:18). The work of the Lord must be done by fire.

As you pray these prayer points, fresh fire will fall from heaven and fill every department of your life.

• CONFESSION

Phil. 4:13: *I can do all things through Christ which strengtheneth me.*

• PRAISE WORSHIP

1. O Lord, cleanse all the soiled part of my life.
2. O Lord, refresh every dry area of my life.
3. O Lord, heal every wounded part of my life.
4. O Lord, bend every evil rigidity in my life.
5. O Lord, re-align every satanic straying in my life.
6. O Lord, let the fire of the Holy Spirit warm every satanic freeze in my life.
7. O Lord, give me a life that kills death.
8. O Lord, kindle in me the fire of charity.
9. O Lord, glue me together where I am opposed to myself.
10. O Lord, enrich me with Your gifts.
11. O Lord, quicken me and increase my desire for the things of heaven.
12. By Your rulership, O Lord, let the lust of the flesh in my life die.
13. Lord Jesus, increase daily in my life.
14. Lord Jesus, maintain Your gifts in my life.
15. O Lord, refine and purge my life by Your fire.
16. Holy Spirit, inflame and fire my heart, in the name of Jesus.
17. Lord Jesus, lay Your hands upon me and quench every rebellion in me.
18. Holy Ghost fire, begin to burn away every self-centeredness in me, in the name of Jesus.
19. Father Lord, breathe Your life-giving breath into my soul, in the name of Jesus.
20. O Lord, make me ready to go wherever You send me.
21. Lord Jesus, never let me shut You out.

22. Lord Jesus, never let me try to limit You to my capacity.

23. Lord Jesus, work freely in me and through me.

24. O Lord, purify the channels of my life.

25. Let Your heat O Lord, consume my will, in the name of Jesus.

26. Let the flame of the Holy Spirit blaze upon the altar of my heart, in the name of Jesus.

27. Lord Jesus, come like blood into my veins.

28. O Lord, order my spirit and fashion my life in Your will.

29. O Lord, let Your fire burn all that is not holy in my life.

30. O Lord, let Your fire generate power in my life.

31. Lord Jesus, impart to me thoughts higher than my own thoughts.

32. Holy Spirit, come as dew and refresh me, in the name of Jesus.

33. Holy Spirit, guide me in the way of liberty, in the name of Jesus.

34. Holy Spirit, blow upon me such that sin would no more find place in me, in the name of Jesus.

35. Holy Spirit, where my love is cold, warm me up, in Jesus' name.

36. Thank God for His mighty presence in your life.

37. Let my hand become the sword of fire to cut down evil trees, in the name of Jesus.

38. Let my feet become the thunder of God, as I stamp them. Let them deafen the enemy, in the name of Jesus.

39. Let the spiritual rag of poverty in my life be destroyed by the fire of God, in the name of Jesus.

40. Every enemy of excellence in my life, be paralysed, in Jesus' name.

41. Let every past satanic achievements in my life be converted to my promotion, in the name of Jesus.

42. O Lord, let the shame of my enemies be multiplied greatly.

43. O Lord, let the defeat and disgrace of enemy of my progress be multiplied beyond measure.

44. Let every power planning to turn my life upside down, fall down and die now, in the name of Jesus.

45. I paralyse every satanic inspiration targeted against me, in the name of Jesus.

46. I barricade my life from every satanic opinion, in the name of Jesus.

47. Let my divinely-appointed helpers begin to locate me from now, in the name of Jesus.

48. Every lame glory, receive life now, in the name of Jesus.

49. Thank God for answers to your prayer.

HOLY DISTURBANCE
Luke 18:1-7

- *For creating open heavens.*
- *For paralysing angels that are contending with our angels of blessing.*

The Bible is replete with examples of people who pestered God unceasingly for their needs. God is not like man who can become weary of importunate petitions. He rather arises to help you in the time of need.

James 5:16: *"The effectual fervent prayer of a righteous man availeth much."*

The man who can pray has nothing to fear. The key that changes God's promises to reality is prayer. We are told to Apray without ceasing " (1 Thessolonians 5:17). And Isaiah says, "And give him no rest, till he establish, and till he make Jerusalem a praise in the earth." (Isaiah 62:7). We need to pray continually because there are unseen forces which seek to hinder our prayers (Daniel 10). They wage war against the angels bringing the answers to our prayers. If Heaven seems silent and it looks like your prayers are bouncing back to you from a brass wall, then you need to forcefully open the heaven.

Our prayer has to be:

- Effectual: They have to be able to produce the desired results; they have to be productive and fruitful. –

- Fervent: they have to be boiling, hot, warfare prayers said passionately from the heart. Violent. Strong. –

There are two important ingredients that we need in our prayers. Only a righteous man can pray. The prayer of a sinner is an abomination to the Lord. Holiness is a must for prayers to be answered. When prayer is effectual and fervent and the person praying is righteous, then power will be made available for supernatural and unprecedented breakthroughs!

• CONFESSION

Isa. 62:7: *And give him no rest, till he establish, and till he make Jerusalem a praise in the earth.*

• PRAISE WORSHIP

1. O Lord, advertise Yourself as the living God in my life.

2. Let the hand of the Lord lift me to my desired mountain, in the name of Jesus.

3. Let the spirit of the valley in my life be suffocated unto death, in the name of Jesus.

4. Let every satanic revival organised against my life be shattered into nothingness, in the name of Jesus.

5. Let the fire of the Holy Ghost melt away every spiritual blindness in my life, in the name of Jesus.

6. Holy Ghost, pump favour into my life, in the name of Jesus.

7. I refuse to follow any evil procedure for my life, in Jesus' name.

8. Let every evil camp set up against me be scattered unto desolation, in the name of Jesus.

9. I speak failure unto every satanic weapon fashioned against me, in the name of Jesus.

10. I speak frustration unto every evil snare prepared against me, in the name of Jesus.

11. Every satanic pit against my being, be neutralized, in Jesus' name.

12. Every owner of evil load in my life, begin to carry your evil luggage with both hands, in the name of Jesus.

13. Every satanic decoder being used against my desired breakthroughs, fall down and scatter, in the name of Jesus.

14. Let every blood altar erected against me be destroyed by Holy Ghost fire, in the name of Jesus.

15. O Lord, let my cries in this programme provoke angelic violence against my enemies.

16. Lord, empty every satanic vessel filled for my sake.

17. Let every jungle consultation on my behalf be rendered null and void, in the name of Jesus.

18. Let every satanic judge installed against me fall down and die, in the name of Jesus.

19. Wind of God, blow on all my dead bones now, in Jesus' name.

20. I arise out of the minimum to the maximum in every area of my life, in the name of Jesus.

21. I arise out of poverty to prosperity, in the name of Jesus.

22. Let every satanic wisdom against me be rendered impotent, in the name of Jesus.

23. O Lord, let my life demonstrate Your power.

24. O Lord, let my life disgrace every satanic power.

25. O Lord, let my words carry holy fire and power.

26. Every power swallowing the result of my prayer, fall down and die, in the name of Jesus.

27. Every power of household witchcraft troubling my life, fall down and die now, in the name of Jesus.

28. I reject every witchcraft burial of prosperity, in the name of Jesus.

29. Let every good road closed against me by the enemy open now, in the name of Jesus.

30. Every power activating failures against me, fall down and die, in the name of Jesus.

31. Every satanic insect polluting my breakthroughs, fall down and die now, in the name of Jesus.

32. My season of breakthroughs, reject satanic delays, in Jesus' name.

33. I over-rule every satanic decree against my person, in Jesus' name.

34. Let my breakthroughs be pursued unto completion by the angels of the living God, in the name of Jesus.

35. Every satanic animal in the dream, fall down and die, in the name of Jesus.

36. O Lord, let Your blessings have foothold in my life.

37. Let my hand become the sword of fire to cut down evil trees, in the name of Jesus.

38. Thank God for answers to your prayer.

FREEDOM FROM INORDINATE AFFECTIONS AND SOUL-TIES

Gal. 5:24

People who maintain that nobody can be free from willful sin or ties with demonic world are ignorant of God's provision to set man free, and make him free indeed. Appropriate this provision for your life by ensuring that you crucify your flesh with all its affections and lusts today.

1 Corinthians 6:16: "What? Know ye not that he which is joined to an harlot is one body? for two, saith he shall be one flesh."

A soul-tie is an obsessive affection for a person, which is often strengthened by sexual intercourse or blood covenants. When there is soul-tie one's actions are controlled and subject to those of the other person. An unholy union is formed with this person and is consecrated so that the two share mind, purpose and life. One is living for the other person.

Soul ties can be between a man and a woman; a mother and a son (this is called Olympus complex), a boyfriend and a girlfriend;. When a man or woman is being manipulated or controlled in the name of love, this bond has to be broken because as far as God is concerned, this is witchcraft.

● CONFESSION

Gal 6:17: *From henceforth let no man trouble me: for I bear in my body the marks of the Lord Jesus.*

● PRAISE WORSHIP

1. Thank the Lord for His redemptive power.

2. Prayers of confession of sins and forgiveness.

3. I release myself from all unprofitable friendships, in Jesus' name.

4. I come against the dark powers which have manipulated my friendship with . . . (*mention the name of the person*) and I break their powers over my life, in the name of Jesus.

5. I bind all demonic authorities which motivated and controlled my relationship with . . . (*mention the name of the person*) and break their authority and power over my affections, in the name of Jesus.

6. I command all evil 'remote controllers' to loose their hold upon my affections, in the name of Jesus.

7. I release myself from the hold of every bewitched relationship, in the name of Jesus.

8. By the blood of Jesus, I remove myself from any strange authority ever exercised over me.

9. I remove all evil soul ties and affections, in the name of Jesus.

10. I come against every desire and expectation of the enemy to engage me in any unprofitable relationship, in the name of Jesus.

11. I break every ungodly relationship, in the name of Jesus.

12. I break and renounce evil soul ties I have had or may have had with

    - secret societies   - cults

    - adulterers   - family members

    - close friends   - organisations

    - husbands   - past or present friends

    - acquaintances   - wives

    - engagements   - doctors

    - clubs   - religious leaders

    - social organisations   - preachers, etc.,

    in the name of Jesus.

13. I renounce all hidden evil soul ties, in the name of Jesus.

14. I renounce, break and loose myself from all demonic subjection to any relationship, in the name of Jesus.

15. I break all evil soul-ties and wash them away with the blood of the Lord Jesus.

16. I remove myself from any strange authority exercised over me, in the name of Jesus.

17. I remove all mind controlling manipulations between me and any friend or family member, in the name of Jesus.

18. I claim deliverance from any negative affection towards anyone, in the name of Jesus.

19. Let evil affections towards me be wiped off the mind of . . . (*mention the name of the person*), in the name of Jesus.

20. Lord Jesus, I give You my affections, emotions and desires and I request that they be in submission to the Holy Spirit.

21. Praise the Lord for answered prayer.

WAR AGAINST ANTI-MARRIAGE FORCES

Matt. 19:6

• *When your marriage is being threatened.*

One of the devices of the enemy to make people objects of ridicule is preventing them from getting married. You must take up all the armours of God to counter all the measures taken by the enemy to subject you to perpetual frustration.

S. Sol. 8:6,7: *"Set me as a seal upon thine heart, as a seal upon thine arm; for love is strong as death; Jealousy is cruel as the grave: the coals of fire which hath a most vehement flame. Many waters cannot quench love, neither can the floods drown it; if a man were to give all the substance of his home for love, it will be utterly contemned."*

Love is the greatest weapon we have against anti-marriage forces! Let me ask you a question. If a husband and a wife fight, who should apologize? Answer: The person who was wrong. If you believe that answer, then you have just failed the entrance examination into the institution of marriage. The correct answer is this: The person who loves the most will apologize first. - "Hatred stirreth up strife; but love covereth a multitude of sins" (Proverbs 10:12).

Beloved, the Bible says that, "Love never fails" (1 Cor. 13:18). If you truly and honestly love your spouse, you will be determined to make your marriage work and no anti-marriage force can come between you to cut anything asunder.

Love is as **STRONG** as death . . .only death can break the power of love.

Many waters cannot quench love . . . No matter how deep or turbulent the waters of tribulation and affliction are they cannot drown love (Isaiah 43:2). Neither can the floods of crisis drown love . . . No disaster or satanic storm can destroy true love.

Love cannot be bought. Love is unconditional and it is priceless, it is a gift from God. The love of God was shed into our heart by the Holy Ghost (Romans 5:5).

Pray to God to give you true love for your spouse. Ask the Lord to teach you how to love your spouse and meet his/her needs (emotional, financial, material, physical and spiritual).

The love you have for your spouse will cause you to continually intercede for him/her in prayer. These prayer points have been designed to destroy all anti-marriage forces. As you pray them from a heart of love, God will give you the victory

• CONFESSION

Obad. 1:3-4: *The pride of thine heart hath deceived thee, thou that dwellest in the clefts of the rock, whose habitation is high; that saith in his heart, Who shall bring me down to the ground? Though thou exalt thyself as the eagle, and though thou set thy nest among the stars, thence will I bring thee down, saith the LORD.*

• PRAISE WORSHIP

1. All evil counsels against my marital life, collapse, in Jesus' name.
2. Any association between my husband/wife and any strange man/woman, be scattered now, in the name of Jesus.
3. Every demonic in-law, loose your hold upon my life, in Jesus' name.
4. Spirit husbands and spirit wives, loose your hold in the name of Jesus (*place your hand below your stomach*).
5. Every curse that has been issued against my marriage, be cancelled, in the name of Jesus.
6. Every demonic mark contrary to settled homes, be wiped off with the blood of Jesus.
7. Every inherited spirit that is not of God, go, in the name of Jesus.
8. Every curse issued against my marriage or against my marital life, be broken, in the name of Jesus.
9. Let the effect of every ceremony done on the day of my wedding and which has been working against me, be cancelled and destroyed, in the name of Jesus.
10. Every spiritual dowry collected on my behalf, I return you to the sender, in the name of Jesus.
11. The spiritual marriage of my husband/wife to his / her mother, be dissolved, in the name of Jesus.
12. Any power which says that I will not enjoy my marital life, be roasted, in the name of Jesus.
13. I command my run-away husband/wife to come back, in the name of Jesus.

14. You spirit of marriage destruction, be bound, in the name of Jesus.

15. I command every curse on my marriage to be converted to blessing, in the name of Jesus.

16. I command every evil which strange friends have done against my home to be reversed, in the name of Jesus.

17. I release my partner from every demonic cage, in Jesus' name.

18. Thank God for answers to your prayer.

SAFEGUARDING YOUR HOME
Eccl. 10:8

• *To scrutinize your home and pull down past or present anti-marriage strongholds.*

Be warned that the forces of home breakers are hovering around like a hawk looking for a prey. Be vigilant and jealously guard your home by praying aggressively at all times.

Ecclesiastes 10:8: *"He that diggeth a pit shall fall into it; and whoso breaketh an hedge a serpent shall bite him."*

Beloved, we need to safeguard our homes. Many external forces are waging war against Christian homes. It was reported that some satanists in South Africa fasted for 201 days just to destroy Christian homes. Are you concerned for your home?

We need to check the foundation on which we have built our homes. Is it according to the will of God, or are there compromises here and there? If there are gaps or compromises, that means you are giving the devil a foothold in that home. The things that will break the hedge of protection God has built around our homes and allow the serpent (devil) to bite are:

- sin . . . adultery
- lack of submission
- lack of love
- selfishness
- interference by in-laws
- demonic traditions and covenants
- satanic marriages

As you use these prayer points every broken hedge will be re-built by fire!

• CONFESSIONS

Mark 10:8-9: *And they twain shall be one flesh: so then they are no more twain, but one flesh. What therefore God hath joined together, let not man put asunder.*

Ps. 145:16: *Thou openest thine hand, and satisfiest the desire of every living thing.*

Col. 3:18-19: *Wives, submit yourselves unto your own husbands, as it is fit in the Lord. Husbands, love your wives, and be not bitter against them.*

1 Cor. 7:14-15: *For the unbelieving husband is sanctified by the wife, and the unbelieving wife is sanctified by the husband: else were your children unclean; but now are they holy. But if the unbelieving depart, let him depart. A brother or a sister is not under bondage in such cases: but God hath called us to peace.*

Isa. 43:18-19: *Remember ye not the former things, neither consider the things of old. Behold, I will do a new thing; now it shall spring forth; shall ye not know it? I will even make a way in the wilderness, and rivers in the desert.*

Ps. 68:1: *Let God arise, let his enemies be scattered: let them also that hate him flee before him.*

Job 22:28: *Thou shalt also decree a thing, and it shall be established unto thee: and the light shall shine upon thy ways.*

● **PRAISE WORSHIP**

1. You who conspired with my husband/wife to destroy our marriage and good home, I command you to remove your hand from my husband/wife, in the name of Jesus. It is against God's word for you to separate us.

2. All evil counsels against our home, collapse, in the name of Jesus.

3. I scatter all arrangements between you and my husband/wife, in the name of Jesus.

4. You will dislike each other as from now, in the name of Jesus.

5. I will get the favour and love of my husband/wife, in Jesus' name.

6. Thank the Lord for His mercies and grace.

7. Ask the Holy Spirit to help you pray to the point of breakthrough.

8. *(Gird up your spiritual loins and aggressively stand against the following local home-wreckers. Pray as follows:)* I stand against any . . ., (fix in the items listed below) and command them to 'release me and my marriage, in the name of Jesus.'

- competition by strange women or girls/men
- demonic in-laws
- financial failure and poverty, especially after the wedding
- spirit husbands and wives
- demonic marks
- anti-marriage destruction
- spirit of fear
- spirit of Jezebel (domineering nature)
- inherited spirit from the father's and mother's sides
- marriage curses
- anti-marriage covenants
- spirit of misunderstanding, misinterpretation and exaggeration
- ungodly attachment to parents.

9. *(Cancel the effects of the following things. Please pray aggressively if you are involved or feel you may be involved in them. Pray as follows:)* I cancel the satanic influence of . . . upon my marriage; I bind the connected spirits and command them to loose their hold upon my marriage, in the name of Jesus.

- demonic water pouring on the feet on the wedding day
- contaminated wedding rings and shoes
- background of polygamy and multiple husbands
- familiar spirits and witchcraft spirits
- satanic deposits in the home
- collection of spiritual bride-price
- incest

10. I break and loose myself, in the name of Jesus, from any anti-marriage curse issued upon my family.

11. Father, let the Prince of Peace reign in my marriage without any hindrance, in the name of Jesus.

12. I decree reconciliation between myself and my partner, in the name of Jesus.

13. All powers conspiring with anyone to destroy our home/marriage loose your hold, in the name of Jesus.

14. All evil counsels against our home be frustrated, in Jesus' name.

TO DISSOLVE PLANS FOR SEPARATION AND DIVORCE

Mal. 2:15

Demonic intelligent operatives are busy planning and working to scatter your marriage. Their goal? Divorce or separation. Hence, make sure you effectively take care of this area in your prayer life.

Mark 10:7-9: *"For this cause shall a man leave his father and mother, and cleave to his wife; and the twain shall be one flesh: so they are no more twain, but one flesh. Wherefore what God has joined together let no man put asunder."*

When you understand God's purpose for the institution of marriage, you will not seek divorce. When you do not understand the purpose of a thing you will abuse it. Divorce is an abuse and a bastardization of the institution of marriage.

God's ingredients for marriage are three-fold: (i) A man will LEAVE his parents and form a covenant with his wife. (ii) The husband and wife CLEAVE together and become committed to each other. (iii) They take responsibility for their welfare, etc. Once these three things are present, separation becomes impossible.

When you divide one, you can never get a whole number, you will always get a fraction when there is separation or divorce you are going to hurt and damage your life and you can never be whole again. Your life will become fragmented.

Repent and ask God to forgive you for the role you have played that is causing your spouse to ask for a divorce. Then begin to violently pray these prayer points and every evil trend and stronghold of divorce will dissolve, in Jesus' name.

● **CONFESSION**

Matt. 19:6: *Wherefore they are no more twain, but one flesh. What therefore God hath joined together, let not man put asunder.*

● **PRAISE WORSHIP**

1. Thank God for the institution of marriage.

2. Lord, forgive me for any unprofitable contribution that brings about my present marital situation.

3. Lord, forgive me if the choice of my partner has been wrong from the beginning.

4. Lord, walk back to the foundation of my marriage and carry out the necessary surgical operation.

5. I register my protest in the demonic world for the wounds and injury done to my home by the enemy, in the name of Jesus.

6. I bind every strongman militating against my home, in Jesus' name.

7. Let every evil spiritual marriage contacted by me or on my behalf be dissolved, in the mighty name of Jesus.

8. Let every evil spiritual marriage with spirit husband/wife be divorced, in the name of Jesus.

9. Let every evil spiritual home involving me be destroyed, in the name of Jesus.

10. I pursue, overtake and recover my marriage from the hands of home breakers, in the name of Jesus.

11. Lord, dissolve and render to nought every evil counsel fashioned against my home.

12. I bind every spirit of Ahab, Jezebel, strife and home wreckers, in the name of Jesus.

13. Lord, let Your axe of fire fall on the root of my marital problems and cut them to pieces, in the name of Jesus.

14. Let every power militating against the divine purpose of marriage in my home be destroyed. That is,
    - powers militating against companionship and completeness.
    - powers militating against marital faithfulness and encouraging adultery and fornication.
    - powers militating against procreation.

15. Let every wicked device of the enemy to defeat these purposes in our

lives be frustrated, in the name of Jesus.

16. Let every gadget of marriage destruction be frustrated in my home, in the name of Jesus.

17. Let every evil arrow fired by demonic relatives be uprooted, in the name of Jesus.

18. Let every evil anti-marriage linkage with our parents be dashed to pieces, in the name of Jesus.

19. Let every evil effect of external interferences in our marriage be completely neutralized, in the name of Jesus.

20. Every power preventing me as a wife from accepting the headship of my husband should become paralyzed, in the name of Jesus.

21. Every power preventing me as a husband from living as a true head should become paralyzed, in the name of Jesus.

22. The Lord should forgive any sin of abortion that may lead to blood crying against our home, in the name of Jesus.

23. The Lord should help us make the proper corrections in our marriage.

24. Let every imagination, thought, plan, decision, desire and expectation of divorce and separation against my home be nullified, in the name of Jesus.

25. I bind and render to nought the power and activities of the spirits that put marriage asunder, in the name of Jesus.

26. Satan, hear the word of the Lord, you will not break my home, in the name of Jesus.

27. I paralyze every spirit of misunderstanding between me and my wife/husband, in the name of Jesus.

28. I bind all powers eating away the determination of my wife/husband to stay married to me, in the name of Jesus.

29. Let the satanic birds eating away my love from the heart of my wife/husband vomit it, in the name of Jesus.

30. Pray in the spirit for at least 10 minutes.

DELIVERANCE FROM THE SPIRIT OF MARRIAGE DESTRUCTION

Rev. 13:10

The major focus of the enemy of man since the world began is to unleash destruction on marriage, with a view of exterminating the human race. You as a believer, should seek to install spiritual security apparatus around your marriage.

John 10:10: *"The thief cometh not, but for to steal, and to kill and to destroy: I am come that they might have life, and that they might have it more abundantly."*

The spirit of marriage destruction can be internal, i.e. working in the lives of the husband and the wife. It can also be external.

The internal forces could be spirit husbands or spirit wives. They will create a deep suspicion in either spouse and he/she will develop an intense hatred for the other. They also work using the spirit of anger. They can affect the finances in the home and work against the peace and unity of the home. Selfishness, unbrokenness and pride in the life of either spouse will also cause division.

External forces include demonic in-laws, household wickedness, unfriendly friends, satanic strongmen. Strange children, strange women/men, demonic tradition leading to bondage.

These prayer points are to be said violently, not with the hope of controlling your spouse but to restore love in the home.

• CONFESSION

Isa. 33:1: *Woe to thee that spoilest, and thou wast not spoiled; and dealest treacherously, and they dealt not treacherously with thee! when thou shalt cease to spoil, thou shalt be spoiled; and when thou shalt make an end to deal treacherously, they shall deal treacherously with thee.*

• **PRAISE WORSHIP**

1. Father, let Your kingdom be established in every department of my marriage, in the name of Jesus.

2. I renounce and denounce every evil spiritual marriage contract I have consciously or unconsciously entered into, in Jesus' name.

3. Let all spirits of marriage destruction release me, in the name of Jesus. E.g. the spirit of

- anger	- Ahab	- criticisms
- strife	- Jezebel	- infirmity
- pride	- hatred	- worry
- selfishness	- impatience	- fear
- bad speaking	- familiar spirit	- competition
- adultery	- prayerlessness	- apathy
- fornication	- failure	- power struggling
- harsh words	- cruelty	- lying
- extravagance	- pride	- marital unfaithfulness
- lack of submission by wife		- poor communication
- poor leadership from husband		- domineering character
- spiritual backsliding		

4. I release myself from the school of broken homes, in Jesus' name.

5. I fire back to the camp of the enemy every arrow fired at my marriage, in the name of Jesus.

6. I spoil and cancel every satanic plan against my home, in the name of Jesus.

7. Let every evil design fashioned by the enemy against my life be completely destroyed, in the name of Jesus.

8. Let every curse issued against my home be cancelled and replaced by blessings, in the name of Jesus.

9. Let every evil covenants fashioned against my home be broken and shattered to pieces, in the name of Jesus.

10. Let the powers of household wickedness fashioned against my home be dashed to pieces, in the name of Jesus.

11. Let every cage of the enemy fashioned against my home be broken to pieces, in the name of Jesus.

12. Let every negative word spoken against my home be nullified, in the name of Jesus.

13. Let any spiritual wife and husband sent against me be bound, in the name of Jesus.

14. Every evil wedding ring and garment, be roasted, in Jesus' name.

15. I deliver my marriage from the hands of home-wreckers, in the name of Jesus.

16. I command all evil counsellors and spiritual emptier to loose their hold upon my marriage, in the name of Jesus.

17. Let the Prince of Peace reign in my marriage, in the name of Jesus.

18. Let every satanic agent hired against my marriage fall after the order of Balaam, in the name of Jesus.

19. Let the anointing to prosper in the marital life come upon my home, in the name of Jesus.

20. Let the Holy Spirit transform my marriage to be heaven on earth, in the name of Jesus.

21. Thank God for answers to your prayer.

WAR AGAINST CONFLICTS AND HOSTILITY IN THE HOME

Eph. 5:22-33

Conflicts and hostilities are common pheno-mena in these last days. They are engineered by Satan and his cohorts to prevent the flow of God's anointing. Deliberate efforts must be made by Christian couples to deal with them.

Amos 3:3: *"Can two walk together except they be agreed?"*

Love and hate are two sides of a coin according to Greek mythology. The intense love you have for a person can be changed to intense hatred. Conflicts and hostility arise in the home when the Scripture (Ephesians 4:26), *"Do not let the sun go down upon your wrath"*, is ignored.

When disagreements are not settled immediately, the couple raise up an invisible barrier that will separate them. They break the hedge of protection on the home and open the door for the enemy to strike them.

There is nothing like a perfect marriage. Each relationship has its set of problems. When we choose the path of love and maturity all the time, we will quickly resolve our differences, and will be building our home on the right foundation.

When we have problems and we don't deal with them immediately, we will have conflicts and hostility. This is what the devil wants. Being broken and manifesting pride and selfishness cause many to choose this path.

As you use these prayer points, all the walls of disagreement, unresolved conflicts and hostility in your home will be destroyed by the power of God.

● **CONFESSION**

Gen. 2:24-25: *Therefore shall a man leave his father and his mother, and shall cleave unto his wife: and they shall be one flesh. And they were both naked, the man and his wife, and were not ashamed.*

• PRAISE WORSHIP

1. *Make a list of all the things that are presently wrong in the home.*

2. *Now take these items one by one and pray aggressively as follows:*
   You . . ., (e.g. weakness, faults or problems) in my home, I root you out, I pull you down and I destroy you, in the name of Jesus.

3. Let all the enemies of my good dreams and visions concerning my home be rendered impotent, in the name of Jesus.

4. I paralyze every architect of conflict and hostility in my home, in the name of Jesus.

5. Let every factor leading to maladjustment in the home be dissolved by the fire of the Holy Spirit.

6. I decree that divine character be planted and built in my home, in the name of Jesus.

7. I withdraw my marriage from the hands of evil designers, in the name of Jesus.

8. Let every evil power trying to re-draw my marriage map be put to shame, in the name of Jesus.

9. I refuse to pattern my marriage contrary to God's original design, in the name of Jesus.

10. Household wickedness, release my home, in the name of Jesus.

11. Let every negative influence on my home by parents from both sides be nullified, in the name of Jesus.

12. Every disease of our family altar, be healed, in the name of Jesus.

13. I break every curse affecting my home negatively, in Jesus' name.

14. Devil, I command you to take all your properties and be gone from my life, in the name of Jesus.

15. Lord, restore all that the enemies have stolen from my home.

16. Father Lord, convert all my marital failure to success, in the name of Jesus.

17. Lord, keep the wall of defence of my family constantly strong, in the

mighty name of Jesus.

18. Lord, heal all broken and sore family relationships, in the mighty name of Jesus.

19. I receive deliverance from every evil plantation designed to bring myself and my children under the bondage of the devil, in the name of Jesus.

20. I deliver myself from bondage that my sins and those of my ancestors have provoked, in the name of Jesus.

21. Holy Spirit, break every yoke of marital failure in my life, in the name of Jesus.

22. I paralyse every spirit of hatred and hostility militating against my home, in the name of Jesus.

23. Let peace flow like water into my home, in the name of Jesus.

24. I stand against every spirit of . . .,

-talkativeness	- lack of appreciation	- stubbornness
- laziness	- manipulation	- callousness
- self-centeredness	- impotence	- passiveness
- accusation	- masturbation	- unreasonable- ness
- aggression	- oral sex	- egotism
- unscriptural ambition	- possessiveness	- rigidity
- child molestation	- negative emotion	- inconsistency
- flirtation	- insensitivity	- despondency
- intolerance	- unbelief	- unforgiveness
- rejection	- humiliation	- anger
- frustration	- impatience	

loose your hold upon my life, in the name of Jesus. I command you to be separated from me. I place the cross of Jesus between me and you. I forbid you to ever return or ever to send any other spirits, in the mighty name of Jesus.

25. All demonic maternal and paternal strings, break, in Jesus' name.

DELIVERANCE FROM THE GRIP OF HOME DESTROYERS

Rev. 13:10

Those who experience mysterious misunderstanding borne out of naive and petty differences should be aware that they are under the grip of home destroyers. Therefore, if your home falls into this category, seek to loose the grip through constant bombardment with prayers.

Ecclesiastes 4: 9-12: *"Two are better than one, because they have a good reward for their labour. For if they fall, the one will lift up his fellow: but woe to him that is alone when he falleth for he hath not another to help him up, Again, if two lie together, then they have heat: but how can one be warm alone! And if one prevail against him, two shall withstand him; and a threefold cord is not quickly broken."*

Two are better than one. There is more power when people pray in unity. That is why the Bible says, "One shall chase a thousand and two ten thousand" (Deuteronomy 32:30). On of the symbols of marriage is a triangle. You have God at the top, the husband and the wife at the bottom. This signifies that God is the one holding the marriage together. There is a line joining the woman to God and a line joining the man to God. These lines signify their relationship with God. There is also a line joining the man and the woman. The threefold cord is not quickly broken. If we can maintain these relationships, the home destroyers will not succeed.

When the couple do not neglect the family altar, the enemy cannot penetrate. The family that prays together stays together. As you embark on this prayer programme, God will deliver your home from the grip of home destroyers.

• CONFESSION

Isa. 59:19: *So shall they fear the name of the LORD from the west, and his glory from the rising of the sun. When the enemy shall come in like a flood, the Spirit of the LORD shall lift up a standard against him.*

● PRAISE WORSHIP

1. Confession of sins and prayer of forgiveness.
2. Ask the Holy Spirit to direct you in this prayer session.
3. Take the problem areas listed hereunder one by one and pray these three violent prayer points on each of them.

   (i) Let the axe of fire from heaven uproot the problem from the roots, in the name of Jesus.

   (ii) Let the finger of God pull down the stronghold of the problem, in the name of Jesus.

   (iii)Let the finger of God build up the right replacements, in the name of Jesus.

   - evil association
   - carelessness
   - pride
   - foolishness
   - unprofitable imitation
   - unprofitable comparison
   - communication gap
   - suspicion
   - evil counsellors

   - planlessness
   - weak family altar
   - unsaved partner or children
   - lack of knowledge of the word of God
   - deterioration of relationship
   - selfishness
   - misplaced priority
   - evil attachment to parents
   - incomplete 'leaving' and incomplete 'cleaving' of couple.

4. Let my home be released from the hands of evil remote controlling forces, in the name of Jesus.
5. I command every evil wind directed at my family to be re-directed by the Holy Spirit, in the name of Jesus.
6. Let all the eaters of love and drinkers of joy release my family, in the name of Jesus.
7. Let every problem arising from the issue of sex in the family receive divine solution, in the name of Jesus.

8. Let all extra-marital relationships with other "partners" collapse and die, in the name of Jesus.

9. Let every problem from the issue of finance receive divine solution, in the name of Jesus.

10. Let the anointing to prosper come upon my family, in Jesus' name.

11. Let every problem arising from the issue of relatives receive divine solution, in the name of Jesus.

12. Let every problem arising from the issue of children receive solution, in the name of Jesus.

13. Lord, arise and put the enemies responsible for . . . (pick from the under listed) in my marriage to flight.

- inability to produce children

- replacing love for wife/husband with love for children

- showing more love to one child than the other

- disrespectful children

- inability to cater spiritually, physically and materially

- production of strange children (Psalm 144:11)

- Godless children

- contaminated children

- bad parental example to children

- homes that are not attractive to children

- parental disagreement on child discipline

- children possessed by demons.

- in-laws conflict

- financial difficulties

- loneliness, isolation and boredom

- sexual problems

- absence of romantic love in marriage

DISSOLVING DEADLOCK IN MARRIAGE SETTLEMENT DISCUSSIONS

Mark 3:27

Obviously, some misunderstandings are cau- caused by the enemy to create confusion amidst the brethren and disrupt the free flow of God's power and anointing. If you find yourself in this situation, endeavour to break the power behind it before you go for reconciliatory discussions.

Hebrews 12:14,15: *"Follow peace with all men, and holiness, without which no man shall see the Lord. Looking diligently lest any man fail of the grace of God; lest any root of bitterness spring- ing up trouble you and thereby many be defiled."*

Whatever happens in our relationships we must seek to main- tain peace. When there are disagreements, discord and strife, we should always seek a peaceful solution. When we are hurt, bruised or battered in a relationship, there is a tendency for re- sentment and bitterness. But when we become bitter, we hurt ourselves. Many are sick because of bitterness which affects their relationship with God. Bitterness defiles a person.

The Bible tells us that before we can see God, before we can enter into His presence through acceptable praise worship, we must have a right relationship with man.

As you pray these prayer points, the love of God will melt all the bitterness in your heart and you will reach peaceful agreement with those you disagree with.

● CONFESSIONS

Matt. 19:26: *But Jesus beheld them, and said unto them, With men this is impossible; but with God all things are possible.*

Jer. 32:17: *Ah Lord GOD! behold, thou hast made the heaven and the earth by thy great power and stretched out arm, and there is nothing too hard for thee:*

● **PRAISE WORSHIP**

1. Thank God for all the settlement initiatives.
2. Thank God because with Him nothing shall be impossible.
3. Let the spirit of peace reign within the heart of my . . ., in the name of Jesus.
4. I command every strange hand to be taken off my marriage, in the name of Jesus.
5. I disengage the hand of evil manipulators from my home, in the name of Jesus.
6. Every spirit of rebellion and strife, be put to shame, in Jesus' name.
7. Let every yoke of creating deadlocks in the settlement be melted away, in the name of Jesus.
8. Lord, re-write my name in the heart of . . . *(mention the name of the person)*.
9. I paralyse all the enemies of peace in my home, in Jesus' name.
10. Every yoke of disagreement, be completely broken, in Jesus' name.
11. Let all fake sympathizers be put to shame, in the name of Jesus.
12. Holy Spirit, take the control over all subsequent meetings and dialogues.
13. Holy Spirit, put Your own words into all contributing mouths in this matter.
14. I arrest every creator of deadlocks and paralyse them, in the name of Jesus.
15. Let every acidic contributions to settlement discussions be dissolved, in the name of Jesus.
16. Let every demonic storm rising against my home be punctured, in the name of Jesus.
17. I bind the spirit of hatred and lack of compromise, in Jesus' name.
18. Lord, let the hedge of thorns go into operation in every area where it is needed in my marriage.

19. Let all the activities of strange man/woman fueling the strife be rendered null and void, in the name of Jesus.

20. O God, let Your face shine upon our marital relationship, in the name of Jesus.

21. O Lord, heal all marital diseases plaguing my home.

22. Thank God for answers to your prayer.

TO RESUSCITATE A DEAD MARRIAGE

Eze. 37:1-10

Whatever is dead is regarded as irrecoverable. But the paradox of red-hot prayer is that when embarked upon, it is capable of calling dead things into life. To this end, you can call your long forgotten dead marriage back to life.

Luke 1:37: *"For with God nothing shall be impossible."*

We serve a God that knows no impossibility! The word impossible is not in His vocabulary. The angel asked Sarah, "Is anything too hard for God?" (Genesis 18:14). I am asking you today, "Is anything too hard for God? Is it impossible for God to resurrect your dead marriage?" The answer you give to these questions will determine the outcome of this prayer. If you believe that nothing is too difficult for God and it is possible for God to resurrect your dead marriage, then God will step into your situation and restore the love between your spouse and yourself.

There have been testimonies of couples who were separated for several years, coming together again by the sovereign decision of God. One spouse could get born again and begin to pray, and God will reunite the two. If your case seems hopeless, these prayer points are for you. God who specializes in doing the impossible will step into your situation and resurrect your dead marriage.

• CONFESSIONS

John 11:25: *Jesus said unto her, I am the resurrection, and the life: he that believeth in me, though he were dead, yet shall he live:*

Rom. 4:17: *(As it is written, I have made thee a father of many nations) before him whom he believed, even God, who quickeneth the dead, and calleth those things which be not as though they were.*

• PRAISE WORSHIP

1. Thank the Lord for His resurrection power.
2. Ask the Lord to forgive you or whoever may be directly or indirectly involved in the death of the marriage.
3. I command my marriage to come alive, in the name of Jesus.
4. Lord Jesus, walk back into every second of my marital life and heal all the wounds created by the enemy.
5. Let the breath of life enter into the foundations of my marriage and make it whole, in the name of Jesus.
6. Let all satanic forces contributing to killing my marriage be paralysed, in the name of Jesus.
7. Let all marriage killers be paralysed, in the name of Jesus.
8. Let every activity of household enemies of my marriage be paralysed, in the name of Jesus.
9. Let my partner begin to have dreams and visions that would lead to the resurrection of my marriage, in the name of Jesus.
10. Let God arise and let the enemies of my home scatter, in the name of Jesus.
11. I remove my marriage from the grip of powers that put it asunder, in the name of Jesus.
12. Let all the enemies of settled home living around me scatter, in the name of Jesus.
13. Let the spirit of life enter into the blood of my marriage, in the name of Jesus.
14. Let all the glory that has departed from my marriage be restored, in the name of Jesus.
15. Let all the virtues stolen from my marriage be restored seven-fold, in the name of Jesus.
16. Let the anointing to prosper maritally fall upon me, in Jesus' name.
17. Lord, let divine sense enter into our relationship.

18. I fire back every arrow of the enemy fired at my marriage, in the name of Jesus.

19. Let all the powers sucking the peace of my home be rendered impotent, in the name of Jesus.

20. I retrieve my marriage from the altar of satanic destruction, in the name of Jesus.

21. Let the blood of Jesus erase all past unprofitable memories of my marital relationship.

22. I bind every spirit of demonic independence, in the name of Jesus.

23. Let the resurrection power of the Lord Jesus Christ fall upon my marriage, in the name of Jesus.

24. I remove my name from the book of broken homes , in Jesus' name.

25. Lord, remove from the heart of . . . all excuses for not wanting to face the difficulties of marriage.

26. Lord, remove from the heart of . . . the intention of seeking 'greener grass' in marriage.

27. Let the corpse of my marriage receive fire, in the name of Jesus.

28. Pray in the spirit for at least 10 minutes.

29. Thank the Lord for answered prayer.

RELEASING CHILDREN FROM BONDAGE

Psalm 127

In these last days, the devil is waging a serious war against children knowing fully well that they are the leaders of tomorrow. Therefore you are advised to make sure you seek constant deliverance of your children from evil bondage that is rife among the youth today.

Psalm 8:2: *"Out of the mouth of babes and sucklings hast thou ordained strength because of thine enemies, that thou mightiest still the enemy and the avenger."*

God has a plan for children. He wants to use them to defeat the enemy. But they are constantly receiving information and they sometimes find it difficult to distinguish between the true and the counterfeit. Also social and moral values provide fertile ground for the entrance of demons into their lives.

Points of demonic entry are;

- The senses: what they see, hear, touch and eat,

- The womb: If the mother goes to strange places, spirits can enter the babe in her womb.

- Inheritance: If the mother or grandmother is a witch she can transfer the spirit to the child up to the third and the fourth generations. Diseases such as sickle cell, diabetes, and Asthma can also be transferred. —

- Fear, insecurity as well as physical and sexual abuse.

One of the most effective ways of children deliverance is for the parents to pray over them when they are sleeping. They must be ministered to gently and in love.

● CONFESSIONS

Ps. 32:8: *I will instruct thee and teach thee in the way which thou shalt go: I will guide thee with mine eye.*

Job 22:28: *Thou shalt also decree a thing, and it shall be established unto thee: and the light shall shine upon thy ways.*

Col. 1:9-10: *For this cause we also, since the day we heard it, do not cease to pray for you, and to desire that ye might be filled with the knowledge of his will in all wisdom and spiritual understanding; That ye might walk worthy of the Lord unto all pleasing, being fruitful in every good work, and increasing in the knowledge of God;*

1 Cor. 7:14: *For the unbelieving husband is sanctified by the wife, and the unbelieving wife is sanctified by the husband: else were your children unclean; but now are they holy.*

Luke 1:37: *For with God nothing shall be impossible.*

1 Jn. 4:4: *Ye are of God, little children, and have overcome them: because greater is he that is in you, than he that is in the world.*

Isa. 8:10,18: *Take counsel together, and it shall come to nought; speak the word, and it shall not stand: for God is with us. . . . Behold, I and the children whom the LORD hath given me are for signs and for wonders in Israel from the LORD of hosts, which dwelleth in mount Zion.*

Deut. 28:7: *The LORD shall cause thine enemies that rise up against thee to be smitten before thy face: they shall come out against thee one way, and flee before thee seven ways.*

Rom. 16:20: *And the God of peace shall bruise Satan under your feet shortly. The grace of our Lord Jesus Christ be with you. Amen.*

● **PRAISE WORSHIP**

1. I bind every spirit, contrary to the Spirit of God, preventing me from enjoying my children, in the name of Jesus.

2. I bind every spirit blinding their minds from receiving the glorious light of the Gospel of our Lord Jesus Christ, in the name of Jesus.

3. Let all spirits of stubbornness, pride and disrespect for parents flee from their lives, in the name of Jesus.

4. Father, destroy everything in my children preventing them from doing Your will, in the name of Jesus.

5. Every curse, evil covenant and all inherited problems passed down to

the children, be cancelled, in the name of Jesus.

6. Mention their names one by one and tell the Lord what you want them to become.

7. Let every association and agreement between my children and my enemies be scattered, in the name of Jesus.

8. My children will not become mis-directed arrows, in Jesus' name.

9. I release my children from the bondage of any evil domination, in the name of Jesus.

10. Let all evil influences by demonic friends clear away, in the name of Jesus.

11. You . . . *(mention the name of the child)*, I dissociate you from any conscious or unconscious demonic groupings or involvement, in the name of Jesus.

12. In the name of Jesus, I receive the mandate and now exercise it to release my children from the prison of any strongman.

13. Let God arise and all the enemies of my home be scattered, in the name of Jesus.

14. Every evil influence and activity of strange women on my children be nullified, in the name of Jesus.

15. Thank God for answers to your prayer.

DELIVERANCE FOR CHILDREN
Mark 10:14-16

We often tend to forget that teaching the gospel of deliverance produces greater result in children who are in their tender ages than adults. It is high time you, as a Christian minister or parent, sought for early deliverance of your children or wards before they graduate to "dry fish that can no longer be folded".

Luke 18:15: *"And they brought unto Him infants that He would touch them, ..."*

One touch from Jesus was enough to open blind eyes, heal long standing infirmities and set the captives free. No matter the strength or the duration of the bondage, one touch was enough.

I don't know what your child needs deliverance from, but one touch from Jesus will solve the problem. These prayer points will invite Jesus into your situation to take control. They are designed for the unborn child as well as young children. Children in the womb can hear and there have been cases where an infirmity like asthma has been traced to the parents fighting while the woman was pregnant.

Infants and young children need to be prayed for against unfriendly friends and demonic initiation through food. They need to be constantly placed under the protection of the blood of Jesus.

As you use these prayer points, your child/children will "increase in wisdom and stature, and in favour with God and man" (Luke 2:52).

A. PRAYER POINTS FOR BABIES IN THE WOMB

• CONFESSIONS

Luke 1:41: *And it came to pass, that, when Elisabeth heard the salutation of Mary, the babe leaped in her womb; and Elisabeth was filled with the Holy Ghost:*

Ps. 139:13: *For thou hast possessed my reins: thou hast covered me in my mother's womb.*

Isa. 44:2: *Thus saith the LORD that made thee, and formed thee from the womb, which will help thee; Fear not, O Jacob, my servant; and thou, Jeshurun, whom I have chosen.*

Gal. 1:15: *But when it pleased God, who separated me from my mother's womb, and called me by his grace,*

Jer. 1:5: *Before I formed thee in the belly I knew thee; and before thou camest forth out of the womb I sanctified thee, and I ordained thee a prophet unto the nations.*

● **PRAISE WORSHIP**

1. I thank You Lord for the provision of this child.
2. I thank You Lord for this child shall be great before You and shall do exploits in Your name.
3. I decree that no sickness or plague will come upon the baby, in the name of Jesus.
4. I decree soundness, health and wholeness into the spirit, soul and body of the baby, in the name of Jesus.
5. I ban this baby from inheriting any evil thing from our own family line, in the name of Jesus.
6. I speak wholeness, soundness and perfection into the heart, eyes, ears, skin, bones, teeth of the baby, in the name of Jesus.
7. Let the baby be covered with the blood of Jesus and surrounded by the hedge of divine fire, in the name of Jesus.
8. I disallow the baby from having/accepting any form of infirmity, in the name of Jesus.
9. Let the respiratory, digestive and circulatory systems of the baby be normal, strong and healthy, in the name of Jesus.
10. You baby, hear the word of the Lord. Your position must be head down at birth, in the name of Jesus. The cord must be the perfect length and position, not around the baby's neck, in Jesus' name.
11. O Lord, let the child be saved at an early age.

12. O Lord, let the child be filled with the Holy Spirit even from the womb.

B. PRAYER POINTS FOR PROTECTION AND DELIVERANCE FOR CHILDREN

• CONFESSION

Col. 2:14-15: *Blotting out the handwriting of ordinances that was against us, which was contrary to us, and took it out of the way, nailing it to his cross; And having spoiled principalities and powers, he made a shew of them openly, triumphing over them in it.*

Isa. 26:3: *Thou wilt keep him in perfect peace, whose mind is stayed on thee: because he trusteth in thee.*

Ps. 91:10: *There shall no evil befall thee, neither shall any plague come nigh thy dwelling.*

• PRAISE WORSHIP

1. I cut off the flow of hereditary problem's into the child, in the name of Jesus.

2. I bind every negative ancestral spirit and command it to loose its hold upon the child, in the name of Jesus.

3. Let every problem arising from the power of bad parental example receive solution, in the name of Jesus.

4. I break every hereditary curse and bondage upon the child, in the name of Jesus.

5. Let the child be cleansed from every hereditary problems with the blood of Jesus.

6. I command everything that will prevent my child from being a blessing to be totally shattered, in the name of Jesus.

7. I command any power that wants to convert my child to a nuisance to be completely paralysed, in the name of Jesus.

8. You spirit of . . . (*pick from the under listed*), release my child, in the name of Jesus.

- rejection	- abnormal fears	- familiar spirit
- sexual lust	- addiction	- unreasonable silence
- rebellion	- forgetfulness	- anger
- mind darkness	- confusion	- day dreaming
- stupidity	- slowness	- inactivity
- inability to read	- infirmity	- indifference
- dullness	- spiritual blindness	- ostrich behaviour
- bad sleeping	- bad dreams	

9. Let every problem arising from . . . (*Pick from the under listed*) receive divine solution, in the name of Jesus.

- child birth after long and protracted labour
- child birth by caesarean operation or with instrumental assistance
- child birth with cord around the neck
- father dying or leaving the mother
- polygamous set up
- parents addiction to alcohol, smoking or others sins
- child conceived outside wedlock
- child conceived as a result of rape or accidental pregnancy
- child conceived as a result of incest
- child born to parents who do not want them
- child being spoilt and pampered
- child born to unhappy parents who argue, fight or do not communicate
- child born to harsh parents
- destruction of home by fire or encountering some natural disasters
- sudden drop in the family standard of living
- child not believed when telling the truth
- constant criticism by parents

- unjust discipline
- subjection to sexual molestation
- children with some birth deformity
- children born with sex opposite to what the parents desired
- sexual aggression to wife by a father in the presence of the child.
- adopted child
- separation or divorce of the parents
- death of one or both parents
- boarding school
- lack of parental love and discipline
- attempted abortion during pregnancy, etc.

10. I render every bad spirit powerless in the life of . . . *(put the name of the child)*, in the name of Jesus.

11. I bind the power and break the influence of every negative spirit militating against . . .*(put the name of the child)*, in Jesus' name.

12. You harmful hereditary and other wicked spirits, loose . . . *(put the name of the child)* from your grip, in the name of Jesus.

13. Father Lord, let the blood of Jesus cleanse the mind, emotions, imaginations and will of . . . *(put the name of the child)*, in the name of Jesus.

14. Lord, fill this child with Your joy, glory, peace and love.

15. Thank God for answering your prayer.

I REFUSE TO LOSE
Genesis 50

- *For those who are under satanic pressure to give up.*
- *For those who refuse to quit.*

The activities of the emptier and wasters are on the increase. They are working to make you lose your spiritual, physical and material blessings; don't give up, resist them sternly in prayer.

Phillipians 4:13: "*I can do all things through Christ who strengthens me.*"

If you want to win in life you have to develop the right mental attitude. Man is a product of his thoughts. That is why the Bible says in Proverbs 23:7, "As he thinketh in his heart, so is he." If you think you are a failure then you are a failure. If you believe you are a winner, you are a winner.

One of the places the enemy builds a stronghold is in our minds. That is why we are told to cast down every negative imagination. "Casting down imaginations, and every high thing that exalteth itself against the knowledge of God, and bringing into captivity every thought to the obedience of Christ; (2 Corin. 10:5).

Don't be moved by sight, the things you see or the circumstances around you. You should only be moved by the word of God. Your future is not determined by your present situation or circumstances. It is determined by God's pre-ordained will concerning you (2 Tim. 1:4). God is able to bring growth and life out of the most unlikely places. "for he shall grow up before him as a tender plant and as a root out of dry ground: . . ." Plants don't normally grow and blossom on dry ground.

Stop limiting God by your thinking. Think big, plan big. God is able to do all things.

Know this; the ridiculous goes before the miraculous. As you use these prayer points, God will turn your points of ridicule into streams of miracles.

- **CONFESSION**

Ps. 27:1-2: *The LORD is my light and my salvation; whom shall I fear? the LORD is the strength of my life; of whom shall I be afraid? When the wicked, even mine enemies and my foes, came upon me to eat up my flesh, they stumbled and fell.*

● **PRAISE WORSHIP**

1. Let every imagination of destruction against me wither from the source, in the name of Jesus.

2. Those laughing me to scorn shall glorify God because of me, in the name of Jesus.

3. Let the destructive plan of the enemies aimed against me blow up in their faces, in the name of Jesus.

4. Let my point of ridicule be converted to a source of promotion, in the name of Jesus.

5. Let all powers sponsoring evil activities against me be disgraced, in the name of Jesus.

6. Let the stubborn strongman delegated against me fall down to the ground and become impotent, in the name of Jesus.

7. Let the stronghold of every spirit of Korah, Dathan and Abiram militating against me be smashed to pieces, in Jesus' name.

8. Let every spirit of Balaam hired to curse me fall after the order of Balaam, in the name of Jesus.

9. Let every spirit of Sanballat and Tobiah hindering my progress receive the stones of fire, in the name of Jesus.

10. Let every spirit of Egypt militating against me fall after the order of Pharaoh, in the name of Jesus.

11. Let every spirit of Herod planning my fall be disgraced, in the name of Jesus.

12. Let every spirit of Goliath boasting against me receive the stones of fire, in the name of Jesus.

13. Let every spirit of Pharaoh pursuing me fall into the Red Sea of their own making, in the name of Jesus.

14. Let all satanic manipulations aimed at reversing my divine destiny be frustrated, in the name of Jesus.

15. Let all destructive broadcasters of my goodness be silenced, in the name of Jesus.

16. Let all leaking bags and pockets be sealed up, in Jesus' name.

17. Let all evil monitoring eyes fashioned against me receive blindness, in the name of Jesus.

18. Let every evil effect of strange touches be removed from my life, in the name of Jesus.

19. Let all my blessings confiscated by witchcraft spirits be released, in the name of Jesus.

20. Let all my blessings confiscated by familiar spirits be released, in the name of Jesus.

21. Let all my blessings confiscated by ancestral spirits be released, in the name of Jesus.

22. Let all my blessings confiscated by envious enemies be released, in the name of Jesus.

23. Let all my blessings confiscated by satanic agents be released, in the name of Jesus.

24. Let all my blessings confiscated by principalities be released, in the name of Jesus.

25 Let all my blessings confiscated by rulers of darkness be released, in the name of Jesus.

26. Let all my blessings confiscated by evil powers be released, in the name of Jesus.

27. Let all my blessings confiscated by spiritual wickedness in the heavenly places be released, in the name of Jesus.

28. I command all demonic reverse gears installed to hinder my progress to be roasted, in the name of Jesus.

29. Any evil sleep undertaken to harm me should be converted to dead sleep, in the name of Jesus.

30. Let all weapons and devices of oppressors and tormentors be rendered impotent, in the name of Jesus.

31. Let the fire of God destroy the power operating any spiritual vehicle working against me, in the name of Jesus.

32. Let all evil advice given against my favour crash and disintegrate, in the name of Jesus.

33. Let all the eaters of flesh and drinkers of blood, stumble and fall, in the name of Jesus.

34. I command stubborn pursuers to pursue themselves, in the name of Jesus.

35. Let the wind, the sun and the moon run contrary to every demonic presence in my environment, in Jesus' name.

36. You devourers, vanish from my labour, in the name of Jesus.

37. Let every tree planted by fear in my life dry up to the roots, in the name of Jesus.

38. I cancel all enchantments, curses and spells that are against me, in the name of Jesus.

39. Let all iron-like curses break, in the name of Jesus.

40. Let divine tongue of fire roast any evil tongue against me, in the name of Jesus.

41. O Lord, establish me in every good work.

42. I claim long life and prosperity, in the name of Jesus.

43. God of peace, sanctify me wholly, in the name of Jesus.

44. Let Christ dwell in my heart by faith, in the name of Jesus.

45. I paralyze every power of death and hell targeted against me, in the name of Jesus.

46. I claim deliverance from the attack of any satanic sword of death, in the name of Jesus.

47. I shall not die but live to declare the works of God, in Jesus' name.

48. Let my body, soul and spirit be preserved blameless unto the coming of our Lord Jesus Christ.

49. I claim angelic assistance and protection, in the name of Jesus.

50. Lord, let me be fruitful in every good work.

51. I decree every satanic stranger in my body to depart now, in the name of Jesus.

52. Let the word of the Lord have free course and be glorified by me, in the name of Jesus.

53. I command all my pursuing enemies to turn back and flee, in the name of Jesus.

54. I command every enemy of my life to stumble and fall, in the name of Jesus.

55. Lord, let me be above and never beneath.

56. Let me be filled with the knowledge of God's will, in Jesus' name.

57. God will bless them that bless me and curse them that curse me, in the name of Jesus.

58. Let the anointing to be more than a conqueror fall upon me, in the name of Jesus.

59. Let me walk worthy of the Lord unto all, in the name of Jesus.

60. I trample upon every problem serpent and scorpion, in Jesus' name.

61. Lord, set me on high and honor me.

62. Let me be filled with all wisdom and spiritual understanding, in the name of Jesus.

63. I come against every fear of the enemy in my life, in Jesus' name.

64. Let me be rooted and grounded in love, in the name of Jesus.

65. The terror of the night shall not be my portion, in Jesus' name.

66. The arrow of the day willnot be my lot, in the name of Jesus.

67. The pestilence of darkness shall be disgraced before me, in the name of Jesus.

68. The destruction of the noonday shall not be my portion, in the name of Jesus.

69. I forbid evil to befall me or any plague near my camp, in the name of Jesus.

70. Oh God, help me to comprehend the breadth, length, depth and height of the love of Christ, in the name of Jesus.

71. Let the wrath of God be upon every enemy of my life, in the name of Jesus.

72. Let me be filled with all the fullness of God, in the name of Jesus.

73. I render every divination and enchantment of hell against my life impotent, in the name of Jesus.

74. I forbid the storm of the world from troubling my dwelling place, in the name of Jesus.

75. Let every false allegation and accusation against me fall down to the ground and die, in the name of Jesus.

76. Let there be a divine cover of the glory of God upon me, in the name of Jesus.

77. Lord, let the eyes of my understanding be enlightened, in the name of Jesus.

78. I decree all diseases of Egypt out of my life, in the name of Jesus.

79. Begin to command all afflictions to depart, in the name of Jesus.

80. O Lord, perfect what is lacking in my faith.

81. I revoke every satanic decree issued against my promotion, in the name of Jesus.

82. I silence every evil dog barking against my breakthroughs, in the name of Jesus.

83. Let the finger of God unseat my household strongman, in the name of Jesus.

84. Every evil bird flying for my sake, be trapped, in the name of Jesus.

85. Every agent of disgrace, backward movements and shame, release me, in the mighty name of Jesus.

86. I overthrow every evil throne installed against my life, in the name of Jesus.

87. Every agent of disorder in my life, be scattered unto desolation, in the name of Jesus.

88. Every power fueling my problems, fall down and die, in Jesus' name.

89. I release myself from any curse working in my family, in the name of Jesus.

90. Let every spiritual vulture delegated against me eat its own flesh, in the name of Jesus.

91. I receive the shoes of iron and trample upon serpents and scorpions, in the name of Jesus.

92. Every cleverly concealed problematic root, be uprooted, in the name of Jesus.

93. I disgrace every evil wisdom working against my breakthroughs, in the name of Jesus.

94. In the power of the Holy Spirit, I crush all my enemies, in the name of Jesus.

95. In the power of the Holy Spirit, I put every evil under my feet, in the name of Jesus.

96. Lord, let me be extraordinary.

97. Holy Spirit, deposit Your wonders in my life, in the name of Jesus.

98. Lord Jesus, break my infirmity and destroy my disease.

99. Lord Jesus, destroy satanic foundations and build me upon Your word.

100. Lord Jesus, set me ablaze with Your Spirit.

101. Let divine earthquake shake down the foundation of every satanic prison, in the name of Jesus.

102. I loose confusion, shame and reproach into the camp of the enemy, in the name of Jesus.

103. I bind every evil spirit withstanding good testimonies in my life, in the name of Jesus.

104. Every satanic river of backwardness, dry up, in the name of Jesus.

105. I destroy every evil dedication made by my parents for my sake, in the name of Jesus.

106. Let all prayer failures cease in my life, in the name of Jesus.

107. Holy Ghost, fulfil Your purpose in me now, in the name of Jesus.

108. I refuse to be moved by environment based situations or satanic re vival, in the name of Jesus.

109. I will receive all that the Lord purposed for me in this programme, in the name of Jesus.

110. O Lord, create within me hunger and thirst after purity and holiness.

111. Holy Spirit, promote divine possibility in my life, in Jesus' name.

112. Holy Spirit, liberate my spirit that I may scorn the works of the flesh, in the name of Jesus.

113. I take the thoughts of accusation against me captive, in the name of Jesus.

114. I command everything working contrary to the obedience of Christ in my life to wither away, in the name of Jesus.

115. Holy Spirit, transform me from weakness to strength, in the name of Jesus.

116. Holy Spirit, unmask any portion of me that is unsurrendered, in the name of Jesus.

117. Holy Spirit, begin to expose all the hidden sins in my life, in the name of Jesus.

118. Let every circle of backwardness in my life be dashed to pieces, in the name of Jesus.

119. All my Goliaths, receive the stones of fire, in the name of Jesus.

120. All satanic consultations against me, be frustrated, in the name of Jesus.

121. All satanic confrontations against me, disintegrate, in the name of Jesus.

122. I render every weapon fashioned against me impotent, in the name of Jesus.

123. Every monitoring and regulatory gadgets working against me, be destroyed, in the name of Jesus.

124. I refuse to shed tears to glorify the enemy, in the name of Jesus.

125. I disarm every vagabond spirit in my life, in the name of Jesus.

126. I paralyse every opposition to my breakthroughs in every area of my life, in the name of Jesus.

127. Every financial coffin fashioned against my finances, be smashed to pieces, in the name of Jesus.

128. I break every grip of witchcraft over my life, in the name of Jesus.

129. All unfavourable situations confronting me, begin to re-align your selves to favour me now, in the name of Jesus.

130. Every mountain of satanic confrontation in every department of my life, crumble now, in the name of Jesus.

131. Every mountain of impossibility in every department of my life, crumble now n the name of Jesus.

132. O Lord, bear me up on eagle's wings before my enemies.

133. I destroy every financial and progress coffins constructed against me with the thunder fire of God, in Jesus' name.

134. I receive power to leap over every wall that the enemy has built against my progress, in the name of Jesus.

135. Let the root of any oppression in my life dry up from its source, in the name of Jesus.

136. I render every Goliath defying my prayers impotent, in the name of Jesus.

137. I paralyse every unrepentant adversity, in the name of Jesus.

138. Let every incantation against me wither from the source, in the name of Jesus.

139. O Lord, begin to convert my mockery to advancement.

140. Let every opposition by household wickedness melt away, in the name of Jesus.

I AM SENTENCED TO VICTORY AND CONDEMNED TO WIN

Acts 12

- *For those who have made up their minds that complete victory is a must.*

People may join to take an evil decision over your life or take actions that are geared towards relegating you to the background. Such decision or actions will eventually turn out for your good if you can pray.

1 John 5:4: *"Whosoever is born of God overcomes the world and this is the victory that overcomes the world even our faith."*

Every born again child of God has been sentenced to win: Jesus won the victory for us on the cross of Calvary. As many as will appropriate these blessings into their lives are winners:

- we have been blessed with all spiritual blessings in heavenly places. Ephesians 1:3.

- we are His workmanship. created in Christ Jesus unto good works. Ephesians 2:10. God's creation is always good! God has never created a failure.

- we have eternal life (John 1:12)

- we have the righteousness of God (2 Corinthians 5:21)

- Jesus became poor that I might become rich. (2 Cor. 8:9)

- Jesus carried my infirmities so I can have divine health (1 Peter 2:24)

- Christ has been made unto us wisdom and righteousness, and sanctification, and redemption: (1 Cor. 1:30)

- God has given us peace (Phillipians 4:7).

Since God has done so much for us, why are we living as failures? Why don't we believe that we have what God says we have, and we are who God says we are?

These prayer points will help losers to become victors and failures; winners.

● CONFESSION

Isa. 40:31: *But they that wait upon the LORD shall renew their strength; they shall mount up with wings as eagles; they shall run, and not be weary; and they shall walk, and not faint.*

● PRAISE WORSHIP

1. Let all my enemies fall into their own traps, in the name of Jesus.
2. O Lord, convert my struggle to prosperity.
3. O Lord, I refuse to let You go unless You bless me.
4. Every evil preparation against my life, be frustrated, in Jesus' name.
5. O Lord, let my joy, peace and blessings be multiplied.
6. Blood of Jesus, disconnect my life from failure at the edge of break-throughs, in the name of Jesus.
7. I refuse to reap any evil harvest in every department of my life, in the name of Jesus.
8. Let divine favour in every blessing of life be my lot, in Jesus' name.
9. I cut off and reject every inherited poverty, in the name of Jesus.
10. Let the foundations of my life be repaired to carry divine prosperity, in the name of Jesus.
11. Let every territorial power hindering answers to my prayers be brought down to the pit, in the name of Jesus.
12. I refuse to offer unacceptable offerings, in the name of Jesus.
13. I refuse to run ahead of God in all my endavours, in Jesus' name.
14. I refuse to ask in contrast to God's will, in the name of Jesus.
15. I refuse to harbour any prayer killer in every department of my life, in the name of Jesus.
16. *Spend quality time to stand against the effects of the evil designs listed hereunder. Take one fruit at a time and be violent. If you notice any reaction, stop and deal thoroughly with it before you proceed to the next one. Pray aggressively as follows:* "I speak destruction unto

the fruits of . . ., loose your hold upon my life, in the name of Jesus. I command you to be separated from me. I place the cross of Jesus between me and you. I forbid you to never return or deposit or any other evil thing, in Jesus' name."

- blood pollution
- failure of divine promise
- parental curses
- examination failure
- hair manipulation
- debts
- unexplainable hatred
- incomplete victories
- closed roads
- spiritual confiscation
- miracle delayers
- self-declared antagonists
- slow-down progress
- circle of problems
- satanic time-table
- infirmity
- enchantment

- success manipulation
- polygamous contamination
- peppery arrows
- satanic syringe
- drug dependence
- caged finances
- lukewarmness in prayer
- open curses and threats
- marital downgrading
- night feeding
- anti-promotion spirits
- lack of direction
- dream harassment
- periodic problems
- parental hatred
- false vision
- rejection

17. I dismantle every satanic dustbin fashioned against me, in the name of Jesus.

18. I recover every fragment of my life from the hands of household wickedness, in the name of Jesus.

19. Every evil grip upon my spirit, loose your hold, in Jesus' name.

20. Every evil grip upon my soul, loose your hold, in the name of Jesus.

21. Every evil grip upon my body, loose your hold, in Jesus' name.

22. I overthrow every demonic judgement directed against me, in the name of Jesus.

23. I dismantle by the blood of Jesus, every evil throne installed against me, in the name of Jesus.

24. I challenge and disgrace every satanic prophet hired against me by fire, in the name of Jesus.

25. Every evil authority backing up my enemies, be withdrawn, in the name of Jesus.

26. Let the foothold of satanic oppressors become slippery, in the name of Jesus.

27. Holy Ghost fire, destroy every garment of reproach in my life, in the name of Jesus.

28. I refuse every evil design and label placed upon my life, in the name of Jesus.

29. Let riot and confusion baptize the camp of my enemies, in the name of Jesus.

30. I close down every satanic broadcasting station fashioned against me, in the name of Jesus.

31. Any conscious or unconscious material eaten from the table of the enemy, depart from my life now, in Jesus' name.

32. I dismantle every demonic opposition to my breakthroughs, in the name of Jesus.

33. Every anti-excellence spirit, loose your hold upon my life, in the name of Jesus.

34. I cast the spirits behind my problems unto the fire of judgement, in the name of Jesus.

35. Every agent of oppression, be punished and tormented unto submission, in the name of Jesus.

36. Every satanic case-file against my life, be closed by the blood of Jesus.

37. Every agent of oppression, be disgraced after the order of the gods of Egypt, in the name of Jesus.

38. Let every agent of oppression experience God as a mighty terrible one, in the name of Jesus.

39. Holy Spirit, empower me to pray destiny-changing prayers, in the name of Jesus.

40. Let all my prayers in this programme arrest divine attention, in the name of Jesus.

41. I withdraw my benefits from the altar of (pick from the under listed), in the name of Jesus.

- household wickedness
- unfriendly friends
- iron-like curses
- ancestral handwriting
- spirit of failure
- evil broadcasters
- evil breeze
- devourers
- evil consumption
- placental bondage
- ancestral bondage
- satanic handwriting
- wicked superiors
- unconscious evil invitation
- ignorant satanic assistance
- serpentine attacks
- arrows of infirmity
- wicked stronghold

- envious friends
- evil covenants
- imported demons
- evil hands
- uncertainty
- collective captivity
- emptier
- bewitchment
- evil transfer
- satanic decision
- bad names
- dream defeats
- marital demotion
- evil parental design
- attack through polygamy
- evil summons
- evil spiritual consumption

42. I command all my foes to prostrate before me in surrender, in the name of Jesus.

43. Every evil river mocking my efforts, dry up now, in Jesus' name.

44. I dismantle every satanic protocol affecting my breakthroughs, in the name of Jesus.

45. Every evil guest, do not locate my address, in the name of Jesus.

46. Let all my Marah receive sweetness and my Jericho receive demolition, in the name of Jesus.

47. I paralyse every merciless tormentor, in the name of Jesus.

48. Let the blood of Jesus rub off every handwriting of poverty in my life, in the name of Jesus.

49. Lord, bring miracles into my life by ways which Herod cannot find.

50. Just as the grave cannot hold Jesus, no grave will hold my miracles, in the name of Jesus.

51. Let every inherited poison begin to come out from their hidden places in my life now, in the name of Jesus.

52. I destroy all secret power sources fashioned against me, in the name of Jesus.

53. I withdraw the authority belonging to any demonic object fashioned against me, in the name of Jesus.

54. O Lord, turn my mountains to miracles.

55. I refuse to pick the wrong materials from the bank of life, in the name of Jesus.

56. I refuse to loose any ground in my life to the enemy, in Jesus' name.

57. Let every inherited wicked plantation in my life be uprooted, in the name of Jesus.

58. My prosperity will not become history while I am yet living, in the name of Jesus.

59. I paralyse every progress arrester, in the name of Jesus.

60. O Lord, satisfy me till my satisfaction overflows.

61. Let my breakthroughs baffle my enemies, in the name of Jesus.

62. I defy the camp of the enemy with the blood of Jesus.

63. Let every instrument of bewitching be rendered impotent now, in the name of Jesus.

64. You stubborn problems, I trample upon your serpents and scorpions, in the name of Jesus.

65. Let the military angels of the Almighty pursue and attack my attackers, in the name of Jesus.

66. Let confusion be created in the camp of my oppressors, in the name of Jesus.

67. Let every battle in the heavenlies be won in favour of the angels conveying my blessings, in the name of Jesus.

68. Let every satanic law programmed into my life be terminated, in the name of Jesus.

69. Let every evil ancestral law programmed into my genes be terminated, in the name of Jesus.

70. Let my prayers release angelic intervention to my favour, in the name of Jesus.

71. I receive the anointing to disgrace satanic arrows, in Jesus' name.

72. I cut off every supply of food to my problems, in the name of Jesus.

73. Let thunder from the Lord destroy every evil altar constructed against me, in the name of Jesus.

74. Lord, release me from known and unknown curses.

75. I rebuke every power working against the soundness of my mind, in the name of Jesus.

76. I seal the rebuke with the blood of Jesus.

77. Let every untamed enemy be tamed by the Holy Ghost, in the name of Jesus.

78. I break every evil padlock put upon my business, in Jesus' name.

79. Let the blood of Jesus rub off evil creams and ointments put upon my body, in the name of Jesus.

80. Let every witchcraft meeting summoned for my sake be scattered unto desolation, in the name of Jesus.

81. Let every chain of satanic accusation be shattered, in Jesus' name.

82. Let every resistance to my breakthroughs crumble, in Jesus' name.

83. I will become all that God created me to be, in the name of Jesus.

84. Every good area in my life that the enemy has denied expression, receive resurrection power, in the name of Jesus.

85. Let every . . . (pick from the under listed) receive the resurrection power of the Lord Jesus Christ now.

    - paralysed potential - buried virtue   - dead talent
    - slow progress   - battered emotion - amputated blessing
    - fainting spirit   - dead organ   - lifeless business
    - dead certificate   - dead spiritual life - dead prayer altar
    - slumbering spirit   - dead marriage

86. Every roar of satanic lions against me, be silenced, in Jesus' name.

87. Let the activities of vagabond evil broadcasters be terminated, in the name of Jesus.

88. Every satanic programme against me, be nullified, in Jesus' name.

89. Every power hunting for my secrets, be confounded, in Jesus' name

90. I paralyse every power of bewitching fashioned against me, in the name of Jesus.

91. Let any demon living inside any member of my household depart now, in the name of Jesus.

92. Every spirit of 'pocket with holes', be mended by the blood of Jesus.

93. Let all evil rivers flowing down to me from my ancestral line dry up now, in the name of Jesus.

94. I quench the power of 'star paralyzers', in the name of Jesus.

95. Let every power of unrepentant witchcraft be disgraced, in the name of Jesus.

96. Let all satanic check-points hindering my prayers be bulldozed by divine fire, in the name of Jesus. *Sing any song about the blood of Jesus (for at least 5 minutes).*

97. Angels of the living God, arrest, detain and prosecute all agents of darkness working against me, in the name of Jesus.

98. I destroy the walls of security around my enemies, in Jesus' name.

99. Every power obstructing the manifestations of my goodness, fall down and die now, in the name of Jesus.

100. I refuse to supply my enemies with ammunition, in Jesus' name.

101. Let the fire of God begin to melt every evil resistance to my progress, in the name of Jesus.

102. I paralyse every satanic siege mounted against any area of my life, in the name of Jesus.

103. My prayers will not return to my chest, in the name of Jesus.

104. My heavens shall not become brass, in the name of Jesus.

105. My prayers shall not fall down to the ground, in Jesus' name.

106. My cries shall arrest divine attention and sponsor divine action in this programme, in the name of Jesus.

107. Every spirit serpent delegated against me, I command you to run into the desert and be buried in the hot sand, in Jesus' name.

108. I forbid the downgrading of my potentials, in the name of Jesus.

109. Let the demons delegated against my prayers fall down and die now, in the name of Jesus.

110. All satanic traffic wardens diverting good things from me, be paralysed, in the name of Jesus.

111. I release myself from hereditary spiritual handicap, in the name of Jesus.

112. Let all stubborn demons be starved to death, in Jesus' name.

113. I reject every evil peace in any department of my life, in the name of Jesus.

114. I seize power from every wicked spirit militating against my life, in the name of Jesus.

115. O Lord, open my eyes, and let me have a revelation vision of Christ in this programme.

116. O Lord, clean away from my life all that does not reflect You.

117. Holy Spirit, deposit Your wonders in my life in this programme, in the name of Jesus.

118. Holy Ghost, fill me that I might bring forth good fruit, in the name of Jesus.

119. Let the healing power of the Holy Spirit fall on me now, in the name of Jesus.

120. I use the blood of Jesus to defy every satanic power fashioned against any department of my life, in the name of Jesus.

121. I put every evil hindrance to my breakthroughs under my feet now, in the name of Jesus.

122. From the north, south, east and west, I claim all my blessings now, in the name of Jesus.

123. I receive all that God has for me in this programme, in the name of Jesus.

124. I render every aggressive altar impotent, in the name of Jesus.

125. Every evil altar erected against me, be disgraced, in Jesus' name.

126. Anything done against my life under demonic anointing be nullified, in the name of Jesus.

127. I curse every local altar fashioned against me, in the name Jesus.

128. Let the hammer of the Almighty God smash every evil altar erected against me, in Jesus, name.

129. O Lord, send Your fire to destroy every evil altar fashioned against me, in the name of Jesus.

130. Every evil priest ministering against me at the evil altar, receive the sword of God, in the name of Jesus.

131. Let the thunder of God smite every evil priest working against me, on the evil altar, and burn them to ashes, in Jesus' name.

132. Let every satanic priest ministering against me, on evil altars, fall down and die, in the name of Jesus.

133. Any hand that wants to retaliate or arrest me because of all these prayers I am praying, dry up and wither, in Jesus' name.

134. Every stubborn evil altar priest, drink your own blood, in the name of Jesus.

135. I possess my possession stolen by the evil altar, in Jesus' name.

136. I withdraw my name from every evil altar, in the name of Jesus.

137. I withdraw my blessings from every evil altar, in the name of Jesus.

138. I withdraw my breakthroughs from every evil altar, in the name of Jesus.

139. I withdraw my glory from every evil altar, in the name of Jesus.

140. I withdraw my prosperity from every evil altar, in Jesus' name.

DEATH MUST DIE
1 Cor. 15

• *For those who desire to hold on to the promise, 'I shall not die but live to declare the works of God'.*

Do you know that the unfathomable power of the risen Christ has shattered the power of death which is known to be the last enemy of man? This power is also at your disposal to wield against the spirit of death haunting your life.

Hebrews 5:7: *"Who in the days of His flesh when He had offered up prayers and supplications with strong crying and tears unto Him that was able to save him from death, and was heard in that He feared."*

Death was defeated the day Jesus rose from the dead. The resurrection morning marked the defeat of death. As believers we are not to fear death (1 Corin. 15:54-56). God wields power over death.

The Scripture says, "I shall not die but live and declare the works of God" (Psalm 118:17). If you are being pursued of the spirit of death and hell and you desire to live long, these prayer points are for you.

God has promised that He will satisfy us with long life (Ps 91:16). This means when you are satisfied and fulfilled in life then you can go. As long as you are not satisfied, and you have not fulfilled your destiny, death has no business with you.

Rebuke the spirit of death, using these prayer points and you will fulfil the number of your days.

• **CONFESSION**

Ps. 118:17: *"I shall not die, but live, and declare the works of the LORD."*

• **PRAISE WORSHIP**

1. I withdraw anything representing me from every evil altar, in the name of Jesus.

2. *Mention the organ that you know is not behaving the way it should. When you have done this begin to say, "I withdraw you from every evil altar, in the name of Jesus." Say this seven hot times.*

3. Let the wind of the Holy Spirit bring all scattered bones together now, in the name of Jesus.

4. I use the blood of Jesus to reverse every poor record of the past about my life, in the name of Jesus.

5. I refuse to accept satanic substitute for my destiny, in Jesus' name.

6. I refuse to be caged by the enemy of good things, in Jesus' name.

7. Let every internal coffin in my life receive the fire of God and be roasted now, in the name of Jesus.

8. Every destiny-paralysing power fashioned against my destiny, fall down and die, in the name of Jesus.

9. Every inherited evil limitation in any area of my life, depart now, in the mighty name of Jesus.

10. Every architect of spiritual coffins, I command you to fall down and die, in the name of our Lord Jesus Christ.

11. Every cloud of uncertainty, clear away now, in the name of Jesus.

12. I refuse to be converted to a living dead, in the name of Jesus.

13. Let every evil laying on of hands and shaking of evil hands be nullified, in the name of Jesus.

14. Every satanic consultation concerning my life, be nullified, in the name of Jesus.

15. Every decision taken against my life by witchcraft spirits, be nullified, in the name of Jesus.

16. I reject aborted victories in every area of my life, in Jesus' name.

17. Every caged star, be released now, in the name of Jesus.

18. My imagination and dreams will not be used against me, in the name of Jesus.

19. Let every germ of infirmity die, in the name of Jesus.

20. Let every agent of sickness die, in the name of Jesus.

21. Hidden sicknesses, disappear now, in the name of Jesus.

22. Fountain of discomfort in any part of my body, dry up, in the name of Jesus.

23. Every dead organ in my body, receive life, in the name of Jesus.

24. Let my blood be transfused with the blood of Jesus.

25. Every internal disorder in my body, receive order, in Jesus' name.

26. Every infirmity, come out with all your roots, in the name of Jesus.

27. I withdraw every conscious and unconscious cooperation with sickness, in the name of Jesus.

28. Let the whirlwind of the Lord blow away every wind of infirmity, in the name of Jesus.

29. I release my body from every curse of infirmity, in Jesus' name.

30. Let the blood of Jesus flush out every evil deposit from my blood, in the name of Jesus.

31. I recover every organ of my body from every evil altar, in the name of Jesus.

32. Help me, O Lord, to recognise Your voice.

33. Lord, where I am blind, give me sight.

34. I command my fears to evaporate now, in the name of Jesus.

35. I throw off every burden of worry, in the name of Jesus.

36. I refuse to be entangled with evil friends, in the name of Jesus.

37. I cast down every road-block hiding my progress, in Jesus' name.

38. Let my spiritual climate send terror to the camp of the enemy, in the name of Jesus.

39. O Lord, release me from evil words or evil sentences.

40. O Lord, let all my enemies be boxed to a corner.

41. I bind every jungle and desert spirit working in any area of my life, in the name of Jesus.

42. O Lord, deliver me by signs and wonders.

43. O Lord, make me a divine phenomenon.

44. Let spiritual violence that confuses the enemy be set into the camps of my enemies, in the name of Jesus.

45. Let heavenly fire ignite my prayer life, in the name of Jesus.

46. Let the divine anointing for spiritual breakthroughs fall upon me now, in the name of Jesus.

47. Let my prayer altar receive power today, in the name of Jesus.

48. O Lord, make me a prayer addict.

49. O Lord, forgive me of the sin of ingratitude.

50. Lord Jesus, make me a burning flame for You.

51. Lord Jesus, revive and ignite my prayer altar.

52. Let the calculations of the enemy upon my life backfire, in the name of Jesus.

53. Let the glory of the enemy upon my life be put to shame, in the name of Jesus.

54. No enemy will use my life for promotion, in the name of Jesus.

55. I disband every host of wickedness organised against my life, in the name of Jesus.

56. Let the cross of Christ come between me and the oppressors, in the name of Jesus.

57. I close every door opened to satan by me or by my ancestors with the blood of Jesus.

58. I break and loose myself from all problems emanating from the womb, in the name of Jesus.

59. I break and loose myself from any evil spiritual agreement, in the name of Jesus.

60. I break and loose myself from any bondage of physical illness, in the name of Jesus.

61. I break and loose myself from every curse, bewitching, witchcraft and charms put upon my family line.

62. I break and loose myself from every dark spirit and satanic bondage, in the name of Jesus.

63. Let every strongman attached to any area of my life be bound by hot chains of fire, in the name of Jesus.

64. Power preventing my life from growing the seed God wants to grow, depart, in the name of Jesus.

65. I refuse to reap any bad harvest, in the name of Jesus.

66. All wolves working in my life, be bound and receive the thunder fire of God, in the name of Jesus.

67. Whatever hinders me from my goodness, give way now, in the name of Jesus.

68. My buried goodness, come forth now, in the name of Jesus.

69. Holy Spirit, reveal Yourself to me, in the name of Jesus.

70. Holy Spirit, overshadow my life, in the name of Jesus.

71. Lord, let Your glory be manifested in my life.

72. Lord, let Your fire make my body too hot for to any evil spirit to inhabit.

73. Lord, drain sickness and worry out of my spirit.

74. Let all remnants of evil deposits be melted with the fire of God, in the name of Jesus.

75. Holy Spirit, energise me to pray to arrest God's attention, in the name of Jesus.

76. Holy Spirit, empower me to pray destiny-changing prayers, in the name of Jesus.

77. Poisons, come out of my life now, in the name of Jesus.

78. I destroy all secret power sources, in the name of Jesus.

79. I tear down and destroy the hidden works of the enemy, in the name of Jesus.

80. I break any evil stronghold over my life, in the name of Jesus.
81. I bind and cast out any spirit executing evil curse against me, in the name of Jesus.
82. I come against every evil pronouncement against me, in the name of Jesus.
83. I overthrow and release myself from evil domination and control, in the name of Jesus.
84. I withdraw the authority belonging to any demonic object fashioned against me, in the name of Jesus.
85. All demonic gifts, loose your activity upon my life, in Jesus' name.
86. Evil magnets, loose your activity upon my life, in the name of Jesus.
87. I terminate any evil tenancy in any department of my life, in the name of Jesus.
88. I refuse to pick the wrong materials in the bank of life, in the name of Jesus.
89. I refuse to travel along the wrong road, in the name of Jesus.
90. I refuse to loose ground to the enemy, in the name of Jesus.
91. O Lord, turn my mountains to miracles.
92. I refuse to be crushed by satanic mountains, in the name of Jesus.
93. I receive the anointing to disgrace satanic arrows, in Jesus' name.
94. I cut off every supply of food to my problems, in the name of Jesus.
95. Let the thunder from the Lord destroy every evil altar constructed against me, in the name of Jesus.
96. Lord, release me from known and unknown curses.
97. I rebuke every power working against the soundness of my mind, in the name of Jesus.
98. I seal the rebuke with the blood of Jesus.
99. Let every untamed enemy be tamed by the Holy Ghost, in the name of Jesus.

100. I use the hammer of the Lord to break every padlock put upon my progress, in the name of Jesus.

101. Let the blood of Jesus rub off evil creams and ointments put upon my body against my goodness, in the name of Jesus.

102. Blood of Jesus, flood out and scatter witchcraft meetings summoned for my sake, in the name of Jesus.

103. Let every chain of satanic excuse against my progress be shattered, in the name of Jesus.

104. Let every satanic resistance to my breakthroughs in the heavens, on earth and underneath the earth crumble, in the name of Jesus.

105. I will become all that God created me to be, in Jesus' name.

106. Every good area in my life that the enemy has denied breakthroughs, receive resurrection power now, in Jesus' name.

107. By the blood of Jesus, I cast every spiritual viper attached to my hands against my progress into the fire of judgement, in the name of Jesus.

108. By the blood of Jesus, I rebuke every attacking and fearful dreams, in the name of Jesus.

109. By the blood of Jesus, I recover my l ost land and blessings, in the name of Jesus.

110. By the blood o f Jesus, I challenge spiritual poisons with the Holy Ghost fire, in the name of Jesus.

111. I command every seat of satanic diviners erected against my progress in life to be overturned now, in the name of Jesus.

112. Every power siting on evil mats against my progress in life, fall down and die now, in the name of Jesus.

113. I speak destruction unto every oracle speaking against my progress in life, in the name of Jesus.

114. Every power speaking impossibility unto my present unfavourable situation, fall down and die, in the name of Jesus.

115. I terminate every evil progress in every area of my life, in the name of Jesus.

116. Every satanic power that has swallowed my money, vomit it now, in the name of Jesus.

117. Every agent of health destruction working in my life, fall down and die, in the name of Jesus.

118. Every problem masquerading as something else, be exposed and disgraced by fire, in the name of Jesus.

119. Let favour meet favour in my life and be increased mightily, in the name of Jesus.

120. Every good thing stolen from my life, be restored in 21 fold, in the name of Jesus.

121. O Lord, reveal every beneficial secret about my life to me.

122. I refuse to enter into any satanic coffin constructed for my sake, in the name of Jesus.

123. Let every anti-marriage stronghold organised against my life be pulled down by fire, in the name of Jesus.

124. Let all my Red Sea situations receive divine solution now, in the name of Jesus.

125. Every unrepentant opposition against my breakthroughs, fall down and die, in the name of Jesus.

126. Let the river of poverty flowing into my life from my family line dry up now, in the name of Jesus.

127. Any problem in my finances associated with the consumption of concoctions receive solution now, in the name of Jesus.

128. Let every satanic oppression be dissolved by fire, in Jesus' name.

129. O God, arise in Your anger and set me free from every grip of the oppressors, in the name of Jesus.

130. I speak failure unto every satanic weapon fashioned against me, in the name of Jesus.

131. I speak frustration unto every evil snare fashioned against me, in the name of Jesus.

132. Every satanic pit, be neutralised now, in the name of Jesus.

133. Let the strength of evil in my life wither to nothingness, in the name of Jesus.

134. Let every evil angel contending with the angel bringing my blessings fall down, like lightening and be disgraced, in the name of Jesus.

135. Let my personal Jeroboam be disgraced, in the name of Jesus.

136. Every visible and invisible altar, I sentence you to trouble today, in the name of Jesus.

137. I hammer to pieces every internal evil altar, in the name of Jesus.

138. Every evil king enthroned against me, fall down and die now, in the name of Jesus.

139. I tear down every evil altar and I disgrace their priests, in the name of Jesus.

140. Let the hands of evil priests offering evil sacrifices on evil altars against me wither, in the name of Jesus.

WEALTH MUST CHANGE HANDS

2 Kings 7

- *For abundance, prosperity and financial breakthroughs.*
- *To release wealth into your bossom.*
- *To paralyse the spirit of poverty.*
- *To recover lost benefits.*

We must accept the fact that the earth is the Lord's and the fullness thereof. We, as Christians, should make deliberate effort to ensure that there is transfer of wealth from the enemies of God to us.

Proverbs 13:22: *"A good man leaveth an inheritance to his children's children: the wealth of the sinner is laid up for the just."*

The wealth of the sinner has been stored up for the righteous. These prayer points have been specially vomited by the Holy Spirit to cause the transfer of this wealth into the hands of the children of God, from the hands of the sinners. Poverty must die in the lives of the children of God. God is the one that gives the power to get wealth (Deuteronomy 8:18).

Believers have to pray to God for the power to get wealth, so that the law relating to divine prosperity will function in their lives.

The laws concerning money are:

- **MAKE:** A true child of God has to be able to make money legally. He needs the wisdom of God to generate unique idea's that will enable him to get wealth.

- **MANAGE:** A true child of God has to have the right perspective on how to manage money. There are some people, even if you give them 1million, they will mismanage it and get back into begging and borrowing.

- **MULTIPLY:** Each child of God has to learn how to multiply the wealth God has given him. It is not enough to make money, you need to multiply it. Pray for discernment to make the right investments. When God blessed I saac, the Bible says, *"And the man waxed great, and went forward, and grew until he became very great:"* (Gen. 26:13).

As you pray these prayer points, God will baptize you with the power to get wealth and wealth will change hands in your life.

● CONFESSIONS

Ps. 84:11-12: *For the LORD God is a sun and shield: the LORD will give grace and glory: no good thing will he withhold from them that walk uprightly. O LORD of hosts, blessed is the man that trusteth in thee.*

Deut. 8:18: *But thou shalt remember the LORD thy God: for it is he that giveth thee power to get wealth, that he may establish his covenant which he sware unto thy fathers, as it is this day.*

● PRAISE WORSHIP

1. O Lord, let my Jacob become Israel today.
2. Let my bald Samson begin to grow hair now, in the name of Jesus.
3. Let every evil conspirator gathering against me be disbanded by fire, in the name of Jesus.
4. Let evil vows against my future be rendered null and void, in the name of Jesus.
5. You powers that quench the fire of God in one's life, I am not your candidate, in the name of Jesus.
6. Every deeply-rooted problem in my life, be uprooted by fire, in the name of Jesus.
7. I reject every evil domination and bondage in my life, in the name of Jesus.
8. My angel of blessings will locate me today, in the name of Jesus.
9. My angel of blessing will not go unless he blesses me, in the name of Jesus.
10. Lord, let my cries provoke angelic assistance today.
11. Lord, give me the name that would bless me today.
12. Let every satanic hindrance targeted against my angel of blessing be dissolved by fire, in the name of Jesus.
13. O Lord, deliver me from evil stones thrown at me by unfriendly friends.
14. Every evil riot and rage against me, be disgraced, in Jesus' name.

15. O Lord, deliver me from every satanic noise.

16. O Lord, deliver me from the tumult of the people.

17. Let every evil crowd seeking to take my life be scattered unto desolation, in the name of Jesus.

18. Let all sicknesses come out with all their roots now, in the name of Jesus.

19. Let the poison of sickness be drained out of my system now, in the name of Jesus.

20. Let every abnormality within my body receive divine healing now, in the name of Jesus.

21. Let every fountain of infirmity dry up now, in the name of Jesus.

22. Every hunter of my health, be disappointed, in the name of Jesus.

23. Let every stubborn pursuer of my health fall down and die now, in the name of Jesus.

24. My head will not be anchored to any evil, in the name of Jesus.

25. Let evil pursue all unrepentant evil workers, in the name of Jesus.

26. I neutralize every power of tragedy, in the name of Jesus.

27. No evil shall overtake me, in the name of Jesus.

28. Every evil preparation against me, be frustrated, in Jesus' name.

29. Let every dead area of my blessings receive resurrection now, in the name of Jesus.

30. Let the resurrection power of the Lord Jesus come upon the works of my hands now, in the name of Jesus.

31. O Lord, bless me to a dumbfounding degree.

32. O Lord, enlarge my coast.

33. Let every embargo on my progress fall down and scatter, in the name of Jesus.

34. I reject satanic restrictions in every area of my life, in Jesus' name.

35. Let the mighty hands of God be upon me for good, in Jesus' name.

36. Lord, keep me from all evil wisdom and manipulation.

37. I reject any invitation to appointment with sorrow, in Jesus' name.

38. I scatter evil multitudes gathered against me, in the name of Jesus.

39. Let God be God against my oppressors, in the name of Jesus.

40. The Lord will not be a spectator in my affairs, but a participant, in the name of Jesus.

41. Lord, save me from sinking in the sea of life.

42. My head will not be anchored to doubt, in the name of Jesus.

43. I refuse any evil diversion, in the name of Jesus.

44. I will not take my eyes off the Lord Jesus, in the name of Jesus.

45. O Lord, anchor Your mercy to my head.

46. Lord Jesus, let me receive the touch of signs and wonders now.

47. Let God be God in my Red Sea situation, in the name of Jesus.

48. O God, let it be known that you are God in every department of my life, in the name of Jesus.

49. O Lord, do a new thing to my enemies that would permanently dismantle their power.

50. O Lord, let uncommon techniques be utilised to disgrace any opposition against my life.

51. Let the earth open up and swallow every stubborn pursuer in my life, in the name of Jesus.

52. O Lord God of Abraham, Isaac and Jacob, manifest Yourself in Your power to bless me.

53. O Lord, begin to answer every evil stronghold by fire and roast them to ashes.

54. Every power challenging the power of God in my life, be disgraced now, in the name of Jesus.

55. Let every rage of the enemy against my coming breakthroughs be disgraced now, in the name of Jesus.

56. Let every evil imagination fashioned against me be frustrated and be disgraced by fire, in the name of Jesus.

57. Let every satanic plan against my future glory be rendered a useless, in the name of Jesus.

58. Evil rulers assembled against me, be scattered unto desolation, in the name of Jesus.

59. O Lord, behold the threatening of my enemies, give unto me divine boldness to prosper over them.

60. O Lord, stretch Your mighty hand to perform signs and wonders in my life.

61. I speak destruction unto every desert spirit of poverty in my life, in the name of Jesus.

62. I speak disgrace unto the spirit of failure in my life, in Jesus' name.

63. I speak failure unto spirit of impossibility in my life, in Jesus' name.

64. Let every spirit of fruitlessness in my life, be paralysed now, in the name of Jesus.

65. I reject every spirit of debt and bankruptcy in my life. Be paralysed now, in the name of Jesus.

66. I reject every spirit of business and work failure in my life. Be paralysed now, in the name of Jesus.

67. Spirit of infirmity in my life, be paralysed now, in Jesus' name.

68. Spirit of marriage destruction in my life, be paralysed now, in the name of Jesus.

69. Every desert security man assigned against my life, fall down and die now, in the name of Jesus.

70. I release every faculty of my life from the dominion of desert spirit, in the name of Jesus.

71. I paralyse the activities of desert spirit in my life, in Jesus' name.

72. Every evil load of desert spirit in my life, go back to your sender, in the name of Jesus.

73. Every anointing of desert spirit upon my life, dry up by the fire of the Holy Ghost, in the name of Jesus.

74. Blood of Jesus, block every doorway of poverty.

75. All the powers assisting poverty in my life, be bound, in the name of Jesus.

76. My life, receive the anointing of fruitfulness, in the name of Jesus.

77. My life, refuse to be anchored to any evil, in the name of Jesus.

78. My head, refuse to bear any evil burden, in the name of Jesus.

79. I refuse to walk into any problem, in the name of Jesus.

80. My hands, refuse to magnetise problems to me, in Jesus' name.

81. Every satanic architect of problems assigned against me, be roasted, in the name of Jesus.

82. I break the backbone of any problem associated with every second of my life, in the name of Jesus.

83. Any power that has been supplying strength to problems in my life, be wasted, in the name of Jesus.

84. I refuse to swim in the ocean of problems in my life, in the name of Jesus.

85. Every remotely controlled problem energised by household wickedness, be devoured by the Lion of Judah, in Jesus' name.

86. I sack and disband any power behind the problems of my life, in the name of Jesus.

87. Lord Jesus, I refuse to be kept busy by the devil.

88. I receive power to convert failures designed for my life to outstanding successes, in the name of Jesus.

89. I receive power to close down every satanic factory designed for me, in the name of Jesus.

90. Angels of blessings, begin to locate me for my own blessings in this programme now, in the name of Jesus.

91. Powers behind accidental problems, I am not your candidate. Fall down and die, in the name of Jesus.

92. I receive the power to break every circle of problems, in the name of Jesus.

93. Every attempt being made by destiny killers against my destiny, be frustrated unto death, in the name of Jesus.

94. I command the fire of God to come upon every destiny killer working against my destiny, in the name of Jesus.

95. I remove my destiny from the camp of destiny killers, in the name of Jesus.

96. I use the fire of God and the blood of Jesus to surround my destiny, in the name of Jesus.

97. Every power working against the fulfilment of my destiny, be disgraced, in the name of Jesus.

98. I command my destiny to reject every bewitchment, in the name of Jesus.

99. I deliver my destiny from the grip of destiny killers, in Jesus' name.

100. Every evil done to my destiny by household wickedness, be reversed now, in the name of Jesus.

101. Every vessel of destiny killers fashioned against my destiny, fall down and die, in the name of Jesus.

102. Let the ground open now and swallow all destiny killers working against me, in the name of Jesus.

103. Every evil gathering against my destiny, be scattered, in the name of Jesus.

104. My destiny, you will not manage poverty, in the name of Jesus.

105. My destiny, you will not manage failure, in the name of Jesus.

106. I command my destiny to begin to change to the best now, in the name of Jesus.

107. My head will not carry evil load, in the name of Jesus.

108. Every enemy of progress in my life, fall down and die now, in the name of Jesus.

109. I reject every evil manipulation against my destiny, in the name of Jesus.

110. I paralyse every activity of destiny killers in every area of my life, in the name of Jesus.

111. I smash every giant of 'almost there' to pieces, in Jesus' name.

112. I destroy every castle of backwardness, in the name of Jesus.

113. I receive the anointing to destroy every destiny killer, in the name of Jesus.

114. Let every satanic guard organised against my life be paralysed, in the name of Jesus.

115. I frustrate every evil network designed against my life, in the name of Jesus.

116. The enemies shall not understand the issues of my life, in the name of Jesus.

117. The enemies shall not understand the issues of my finances and blessings, in the name of Jesus.

118. Anything that has been done with snail to slow down my life, be destroyed by the blood of Jesus, in the name of Jesus.

119. I reject every spirit of backwardness, in the name of Jesus.

120. I reject caged life, in the name of Jesus.

121. I reject caged finances, in the name of Jesus.

122. I reject caged health, in the name of Jesus.

123. I reject caged marriage, in the name of Jesus.

124. I reject every spirit of stagnation, in the name of Jesus.

125. Every satanic chain on my legs, break now, in the name of Jesus.

126. Let every hole in my hands be blocked by the blood of Jesus, in the name of Jesus.

127. My life shall not be hung on the shelf, in the name of Jesus.

128. The hair of my Samson shall not be shaved, in the name of Jesus.

129. Every anti-progress spirit, be bound by chains of fire, in the name of Jesus.

130. Every satanic prison warden, fall down and die, in Jesus' name.

131. I shall not crash in the race of life, in the name of Jesus.

132. My progress shall not be terminated, in the name of Jesus.

133. Let my life be too hot for the enemy to handle, in Jesus' name.

134. Every power set up to pull me down spiritually, be disgraced, in the name of Jesus.

135. Every power set up to pull me down physically, be disgraced, in the name of Jesus.

136. Every power set up to pull my marriage down, be disgraced, in the name of Jesus.

137. Every power set up to pull my finances down, be disgraced, in the name of Jesus.

138. No 'progress arrester' shall prevail over my life, in Jesus' name.

139. I receive power to excel in every area of my life, in Jesus' name.

140. I shall mount up on wings as the eagles, in the name of Jesus.

141. I withdraw my wealth from the hand of the bondwoman and her children, in the name of Jesus.

142. I will not squander my divine opportunities, in the name of Jesus.

143. I must pray to get results in this programme, in Jesus' name.

144. I dismantle any power working against my efficiency, in the name of Jesus.

145. I refuse to lock the door of blessings against myself, in the name of Jesus.

146. I refuse to be a wandering star, in the name of Jesus.

147. I refuse to appear to disappear, in the name of Jesus.

148. Let the riches of the Gentiles be transferred to me, in the name of Jesus.

149. Let the angels of the Lord pursue every enemy of my prosperity to destruction, in the name of Jesus.

150. Let the sword of the Goliath of poverty turn against it, in the name of Jesus.

151. Let wealth change hands in my life, in the name of Jesus.

152. O Lord, make a hole in the roof for me for my prosperity.

153. Let the yoke of poverty upon my life be dashed to pieces, in the name of Jesus.

154. Let every satanic siren scaring away my helpers be silenced, in the name of Jesus.

155. Let every masquerading power swallowing my prosperity be destroyed, in the name of Jesus.

156. Let every coffin constructed against my prosperity swallow the owner, in the name of Jesus.

157. Let the ways of the evil angels of poverty delegated against me be dark and slippery, in the name of Jesus.

158. Lord Jesus, hold my purse.

159. Every demonic scarcity, be dissolved by fire, in Jesus' name.

160. By the wealthy name of Jesus, let heavenly resources rush to my door.

161. I attack my lack with the sword of fire, in the name of Jesus.

162. Satanic debt and credit, be dissolved, in the name of Jesus.

163. O Lord, be my eternal cashier.

164. I bind the spirit of debt. I shall not borrow to eat, in Jesus' name.

165. Every evil meeting summoned against my prosperity, scatter without repair, in the name of Jesus.

166. Every arrow of wickedness fired against my prosperity, be disgraced, in the name of Jesus.

167. Let my life magnetize favour for breakthroughs, in Jesus' name.

168. I arrest every gadget of poverty, in the name of Jesus.

169. I recover my blessings from any water, forest and satanic banks, in the name of Jesus.

170. Let all my departed glory be restored, in the name of Jesus.

171. Let all my departed virtues be restored, in the name of Jesus.

172. Let God arise and let all my stubborn pursuers scatter, in the name of Jesus.

173. Every attack by evil night creatures, be disgraced, in the name of Jesus.

174. Let the wings of every spirit flying against me be dashed to pieces, in the name of Jesus.

175. Angels of the living God, search the land of the living and the land of the dead and recover my stolen properties, in the name of Jesus.

176. Every gadget of frustration, be dashed to pieces, in Jesus' name.

177. I break every curse of poverty working upon my life, in the name of Jesus.

178. I bind every spirit drinking the blood of my prosperity, in the name of Jesus.

179. O Lord, create new and profitable opportunities for me.

180. Let ministering angels bring customers and favour to me, in the name of Jesus.

181. Anyone occupying my seat of prosperity, clear away, in the name of Jesus.

182. Lord, make a way for me in the land of the living.

183. I bind the spirit of fake and useless investment, in Jesus' name.

184. All unsold materials, be sold with profit, in the name of Jesus.

185. Let all business failures be converted to success, in Jesus' name.

186. Every curse on my hands and legs, be broken, in Jesus' name.

187. O Lord, embarrass me with abundance in every area of my life.

188. Every effect of strange money affecting my prosperity, be neutralized, in the name of Jesus.

189. Let brassy heavens break forth and bring rain, in Jesus name.

190. I break the control of every spirit of poverty over my life, in the name of Jesus.

191. Lord Jesus, anoint my eyes to see the hidden riches of this world.

192. Lord Jesus, advertise Your breakthroughs in my life.

193. Let the riches of the ungodly be transferred into my hands, in the name of Jesus.

194. I will rise above the unbelievers around me, in the name of Jesus.

195. O Lord, make me a reference point of divine blessings.

196. Let blessings invade my life, in the name of Jesus.

197. Let the anointing of excellence fall on me, in the name of Jesus.

198. I disarm satan as king and authority over my prosperity, in the name of Jesus.

199. Let harvest over take harvest in my life, in the name of Jesus.

200. Let harvest overtake the sower in my life, in the name of Jesus.

201. Every curse pronounced against my source of income, be broken, in the name of Jesus.

202. Let my breakthroughs turn around for good, in Jesus' name.

203. Curses working against my destiny, break, in the name of Jesus.

204. O Lord, network me with divine helpers.

205. Let life-transforming breakthroughs overtake me, in Jesus' name.

206. Let divine ability overtake me, in the name of Jesus.

207. O Lord, lead me to those who will bless me.

208. Let my favour frustrate the plans of the enemy, in Jesus' name.

209. I will witness the downfall of my strongman, in Jesus' name.

210. I will be a lender and not a borrower, in the name of Jesus.

211. My labour shall not be in vain, in the name of Jesus.

212. Let the embarrassing blessings overtake me, in Jesus' name.

213. O Lord, plant me by the rivers of prosperity.

214. Unknown evil seeds in my life, I command you to refuse to germinate, in the name of Jesus.

215. I refuse to get stuck on one level of blessing, in Jesus' name.

216. I shall posses all the good things I pursue, in the name of Jesus.

217. Every effect of cursed house and land upon my prosperity, break, in the name of Jesus.

218. Every power shielding me away from breakthroughs, fall down and die, in the name of Jesus.

219. Let the garden of my life yield super abundance, in Jesus' name.

220. Every desert spirit, loose your hold upon my life, in Jesus' name.

221. Holy Spirit, plug my life into divine prosperity, in Jesus' name.

222. Every Achan in the camp of my breakthroughs, be exposed and be disgraced, in the name of Jesus.

223. Every power operating demonic gadget against my prosperity, fall down and die, in the name of Jesus.

224. Every power passing evil current into my finances, loose your hold, in the name of Jesus.

225. I break every circle of financial turbulence, in the name of Jesus.

226. I smash the head of poverty on the wall of fire, in Jesus' name.

227. Ugly feet of poverty, walk out of my life now, in Jesus' name.

228. Every garment of poverty, receive the fire of God, in Jesus' name.

229. I reject financial burial, in the name of Jesus.

230. Every garment of poverty, receive the fire of God, in Jesus' name

231. I reject financial burial, in the name of Jesus.

232. I reject every witchcraft burial of my goodness, in Jesus' name.

233. Woe unto every vessel of poverty pursuing me, in Jesus' name.

234. Let the fire of God burn away evil spiritual properties, in the name of Jesus.

235. Poverty-identification marks, be rubbed off by the blood of Jesus.

236. O Lord, heal every financial leprosy in my life.

237. Let my foundation be strengthened to carry divine prosperity, in the name of Jesus.

238. Every stolen property and satanical transfer of virtue, be restored, in the name of Jesus.

239. Let every ordination of debt over my life be cancelled, in the name of Jesus.

240. O Lord, create newer and profitable opportunities for me.

241. Every strange fire ignited against my prosperity, be quenched, in the name of Jesus.

242. Let those sending my money to spiritual mortuary fall down and die, in the name of Jesus.

243. Every power scaring away my prosperity, be paralysed, in the name of Jesus.

244. Every familiar spirit sharing my money before I receive it, be bound permanently, in the name of Jesus.

245. Let every inherited design of poverty melt away by fire, in the name of Jesus.

246. Let every evil re-arrangement of prosperity be dismantled, in the name of Jesus.

247. Lead me O Lord, to my own land that flows with milk and honey.

248. Let satanic giants occupying my promised land fall down and die, in the name of Jesus.

249. O Lord, empower me to climb my mountain of prosperity.

250. Strongman of poverty in my life, fall down and die, in the name of Jesus.

251. Spirits of famine and hunger, my life is not your candidate, in the name of Jesus.

252. I remove my name from the book of financial embarrassment, in the name of Jesus.

253. Every power reinforcing poverty against me, loose your hold, in the name of Jesus.

254. I release myself from every bondage of poverty, in Jesus' name.

255. The riches of the gentiles shall come to me, in the name of Jesus.

256. Let divine magnets of prosperity be planted in my hands, in the name of Jesus.

257. I retrieve my purse from the hand of Judas, in the name of Jesus.

258. Let there be a reverse transfer of my satanically transferred wealth, in the name of Jesus.

259. I take over the wealth of the sinner, in the name of Jesus.

260. I recover the steering wheel of my wealth from the hand of evil drivers, in the name of Jesus.

261. I refuse to lock the door of blessings against myself, in the name of Jesus.

262. O Lord, revive my blessings.

263. O Lord, return my stolen blessings.

264. O Lord, send God's angels to bring me blessings.

265. O Lord, let everything that needs change in my life to bring me blessings be changed.

266. O Lord, reveal to me the key to my prosperity.

267. Every power sitting on my wealth, fall down and die, in the name of Jesus.

268. O Lord, transfer the wealth of Laban to my Jacob.

269. Let all those who hate my prosperity be put to shame, in the name of Jesus.

270. Every evil bird swallowing my money, fall down and die, in the name of Jesus.

271. Every arrow of poverty, go back to where you came from, in the name of Jesus.

272. I bind every word spoken against my breakthroughs, in the name of Jesus.

273. Every business house energised by satan, fold up, in the name of Jesus.

274. I destroy every clock and timetable of poverty, in Jesus' name.

275. Every water spirit, touch not my prosperity, in the name of Jesus.

276. Let men and women rush wealth to my doors, in Jesus' name.

277. I reject temporary blessings, in the name of Jesus.

278. Every arrow of poverty energised by polygamy, fall down and die, in the name of Jesus.

279. Every arrow of poverty energised by household wickedness, fall down and die, in the name of Jesus.

280. Let power change hands in my finances, in the name of Jesus.

281. Every serpent and scorpion of poverty, die, in the name of Jesus.

282. I refuse to eat the bread of sorrow. I reject the water of affliction, in the name of Jesus.

283. Let divine explosion fall upon my breakthroughs, in Jesus' name.

284. The enemy will not drag my finances on the ground, in the name of Jesus.

285. O Lord, advertize Your wealth and power in my life.

286. Let promotion meet promotion in my life, in the name of Jesus.

287. I pursue and overtake my enemy and recover my wealth from him, in the name of Jesus.

288. Holy Spirit, direct my hands into prosperity, in the name of Jesus.

I SHALL LAUGH LAST
1 Samuel 17

- *For those who are subjects of ridicule and would like to have the last laugh over their enemies.*

In the story of David versus Goliath, a bad beginning made a good end for the nation of Israel. So a true believer is not running the Christian race as one "beating the air". While taking cognizance of the rules of the race, you will surely laugh last.

Psalm 126:2 & 2: *"When the Lord turned again the captivity of Zion, we were like them that dream. Then was our mouth filled with laughter, and our tongue with singing: then said they among the heathen, the Lord has done great thing for them."*

He who laughs last laughs best, says an old English proverb. Indeed this is true for every child of the living God. The devil might feel that he has you where he wants you with your back against the wall with any hope of salvation dashed. Your enemies might be mocking and ridiculing you. Beloved, as long as you place your complete trust in God, He will perfect that which concerns you. He will begin a great deliverance that will turn around all captivity and put laughter into your mouth.

I don't know what your captivity is or what is making the devil feel he is winning in your life. These prayer points will destroy every bondage, and every garment of shame and reproach will be torn off. The Bible says, Against all hope Abraham believed in hope and he became the father of many nations (Romans 4:18). The name of the promised child was Isaac, which means laughter. When the captivity of barrenness was turned around, Abraham and Sarah laughed (Genesis 21:1-6). God filled their mouths with laughter.

As you use these prayer points every captivity that is causing shame and reproaches well as everything that is causing you to cry, will be destroyed and the Almighty God will fill your mouth with laughter.

● CONFESSION

Zeph. 3:17: *The LORD thy God in the midst of thee is mighty; he will save, he will rejoice over thee with joy; he will rest in his love, he will joy over thee with singing.*

● PRAISE WORSHIP

1. The Lord shall promote me in multiple folds, in the name of Jesus.
2. Every inherited evil cage in my life, be dismantled by fire, in the name of Jesus.
3. Any evil door opened in my life, be sealed by the blood of Jesus, in the name of Jesus.
4. Holy Ghost fire, begin to arrest the spirit of fear in every department of my life, in the name of Jesus.
5. Holy Ghost fire, begin to arrest the spirit of doubt in every department of my life, in the name of Jesus.
6. Holy Ghost fire, begin to arrest the spirit of deceit in every department of my life, in the name of Jesus.
7. Holy Ghost fire, begin to arrest the spirit of unbelief in every department of my life, in the name of Jesus.
8. Holy Ghost fire, begin to arrest the spirit of strife in every department of my life, in the name of Jesus.
9. Holy Ghost fire, begin to arrest unforgiving spirit in every department of my life, in the name of Jesus.
10. Holy Ghost fire, begin to arrest murmuring spirits in every department of my life, in the name of Jesus.
11. My life, be delivered from internal cage, in the name of Jesus.
12. I fire back every arrow of poverty in every department of my life, in the name of Jesus.
13. I come against every hidden and clever devourer in every department of my life, in the name of Jesus.
14. I bind every profit starvation, in the name of Jesus.

15. I disconnect myself from every financial trap, in the name of Jesus.
16. I uproot every seed of failure in my life with the fire of God, in the name of Jesus.
17. I nullify every spirit of leaking pocket in my finances, in the name of Jesus.
18. I nullify and destroy every activity of success polluters, in the name of Jesus.
19. Financial embarrassment will never continue to be my lot, in the name of Jesus.
20. I will not follow evil pattern of failure, in the name of Jesus.
21. Dead account, you will never be my lot, in the name of Jesus.
22. I shall not work for others to eat, in the name of Jesus.
23. My blessings, you will not slip off my hands, in the name of Jesus.
24. I come against every poverty activator in every department of my life, in the name of Jesus.
25. O Lord, let my angelic assistants scatter every evil activator assigned against me.
26. You powers of the emptier, you will not empty my life, in the name of Jesus.
27. You powers of the emptier, you will not empty my marriage, in the name of Jesus.
28. You powers of the emptier, you will not empty my finances, in the name of Jesus.
29. You powers of the emptier, you will not empty my health, in the name of Jesus.
30. You powers of the emptier, you will not empty my children, in the name of Jesus.
31. O Lord, enlarge my coast and silence my enemies.
32. Father Lord, let Your floods of success overwhelm my life, in the name of Jesus.

33. O Lord, put to shame and disgrace every evil activator pursuing my progress, in the name of Jesus.

34. Every arrow of vagabond spirit fired at me by household wickedness, come out and die now, in the name of Jesus.

35. Every spirit of double left hand that walked into my life through household wickedness, walk out now, in the name of Jesus.

36. I paralyse every inner heat in my life, in the name of Jesus.

37. Every arrow of madness in any area of my life, come out and die now, in the name of Jesus.

38. Every arrow of poverty in any area of my life, come out and die now, in the name of Jesus.

39. Every arrow of non-achievement in any area of my life, come out and die now, in the name of Jesus.

40. Every arrow of backwardness in any area of my life, come out and die now, in the name of Jesus.

41. Every arrow of worry in any area of my life, come out and die now, in the name of Jesus.

42. Every evil arrow of the enemy in my private part, jump out now and die, in the name of Jesus.

43. Every household arrow fired at my business, be neutralised by the blood of Jesus, in the name of Jesus.

44. Every arrow of death and hell in my life, come out and die now, in the name of Jesus.

45. Any evil arrow fired at any of my organs by household wickedness, jump out now and die, in the name of Jesus.

46. I pull out every arrow fired into my foundation by household wickedness, in the name of Jesus.

47. Every household arrow putting stubbornness into my problems, fly out and die, in the name of Jesus.

48. Every arrow of prayerlessness, fly out of my life now, in the name of Jesus.

49. I loose myself from the bondage of profitless hard-work, in the name of Jesus.

50. Let all evil enquiries about my life be rendered null and void, in the name of Jesus.

51. Let all evil pronouncements made against me by evil reporters be nullified by the blood of Jesus, in the name of Jesus.

52. Let every imagination of evil reporters against my life be nullified by the blood of Jesus, in the name of Jesus.

53. I withdraw all my co-operation with evil reporters, in Jesus' name.

54. Let every tree of sorrow planted by the evil reporter be uprooted by fire, in the name of Jesus.

55. I command all the secrets of the evil reporter to be reviewed and let them be disgraced by fire, in the name of Jesus.

56. O Lord, plant good things into my life that will elevate me, in the name of Jesus.

57. Father Lord, let Your name alone be glorified in my life as a result of this programme, in the name of Jesus.

58. Let the fire of the Lord consume every evil report about my life, in the name of Jesus.

59. Let God arise and let all the evil reporters be scattered, in the name of Jesus.

60. Let every power assigned against my life fall down and die, in the name of Jesus.

61. Let every power that is against the plan of God for my life in this programme fall down and die, in the name of Jesus.

62. I will never turn back at the edge of my miracles in this programme, in the name of Jesus.

63. Let every progress of evil reporters in my life be destroyed, in the name of Jesus.

64. I remove my name from the book of failure, in the name of Jesus.

65. Let the rain of fire fall upon the camp of all evil reporters working against my life, in the name of Jesus.

66. Let every evil hand-writing fashioned against my life be washed away by the blood of Jesus.

67. Let every evil hand-writing fashioned against my home be nullified by the blood of Jesus.

68. Let every evil hand-writing fashioned against my promotion be nullified by the blood of Jesus.

69. Let every evil hand-writing fashioned against my peace be nullified by the blood of Jesus.

70. Let every evil hand-writing fashioned against my joy be nullified by the blood of Jesus.

71. Let every evil hand-writing fashioned against my promotion be nullified by the blood of Jesus.

72. Let every evil hand-writing fashioned against my business be nullified by the blood of Jesus.

73. Let every evil hand-writing fashioned against my spiritual growth be nullified by the blood of Jesus.

74. Let every evil hand-writing fashioned against my finances be nullified by the blood of Jesus.

75. I receive divine anointing to quench the fire of any evil arrow in my life, in the name of Jesus.

76. Every inherited arrow of family destruction, receive the fire of God and come out of my life now, in the name of Jesus.

77. Every arrow of marriage destruction, receive the fire of God and come out of my life now, in the name of Jesus.

78. Every arrow of financial failure, receive the fire of God and come out of my life now, in the name of Jesus.

79. Every arrow of infirmity, receive the fire of God and come out of my life now, in the name of Jesus.

80. Every arrow of untimely death, receive the fire of God and come out of my life now, in the name of Jesus.

81. Every arrow of sudden tragedy, receive the fire of God and come out of my life now, in the name of Jesus.

82. Every arrow of prayerlessness, receive the fire of God and come out of my life now, in the name of Jesus.

83. Every arrow of spiritual blindness, receive the fire of God and come out of my life now, in the name of Jesus.

84. Every arrow of spiritual stagnancy, receive the fire of God and come out of my life now, in the name of Jesus.

85. Every arrow of failure at the edge of testimonies, receive the fire of God and come out of my life now, in the name of Jesus.

86. Every arrow of fear and sorrow, receive the fire of God and come out of my life now, in the name of Jesus.

87. Every arrow of depression, frustration and discouragement, receive the fire of God and come out of my life now, in the name of Jesus.

88. Every arrow shot through witchcraft operation, receive the fire of God and come out of my life now, in the name of Jesus.

89. Every arrow from water spirits, receive the fire of God and come out of my life now, in the name of Jesus.

90. Every arrow shot by household wickedness, receive the fire of God and come out of my life now, in the name of Jesus.

91. Every evil arrow that has come out of my life through these prayers, be gathered together, be coated with fire, and spiritual poison and go back to your senders now, in the name of Jesus.

92. Let the power in the blood of Jesus repair every damage done to my life by evil arrows, in the name of Jesus.

93. Let the fire of the Holy Ghost occupy every space vacated by evil arrows in me, in the name of Jesus.

94. I receive spiritual garment that will make my life impenetrable to evil arrows, in the name of Jesus.

95. Every weakness in me that can cause tragedy, be electrocuted, in the name of Jesus.

96. Let the root of tragedy in the foundation of my life, be electrocuted, in the name of Jesus.

97. Let every pollution in my life and family receive divine cleansing now, in the name of Jesus.

98. No member of my family will bring tragedy to my life, in the name of Jesus.

99. You arrow of tragedy, I send you back to your sender, in the name of Jesus.

100. Every information of tragedy that is against my life, be nullified, in the name of Jesus.

101. Let every reporter of tragedy receive mental paralysis now, in the name of Jesus.

102. I refuse to do what will entertain tragedy in my life, in the name of Jesus.

103. My family will not be involved in any tragedy, in Jesus' name.

104. I arrest every agent of tragedy, in the name of Jesus.

105. You spirit of tragedy, I overcome you. You are not my portion, in the name of Jesus.

106. You arrows of tragedy, I make my life invisible to you. You will never locate me, in the name of Jesus.

107. Every strongman behind the spirit of tragedy fashioned against me, I paralyse your strength unto death, in the name of Jesus.

108. All you powers that plan tragedy against one's life, I am not your candidate, in the name of Jesus.

109. Every architectural design of tragedy against my life, be roasted to ashes, in the name of Jesus.

110. O Lord, give me power to overcome every device of tragedy.

111. Holy Spirit, help me to locate and overcome every snare of tragedy, in the name of Jesus.

112. Instead of tragedy, success and promotions shall be my lot, in the name of Jesus.

113. Instead of tragedy, dumbfounding promotions shall pursue and over take me, in the name of Jesus.

114. O Lord, I recall every satanic meeting ever held against my finances, and I reverse the evil decisions taken.

115. I vandalise and destroy any demonic channel through which the money of my labour is being siphoned, in the name of Jesus.

116. Let all satanic agents delegated to monitor my money and progress fall down and die, in the name of Jesus.

117. O Lord, let every power behind the spirit swallowing the money of my labour be paralysed, in the name of Jesus.

118. Let the strongman assigned to watch over my swallowed money be unseated by the fire of God, in the name of Jesus.

119. Let the satanic bank where my swallowed money is being stored receive the thunder of God, the stones of fire and be scattered unto desolation, in the name of Jesus.

120. All those who swallowed my money, s ince I have been working or doing business, I command you to begin to vomit it now, in the name of Jesus.

121. I collect all my vomited money back seven-fold, in Jesus' name.

122. Any money that I have given in good faith to anybody, that is being used as a source of evil against my finances, be roasted to ashes, in the name of Jesus.

123. Let all my money presently in any demonic altar receive the fire of God and be burnt to ashes, in the name of Jesus.

124. I recover the money of my labour from powers that swallow money, in the name of Jesus.

125. I loose my spirit, soul and body from the effect of any evil vow taken on my behalf by household wickedness concerning my money, in the name of Jesus.

126. You household wickedness that have renewed the vow that I will go begging for money, fall down to the ground and die, in the name of Jesus.

127. Let the spirit of baseless basket assigned to my money and business fall to the ground and die, in the name of Jesus.

128. Father Lord, cause the spirit of profitless spending in my life to fall down and die, in the name of Jesus.

129. Let the evil effect of any strange money I have received or touched be neutralised, in the name of Jesus.

130. O Lord, give unto me today, the key to my supernatural financial break throughs.

131. You the spirits of poverty and wasters, I am not your candidate, in the name of Jesus.

132. Every power sitting on my finances, be unseated by fire, in the name of Jesus.

133. Anointing for financial excellence, financial breakthroughs and financial prosperity, fall upon my life now, in the name of Jesus.

134. Every faulty foundation affecting my finances, be repaired by the blood of Jesus, in the name of Jesus.

135. I will not labour in vain in my life, in the name of Jesus.

136. I withdraw my name from the book of financial collapse, in the name of Jesus.

137. Every power of the devourer that has swallowed my finances, begin to vomit them now, in the name of Jesus.

138. I command my dead financial life to receive the power of the resurrection of Jesus, in the name of Jesus.

139. Lord, let my financial life be too hot for the enemy to handle, in the name of Jesus.

LET EVIL STONES BE ROLLED AWAY

Matt. 28

- *To clear away stubborn hindrances.*

You owe it a duty to roll away any stone of sin and unbelief which may can block your miracles. That way, the voice of the Almighty would be able to reach your own Lazarus in the grave yard of sorrow.

John 11:39: *"Jesus said, Take ye away the stone"*

The stone represents anything standing between you and your desired breakthrough! It is that thing which stands between you and your dead situation and hinders your breakthrough from coming forth.

At the tomb of Lazarus, Jesus said, "Roll away the stone!" The stone had to be rolled away before Lazarus could come forth. If the stone had been standing, then there would be no way Lazarus could come forth. For your breakthroughs and desired miracles to come forth you need to roll away all evil stones.

When you've fasted, you've prayed, encouraged yourself in the Lord and you cannot see a change in your situation, and your desired miracle is not coming forth, then these prayer points to roll away evil stones for you!

• CONFESSION

Ps. 103:1-5: *Bless the LORD, O my soul: and all that is within me, bless his holy name. Bless the LORD, O my soul, and forget not all his benefits: Who forgiveth all thine iniquities; who healeth all thy diseases; Who redeemeth thy life from destruction; who crowneth thee with lovingkindness and tender mercies; Who satisfieth thy mouth with good things; so that thy youth is renewed like the eagle's.*

• PRAISE WORSHIP

1. Father Lord, I dedicate and consecrate my financial life to You, in the name of Jesus.

2. Every satanic broadcasting station fashioned against my life, be burnt to ashes, in the name of Jesus.

3. I command all unfriendly friends to receive their spiritual obituaries now, in the name of Jesus.

4. Let all wicked broadcasters become fertilisers for my divine promotion, in the name of Jesus.

5. All evil broadcasters, be buried in the desert, in the name of Jesus.

6. I command every spiritual Sanballat and Tobiah to receive incurable insanity, in the name of Jesus.

7. All my enemies shall bite their fingers in regret, in Jesus' name.

8. Let every satanic agent circulating my name for evil fall down and die now, in the name of Jesus.

9. O Lord, avenge me of my enemies speedily.

10. Let every effect of wicked broadcasting station against my life and destiny be nullified, in the name of Jesus.

11. Let every evil desire and expectation against me and my family fail woefully, in the name of Jesus.

12. Let the works of wicked broadcasters be frustrated, in the name of Jesus.

13. I fire the arrows of disarray into the camp of my enemies, in the name of Jesus.

14. I will not be put to shame, but my enemies shall drink their cup of shame, in the name of Jesus.

15. Let all curses issued against me be converted to blessings, in the name of Jesus.

16. Holy Spirit, broadcast Jesus in my life, in the name of Jesus.

17. Whether the devil likes it or not, goodness and mercy shall follow me, in the name of Jesus.

18. I receive the anointing to succeed against all odds after the order of Nehemiah, in the name of Jesus.

19. I receive the spirit of wisdom and excellence to confound my accusers, in the name of Jesus.

20. I shall laugh my enemies to scorn, in the name of Jesus.

21. Every evil tongue rising against me in judgement, receive the thunder-fire of God, in the name of Jesus.

22. I command every anti-marriage strongman to fall down and die, in the name of Jesus.

23. Father Lord, destroy the yoke of hatred and unhappiness in my marriage, in the name of Jesus.

24. I paralyse the powers behind every for of marriage interference, in the name of Jesus.

25. O Lord, cause the noise of the strangers to cease in my marriage.

26. I bridle the jaw of every power opposing my marriage, in the name of Jesus.

27. Let the sun of my marriage rise in its full strength, in Jesus' name.

28. Lord, cause Your glorious voice of peace to be heard in my marriage.

29. I command every anti-marriage yoke to crumble to pieces, in the name of Jesus.

30. I break every hold of witchcraft working against my marriage, in the name of Jesus.

31. Let every spiritual padlock holding my marriage in bondage break to pieces, in the name of Jesus.

32. Lord, turn the enchantment and divination of my enemy to wind and confusion.

33. Let the whirlwind of God fall grievously upon every strongman in my marriage, in the name of Jesus.

34. Lord, overturn the evil desire of strangers upon my marriage.

35. Evil wall in my marriage, crumble to pieces, in the name of Jesus.

36. I take authority over every marriage destroyer, in Jesus' name.

37. I command every wind of bitterness and fighting in my marriage to stop immediately, in the name of Jesus.

38. Let the attacks by household wickedness be rendered null and void by the blood of Jesus, in the name of Jesus.

39. Let the blood of Jesus destroy the foundation of problems and failure in my marriage, in the name of Jesus.

40. I pronounce the blessings of God upon my marriage, in Jesus' name.

41. Father Lord, heal my marriage and restore happiness to my home, in the name of Jesus.

42. The sun of my marriage shall not set, in the name of Jesus.

43. The banner of love over my marriage shall not tear, in Jesus' name.

44. The glory of my marriage shall not fade, in the name of Jesus.

45. I use the blood of Jesus to unseat every power sitting on my promotion, in the name of Jesus.

46. I use the blood of Jesus to bind all inherited hidden mysterious diseases in my life, in the name of Jesus.

47. By the power in the blood of Jesus, I utilise my divine capital, in the name of Jesus.

48. O Lord, make me a blessing today.

49. I use the blood of Jesus to loose myself from every spirit in me which is not a spirit of God, in the name of Jesus.

50. By the blood of Jesus, I take authority over, and order the binding of, the strongman in my life, in the name of Jesus.

51. I bind every spirit of unbelief in my life, in the name of Jesus.

52. I use the blood of Jesus to send confusion into the camp of the enemy of the progress of my life, in the name of Jesus.

53. By the grace of God, I will see the goodness of the Lord in the land of the living, in the name of Jesus.

54. O Lord, envelope me with fire from heaven and make me to become untouchable to my enemies.

55. O Lord, by Your power that knows no failure, let all the blessings I have lost through unbelief, be restored unto me seven-fold, now.

56. Let every blocked way to breakthroughs be opened by divine order now, in the name of Jesus.

57. Let the fire of the Holy Ghost revive my spiritual life, in Jesus' name.

58. Father Lord, let every habitation of sickness in my life become desolate, in the name of Jesus.

59. Let the blood of Jesus begin to remove every hidden sickness in my body, in the name of Jesus.

60. I command the very cause of any sickness, open or hidden, in my life to leave now, in the name of Jesus.

61. O Lord, carry out every surgical operation necessary in my body now, in the name of Jesus.

62. O Lord, pour Your healing oil of anointing upon my life now.

63. Let my Jacob become Israel today, in the name of Jesus.

64. Let all evil conspirators gathering against me be disbanded, in the name of Jesus.

65. Let all evil vows taken against me be rendered null and void, in the name of Jesus.

66. Let all quenchers of the fire of God in my life be quenched by the fire of the Holy Ghost, in the name of Jesus.

67. Let every deeply rooted problem in any area of my life be uprooted and roasted to ashes, in the name of Jesus.

68. I reject every evil domination and bondage over my life, in the name of Jesus.

69. You oppressive spirits doing havoc in my life, come out with all your roots now, in the name of Jesus.

70. I bind the strongman and cast out his armour, in the name of Jesus.

71. Satan, by the blood of Jesus, I recover all my blessings you and your agents have stolen from me, in the name of Jesus.

72. I break the curse of eating from the dustbin in sorrow, in the name of Jesus.

73. I break the curse of thorns and thistles, in the name of Jesus.

74. I break the curse of eating by the sweat of the face, in the name of Jesus.

75. I stand against all the tricks of satan to hinder my prayer life, in the name of Jesus.

76. Lord, let not my name disappear from Your book of remembrance.

77. Every power trying to remove my name from the mind of my helpers, fall down and die now, in the name of Jesus.

78. Every power trying to pollute the mind of my helpers, fall down and die now, in the name of Jesus.

79. I crush every satanic lion roaring against my success, in the name of Jesus.

80. Any power planning to rebuild my fallen Jericho, fall down and die, in the name of Jesus.

81. Let my mountains be overthrown by fire now, in the name of Jesus.

82. Let my Red Sea begin to divide now, in the name of Jesus.

83. I refuse to live under any satanic cloud, in the name of Jesus.

84. Let every evil power increasing against me fall down and die now, in the name of Jesus.

85. I come against every power in heaven, on earth and underneath the earth, that is against my wealth, by the blood of Jesus.

86. Let the Lord arise mightily for me now.

87. Let the glory of the Lord be seen upon me in a mighty and glorious way, in the name of Jesus.

88. Let all those despising me begin to bow to me from now, in the name of Jesus.

89. My sun shall not go down, in the name of Jesus.

90. My moon shall not wane, in the name of Jesus.

91. I shall not live my life in sorrow, in the name of Jesus.

92. I refuse to make peace with all evil powers, in the name of Jesus.

93. Let any area of my life that is obeying demonic instructions begin to disobey them, in the name of Jesus.

94. Forces of affliction and oppression in any area of my life, be paralysed, in the name of Jesus.

95. All chronic diseases, return to your sender, in the name of Jesus.

96. I stand against the operations of the spirit of death in my life, in the name of Jesus.

97. Let the counsel of the devil to destroy my home be frustrated, in the name of Jesus.

98. I bind every spirit of doubt set up to disgrace my life, in the name of Jesus.

99. I bind every spirit of unbelief set up to disgrace my life, in the name of Jesus.

100. I bind every spirit of fear set up to disgrace my life, in the name of Jesus.

101. I bind every spirit of tradition set up to disgrace my life, in the name of Jesus.

102. I destroy every stronghold of the powers of darkness in my family by the sword of fire, in the name of Jesus.

103. Let every evil effect of ritual killing upon my life by my ancestors be nullified, in the name of Jesus.

104. Let every evil effect of terminal sickness upon my life be nullified, in the name of Jesus.

105. Let every evil effect of genetic sickness upon my life be nullified, in the name of Jesus.

106. Let every evil effect of ancestral sickness upon my life be nullified, in the name of Jesus.

107. I curse every sickness and its evil trees from the roots, in the name of Jesus.

108. I refuse to reap any bad harvest, in the name of Jesus.

109. Every spirit of wolves working against my life, be bound and receive divine judgement now, in the name of Jesus.

110. Let whatever hinders me from my greatness begin to give way now, in the name of Jesus.

111. Let all my buried goodness come forth powerfully now, in the name of Jesus.

112. Any evil door in my life that was opened by my ancestors, I command you to be closed now by the blood of Jesus.

113. Every evil doo r that is giving my enemies way in my life, be closed now by the blood of Jesus, in the name of Jesus.

114. I loose myself from all the effects of any evil spiritual agreement upon my life, in the name of Jesus.

115. I loose myself from all the effects of any evil bondage of physica ill-ness in my life, in the name of Jesus.

116. I loose myself from all the effects of evil curses, bewitching, witch-craft and charms put upon my family line, in Jesus' name.

117. I break and loose myself from every dark spirit and satanic bondage, in the name of Jesus.

118. Let the strongman attached to my promised land be bound by the chains of fire, in the name of Jesus.

119. The good seed of God in me shall not die, in the name of Jesus.

120. The glory of God buried in me shall not die, in the name of Jesus.

121. I refuse to fish in the wrong waters, in the name of Jesus.

122. I will not run myself down, in the name of Jesus.

123. I command the heavens to open to me right now, in Jesus' name.

124. Let the sword of my Goliath turn against him, in Jesus' name.

125. Let the evil vision and dream on my life evaporate from the camp of the enemy, in the name of Jesus.

126. Let every mention of my name for evil become dangerous poison in the mouth of the enemy, in the name of Jesus.

127. O Lord, send divine plagues upon my Pharaoh.

128. Let every satanic ambush be frustrated, in the name of Jesus.

129. Let the confidence of the wicked over my life be broken, in the name of Jesus.

130. Inherited limitations to obtaining good things in my life, depart now, in the name of Jesus.

131. Anti-miracle forces, be paralysed, in the name of Jesus.

132. Let the spirits of revelation and wisdom fall upon my life now, in the name of Jesus.

133. Let the fire of the Holy Ghost clear away every dirtiness from my spirit, in the name of Jesus.

134. Let faith arise in me and let doubt be scattered, in Jesus' name.

135. Let the divine power to speak peace to storms fall upon my life now, in the name of Jesus.

136. Let the divine anointing for spiritual breakthroughs fall upon my life now, in the name of Jesus.

137. O Lord, open my spiritual eyes.

138. I tear up every application I have written to the school of poverty in my life, in the name of Jesus.

139. I tear up all the invitation letters to the demons of poverty, in the name of Jesus.

140. O Lord, open the gates of the showers of blessing to me.

BAPTISM OF PROMOTIONS AND TESTIMONIES

Daniel 3

- *For those who desire dumbfounding break-throughs.*

Perhaps you are passing through series of persecutions and hardships, allowed by God to create an opportunity for your promotion, so that your mouth would be able to share testimonies of His wonders and goodness.

Psalm 71:21: *"Thou shalt increase my greatness, and comfort me on every side."*

"God is able to do exceeding abundantly above all we ask or think, according to the power that worketh in us" (Ephesians 3:20). These prayer points will draw the attention of the God of exceeding abundance. Get God of exceeding abundance to bombard us with blessings and testimonies to the level we will cry out, "O Lord, this is too much. It is enough, please, stop." God wants to 'over-bless' us. He wants to give us more than we need, so we can give out to others. We are blessed to be a blessing.

These prayer points will cause divine increase in all areas of your life. You will grow from strength to strength, glory to glory and favour to favour. God will surely increase your greatness and cause you to be comforted (increased) on every side.

- ## CONFESSION

Luke 4:18: *The Spirit of the Lord is upon me, because he hath anointed me to preach the gospel to the poor; he hath sent me to heal the broken-hearted, to preach deliverance to the captives, and recovering of sight to the blind, to set at liberty them that are bruised,*

- ## PRAISE WORSHIP

1. O Lord, begin to transport me from minimum to maximum.
2. O Lord, let Your renewing power renew my life like the eagles.
3. O Lord, touch my spirit with Your fire.

4. O Lord, let Your wonder-working power close every door to devourers in my life.

5. I rebuke every devourer working on my finances, in Jesus' name.

6. I rebuke every bad feet in my finances, in the name of Jesus.

7. I remove every hand and leg of evil people from my finances, in the name of Jesus.

8. Let the little foxes spoiling my finances be chased out by fire, in the name of Jesus.

9. O Lord, wash my handiwork with the blood of Jesus.

10. O Lord, let Your reviving power revive my blessings.

11. Let the angels of the living God begin to return all my stolen blessings, in the name of Jesus.

12. I loose myself from every satanic seduction, in the name of Jesus.

13. I loose myself from every satanic senselessness, in Jesus' name.

14. I command the cloud of darkness to lift up from me, in the name of Jesus.

15. I arrest myself from the path of death and destruction, in the name of Jesus.

16. Let every destruction and danger to my lifting up be banished, in the name of Jesus.

17. I loose myself from every cobweb of ancestral frustration and backwardness, in the name of Jesus.

18. Every darkness, be dispersed from my life by fire, in Jesus' name.

19. Every stubborn problem in my life, receive the arrow of the Holy Ghost, in the name of Jesus.

20. Every anti-profit, anti-testimony and anti-miracle forces, working in any area of my life, be paralysed by fire, in the name of Jesus.

21. I renounce every evil parental dedication of my life, in Jesus' name.

22. Let my peace drown every trouble fired at me, in Jesus' name.

23. O Lord, begin to make a way for me in the wilderness of life.

24. I refuse to feed my doubt. Doubt, I command you to die, in the name of Jesus.

25. Every evil campaign against my calling, be disgraced, in the name of Jesus.

26. Let the fire of God pursue and consume all repairers of evil in my life, in the name of Jesus.

27. Every dirt in my spirit, be sanitised by the blood of Jesus, in the name of Jesus.

28. I shall be the victor and not the victim, in the name of Jesus.

29. I claim all my covenant rights now, in the name of Jesus.

30. O Lord, touch every department of my life with Your right hand of power.

31. O Lord, deliver me from the oppressors by Your outstretched hand.

32. Let the power to box stubborn forces to a corner fall upon my life now, in the name of Jesus.

33. I repent from every disobedience, in the name of Jesus.

34. O Lord, examine my life and purge me clean.

35. O Lord, guide my steps into the way of peace.

36. O Lord, send help from above to me, to be able to stop every activity of the devil in my life.

37. O Lord, disallow the enemy from making me a bad example.

38. I bind every spirit that beats the air, in the name of Jesus.

39. O Lord, anoint me with the oil of gladness.

40. I put the curse of the Lord upon every sickness and satanic marks upon my life, in the name of Jesus.

41. Let every satanic kingdom mounted against my life crumble to pieces, in the name of Jesus.

42. The enemy is the grasshopper, I am the giant, in Jesus' name.

43. Blood of Jesus, boil my spirit, soul and body, in the name of Jesus.

44. Holy Spirit, charge me with Your fire, in the name of Jesus.

45. Strength and health of God, enter into my body, in Jesus' name.

46. O Lord, in the name of Jesus, let heavens open for me now.

47. Let the anointing for supernatural breakthroughs fall mightily upon me, in the name of Jesus.

48. I command every evil progress in my life to cease now, in the name of Jesus.

49. Evil yoke, go out of my life now, in the name of Jesus.

50. Spiritual weakness, I cast you out of my life now, in Jesus' name.

51. O Lord, dethrone self in my life.

52. I want to die to self, in the name of Jesus.

53. I want to die to my opinions, preferences, tastes and will, in the name of Jesus.

54. I want to die to the world, its approval and blame, in Jesus' name.

55. Every inherited problem in any area of my life, no regrouping, no violence, no reinforcements, no arguing. I command you to go out of my life, in the name of Jesus.

56. I rebuke every family evil burden and bondage in my life, in the name of Jesus.

57. I reject every bad name, in the name of Jesus.

58. All the 'negative' I have said in this programme, any evil power that would say 'yes', be bound now, in the name of Jesus.

59. Let every 'evil arrester' of my blessing receive blindness now, in the name of Jesus.

60. Every power arresting my progress, fall down and die now, in the name of Jesus.

61. I reject every demonic alteration of destiny, in the name of Jesus.

62. Every power contributing stubbornness to problems in my life, fall down and die now, in the name of Jesus.

63. Every power re-arranging problems in my life, fall down and die now, in the name of Jesus.

64. O Lord, forgive me for ever making myself an object to be pursued.

65. I command blindness to fall on every stubborn pursuer of my life, in the name of Jesus.

66. You pursuer of my destiny, be pursued by angels of God, in the name of Jesus.

67. O Lord, empower me to surrender all to You.

68. Every cause of torment by wicked intelligent network in my life, be nullified by the blood of Jesus.

69. Every cause of inability to enjoy divine benefits in my life, be nullified by the blood of Jesus, in the name of Jesus.

70. Every cause of constant attack by unrepentant and stubborn household wickedness in my life, be nullified by the blood of Jesus.

71. Every cause of suffering from intensive marital attacks, be nullified by the blood of Jesus.

72. Every root of inability to locate the enemy in my life, dry up by the blood of Jesus.

73. Every curse of seeing goodness but not attaining it, be broken by the blood of Jesus.

74. Every problem attempting to suffocate my faith, be uprooted by the blood of Jesus.

75. Every cause of my life being used to test satanic weapons, be nullified by the blood of Jesus.

76. Every cause of caged husband/wife, be nullified by the blood of Jesus.

77. Every cause of demotion in the dream in my life, be nullified by the blood of Jesus.

78. Every ladder of financial embarrassment in my life, be broken by the blood of Jesus.

79. Every cause of spiritual stagnancy in my life, be nullified by the blood of Jesus.

80. Every cause of demonic delays of miracles in my life, be nullified by the blood of Jesus.

81. Every buried talent and virtue in my life, be exhumed by the blood of Jesus.

82. Every cause of spiritual coldness in my life, be nullified by the blood of Jesus.

83. Every cause of disappearance or unwillingness of would-be helpers in my life, be nullified by the blood of Jesus.

84. Every cause of lack of working capital in my life, be nullified by the blood of Jesus.

85. Every cause of circular problems in my life, be nullified by the blood of Jesus.

86. Every cause of always having to fight seriously to get anything done in my life, be disannulled by the blood of Jesus.

87. Every cause of always occupying wrong positions in my life, be nullified by the blood of Jesus.

88. Every cause of delayed and denied promotions in my life, be nullified by the blood of Jesus.

89. Every cause of desert business/finances in my life, be nullified by the blood of Jesus.

90. Every cause of lame breakthroughs in my life, be nullified by the blood of Jesus.

91. Every cause of evil family pattern in my life, be nullified by the blood of Jesus.

92. Every cause of dead accounts in my life, be nullified by the blood of Jesus.

93. Every cause of accumulated debts in my life, be nullified by the blood of Jesus.

94. Every cause of transferred virtues in my life, be nullified by the blood of Jesus.

95. Every cause of confused and unprogressive dreams in my life, be nullified by the blood of Jesus.

96. I stand against prayer paralysis in my life by the blood of Jesus.

97. Every cause of evil diversion in my life, be nullified by the blood of Jesus.

98. Every effect of bewitching, be nullified by the blood of Jesus.

99. Every captured foreign benefits, be released, in the name of Jesus.

100. Every cause of gradual dispossession of good things in my life, be nullified by the blood of Jesus.

101. Every cause of dead organs in my life, be nullified by the blood of Jesus.

102. Every cause of being trapped in the fowler's net in my life, be nullified by the blood of Jesus.

103. Every cause of being pursued by the spirit of death in my life, be nullified by the blood of Jesus.

104. Every arrow of poverty in my life, be removed, in Jesus' name.

105. Every cause of feeding one's enemy to be able to fight harder, be nullified by the blood of Jesus.

106. Every curse by satanic prophets, be revoked by the blood of Jesus.

107. Every cause of longstanding and resistant infirmities in my life, be nullified by the blood of Jesus.

108. Every cause of spiritual blindness in my life, be nullified by the blood of Jesus.

109. Every curse of vagabond anointing, be broken, in Jesus' name.

110. Every cause of profit starvation in my life, be nullified by the blood of Jesus.

111. Every cause of unexplainable loss of good things in my life, be nullified by the blood of Jesus.

112. Every mark of hatred, be washed away by the blood of Jesus.

113. Every cause of spirit of rejection in my life, be nullified by the blood of Jesus.

114. Every evil broadcasting of my goodness, be revoked, in the name of Jesus.

115. Every tortoise and snail anointing, be broken, in Jesus' name.

116. Every curse of leaking pockets, be broken, in the name of Jesus.

117. Every cause of being harassed in the dreams by familiar faces in my life, be nullified by the blood of Jesus.

118. I destabilise and uproot all dominions contrary to the will of God for my life, in the name of Jesus.

119. I command the fire of judgement on all evil operations, in the name of Jesus.

120. I command the fire of judgement on all evil plans and devices that are against my dominion, in the name of Jesus.

121. Let all contrary powers and authorities in the land of my life be confounded and put to shame, in the name of Jesus.

122. I decree the fire of the Holy Spirit to destroy every stronghold of wickedness mounted against my life, in the name of Jesus.

123. I command the fire of God on all idols delegated against me, in the name of Jesus.

124. I command the fire of God on all sacrifices and rituals delegated against me, in the name of Jesus.

125. I break all the agreements made on my behalf between my parents and satan, in the name of Jesus.

126. Let the presence, dominion, authority and blessings of God be experienced in every department of my life, in the name of Jesus.

127. I destroy and decree total removal of satanic establishment against me, in the name of Jesus.

128. I prophesy and decree that peace and glory of God be established in every department of my life, in the name of Jesus.

129. I command confusion and disagreement among my hardened enemies, in the name of Jesus.

130. I command the judgement of God on the plans and devices of wickedness against my being, in the name of Jesus.

131. I break any covenant made by my enemies against me, in the name of Jesus.

132. I paralyse every spirit of wastage. I shall not borrow, in the name of Jesus.

133. Let the works of the flesh be removed from my life, in the name of Jesus.

134. I take authority over the forces of darkness causing prayer failures in my life, in the name of Jesus.

135. I break down every demonic wall of prayerlessness, frustration and discouragement in my life, in the name of Jesus.

136. I claim and receive from God the mind of Christ, in Jesus' name.

137. Let me live a life of watchfulness and prayer, in Jesus' name.

138. I challenge the forces that cause disobedience to God in my life, in the name of Jesus.

139. O Lord, give me grace to overcome worldliness.

140. I command these blessings upon myself, in the name of Jesus.

- love, longsuffering, faith, joy, gentleness, meekness, peace, goodness, temperance
- spirit of understanding, spirit of revelation, spirit of counsel, spirit of fear of the Lord
- knowledge of God   - divine healing   - divine health
- total submission to God   - obedience   - fruitfulness
- holiness   - progress

141. I break down and destroy all infirmities and weakness in my life, in the name of Jesus.

142. O God, give me the grace to put off
- anger   - malice   - filthy communication   - lying,
in the name of Jesus.

143. O God, give me the grace to put on
- new man   - bowels of mercies   - kindness   - divine love
- beauty and glory of God   - victory over sin and temptation
- supernatural love   - righteousness and holiness,
in the name of Jesus.

144. O Lord, make me part of Your move.

145. O Lord, break me and refill me.

146. O Lord, let the anointing for prayer and witnessing fall mightily upon me now.

147. I will not tempt God by
- murmuring   - unbelief   - rebellion   - provocation
- backsliding   - hardening the heart

148. I refuse to be dominated by any evil manipulation, in Jesus' name

149. I issue death sentence on all my Goliath, in the name of Jesus.

150. Let the sword of God, touch the blood of all my enemies, in the name of Jesus.

151. My miracle will not die, in the name of Jesus.

152. My testimonies will not vanish, in the name of Jesus.

153. My dream will not become a nightmare, in the name of Jesus.

154. Devil, you are a liar, you cannot have my destiny, in Jesus' name.

155. I release myself from every fear of the future, in Jesus' name.

156. I release myself from failure before opportunity, in Jesus' name.

157. Lord, heal my land.

158. I challenge all authorities that hinder the move of God in my life, in the name of Jesus.

159. I decree the will of God into my life, in the name of Jesus.

160. Every power swallowing the results of my prayers, fall down and die now, in the name of Jesus.

161. Every household wickedness power, fall down and die now, in the name of Jesus.

162. Let every demon of adversity be scattered unto desolation, in the name of Jesus.

163. I disarm all vagabond problems in my life, in the name of Jesus.

164. Every satanic informant, I command you to be dumb and deaf, in the name of Jesus.

165. Let all unrepentant and stubborn adversities begin to fall down and die now, in the name of Jesus.

166. Every mockery be converted to honour in my life, in Jesus' name.

167. I shall not serve my enemies in any area by any means, in the name of Jesus.

168. I break the backbone of household wickedness behind any problem in my life, in the name of Jesus.

169. Let every stronghold of poverty in my life be smashed now, in the name of Jesus.

170. Let every vulture spirit begin to eat their own flesh and not mine, in the name of Jesus.

171. Every wicked power spitting and urinating on my property, fall down and die, in the name of Jesus.

172. Any tree or rock housing my blessings, receive divine thunder and scatter unto desolation, in the name of Jesus.

173. Every stubborn satanic deposit in my life, come out with all your roots, in the name of Jesus.

174. Let the weapons of war fashioned against me perish, in the name of Jesus.

175. I refuse to sit on the seat constructed by the enemy, in the name of Jesus.

176. Every stubborn problem tree, be uprooted by fire now, in the name of Jesus.

177. O Lord, give me the violent faith to make smash every problem in my life.

178. I command every strongman shielding my enemy to fall down and die, in the name of Jesus.

179. I paralyse every demonic logic and wisdom targeted against me, in the name of Jesus.

180. I render all stubborn diviners working against me mad, in the name of Jesus.

181. Let every satanic oath made against me be fully disgraced, in the name of Jesus.

182. Every rage of the enemy against me, be quenched, in the name of Jesus.

183. Let every stubborn oracle divining against me be frustrated, in the name of Jesus.

184. Every stubborn familiar spirit and witchcraft, be disgraced, in the name of Jesus.

185. Let any evil river polluting my family line dry up, in Jesus' name.

186. Let the energy of persistent attackers dry up, in Jesus' name.

187. I frustrate every demonic arrest over my spirit-man, in the name of Jesus.

188. I destroy the power of every satanic arrest over my life, in the name of Jesus.

189. All satanic arresting agents, release me now, in Jesus' name.

190. Holy Ghost fire, destroy every satanic garment made for my life, in the name of Jesus.

191. Let divine earthquake shake down the foundations of every satanic prison where my blessings are being kept, in Jesus' name.

192. I loose confusion, shame and reproach into the camp of the enemy, in the name of Jesus.

193. I bind every evil spirit withstanding testimony in my life, in the name of Jesus.

194. Let every satanic river of backwardness dry up in my life, in the name of Jesus.

195. I destroy every evil dedication made by my parents for my sake, in the name of Jesus.

196. I destroy everything that represents me in any demonic meeting, in the name of Jesus.

197. I arrest every demonic assignment against my life, in Jesus' name.

198. Let all satanic strategies designed to divert my blessings be frustrated, in the name of Jesus.

199. Let all emptier and wasters be disgraced, in the name of Jesus.

200. I run into the city of solution, in the name of Jesus.

201. Let all evil meetings held for my sake scatter unto desolation, in the name of Jesus.

202. Let all evil ties with unfriendly friends break, in Jesus' name.

203. Let the angels of God take evil attackers down to the bottom of the pit, in the name of Jesus.

204. Let the rain of fire fall upon every camp of stubborn wickedness, in the name of Jesus.

205. Let every tree planted by fear in my life dry to the roots, in the name of Jesus.

206. Let all stubborn pursuers pursue themselves, in Jesus' name.

207. I refuse to be shaken by the enemy, in the name of Jesus.

208. I close entrance doors of problems and exit doors of blessings, in the name of Jesus.

209. O Lord, avenge me of my adversaries.

210. I refuse every unprofitable reconciliation, in the name of Jesus.

211. I neutralize every satanic attention on my goodness, in the name of Jesus.

WITH HEALING IN HIS WINGS
Isa. 53:5

- **To defeat infirmity.**

You may lack the knowledge that the great salvation you received in Christ brought with it healing in His wings. This means that God in-included His divine healing in His package of salvation for mankind.

Malachi 4:2: *"But unto you that fear my name shall the sun of righteousness arise with healing in his wings; and ye shall go forth, and grow up as calves of the stall."*

Jesus is still in the business of healing the sick. He is not here physically to heal. He uses people like you and I. As long as you are a born again child of God, the power to heal is flowing in your hands. The Bible says we will lay hands on the sick and they shall recover (Mark 16:18). This means you can lay hands on yourself wherever you are sick and believe God for your healing!

It is recorded that when Jesus was hanged on the cross it is recorded that "He was wounded for our transgressions, He was bruised for our iniquities: the chastisement of our peace was laid upon Him; and with his stripes we are healed (Isaiah 53:5). Jesus bore our infirmities on the cross so we can have divine health and healing. This means He has paid the price for whatever disease or sickness is troubling you. All you have to do is appropriate this blessing into your life.

These prayer points are designed to prophesy healing into your situation. They will cause you to have that which is yours by right healing and divine health.

● CONFESSION

Mal 4:2: *But unto you that fear my name shall the Sun of righteousness arise with healing in his wings; and ye shall go forth, and grow up as calves of the stall.*

Make these confessions out loud.

Let praise and glory be unto the God and the Father who has blessed me with all physical spiritual blessings in the heavenly realm through Christ Jesus.

Confession brings about possession, now I receive the healing promises of God in my and I ask my father in heaven to command them to begin to be operational in my spirit, soul and body.

I am a member of the body of Christ. Jesus Christ is the word of God sent into the world to heal me. I confess my faith in God, the father of Jesus. I confess my faith in the word of God. The word of God is my healing capsule and as I take it now it will minister destruction to any inherited infirmity, sickness or disease in my body. It will minister health to my body and minister glory and honour to God, my healer.

It is written that I shall serve the Lord my God, and he shall bless my bread, and my water; and he will take sickness away from the midst of me. Let this scripture come true in my life right now.

It is written, the Lord will strengthen him upon the led of languishing: thou will make all his bed in his sickness. He keepeth all his bones: not one of them is broken. I swallow this promises of God in faith.

Surely He shall deliver me from the snare of the fowler and from the noisome pestilence. There shall no evil befall me, neither shall any plague come nigh my dwelling. The Lord has forgiven me all my iniquities; He has healed all my diseases. He has redeemed my life from destruction, He has crowned me with loving kindness and tender mercies. He has satisfied my mouth with good thing so much so that my youth is renewed as the eagle's. I ask these scriptures to renew my body right now and I receive it in faith.

The Lord upholdeth all that fall, and raiseth up all these that be bowed down. The Lord openeth the eyes of the blind; the Lord raiseth them that are bowed down: the Lord loveth the righteous. He healeth the broken in heart, and bindeth up their wounds. Let the Spirit of God in these scriptures quickened my spirit, soul and body.

It written my son, attend to my words; incline thine ears unto my sayings. Let them not depart from thine eyes; keep them in the midst of thine heart.

For they are life unto those that find them, and health to all their flesh. For by me thy days shall be multiplied and the years of thy life shall be increased. A sound heart is the life of the flesh: But envy the rottenness of the bones. Pleasant words are as a honey-comb, sweet to the soul and health to the bones. Jeremiah also said, "Your words were found by me and I did ate them and they are the joy and the rejoicing of my soul." I eat all the healing capsules in the above scriptures of God and they shall bring healing and refreshing to my flesh and bones.

He giveth power to the faint; and to them that have no might he increaseth strength. For I will restore health unto thee and I will heal thee of thy wounds, saith the Lord. Behold I will bring it health and cure, and I will cure them, and will reveal unto them the abundance of peace and truth. For I will cleanse their blood that I have not cleansed: for the Lord dwelleth in Zion. I am a child of promise and I stand on the covenant promise of God for me. I receive every benefit of divine health made to me through these words of God.

It is written that Jesus himself took away all my infirmities and bore all my sicknesses on the cross of calvary. Jesus Christ bore all my griefs and has taken away all my sorrows. He has stricken, smitten, afflicted and wounded so that I might be saved. He was bruised for my iniquities and the chastisement of my peace was upon him and by his stripes I am healed. The Bible says, when I see this my heart shall rejoice, and my bones shall flourish like an herb: and the hand of the Lord shall be known towards me and his indignation towards my enemies.

Through the death of Jesus Christ on the Cross of calvary, the devil, who had the power of death, sickness and diseases, was destroyed. Therefore, because Jesus Christ has redeemed me from this curse and has come to give me abundant life, you demons of infirmities and sickness you have no more dominion over my body. I have confessed my sins which I committed against my Maker: and as it is written, He is faithful and just to forgive me all my transgressions. Himself said He will be merciful and gracious towards my sins and will remember my deeds of unrighteousness no more. Therefore, let everything the accuser is holding against me in order keep afflicting me, be removed by the blood of Jesus.

With faith in my heart and with all my strength I cry out to you, the Balm of Gilead, my healer: Heal me, O Lord, and I shall be healed; save me, and I shall be saved; for thou hath my praise. Let your thoughts that are not of evil towards me begin to prosper in my life. You wish me above all things that I may prosper and be in health even as my soul prospereth. I receive this prosperity. God has not given me the spirit of fear, rather He has given me the spirit of power, the spirit of love and of a sound mind. I stand against the devil with the blood of Jesus and I bind any further attacks and afflictions.

The Lord is my strength and power, he maketh my health perfect, the Lord is the captain of my salvation, the Lord is my deliverer, redeemer and protector, the joy of the Lord is my strength No longer shall I be weak or become feeble again. I have eaten the flesh of Jesus and drunk His blood I shall no longer die but live to declare His praise who loved me, died for me and washed me in His own blood.

The Lord shall guide me continually, and satisfy my soul in drought, and make fat my bones, and I shall be like a watered garden, and like a spring of water, whose waters fail not.

Now, I am a workmanship of God recreated in Christ. I am one with Christ. Sickness has no place on me any more. I have abundant life. Jesus has restored to me all that the devil has stolen, killed and destroyed. No longer can any negative confession I made in times past about my health prosper; God has started new things in my spirit, soul and body and they have already begun to spring up. Amen.

• PRAISE WORSHIP

1. Praise God for His mighty power that is able to heal all sicknesses.
2. Thank God for He is the Lord God that heals you.
3. Let Your healing hand be stretched out upon my life now, in the name of Jesus.
4. Let Your miracle hand be stretched out upon my life now, in the name of Jesus.

5. Let Your deliverance hand be stretched out upon my life now, in the name of Jesus.

6. I annul every engagement with the spirit of death, in Jesus' name.

7. I rebuke every refuge of sickness, in the name of Jesus.

8. I destroy the grip and operation of sickness upon my life, in the name of Jesus.

9. Every knee of infirmity in my life, bow, in the name of Jesus.

10. Let my negativity be converted to positivity, in the name of Jesus.

11. I command death upon any sickness in any area of my life, in the name of Jesus.

12. I shall see my sickness no more, in the name of Jesus.

13. Let the whirlwind scatter every vessel of infirmity fashioned against my life, in the name of Jesus.

14. Every spirit hindering my perfect healing, fall down and die now, in the name of Jesus.

15. Let all death contractors begin to kill themselves, in Jesus' name.

16. Let every germ of infirmity in my body die, in the name of Jesus.

17. Let every agent of sickness working against my health disappear, in the name of Jesus.

18. Fountain of discomfort in my life, dry up now, in the name of Jesus.

19. Every dead organ in my body, receive life now, in Jesus' name.

20. Let my blood be transfused with the blood of Jesus to effect my perfect health, in the name of Jesus.

21. Every internal disorder, receive order, in the name of Jesus.

22. Every infirmity, come out with all your roots, in the name of Jesus.

23. I withdraw every conscious and unconscious cooperation with sickness, in the name of Jesus.

24. Let the whirlwind of the Lord blow every wind of infirmity away, in the name of Jesus.

25. I release my body from every curse of infirmity, in Jesus' name.

26. Let the blood of Jesus flush every evil deposit out from my blood, in the name of Jesus.

27. I recover every organ of my body from every evil altar, in the name of Jesus.

28. O Lord, I thank You for answering my prayer.

MY HAMAN SHALL DIE IN MY PLACE

Esther 7

If you take your stand for God and avoid any form of compromise in your Christian life, like Mordecai did during his time, any person or group of persons who may conspire to eliminate you from the land of the living shall end up being eliminated in your stead.

Jeremiah 30:16: *"Therefore all they that devour thee shall be devoured; and all thine adversaries, everyone of them, shall go into captivity; and they that spoil thee shall be a spoil, and all that prey upon thee will I give for a prey."*

There is a law of God called the law of divine substitution. This simply means that instead of you, whosoever is planning to kill you will die in your place. Christ become a substitute for all men when He died in our place and took the sin of the whole world. In the book of Esther we read about how Haman died on the gallows he had built for Mordecai. (Esther 7:10).

In the book of Daniel we read about how the people who accused Daniel and caused him to be thrown into the lion's den were cast into the lion's den (Daniel 6:24).

Isa. 43:4 says, "Since thou wast precious in my sight, thou hast been honourable, and I have loved thee: therefore will I give men for thee, and people for thy life." If there is a gang-up against you, then these prayer points are for you. They will activate the law of divine substitution to work for you.

• CONFESSION

Jer 17:18: *Let them be confounded that persecute me, but let not me be confounded: let them be dismayed, but let not me be dismayed: bring upon them the day of evil, and destroy them with double destruction.*

• PRAISE WORSHIP

1. Let every evil geographical hindrance to my praying to breakthroughs in this programme, clear away, in Jesus' name.

2. Any anti-progress material fired into my life through dreams, be nullified, in the name of Jesus.

3. Every power keeping me low, fall down and die, in Jesus' name.

4. Every power tying me down, fall down and die, in Jesus' name.

5. Every power stealing from me, fall down and die, in Jesus' name.

6. Every power scattering my resources and blessings, fall down and die, in the name of Jesus.

7. Let the rock and fire of God destroy every weapon of demotion fashioned against me, in the name of Jesus.

8. Every power suppressing my elevation, fall down and die, in the name of Jesus.

9. Every demonic panel set up against me, scatter unto desolation, in the name of Jesus.

10. Let every fetish material directed against my progress turn against its owner, in the name of Jesus.

11. I overrule every demonic decision made against my elevation, in the name of Jesus.

12. Let my youth be renewed like the eagle's, in the name of Jesus.

13. No evil meeting summoned against me shall prosper, in the name of Jesus.

14. Let the law of substitution begin to operate to my favour, in the name of Jesus.

15. Every anti-gospel establishment in my work-place and business, crash and disintegrate, in the name of Jesus.

16. Every internal stronghold, be broken now, in the name of Jesus.

17. I pull down every external stronghold that is working against my elevation, in the name of Jesus.

18. Every satanic plan to embarrass me, be dissolved by fire, in the name of Jesus.

19. Every gathering of the ungodly against me, physically or spiritually, be scattered unto desolation, in the name of Jesus.

20. I cancel every report brought against me in the kingdom of darkness, in the name of Jesus.

21. I cancel every charge brought against me in the kingdom of darkness, in the name of Jesus.

22. I cancel every accusation brought against me in the kingdom of darkness, in the name of Jesus.

23. I revoke and nullify every judgement passed upon me in the kingdom of darkness, in the name of Jesus.

24. I revoke and nullify every decision passed upon me in the kingdom of darkness, in the name of Jesus.

25. I revoke and nullify every condemnation passed upon me in the kingdom of darkness, in the name of Jesus.

26. I forbid evil hands to perform their enterprise against me, in the name of Jesus.

27. I abort the operations of the powers of darkness commissioned against my life, in the name of Jesus.

28. I abort the assignments of the powers of darkness commissioned against my life, in the name of Jesus.

29. Every labour of the enemy on my prosperity, receive double failure, in the name of Jesus.

30. Every war waged against my staff of bread, receive double disgrace, in the name of Jesus.

31. Satanic hunters of my career, receive double frustration, in the name of Jesus.

32. Any power hiding my key of elevation, fall down and die, in the name of Jesus.

33. Let the angels of the living God prepare special fire for poverty in my life, in the name of Jesus.

34. Every seed of poverty in my family, be roasted to ashes, in the name of Jesus.

35. I refuse to come to the tail compartment, in the name of Jesus.

36. I reject every invitation to the arena of poverty, in Jesus' name.

37. I paralyse all satanic agents trying to drink the blood of my prosperity, in the name of Jesus.

38. Every Sanballat and Tobiah of my breakthroughs, be bound by chains of fire, in the name of Jesus.

39. Thank the Lord for given you the victory.

POWER AGAINST DESTINY KILLERS

2 Cor. 10:3-6

The weapons of the Christian's warfare are the most powerful on earth. They can demolish all the attackers of your destiny who are trying to prevent you from reaching your goal in life.

1 Cor. 2: 7,8: *"But we speak the wisdom of God in a mystery even the hidden wisdom which God ordained before the world unto our glory; which none of the princes of this world knew: for had they known it, they would not have crucified the Lord of glory."*

The devil seeks to destroy the destiny of the children of God. He and his agents have devised many means of discovering the destiny of the children of God. For example, when a baby is born, they use his stars, read his palm, and use light and sand to discover his destiny. They would then manipulate and abort the destiny. They also manipulate people's destiny by manipulating their placenta, using charms and covenants, throwing things in the sea and by witchcraft.

When Jesus was born, Herod, (the spirit that kills good things in infancy) tried to kill Him. Joseph was warned by an angel to take Him to Egypt, thus His life was spared.

The devil, using human agents like Herod and Pilate and the religious rulers of the day, got Jesus crucified. The devil did not realise that the death of Jesus marked the beginning of his defeat. The day Jesus died, he jubilated. He thought he had destroyed God's plan. On the resurrection morning, he wept as the Lord of glory rose from the dead. God's prophecy had come to plant the seed of the woman making it impossible to destroy the destiny of Jesus. By killing Jesus, the devil helped Him fulfil His destiny.

● CONFESSIONS

Obad. 1:17: *But upon mount Zion shall be deliverance, and there shall be holiness; and the house of Jacob shall possess their possessions.*

Mal. 3:6: *For I am the LORD, I change not; therefore ye sons of Jacob are not consumed.*

• **PRAISE WORSHIP**

1. O Lord, let my divine destiny appear and let perverted destiny disappear.

2. I reject every satanic re-arrangement of my destiny, in Jesus' name.

3. I refuse to live below my divine standard, in the name of Jesus.

4. Every evil power having negative awareness of my destiny, be impotent, in the name of Jesus.

5. I paralyse every destiny polluter, in the name of Jesus.

6. Every damage done to my destiny, be repaired now, in Jesus' name.

7. The enemy will not convert my body to rags, in the name of Jesus.

8. The enemy will not convert my destiny to rags, in Jesus' name.

9. O Lord, restore me to Your original design for my life.

10. I reject destiny-demoting names, in the name of Jesus.

11. O Lord, enlarge my coast.

12. I refuse to operate below my divine destiny, in the name of Jesus.

13. O Lord, anoint my eyes, hand and legs to locate my divine purpose.

14. Every power contending with my divine destiny, scatter unto desolation, in the name of Jesus.

15. Let the spirit of excellence come upon me, in the name of Jesus.

16. Satan, I resist and rebuke your efforts to change my destiny, in the name of Jesus.

17. Satan, I remove from you the right to rob me of my divine destiny, in the name of Jesus.

18. I command all powers of darkness assigned to my destiny to leave and never return, in the name of Jesus.

19. Let the earthquake, sea quake, air quake destroy every demoter assigned against my life, in the name of Jesus.

20. I command all the enemies of Jesus Christ that have access to my progress to leave and never return, in the name of Jesus.

21. I paralyse every satanic opportunities contending against my life, in the name of Jesus.

22. Every incantation, ritual and witchcraft power against my destiny, fall down and die, in the name of Jesus.

23. I render null and void the influence of destiny swallowers, in the name of Jesus.

24. Every household wickedness struggling to re-arrange my destiny, loose your hold, in the name of Jesus.

25. The rod of the wicked shall not rest upon my life, in Jesus' name.

26. I refuse to be removed from the divine agenda, in Jesus' name.

27. Holy Spirit, I invite You into my imagination.

28. O Lord, bring to light every darkness shielding my potentials, in the name of Jesus.

29. I break every curse of backwardness, in the name of Jesus.

30. I recover myself from every evil diversion, in the name of Jesus.

31. I shall not come to the world in vain, in the name of Jesus.

32. Every forest and rock demons assigned against me, fall down and die, in the name of Jesus.

33. Every local charm burnt against me, be roasted, in the name of Jesus.

34. I release myself from ungodly parental linkage, in Jesus' name.

35. Lord Jesus, manifest Yourself in my life by Your name called 'Wonderful'.

36. Every bird of death assigned against me, fall down and die, in the name of Jesus.

37. I withdraw the food and drink of my problems, in Jesus' name.

38. No evil family river shall flow into my life, in the name of Jesus.

39. I withdraw my progress from every satanic regulation and domination, in the name of Jesus.
40. Every garment of darkness, be roasted by fire, in Jesus' name.
41. I refuse to live a floating life, in the name of Jesus.
42. Every deeply entrenched problem, dry to the roots, in Jesus' name.
43. I destroy the weapons of satanic night raiders, in Jesus' name.
44. Every stronghold of failure, be broken, in the name of Jesus.
45. Every internal warfare in my life, be quenched, in Jesus' name.
46. Every internal thief, be exposed, in the name of Jesus.
47. Anything planted in my life by my enemies, come out with all your roots, in the name of Jesus.
48. *Use the under listed weapons (marked ●) against the under listed problems (marked ♦) and pray aggressively. For example,: 'Every power expanding power, receive the fire of God, in Jesus' name.*

DESTINY KILLERS

♦ power expanding problems
♦ backward progress
♦ star hijackers
♦ destiny killers
♦ evil spies
♦ power swallowing money
♦ head manipulators
♦ power arresting progress
♦ satanic ministers
♦ poverty activators
♦ coffin spirits
♦ round-about spirits

♦ vagabond anointing
♦ demons of rocks
♦ forest spirits
♦ counterfeit blessings
♦ spirit of death and hell
♦ rain of affliction
♦ evil observers
♦ strange money
♦ witchcraft handwriting
♦ satanic arrows
♦ evil bullets
♦ desert spirits

- spirit of tragedy
- amputated breakthrough
- evil marks
- progress diverters
- evil reporters
- wicked broadcasters
- dark agents
- contenders with my angels of blessing
- iron-like curse
- multiple evil covenants
- business bewitching
- marriage killers
- children killers
- evil spirit marriage
- unprofitable loads
- arrows of infirmity
- late progress
- shame distributors
- satanic prayers
- evil hindering angel
- hidden oppressors
- personal territorial demotion
- financial caging
- pocket with holes
- evil reinforcement
- internal, external demotion

- evil arresters
- satanic opinion
- evil transfer of blessing
- the gates of evil
- personalised strongholds
- evil plantation
- evil deposits
- occultic arrows
- satanic poison
- arrow of fruitless efforts
- changed body
- basket bank
- evil prophecies
- rags of poverty
- evil traffic wardens
- demon idols
- dream manipulators
- satanic programmes
- household arrows
- evil advertisement
- placental manipulators
- internal suicide
- helper-manipulators
- wandering stars
- counterfeit children
- counterfeit money

WEAPONS

- *whirlwind*
- *fire of God*
- *great earthquake*
- *sea-quake*
- *air-quake*
- *horrible tempest*
- *furnace of affliction*
- *thunder and fire*
- *brimstone and fire*
- *destructive oppression*
- *unbearable heat*
- *concentrated acid*
- *destroying flood*
- *great furnace*
- *shock*
- *destruction*
- *anger of the Lord*
- *bread of affliction*
- *water of affliction*

- *red-hot charcoal*
- *cloud of sorrow*
- *raging fire*
- *blindness*
- *madness*
- *worms*
- *continuous plagues*
- *fear of day and night*
- *bitter destruction*
- *double destruction*
- *self-destruction*
- *disappointment*
- *failures*
- *discomfort on all sides*
- *disorderliness*
- *hail and fire mingled with the blood of the Lamb*
- *confusion*

49. Let the handwriting of household wickedness be rubbed off, in the name of Jesus.

50. I do not ask for your co-operation, I command it, in Jesus' name.

51. Thieves that have stolen my divine deposits, return them now, in the name of Jesus.

52. O Lord, lay Your hands of fire upon me and change my destiny.

53. I receive explosive breakthroughs, I reject weak breakthroughs, in the name of Jesus.

54. O Lord, change my destiny to the best.

55. Every evil power struggling to re-programme my life, fall down and die, in the name of Jesus.

56. O Lord, shake me to my senses where I have made mistakes.

57. I thank the Lord Jesus for scattering the enemies of my divine destiny.

58. Every organ of my body, be washed by the blood of Jesus.

59. I withdraw every organ of my body from every satanic altar, in the name of Jesus.

60. Every spiritual parent, release me now, in the name of Jesus.

61. Every unprofitable love targeted against me, be broken now, in the name of Jesus.

62. Every evil load prepared by household wickedness, be smashed unto desolation, in the name of Jesus.

63. Every stubborn curse, be broken by fire, in the name of Jesus.

64. I dash every evil clock controlling my life on the wall of fire, in the name of Jesus.

65. Thank the Lord for answering your prayer.

DEFEATING DEFEAT

Judges 6

It is a fact that satan has power to defeat powerless, Christless people. But God has all powers to defeat that power which satan uses to defeat others. It is this supreme power that is being introduced to you, to use against him (satan).

Colossians 2:16: *"And having spoiled principalities and powers, He made a shew of them openly, triumphing over them in it."*

We defeat defeat when we tap the greatest power that has ever been recorded in human history. On the Cross which the devil had planned to use to defeat Jesus, satan suffered the greatest defeat. The Bible says, Jesus *"spoiled principalities and powers."* This means that Jesus stripped the devil and his agents of their powers to condemn and kill the human race. The law was:

- blotted out
- taken out of the way
- nailed to the cross

And it could no longer hold man in sin and bondage. The devil has lost the right and power to defeat believers by accusing them with the law.

Jesus said in John 16:13, "These things have I spoken to you, that in me ye might have peace. In the world ye shall have tribulation: but be of good cheer; I have overcome the world." This simply means that surely there will be tribulation and the devil will try to defeat us. But we don't have to despair. All we need to do is to tap the victory that Christ won for us on the cross. As you use these prayer points, every defeat in your life will be defeated.

● CONFESSION

Ps. 118:10-17: *All nations compassed me about: but in the name of the LORD will I destroy them. They compassed me about; yea, they compassed me about: but in the name of the LORD I will destroy them. They compassed* *me about like bees; they are quenched as the fire of thorns: for in the name of the LORD I will destroy them. Thou hast thrust sore at me that I might fall: but the LORD helped me. The LORD is my strength and song, and is become my salvation. The voice of rejoicing and salvation is in the tabernacles of the righteous: the right hand of the LORD doeth valiantly. The right hand of the LORD is exalted: the right hand of the LORD doeth valiantly. I shall not die, but live, and declare the works of the LORD.*

• PRAISE WORSHIP

1. Any power sponsoring demotion and embarrassment against me, be disgraced, in the name of Jesus.
2. Let every evil construction against me crumble, in Jesus' name.
3. Every partner in destruction targeted against me, be scattered unto desolation, in the name of Jesus.
4. Every satanic partnership against me, be dismantled, in the name of Jesus.
5. Any power consulting the sun and the moon against me, fall down and die, in the name of Jesus.
6. Anything in my life opening the door to the enemy, go back to your sender, in the name of Jesus.
7. I command all my enemies to surrender to me in shame, in the name of Jesus.
8. I arrest every spiritual transaction with the dead, in Jesus' name.
9. I speak rottenness unto every evil tree planted against me, in the name of Jesus.
10. Angels of the living God, ransack the land of the living and the dead and recover my stolen blessings, in the name of Jesus.
11. Any good thing in my life placed on any evil altar, be withdrawn, in the name of Jesus.
12. Lord, plant me by Your traffic light, to know when to wait, get ready and get going.

13. Let every witchcraft bird flying for my sake receive the arrow of fire, in the name of Jesus.

14. Every spirit of the grave assigned against my life, fall down and die, in the name of Jesus.

15. Let every household fetish fashioned against me be frustrated, in the name of Jesus.

16. Every agent of nakedness and poverty, fall down and die, in the name of Jesus.

17. At the name of Jesus, every satanic knee standing in any area of my life, bow.

18. O Lord, amaze me by signs and wonders.

19. I bury every stubborn doubt today, in the name of Jesus.

20. I lock the jaw of every satanic lion roaring at me, in Jesus' name.

21. I refuse to supply my enemies with ammunition, in Jesus' name.

22. I cut off the head of my Goliath with the sword of the Lord, in the name of Jesus.

23. I paralyse my personal Philistine, in the name of Jesus.

24. I terminate every 'terminator', in the name of Jesus.

25. Satanic carpenters, enter your coffin, in the name of Jesus.

26. Every satanic opposition to my breakthroughs, be paralysed, in the name of Jesus.

27. Let every seed of poverty in the foundation of my life fall down and die now, in the name of Jesus.

28. Let any symbol representing me in the dark world be destroyed, in the name of Jesus.

29. I cut myself free from the hands of serpents and scorpions, in the name of Jesus.

30. Let every evil kingdom reigning against me be torn to pieces, in the name of Jesus.

31. Every labour of the enemy on my life, receive double failure, in the name of Jesus.

32. Every war waged against my staff of bread, receive double disgrace, in the name of Jesus.

33. Satanic hunters of my career, receive double frustration, in the name of Jesus.

34. Any power hiding my key of elevation, fall down and die, in the name of Jesus.

RELEASING GOODS FROM THE HOUSE OF THE STRONGMAN

Mark 3:27

You already have the power, at your disposal, to bind that strongman depriving you of entrance into the storehouse of God, and receiving your benefits. Remember that God will not force you to use the power.

Matthew 12:29: *"Or else how can one enter into a strong man's house and spoil his goods, except he first bind the strongman? and then he will spoil his house."*

The devil and his agents have a prison where they keep the blessings of the people who refuse to exercise their God-given rights or who are ignorant of what is rightfully theirs in Christ. The devil is given a foothold when we sin. Sin opens the door for many virtues and good things to be stolen from a person's life. The devil has three objectives as stated in John 10:10: to steal, to kill and to destroy. He steals people's finances, marriages, joy, health, peace, ministry, calling, children, etc. We need to check our lives to find out where and how we have opened the door for the devil to enter our lives and steal from us. We need to repent and ask for God's forgiveness. Then we will get violent in our spirit and storm into the devil's house to get our goods! With Christ in our lives we are stronger man than the devil. The promise of God is that, "When a stronger than he (the strongman) shall come upon him, and overcome him, he taketh from him all his armour, wherein he trusted, and divided his spoils" (Luke 11:23).

Jesus has given you the power to spoil the enemy and release your goods from the house of the strongman. Use these prayer points to spoil your enemy and collect all your goods.

● **CONFESSIONS**

1 Sam. 30:8: *And David inquired at the LORD, saying, Shall I pursue after this troop? shall I overtake them? And he answered him, Pursue: for thou shalt surely overtake them, and without fail recover all.*

Ps. 18:37: *I have pursued mine enemies, and overtaken them: neither did I turn again till they were consumed.*

Ps. 126:1: *When the LORD turned again the captivity of Zion, we were like them that dream.*

Exod. 3:20: *And I will stretch out my hand, and smite Egypt with all my wonders which I will do in the midst thereof: and after that he will let you go.*

Isa. 45:13: *I have raised him up in righteousness, and I will direct all his ways: he shall build my city, and he shall let go my captives, not for price nor reward, saith the LORD of hosts.*

Phil. 4:19: *But my God shall supply all your need according to his riches in glory by Christ Jesus.*

Rom. 8:31-32: *What shall we then say to these things? If God be for us, who can be against us? He that spared not his own Son, but delivered him up for us all, how shall he not with him also freely give us all things?*

Rom. 9:33: *As it is written, Behold, I lay in Sion a stumbling stone and rock of offence: and whosoever believeth on him shall not be ashamed.*

● PRAISE WORSHIP

1. I recover all my confiscated and stolen properties, in Jesus' name.
2. You devil, take off your legs from my . . ., in the name of Jesus.
3. I bind every strongman holding my privileges and rights captive, in the name of Jesus.
4. I retrieve all properties from the satanic banks, in Jesus' name.
5. Let the angels of God ordain terrifying noises to chase out all stubborn and uncooperative past or present business associates, in the name of Jesus.
6. I possess all my possessions, in the name of Jesus.
7. Lord, restore seven-fold, everything that spiritual thieves have stolen from me.
8. I bind every spirit sitting on my possession, in the name of Jesus.

9. Let all the demonic obstacles that have been established in the heart of . . . against my prosperity be destroyed, in Jesus' name.

10. Lord, show . . . dreams, visions and restlessness that would advance my cause.

11. I command my money being caged by the enemy to be completely released, in the name of Jesus.

12. I break the backbone of any further spirit of conspiracy and treachery, in the name of Jesus.

13. Father, help me to see my mistakes and faults and to do all in my power to overcome and correct them, in the name of Jesus.

14. Father, show me what to do so that business crisis would not arise again in my business, in the name of Jesus.

15. Lord, give unto me the eagle eye and eyes of Elisha to foresee market situations.

16. Lord, give us wisdom to walk out of any unfavorable business situations.

17. Father, help me to formulate a plan of recovery to keep us at the top, in the name of Jesus.

18. Lord, send me divine counsellors who can help me with my business.

19. Lord, always help me to identify evil business traps.

20. Lord, help me to erect safeguards to prevent business failure.

21. Let my proposals be too hot for the enemy to sit upon, in the name of Jesus.

22. Let the riches of the Gentiles be transferred to me, in Jesus' name

23. I recover my blessings from water, forest and satanic banks, in the name of Jesus.

24. O Lord, create new and profitable opportunities for me.

25. Every stolen and satanically transferred virtues, be restored, in the name of Jesus.

26. Any power sitting on an evil mat against my prosperity, fall down and

die, in the name of Jesus.

27. I decree that the angels of prosperity would withdraw the riches of the ungodly and transfer them to me, in the name of Jesus.

28. Every unrepentant adversity working against my prosperity, receive the stones of fire, in the name of Jesus.

29. I shall not pay my tithes to Egypt. I shall not be a servant of the lender, in the name of Jesus.

30. Every past and present satanically diverted money, rush back to my bosom, in the name of Jesus.

OPEN DOORS
Isa. 43:19

When you engage in aggressive and violent prayers coupled with holiness, God would not have any option but to open doors that were previously closed and release your break-through to you.

John 3:27: *"John answered and said, A man can receive nothing except it be given him from heaven."*

Open doors in the Bible signify opportunities that will cause a person to make progress and advance in life. These doors can be marked as marriage, career, ministry, finances, health or fruit of the womb.

It has been said that many people miss opportunities because they come dressed in overalls with a tag saying, 'hard work'. Opportunities can also be lost if a person has an evil failure device working against him. For example, some people can never have more than #200 in their bank account. If they are given #20,000.00, all sorts of problems will come and all the money will come down to #200.

These prayer points will invite Him that hath the key of David, "He that openeth and no man shutteth" (Revelations 3:7) into your situation. He will use His authority and power to open the doors of divine authority for you.

• CONFESSION

Rev. 3:8: *I know thy works: behold, I have set before thee an open door, and no man can shut it: for thou hast a little strength, and hast kept my word, and hast not denied my name.*

• PRAISE WORSHIP

1. Confess any known sin that can increase any satanic storm in your life.

2. O Lord, remember me for good and open the book of remembrance for me.

3. I nullify the activity of any evil thing that I have been fed with, in the name of Jesus.

4. I reverse any damage done to my life from birth, in Jesus' name.

5. I close the entry points of any problem in my life, in Jesus' name.

6. O Lord, restore the years that evil insects have eaten in my life.

7. I take back every single territory held by the enemy in my life, in the name of Jesus.

8. I rise up and escape from any evil prison, in the name of Jesus.

9. Every foundational infirmity, depart from my life, in Jesus' name.

10. I will reign as king over my circumstances, in the name of Jesus.

11. Let every evil family river dry up at my presence, in Jesus' name.

12. Help me O Lord, to recognise Your voice.

13. Lord, where I am blind, give me sight.

14. I throw off every burden of worry, in the name of Jesus.

15. I refuse to be entangled with evil thoughts, in the name of Jesus.

16. I cast down every roadblock hiding my progress, in Jesus' name.

17. Let my spiritual climate send terror to the camp of the enemy, in the name of Jesus.

18. O Lord, release me from evil words and evil silences.

19. Every witchcraft power assigned against my life and marriage, receive . . . (pick from the under listed), in the name of Jesus.
    - the thunder and lighting of God
    - hail and fire mingled with the blood of the Lamb
    - unbearable heat   - concentrated acid
    - destroying flood   - destruction
    - raging fire   - continuous plagues
    - failures   - confusion

20. I release myself from any inherited bondage, in the name of Jesus.

21. I release myself from the grip of any problem transferred into my life from the womb, in the name of Jesus.

22. I break and loose myself from every inherited evil covenant, in the name of Jesus.

23. I break and loose myself from every inherited evil curse, in the name of Jesus.

24. I release myself from every inherited disease, in Jesus' name.

25. Let the blood of Jesus correct any inherited defect in my body, in the name of Jesus.

26. In the name of Jesus, I break any curse of rejection from the womb or illegitimacy which may be in my family back to ten generations on both sides of the family.

27. I reject and renounce every ordination of 'lateness in goodness', in the name of Jesus.

28. I take authority over and order the binding of every strongman in every department of my life, in the name of Jesus.

BREAKING ANTI-MARRIAGE YOKES [1]

Daniel 6:15-22,25-27

● *For spinsters and bachelors of ages 31 and above*

Whatever evil yoke the enemy has put on your marriage, would be broken by the Supreme Headquarters of all powers and authority in heaven and in earth.

Job 14:14: *"If a man die, shall he live again? all the days of my appointed time will I wait, till my change come."*

Beloved, don't let the pressures of society and family push you into marrying the wrong person. "In His time God makes all things beautiful" (Ecclesiastes 3:11). God has a set time for you to get married. You might feel you've made a mistake and you've missed God's best for you. There is still hope. For every Queen Vashti, there is an Esther. God has His own divine replacement. Don't choose a replacement on your own. The Bible says, "He that believeth does not make haste. "(Isaiah 28:16) If you believe that at the right time God will give you His will for you in marriage, then you will stop all the questions, unbelief, doubt and worrying. You will enter into His rest and receive His peace. You will not be moved by the words and opinions of others. You will not be bothered by the reproach, shame and looks of pity they throw your way.

Job said, "All the days of my appointed time will I wait till my change comes." It is only God that will cause a permanent change, that will take you from the class of the single to the married. He is the one that will give you a spouse that will cause your joy to be full.

It has been said that, "love is blind, marriage is an eye opener." Once you are married, there is no room for divorce. Wait patiently on God and let Him give you your spouse. These prayer points will destroy all anti-marriage yokes and cause your God-chosen partner to appear to you by fire!

• CONFESSIONS

1 John 3:8: *For this purpose the Son of God was manifested, that He might destroy the works of the devil.*

Ps. 18:48: *He delivereth me from mine enemies: yea, thou liftest me up above those that rise up against me: thou hast delivered me from the violent man.*

Ps. 91:14-15: *Because he hath set his love upon me, therefore will I deliver him: I will set him on high, because he hath known my name. He shall call upon me, and I will answer him: I will be with him in trouble; I will deliver him, and honour him.*

Ps. 108:13: *Through God we shall do valiantly: for he it is that shall tread down our enemies.*

• PRAISE WORSHIP

1. Praise the Lord and thank Him from the bottom of your heart for what He will do for you in this programme.

2. Worship the Lord and thank Him for His unfailing good promises . . . and what He has promised, He is able to perform (1 Kings 8:56, Rom. 7:21).

3. Thank God for His rainbow of unfailing promises: for His word in Him is yes and amen. (2 Cor.1:20).

4. Confess all your sins to the Lord and ask for forgiveness. As you do that, make a vow that you will sin no more so that you can obtain mercy today.

5. Right now, Holy Father, let Your 'sword of deliverance' touch my blood.

6. Angels of the living God, search the land of the living and the land of the dead, and gather all fragmented parts of my life together, in the name of Jesus.

7. Pick from the under listed, and pray thus: Every . . ., operating in my life against my marriage, fall down and die, in Jesus' name.

   - spirit of the valley   - spirit of the tail

- spirit of the desert
- spirit of lateness in marriage
- spirit of shame and reproach
- spirit of loneliness
- spirit of bitterness
- spirit of unprogressive life

8. Pick from the under listed, and pray thus: Any ground that I have lost to the enemies through . . ., be withdrawn, in Jesus' name.

- sexual perversion
- telling lies
- fornication in the heart
- sex outside marriage
- sale of virginity to strange men/women
- masturbation
- having sex with animals or objects
- abortion
- idolatry
- coveting other people's husbands / wives

9. O Lord, make a way for me in this programme.

10. O grave, where is thy victory? You could not hold back the Lord Jesus Christ. You will not hold back my breakthroughs, in the name of Jesus.

11. In this programme, O Lord, let me receive Your divine mercy and favour.

12. By Your zeal O God of performance, carry out Your strange work and Your strange act in my life and surprise me greatly (Isa. 28: 21^b).

13. O God of new beginnings, do a new thing in my life in this issue of marriage, and let every eye see it, in the name of Jesus.

14. Place your hand on any part of your body that you have sold off to strange men / women through immorality and pray thus: Sword of the Lord's deliverance, touch my (mention it), in the name of Jesus.

15. Lay your hand on your head, and pray with this song:
    Holy Ghost fire, fire fall on me, like the day of Pentecost, fire fall on me.

16. I plead the blood of Jesus over my life and this environment, in the name of Jesus.

17. Every power of the Prince of Persia blocking my prayers all these years, fall down and die, in the name of Jesus.

18. In the name of Jesus, by the blood of Jesus, I release myself from . . . (pick from the under listed)

- any form of parental curse placed on me consciously or unconsciously

- evil effect of placental bondage   - spirit husband / wife

- self-imposed curses   - the spirit of non-achievement

- garment of shame and reproach   - yearly sorrows

- periodic disappointments

19. In the name of Jesus, I denounce every
    - evil spiritual marriage
    - association with familiar spirits
    - association with witchcraft/wizard spirit
    - membership with the dark-world
    - association with God's enemies

20. O Lord, by the blood of Jesus, wash away my reproach.

21. Any power that will attack me as a result of this prayer programme, fall down and die, in the name of Jesus.

22. Cover yourself with the blood of Jesus and pray thus:

    i. Holy Ghost fire, fall on me, burn in my body, soul and spirit, in the name of Jesus.

    ii. Fire of God, go down to my root and burn every evil worm eating up God's plan for my life, in the name of Jesus.

    iii. By the blood of Jesus, I break every evil spiritual marriage vow.

    iv. By the blood of Jesus, I cut myself off from every evil spiritual marriage vow.

    v. In the name of Jesus, I withdraw myself from the evil association of   .   .   . (pick from the under listed).

    - the unmarried   - late marriages   - the bewitched

    - God's enemies   - the self-afflicted   - none achievers

vi. I break every evil vow by my parents on my behalf, in the name of Jesus.

23. I denounce every evil association of . . . (pick from the under listed), in the name of Jesus.

- familiar spirits — - water spirits   - getting married in the dream
- witches   - wizards   - sorcerers
- wandering about in the dream
- star gazers, etc (mention any other ones you know you are involved in)

24. Strange marks on my life, be robbed off by the blood of Jesus.

25. I break every barrier between me and my partner, in Jesus' name.

26. I reject every evil family pattern, in the name of Jesus.

27. Blood of Jesus, arrow of God's deliverance, deliver me now from . . . (pick from the under listed), in the name of Jesus.

- spirit of late marriage   - spirit of error
- spirit of disappointment   - spirit of loneliness

28. O Lord, open Your book of remembrance for me now, in the name of Jesus.

BREAKING ANTI-MARRIAGE YOKES [2]

Obad. 1:3,4,17

- *For spinsters and bachelors of ages 30 and below.*

God shall surely cast down every power that lifted up itself against your marriage, and your expectation of the union shall be realised, as soon as you are ready to slug it out with the enemy in prayer.

Isaiah 28:16: *"Therefore thus saith the Lord God, Behold I lay in Zion for a foundation a stone, a tried stone, a precious corner stone, a sure foundation: he that believeth shall not make haste."*

When you build the foundation of your marriage on Christ it will stand the test of time and conquer the storms of life. When you prayerfully and patiently wait upon the Lord for your marriage partner, by His Spirit, He will magnetise your God chosen partner to you (Isaiah 34:16).

When you hurry into marriage the chances are that you will want to hurry out. The prayer points you refuse to pray before marriage could result in a lifetime of intercession for peace in the home.

Wrong foundation in marriage includes lust, sex before marriage, accidental pregnancies, marrying for money; marrying to fulfil sexual needs; marrying because the man or the woman looks good. These are wrong reasons for getting married.

Your marriage should be based on two things:

- God said it: You know that this is God's revealed will for you. No one is forcing or pushing you into it. You heard God yourself.
- Love: God has given you a deep and gentle love for the person. This love will continue to grow as you relate to each other. The Bible says, "Love never fails." As long as there is love, your marriage will last.

As you use these prayer points, the spirit of error will be removed from your life and every anti-marriage yoke will be destroyed. Remember, it is only the marriage that is built on the right foundation that will stand the test of time and conquer the storms of life. Wait patiently on God, don't be in a hurry.

• CONFESSIONS

Rom. 4:21: *And being fully persuaded that, what he had promised, he was able also to perform.*

2 Cor. 1:20: *For all the promises of God in him are yea, and in him Amen, unto the glory of God by us.*

Isa. 50:7: *For the Lord GOD will help me; therefore shall I not be confounded: therefore have I set my face like a flint, and I know that I shall not be ashamed.*

Ps. 121:2: *My help cometh from the LORD, which made heaven and earth.*

Deut. 33:27: *The eternal God is thy refuge, and underneath are the everlasting arms: and he shall thrust out the enemy from before thee; and shall say, Destroy them.*

• PRAISE WORSHIP

1. Praise the Lord and thank Him from the bottom of your heart for what He will do for you in this programme.

2. Praise God for His exceeding great and precious promises for your life (2 Pet. 1:4).

3. Open your heart before the Lord, and confess all your sins so that your prayers will not be hindered.

4. Right now, Holy Father, let Your 'sword of deliverance' touch my blood.

5. I reject devil's counterfeit. I receive God's original today, in the name of Jesus.

6. I reject and renounce every anti-marriage curse issued on me by my parents.

7. In the name of Jesus, I command the strong East wind of God to blow away every distraction and hindrance often used by satan to block off my partner.

8. O Lord, forgive me of all my sins and those of my ancestors, in the name of Jesus.

9. In this programme, O Lord, I divorce my own will to receive God's will.

10. By Your zeal O God of Jeshurun, send help to me, in Jesus' name.

11. Thou God of performance, do that which no man can do for me.

12. By the blood of Jesus, I nullify every dream of . . . (pick from the under listed).

   - swimming in the water
   - eating strange food
   - drinking coke and fanta
   - having sex with fair or dark women / men
   - running without getting to a stop
   - talking alone without response
   - getting married with dirty garment
   - having children or breast-feeding
   - having bald head or hair falling off
   - sitting on a broken or cracked fence
   - falling inside the mud
   - eating inside a broken plate
   - getting married without wedding suit/dress
   - sleeping/playing in an uncompleted building

13. Every satanic wedding ring, be roasted, in the name of Jesus.

14. In the name of Jesus, every spirit of . . . (pick from the under listed) troubling my life, I reject, I renounce you and I command you to leave me now. By the blood of Jesus, I place the cross of the Lord Jesus Christ between me and you, and I forbid you to ever return to me.

- mammy water	- jealousy	- familiar spirit
- high-mindedness	- unholy thought	
- husband / wife snatching	- wallowing in sins	
- unforgiveness	- sexual thoughts	- seduction
- Delilah	- Jezebel	- abortion and blood shed

15. Lay your right hand on your head and pray: Fire of God, charge my body, soul and spirit, in the name of Jesus.

16. Holy Spirit, energize me to pray to the point of breakthroughs, in the name of Jesus.

17. Pray with this song: *There is power mighty in the blood (2x), there is power mighty in the blood of Jesus Christ, there is power mighty in the blood.*

18. Blood of Jesus, . . .
    - flow into my foundation and cleanse out every evil design
    - rob off every evil mark of anti-marriage from my life
    - nullify every evil spiritual agreement I have made with the spirit husband / wife consciously or unconsciously
    - rob off every contrary handwriting that is against my life
    - flush out every evil dream food and poison from my root.

19. In the name of Jesus, by the fire of the Holy Ghost, I reject . . .
    - every evil prophesy of late marriage on my life
    - every spirit of getting married in the dream
    - every garment of shame and reproach
    - every evil voice speaking defeat into my ears
    - every spiritual marriage certificate signed in the spirit world on my behalf to nullify my marriage here on earth

20. This very day, in the name of Jesus, I shall . . .
    - receive my deliverance   - receive my breakthroughs
    - receive joy instead of sadness   - eceive the touch of God
    - receive divine solution to my life's problem
    - laugh last. My enemies shall cry

21. O Lord, rend the heavens, and send down help for me.

POWER TO EXCEL IN EXAMINATION

Psalms 19; 99;119; Dan. 1:17-20; 1 Kings 3:12; Exod. 31:2-6; Isa. 40:29-31

God is the custodian of wisdom, knowledge and understanding of all things, hence believers stand a better chance than non-believers to tap from the vast resources in all fields of human endeavour. You too can reject failure and embrace the spirit of excellence today.

Job 32:8: *"But there is a Spirit in man: and the inspiration of the Almighty giveth them understanding."*

The only source of true wisdom and intelligence is the Almighty. God has deposited His Spirit into each of His children and as many as will tap from that divine source cannot go wrong. It is recorded that God gave Daniel and the three Hebrew boys knowledge and skill in all learning and wisdom: and Daniel had understanding in all visions and dreams (Daniel 1:17). "And in all matters of wisdom and understanding, that the king enquired of them he found them ten times better than all the magicians and astrologers that were in all his realm" (Daniel 1:20).

When tested, Daniel and his colleagues excelled above all the others. They realised the true source of wisdom and they tapped from it. Child of God, you too have been given the Spirit that will cause you to excel above all your colleagues and unbelievers around you. The Spirit of God is in you and when you ask Him, He will teach you all things (1 John 2:27). He will give you understanding, and like the psalmist you can say, "I have more understanding than all my teachers: (Psalm 119:99).

Beloved, you have to study hard. Read your books, go through past questions and pray hard. When you've prepared well, these prayers will cause you to excel in your examinations.

● *NOTE:*

1. Repent from all known sins

2. Reject every spirit of fear arising from past failures

3. *Believe God for great success in this exam and that you have received already*

4. *Continue to confess that you have passed*

5. *Do not engage in any malpractice*

6. *Resolve not to entertain any doubt and reject all thoughts of failure or dream manipulations*

7. *Always give thanks to God for the answers to your prayers*

DAYS 1 - 3

● **CONFESSIONS**

Exod. 11:3: And the LORD gave the people favour in the sight of the Egyptians. Moreover the man Moses was very great in the land of Egypt, in the sight of Pharaoh's servants, and in the sight of the people.

Ps. 34:7: The angel of the LORD encampeth round about them that fear him, and delivereth them.

Ps. 138:8: The LORD will perfect that which concerneth me: thy mercy, O LORD, endureth for ever: forsake not the works of thine own hands.

Acts 2:4: And they were all filled with the Holy Ghost, and began to speak with other tongues, as the Spirit gave them utterance.

Acts 4:13: Now when they saw the boldness of Peter and John, and perceived that they were unlearned and ignorant men, they marvelled; and they took knowledge of them, that they had been with Jesus.

● **PRAISE WORSHIP**

1. Lord Jesus, I bless You and I confess that all powers belong to You.

2. I nullify all curses of failure in my life, in the name of Jesus.

3. I pull down every stronghold of failure in my life, in my marriage, in my business, both physically and spiritually, in the name of Jesus.

4. Every pipeline of failure in my life, be consumed by the fire of God now, in the name of Jesus.

5. Every spiritual barrier and limitation to success in my life, I command you to break to pieces, in the name of Jesus.

6. Every inherited and self-made failure in my life, I command you to receive repairs, in the name of Jesus.

7. Every area of my life that I have lost to failure, I command you to be restored, in the name of Jesus.

8. Every seed of failure in my life, I command you to be consumed by the fire of God, in the name of Jesus.

9. You spirit of failure, loose your grip over my life, in Jesus' name.

10. O Lord, let me not enter the trap of failure.

11. I refuse to register in the school of failure, in the name of Jesus.

12. Jesus, I thank You because You have given me victory.

DAYS 4 - 6

● CONFESSIONS

Exod. 11:3: *And the LORD gave the people favour in the sight of the Egyptians. Moreover the man Moses was very great in the land of Egypt, in the sight of Pharaoh's servants, and in the sight of the people.*

Ps. 34:7: *The angel of the LORD encampeth round about them that fear him, and delivereth them.*

Ps. 138:8: *The LORD will perfect that which concerneth me: thy mercy, O LORD, endureth for ever: forsake not the works of thine own hands.*

Acts 2:4: *And they were all filled with the Holy Ghost, and began to speak with other tongues, as the Spirit gave them utterance.*

Acts 4:13: *Now when they saw the boldness of Peter and John, and perceived that they were unlearned and ignorant men, they marvelled; and they took knowledge of them, that they had been with Jesus.*

● PRAISE WORSHIP

1. Jesus, I thank You because You are my banner, and by Your name I shall prevail in this exam.

2. You evil follower, I paralyse you and I command you to be roasted, in the name of Jesus.

3. I break evil cycle of failure in my . . . exam, in the name of Jesus.

4. Blood of Jesus, fortify my life against every spell, bewitchment and evil pronouncement, in the name of Jesus.

5. You strong woman sitting on my success, be unseated by the thunder of God, in the name of Jesus.

6. I reject forgetfulness, I reject confusion and I reject error, in the name of Jesus.

7. I stand against every spirit of failure, in the name of Jesus.

8. I reject every satanic re-arrangement of my destiny, in Jesus' name

9. Let every activity of darkness in my academics fail woefully, in the name of Jesus.

10. I receive an excellent spirit after the order of Bezaleel, in the name of Jesus.

11. I receive retentive memory, boldness and a sound mind, in the name of Jesus.

DAY 7

• CONFESSIONS

Exod. 11:3: *And the LORD gave the people favour in the sight of the Egyptians. Moreover the man Moses was very great in the land of Egypt, in the sight of Pharaoh's servants, and in the sight of the people.*

Ps. 34:7: *The angel of the LORD encampeth round about them that fear him, and delivereth them.*

Ps. 138:8: *The LORD will perfect that which concerneth me: thy mercy, O LORD, endureth for ever: forsake not the works of thine own hands.*

Acts 2:4: *And they were all filled with the Holy Ghost, and began to speak with other tongues, as the Spirit gave them utterance.*

Acts 4:13: *Now when they saw the boldness of Peter and John, and perceived that they were unlearned and ignorant men, they marvelled; and they took knowledge of them, that they had been with Jesus.*

• PRAISE WORSHIP

1. I have more understanding than my teachers, because God's testimonies are my meditations, in the name of Jesus.

2. Lord, give me understanding and wisdom.

3. I receive wisdom, knowledge and understanding for my studies, in the name of Jesus.

4. Angels of the living God, encamp round about me now and go before me to lectures and the examination, in the name of Jesus.

5. Father Lord, anoint me for success in my handiwork.

6. All questions directed at Daniel were answered, so I should have right answers to questions in the examination, in Jesus' name.

7. I excel over my colleagues ten times like Daniel, in Jesus' name.

8. I will find favour before all the examiners, in the name of Jesus.

9. The Lord should perfect everything concerning my studies.

10. I shall not study amiss, in the name of Jesus.

11. I bind and render to nothing every spirit of fear, in Jesus' name.

12. I release myself from every spirit of confusion and error, in the name of Jesus.

13. Father Lord, lay Your hand of fire upon my memory and give me retentive memory, in the name of Jesus.

14. Lord, keep me diligent in my private preparations.

15. Lord, let me be very attentive to my lectures/lessons.

16. Father, I dedicate all my faculties to You, in the name of Jesus.

17. Thank You Jesus, because You are the source of my success.

POWER AGAINST HOUSEHOLD WITCHCRAFT

Exodus 22:18; Lev. 20:27; Deut. 18:10,11; Isa. 48:22

Isaiah 8:10: *"Take counsel together, and it shall come to nought; speak the word, and it shall not stand: for God is with us."*

Household witchcraft is something that must be dealt with violently and speedily. It is a sub-group of household wickedness and specifically uses satanic powers to harm, enslave, divert, mislead and overthrow victims through a continuous bombardment with problems. This satanic agent also uses curses, spells and incantations and death to torment its victims.

The victim is placed under evil control, domination and intimidation and will as a result be weary, confused, anxious and depressed. He obeys strange commands and at times experiences accidents.

We thank God that as christians, we are on the winning side. We have been given power over all the power of the enemy (Luke 10:19) and we will overcome them (1 John 5:4).

As you use these prayer points, note the following.

Have the mind that there is nothing and no one you need to fear. "God has not given us the spirit of fear, but of love, power and of a sound mind" (2 Tim. 1:17). God has decided to save us from defeat, not from trouble. AThese things have I spoken to you, that in Me you might have peace. In the world, ye shall have tribulation (trouble): but be of good cheer; I have overcome the world." Many will suffer from the cradle to the grave if they do not learn how to fight. "For we wrestle not against flesh and blood, but against principalities, against powers, against the rulers of darkness of this world, against spiritual wickedness in high places" (Eph. 6:12).

The battle is spiritual and our weapons are spiritual. They are not carnal (2 Cor. 10:3-5). We need to develop spiritual violence because that is all the enemy understands (Matt. 11:12).

As you use these prayer points to attack every household witchcraft, you will have divine victory over it and have its counsels upon your life turned to naught.

● *NOTE:*

You must be a genuine born again child of God before you these prayer points can work for you. You also have to make your way plain before God by confessing your sins and asking the Lord to forgive and wash you with the blood of Jesus.

● **CONFESSIONS**

In the name of Jesus, I believe the word of God is steadfast and unshakeable, endures forever and powerful, and it is the power of God that is able to deliver me out of any bondage.

The word of God is God Himself speaking and not man. Therefore, nothing shall be impossible for me because of the word of God I believe in my heart and confess with my mouth.

Father Lord, as I make this confession now, I pray that You will watch over Your word to perform it, because You are a faithful God. You are not a man that You should lie, neither the son of man that You should repent. You will not break Your covenant, nor alter the word which has gone out of Your mouth.

It is written, when I ask, I should believe and receive. As I make this confession and go into prayer, I will receive dominion and power, according to the word of God, because I know God will prove Himself strong on my behalf, for my heart is stayed on Him.

I know who I am in Christ. I have been purchased by the blood of Jesus Christ that was shed for me on the cross of calvary. I am a child of God. I am called by the name of the Lord. I am bought by the blood of the Lamb of God. I believe the power in the blood of Jesus. Jesus has translated my life from the kingdom of darkness into His own marvelous kingdom of light and peace. I now belong to the kingdom of God. I have the keys of the kingdom of God in my hands to bind and to loose. I have the authority to trample under my feet, serpents, scorpions and all the power of the enemy.

Through death Jesus Christ has destroyed satan, who had the power of death. Jesus has delivered my life from death and damnation. Before

Jesus ascended, He first of all descended into the lower parts of the earth and stripped the devil of all his power over me. Jesus has taken from satan the keys of death and hell and has given me the keys to bind and to loose.

By virtue of the work Jesus Christ did on the cross, I have power over all the power of the enemy. He has wiped out all the handwriting of requirements that were against me, taking them out of the way, having nailed them to the cross. He disarmed principalities and powers and made a show of them openly, triumphing over them in it.

I hold in my hand now the victory won for me on the cross of calvary by my Saviour Jesus Christ, and I say, "Be shattered Oh you witches and powers of wickedness and be broken in pieces. Give ear all you powers of wickedness in my place of birth or origin, gird yourselves and you shall be broken in pieces. Take your counsel together, it will come to nothing. Chant your incantations, they will not stand, for the Lord is with me as a mighty and terrible one. Therefore, you shall stumble and fall.

Encamp against me, my heart shall not fear, for in the name of the Lord, I will destroy you. The Lord is the strength of my life, of whom shall I be afraid. Surround me like bees and I will quench you all like a fire of thorns."

Fashion your weapons of wickedness, they will not prosper. Rise up against me in judgement with all your legal grounds against me, you shall all be condemned because that is my heritage as a servant of God.

I shall not die but live. Any power that has ever led me captive shall go into captivity. They that afflict and oppress me shall be ashamed. God will contend with all who contend with me. He will feed those who oppress me with their own flesh and they shall be drunken with their own blood as with sweet wine, for the Lord will bring upon them the day of doom and destroy them with double destruction.

It is written that God will light my lamp and enlighten my darkness. But every satanic agent or power oppressing me shall grope in the daytime as in thick darkness.

It is written that I should be strong in the Lord and in the power of His might, therefore I ask that as I go into prayer right now the Lord will be my *strength; strength to run through a troop, to leap over any wall, to pursue and overtake my enemies, to recover my stolen properties, to beat them small as the dust, to withstand and overcome all spiritual oppositions and distractions.*

I hold in my hand the shield of faith, for it is written that whosoever is born of God overcometh the world. And this is the victory that overcometh the world and its wickedness, even my faith.

In faith I go into this prayer session. In faith I have the victory. In faith my enemies are all subdued under my feet and none can escape.

My heart steadfastly believes the word of God. I have confessed with my mouth and by the word of my mouth. Let me be justified Oh Lord and let all my enemies be condemned. I seal my confession with the blood of Jesus. Amen."

• PRAISE WORSHIP

1. Let the thunder of God locate and dismantle the throne of witchcraft in my household, in the name of Jesus.

2. Let every seat of witchcraft in my household be roasted with the fire of God, in the name of Jesus.

3. Let the altar of witchcraft in my household be roasted, in the name of Jesus.

4. Let the thunder of God scatter beyond redemption the foundation of witchcraft in my household, in Jesus' name.

5. Every stronghold or refuge of my household witches, be destroyed, in the name of Jesus.

6. Every hiding place and secret place of witchcraft in my family, be exposed by fire, in the name of Jesus.

7. Let every local and international witchcraft network of my household witches be shattered to pieces, in Jesus' name.

8. Let the communication system of my household witches be destroyed, in the name of Jesus.

9. Let the terrible fire of God consume the transportation of my household witchcraft, in the name of Jesus.

10. Every agent ministering at the altar of witchcraft in my household, fall down and die, in the name of Jesus.

11. Let the thunder and the fire of God locate the storehouses and strong-rooms of my household witchcraft harbouring my blessings and pull them down, in the name of Jesus.

12. Let any witchcraft curse working against me be revoked by the blood of Jesus.

13. Every decision, vow and covenant of household witchcraft affecting me, be nullified by the blood of Jesus.

14. I destroy with the fire of God, every weapon of witchcraft used against me, in the name of Jesus.

15. Any materials taken from my body and placed on any witchcraft altar, be roasted by the fire of God, in the name of Jesus.

16. I reverse every witchcraft burial fashioned against me, in the name of Jesus.

17. Every trap set for me by witches begin to catch your owners, in the name of Jesus.

18. Every witchcraft padlock fashioned against any area of my life, be roasted, in the name of Jesus.

19. Let the wisdom of my household witches be converted to foolishness, in the name of Jesus.

20. Let the wickedness of my household enemies overturn them, in the name of Jesus.

21. I deliver my soul from every witchcraft bewitchment, in the name of Jesus.

22. Any witchcraft bird flying for my sake, fall down and die and be roasted to ashes, in the name of Jesus.

23. Any of my blessings traded out by household witches be returned to me, in the name of Jesus.

24. Any of my blessings and testimonies swallowed by witches, be converted to hot coals of fire of God and be vomited, in the name of Jesus.

25. I break myself loose from every bondage of witchcraft covenant, in the name of Jesus.

26. Any witchcraft coven in which any of my blessings are hidden, be roasted by the fire of God, in the name of Jesus.

27. (Lay your right hand on your head) Every witchcraft plantation, pollution, deposit and material in my body, be melted by the fire of God and be flushed out by the blood of Jesus.

28. Every evil ever done to me through witchcraft attack, be reversed, in the name of Jesus.

29. Every damage done to my destiny through witchcraft operations, be reversed now, in the name of Jesus.

30. Every witchcraft hand planting evil seeds in my life through the dream, wither and burn to ashes, in the name of Jesus.

31. Every witchcraft obstacle and hindrance put on the road to my desired miracle and success, be removed by the East wind of God, in the name of Jesus.

32. Every witchcraft chant, spell and projection made against me, I bind you and turn you against your owner, in the name of Jesus.

33. I frustrate every plot, device, scheme and project of witchcraft designed to affect any area of my life, in the name of Jesus.

34. Any witch projecting into the blood of any animal in order to do me harm, be trapped in the body of such an animal forever, in the name of Jesus.

35. Any drop of my blood sucked by any witch, be vomited now, in the name of Jesus.

36. Any part of me shared out amongst household / village witches, I recover you, in the name of Jesus.

37. Any organ of my body that has been exchanged for another through witchcraft operations, be replaced now, in the name of Jesus.

38. I recover any of my virtues / blessings shared out amongst village / household witches, in the name of Jesus.

39. I reverse the evil effect of any witchcraft invocation or summoning of my spirit, in the name of Jesus.

40. I loose my hands and feet from any witchcraft bewitchment and bondage, in the name of Jesus.

41. Let the blood of Jesus wash away every witchcraft identification mark on me or on any of my property, in Jesus' name.

42. I forbid any re-union or re-gathering of household and village witches against my life, in the name of Jesus.

43. Let the entire body system of my household witches be upset until they confess all their wickedness, in the name of Jesus.

As regards the household witches that are contrary to me:

44. Let the mercies of God be withdrawn from them, in Jesus' name.

45. Let them begin to grope in the daytime as in the thickness of a dark night, in the name of Jesus.

46. Let everything that has every worked for them begin to work against them, in the name of Jesus.

47. Let them not have a cloth to cover their shame, in Jesus' name.

48. Let as many of them as are stubbornly unrepentant be smitten by the sun in the day and by the moon at night, in the name of Jesus.

49. Let each step they take lead them to greater destruction, in the name of Jesus.

50. But as for me, let me dwell in the hollow of God's hand, in the name of Jesus.

51. Let the goodness and mercies of God now overwhelm me, in the name of Jesus.

52. Begin to bless the name of the Lord for answering your prayer.

POWER AGAINST THE SPIRIT OF THE SNAIL

Psalm 71:21

- *Prayer points to be used against demonic sluggishness.*
- *To be used against demonic delay.*

Snail is known for its slow movement and sluggishness. If one has this kind of anointing upon his life, progress in life will be retarded. But for you as a child of God, the Scripture says, it is the Lord that giveth you power to run through the troop. This is your portion as a child of God.

• CONFESSION

Luke 10:19: *Behold, I give unto you power to tread on serpents and scorpions, and over all the power of the enemy: and nothing shall by any means hurt you.*

• PRAISE WORSHIP

1. Every power prolonging my journey to breakthroughs, fall down and die, in the name of Jesus.

2. Every problem that I have brought into my life through my association with the spirit of the snail, be cancelled now, in the name of Jesus.

3. I break the covenants and curses of the spirit of the snail over my life, in the name of Jesus.

4. I break the covenants and curses of the spirit of the snail over my life, in the name of Jesus.

5. Every effect of the spirit of the snail over my life, be nullified by the blood of Jesus.

6. Every spirit of sluggishness and backwardness in my life, receive the fire of God now and be destroyed, in the name of Jesus.

7. Every spirit of avoiding good things in my life, be destroyed, in the name of Jesus.

8. O Lord, I reject left-over blessings.

9. I will not feed from waste bins, in the name of Jesus.

10. I refuse to have boneless blessings, in the name of Jesus.

11. Every spirit of irritation in my life, be washed off by the blood of Jesus.

12. I reject the spirit of fear, anxiety and discouragement, in the name of Jesus.

13. Every evil instruction, prophecy or predictions, issued against my life by using snail shell, be cancelled by the blood of Jesus.

14. I reject the spirit of the tall, I claim the spirit of the head, in the name of Jesus.

15. I receive angelic transportation to where God wants me to be now, in the name of Jesus.

16. Every evil deposit in my life as a result of eating snail, be washed away by the blood of Jesus.

17. O Lord, catapult me into greatness as You did for Daniel in the land of Babylon.

18. I reject slippery blessings, in the name of Jesus.

19. I reject the spirit of over-sensitivity, in the name of Jesus.

20. Let all my enemies and their strongholds be shattered to pieces by the thunder of God, in the name of Jesus.

21. I deliver myself from the grip of my enemies, in Jesus' name.

DESTROYING DISEASE GERMS
Isa. 53:5

- **For receiving healing for all manners of infirmities.**

CONFESSIONS

Exod 15:26: *Alf thou wilt diligently hearken to the voice of the LORD thy God, and wilt do that which is right in his sight, and wilt give ear to his commandments, and keep all his statutes, I will put none of these diseases upon thee, which I have brought upon the Egyptians: for I am the LORD that healeth thee.*

Ps 30:2: *O LORD my God, I cried unto thee, and thou hast healed me.*

Ps 34:10: *The young lions do lack, and suffer hunger: but they that seek the LORD shall not want any good thing.*

Ps 34:19: *Many are the afflictions of the righteous: but the LORD delivereth him out of them all.*

Ps 55:18: *He hath delivered my soul in peace from the battle that was against me: for there were many with me.*

Ps 97:10: *Ye that love the LORD, hate evil: he preserveth the souls of his saints; he delivereth them out of the hand of the wicked.*

Ps 103:3: *Who forgiveth all thine iniquities; who healeth all thy diseases;*

Isa 53:4: *Surely he hath borne our griefs, and carried our sorrows: yet we did esteem him stricken, smitten of God, and afflicted.*

John 8:36: *If the Son therefore shall make you free, ye shall be free indeed.*

Rom 8:2: *For the law of the Spirit of life in Christ Jesus hath made me free from the law of sin and death.*

Rom 8:32: *He that spared not his own Son, but delivered him up for us all, how shall he not with him also freely give us all things?*

2 Cor 2:14: *Now thanks be unto God, which always causeth us to triumph in Christ, and maketh manifest the savour of his knowledge by us in every place.*

1 Jn 3:8: *He that committeth sin is of the devil; for the devil sinneth from the beginning. For this purpose the Son of God was manifested, that he might destroy the works of the devil.*

3 Jn 1:2: *Beloved, I wish above all things that thou mayest prosper and be in health, even as thy soul prospereth.*

1 Pet 2:24: *Who his own self bare our sins in his own body on the tree, that we, being dead to sins, should live unto righteousness: by whose stripes ye were healed.*

Ps 138:7: *Though I walk in the midst of trouble, thou wilt revive me: thou shalt stretch forth thine hand against the wrath of mine enemies, and thy right hand shall save me.*

Prov 3:5-8: *Trust in the LORD with all thine heart; and lean not unto thine own understanding. In all thy ways acknowledge him, and he shall direct thy paths. Be not wise in thine own eyes: fear the LORD, and depart from evil. It shall be health to thy navel, and marrow to thy bones.*

Heb 4:12: *For the word of God is quick, and powerful, and sharper than any two-edged sword, piercing even to the dividing asunder of soul and spirit, and of the joints and marrow, and is a discerner of the thoughts and intents of the heart.*

Ezek 16:6: *And when I passed by thee, and saw thee polluted in thine own blood, I said unto thee when thou wast in thy blood, Live; yea, I said unto thee when thou wast in thy blood, Live.*

Joel 3:21: *For I will cleanse their blood that I have not cleansed: for the LORD dwelleth in Zion.*

1 Cor 3:16: *Know ye not that ye are the temple of God, and that the Spirit of God dwelleth in you?*

Prov 4:20-22: *My son, attend to my words; incline thine ear unto my sayings. Let them not depart from thine eyes; keep them in the midst of thine heart. For they are life unto those that find them, and health to all their flesh.*

2 Tim 1:7: *For God hath not given us the spirit of fear; but of power, and of love, and of a sound mind.*

2 Th 3:3: *But the Lord is faithful, who shall stablish you, and keep you from evil.*

Matt 15:13: *But he answered and said, Every plant, which my heavenly Father hath not planted, shall be rooted up.*

Mark 11:23-24 : *For verily I say unto you, That whosoever shall say unto this mountain, Be thou removed, and be thou cast into the sea; and shall not doubt in his heart, but shall believe that those things which he saith shall come to pass; he shall have whatsoever he saith. Therefore I say unto you, What things soever ye desire, when ye pray, believe that ye receive them, and ye shall have them.*

• PRAISE WORSHIP

1. Thank God for His mighty power that is able to heal all sickness.

2. Thank God for He is the Lord God that heals you.

3. Let the blood of Jesus be transfused into my blood vessels, in the name of Jesus.

4. I command every agent of disease in my blood and body organs to die, in the name of Jesus.

5. Let my blood reject every evil foreign entity, in Jesus' name.

6. Holy Spirit, speak deliverance and healing into my life, in the name of Jesus.

7. Let the blood of Jesus speak disappearance unto every infirmity in my life.

8. I hold the blood of Jesus against you spirit of . . . (mention what is troubling you). You have to flee.

9. O Lord, let Your healing hand be stretched out upon my life now.

10. O Lord, let Your miracle hand be stretched out upon my life now.

11. O Lord, let Your deliverance hand be stretched out upon my life now.

12. I disannul every engagement with the spirit of death, in the name of Jesus.

13. I rebuke every refuge of sickness, in the name of Jesus.

14. I destroy the grip and operation of sickness upon my life, in the name of Jesus.

15. Every knee of infirmity in my life, bow, in the name of Jesus.

16. O Lord, let my negativity be converted to positivity.

17. I command death upon any sickness in any area of my life, in the name of Jesus.

18. I shall see my sickness no more, in the name of Jesus.

19. Father Lord, let the whirlwind of God scatter every vessel of infirmity fashioned against my life, in the name of Jesus.

20. Every spirit hindering my perfect healing, fall down and die now, in the name of Jesus.

21. Father Lord, let all death contractors begin to kill themselves, in the name of Jesus.

22. Father Lord, let every germ of infirmity in my body die, in the name of Jesus.

23. Father Lord, let every agent of sickness working against my health disappear, in the name of Jesus.

24. Fountain of discomfort in my life, dry up now, in the name of Jesus.

25. Every dead organ in my body, receive life now, in Jesus' name.

26. Father Lord, let my blood be transfused with the blood of Jesus to effect my perfect health, in the name of Jesus.

27. Every internal disorder, receive order, in the name of Jesus.

28. Every infirmity, come out with all your roots, in the name of Jesus.

29. I withdraw every conscious and unconscious cooperation with sickness, in the name of Jesus.

30. O Lord, let Your whirlwind blow every wind of infirmity away.

31. I release my body from every curse of infirmity, in Jesus' name.

32. O Lord, let the blood of Jesus flush every evil deposit out from my blood.

33. I recover every organ of my body from every evil altar, in the name of Jesus.

34. Thank God for your healing.

RELEASE FROM DESTRUCTIVE COVENANTS

Isa. 49:24-26

- *To break evil covenants.*
- *For freedom from both conscious and unconscious evil covenants.*

A covenant is an agreement between two or more parties to get certain things done on conditional terms. It is legally binding on the parties involved. Any covenant made in the physical is as strong as the one made in the spiritual. A lot of christians are swimming in the sea of the problems caused by unknown evil covenants they entered into to at the time of ignorance. The blood of Jesus, the never failing weapon, can deliver and set free, even, the lawful captive.

Hosea 4:6: *"My people are destroyed for lack of knowledge:"*

As in the court of law ignorance is not an excuse, so it is not in the spiritual realm. If there is an evil covenant in place, it is binding until something serious is done to break it. How do people get into covenants? It could be through parents or by one's personal choice.

Some breakthroughs will refuse to materialise until hidden destructive covenants are broken. There are numerous signs to know if hidden covenants are in place. For example, fear at times is an evidence that there is hidden covenant somewhere. Also, hearing strange voices, constant harassment in the dream, late marriages and unstable homes, uncontrollable anger, etc.

How do you get out of hidden covenants? The first step is repentance. You need to repent from whatever sins you have committed consciously or unconsciously. The second thing to do is to renounce all those evil things you have ever done. The third thing is to revoke and cancel the past covenants, in the name of Jesus and bind the spirits in charge of the evil covenants. Lastly, replace the covenants with Abraham's blessings.

Thanks to God for the victory of the cross (Gal. 3:13,14). Jesus has paid with His blood the price to be. These prayer points are designed to help you do all these.

• CONFESSION

Ps. 18:44-45: *"As soon as they hear of me, they shall obey me: the strangers shall submit themselves unto me. The strangers shall fade away, and be afraid out of their close places."*

• PRAISE WORSHIP

1. I take back all the grounds given to satan by my ancestors, in the name of Jesus.

2. I curse you spirit enforcing evil covenants in my life and I command you to release me, in the name of Jesus.

3. Let everything that has been transferred into my life by demonic laying of hands, loose its hold right now, in the name of Jesus.

4. Let every serpentine poison that has been passed into my life, get out now, in the name of Jesus. I flush you out with the blood of Jesus.

5. Let fire fall on every spirit of death and hell fashioned against my life, in the name of Jesus.

6. I break the head and crush the tail of every serpentine spirit, in the name of Jesus.

7. Let the spiritual bat and spiritual lizard, that have been introduced into my head, receive the fire of God.

8. Let the sword of fire begin to cut off every evil parental attachment, in the mighty name of Jesus.

9. Father Lord, reveal to me any hidden covenant that the devil has arranged against me, in the name of Jesus.

10. Every tree that the Father did not plant in my life, be uprooted, in the name of Jesus.

11. Father Lord, I electrify the ground of this place now. Let every covenant with the feet begin to shatter now, in the name of Jesus.

12. Let every evil hidden covenant break, in the mighty name of Jesus.

13. I refuse to drink from the fountain of sorrow, in Jesus' name.

14. I take authority over all curses issued against my life, in the name of Jesus.

15. Ask God to remove any curse He has placed on your life as a result of disobedience.

16. I command any demon attached to any curse to depart from me now, in the mighty name of our Lord Jesus Christ.

17. Let all curses issued against me be converted to blessings, in the name of Jesus.

18. When you mention any of the underlisted curses, you will aggressively say, "Be broken, be broken, be broken, in the name of Jesus. I release myself from you, in the name of Jesus."

    - Every curse of mental and physical sickness
    - Every curse of failure and defeat
    - Every curse of poverty
    - Every curse of family break-up
    - Every curse of oppression
    - Every curse of bad reputation
    - Every curse of personal destruction or suicide
    - Every curse of chronic sickness
    - Every curse of corruption of the reproductive organ
    - Every curse of family strife
    - Every curse of profitless hard work
    - Every curse of evil dedication
    - Every curse of sickness and infirmity
    - Every curse of witchcraft

19. You will now place blessings on yourself by saying, "There shall be no more poverty, sickness, etc. in my life, in Jesus' name."

POWER AGAINST COLLECTIVE CAPTIVITY

2 Tim. 2:26

- *To dissolve co-operate bondage.*
- *To destroy family bondage.*

Captivity could be selective, partial, individual or collective. Which ever it is, release can come collectively, that is everybody can get out together or individually.

Heb 2:15: *"And deliver them who through fear of death were all their lifetime subject to bondage."*

Collective captivity is when a family is under a spell, or a curse, when there is an evil circle of problems in the family, or bewitchment working in the family. When you begin to notice a trend of evil in your family, then know that you have a battle to fight. There is collective captivity. There are basically three steps to be free from this kind of bondage.

1. Recognise its source.

2. Confess your sins and those of your ancestors and repent of them.

3. Begin aggressive prophetic prayer warfare using the prayer points below.

• CONFESSION

Ps. 68:18: *"Thou hast ascended on high, thou hast led captivity captive: thou hast received gifts for men; yea, for the rebellious also, that the LORD God might dwell among them."*

• PRAISE WORSHIP

1. I apply the blood of Jesus to break all curses.

   Sing this song: "There is power mighty in the blood (2 ce). There is power mighty in the blood of Jesus Christ. There is power mighty in the blood."

2. I apply the blood of Jesus to break all consequences of parental sins.

3. O Lord, turn all the evil directed at me to good.

4. I command all powers of evil directed against me, to return directly to the sender, in the name of Jesus.

5. God, make everything the enemy has said is impossible in my life, possible, in the name of Jesus.

6. I release myself from the umbrella of any collective captivity, in the name of Jesus.

7. I release myself from any inherited bondage, in Jesus' name.

8. O Lord, send Your axe of fire to the foundation of my life and destroy every evil plantation.

9. Let the blood of Jesus flush out from my system every inherited satanic deposit, in the name of Jesus.

10. I release myself from the grip of any problem transferred into my life from the womb, in the name of Jesus.

11. Let the blood of Jesus and the fire of the Holy Ghost cleanse every organ in my body, in the name of Jesus.

12. I break and loose myself from every collective evil covenant, in the name of Jesus.

13. I break and loose myself from every collective curse, in the name of Jesus.

14. I vomit every evil consumption that I have been fed with as a child, in the name of Jesus.

15. I command all foundational strongmen attached to my life to be paralyzed, in the name of Jesus.

16. Let any rod of the wicked rising up against my family line be rendered impotent for my sake, in the name of Jesus.

17. I cancel the consequences of any evil local name attached to my person, in the name of Jesus.

18. Pray aggressively against the following roots of collective captivity. Pray as follows: Every effect of . . . (*pick from the underlisted one by*

one), upon my life, come out with all your roots, in the name of Jesus.

- evil physical design
- parental curses
- envious rivalry
- demonic incisions
- dream pollution
- demonic initiations
- demonic blood transfusion
- demonic alteration of destiny
- fellowship with family idols
- fellowship with demonic consultants
- unscriptural manner of conception

- evil dedication
- demonic marriage
- demonic sacrifice
- inherited infirmity
- evil laying on of hands
- wrong exposure to sex
- exposure to evil diviners
- fellowship with local idols
- destructive effect of polygamy

POWER AGAINST EVIL ALTARS
1 Sam. 7:7-11

- *To break down satanic altars both external and internal.*
- *To shatter the strength of territorial spirits.*
- *To paralyse the activities of satanic priests.*

An altar is a table, platform, or elevated place on which a priest places an offering either to God or to the devil. An altar may be built for evil against someone. The cross of Jesus is the only acceptable altar. All other altars should be demolished by the power of God in prayer.

1 Kings 13:2: *"And he cried against the altar in the word of the LORD, and said, O altar, altar, thus saith the LORD; Behold, a child shall be born unto the house of David, Josiah by name; and upon thee shall he offer the priests of the high places that burn incense upon thee, and men's bones shall be burnt upon thee."*

An altar is a place of sacrifice, a place of covenant, a place of spiritual traffic. When Jacob built an altar to God in Bethel, angels of God were going up and down the altar. If he had built a negative altar, there would have been a traffic of demons. Altars are also places of deliberation, decisions and actions whether negative or positive.

Anytime evil is determined against someone, a priest will go to an altar and offer sacrifice by shedding of blood to make covenants with evil spirits to carry out some evil operations against the person. Anything belonging to the person can be used on the altar to represent him.

Evil occurrences like being pursued by a serpent, restlessness in marriage, amputated breakthroughs, spiritual backwardness, constant failures, consistent errors, etc., will begin to take place in the life of such a person.

In many environments, there are local altars such as crossroads, trees, rocks, images, rivers, forests, family shrines, and so on.

What is the way out if you find yourself a victim of local evil altars? Aggression is needed. Recognise their operations. Repent of anything you have done to make any evil altar to prosper. Renounce them whether you know about them or not. Resist them using the word of God and prayer. Kill the priest at the altar. Withdraw your name, your benefits and your virtues from the altars. Destroy the altar by cursing it and introducing the fire of God upon it. Give praises to God.

● CONFESSION

Isa 8:9-10: *"Associate yourselves, O ye people, and ye shall be broken in pieces; and give ear, all ye of far countries: gird yourselves, and ye shall be broken in pieces; gird yourselves, and ye shall be broken in pieces. Take counsel together, and it shall come to nought; speak the word, and it shall not stand: for God is with us."*

● PRAISE WORSHIP

Every prayer point against evil altars has to be said loudly, with violence, with faith and with an aggressive spirit.

1. I release myself from the bondage of evil altars, in Jesus' name.

2. I vomit every satanic poison that I have swallowed, in Jesus' name.

3. I cancel every demonic dedication, in the name of Jesus. Be repeating, "I cancel you, in the name of Jesus."

4. *(Place your two hands on your head.)* I break every evil authority over my life, in the name of Jesus. Be repeating, "I break you, in the name of Jesus."

5. Mention the underlisted with authority and say, "Break, in the name of Jesus", seven hot times.
   - every evil authority of family shrine or idol
   - every evil authority of witchcraft and family spirits
   - every evil authority of remote control powers
   - every evil authority of the strongman

6. Every owner of evil load, carry your load, in the name of Jesus.

7. I render every aggressive altar impotent, in the name of Jesus.

8. Every evil altar erected against me, be disgraced, in Jesus' name.

9. Anything done against my life under demonic anointing be nullified, in the name of Jesus.

10. I curse every local altar fashioned against me, in the name Jesus.

11. Let the hammer of the Almighty God smash every evil altar erected against me, in the name of Jesus.

12. O Lord, send Your fire to destroy every evil altar fashioned against me, in the name of Jesus.

13. Every evil priest ministering against me at the evil altar, receive the sword of God, in the name of Jesus.

14. Let the thunder of God smite every evil priest working against me at the evil altar and burn him to ashes, in the name of Jesus.

15. Let every satanic priest ministering against me at evil altars fall down and die, in the name of Jesus.

16. Any hand that wants to retaliate or arrest me because of all these prayers I am praying, dry up and wither, in the name of Jesus.

17. Every stubborn evil altar priest, drink your own blood, in the name of Jesus.

18. I possess my possession stolen by the evil altar, in Jesus' name.

19. I withdraw my name from every evil altar, in the name of Jesus.

20. I withdraw my blessings from every evil altar, in the name of Jesus.

21. I withdraw my breakthroughs from every evil altar, in Jesus' name.

22. I withdraw my glory from every evil altar, in the name of Jesus.

23. I withdraw my prosperity from every evil altar, in Jesus' name.

24. I withdraw anything representing me at every evil altar, in the name of Jesus.

25. *(Mention any of your organ that you know is not behaving the way it should and say:)* I withdraw you from every evil altar, in the name of Jesus.

RELEASE FROM EVIL BLOOD COVENANTS

Rev. 12:11
- *To break evil blood covenants.*

- **CONFESSION**

Zech 9:11: *"As for thee also, by the blood of thy covenant I have sent forth thy prisoners out of the pit wherein is no water."*

- **PRAISE WORSHIP**

1. Holy Ghost fire, boil spiritual contamination out of my blood, in the name of Jesus.
2. I release myself from every satanic blood covenant, in Jesus' name.
3. I release my head from every evil blood covenant, in Jesus' name.
4. I dismantle every stronghold of evil covenants, in Jesus' name.
5. I release myself from every covenanted curse, in Jesus' name.
6. Let the blood of Jesus speak against every unconscious evil covenant.
7. I speak destruction unto the fruits of unclean spirits in my life, in the name of Jesus.
8. I break every evil covenant linkage, in the name of Jesus.
9. I dismantle every stronghold of evil blood covenants, in the name of Jesus.
10. I nullify the effects of evil access to my blood, in Jesus' name.
11. I release myself from every covenanted curse, in Jesus' name.
12. I release every organ in my body from the grip of evil blood covenant, in the name of Jesus.

13. I dissociate myself and my family from every territorial blood covenant, in the name of Jesus.

14. I dissociate myself from every tribal blood covenant, in Jesus' name.

15. I dissociate myself from every inherited blood covenant, in the name of Jesus.

16. I withdraw my blood from every evil altar, in the name of Jesus.

17. I withdraw my blood from every satanic blood bank, in Jesus' name.

18. I break every unconscious evil blood covenant, in Jesus' name.

19. Let the blood of any animal shed on my behalf loose its covenant power, in the name of Jesus.

20. Let every drop of blood speaking evil against me, be silenced by the blood of Jesus.

21. I release myself from every collective blood covenant captivity, in the name of Jesus.

22. I release myself from every conscious or unconscious evil blood covenant, in the name of Jesus.

23. Let the blood of every evil covenant loose its power over me, in the name of Jesus.

24. I defy and destroy every evil covenant agreement, in Jesus' name.

25. Let the blood of the new covenant speak against the blood of any evil covenant militating against me, in the name of Jesus.

26. I receive the mandate to disqualify the right of all evil blood covenants, in the name of Jesus.

27. Every evil blood covenant formed with any organ of my body, be nullified by the blood of Jesus.

28. I recover all the good things stolen by the enemies through evil covenants, in the name of Jesus.

29. Let every evil blood covenant along my blood-line be neutralised, in the name of Jesus.

30. I release myself from every curse attached to evil covenants, in the name of Jesus.

31. I release myself from the grip of curse-covenant breakers, in the name of Jesus.

32. Let every repercussion of breaking unconscious covenants be washed away by the blood of Jesus.

THE EARLY RISERS' CRY
Mark 11, Psalm 2

- **To be prayed early in the morning to dismantle evil things programmed into the sun, moon and stars.**
- **Targeted against powers working in conference with spiritual wickedness in the heavenlies that seek to control human destinies.**

• CONFESSION

Phil 4:13: *"I can do all things through Christ which strengtheneth me."*

Ps 16:8: *"I have set the LORD always before me: because he is at my right hand, I shall not be moved."*

• PRAISE WORSHIP

Make these powerful confessions out loud.

I take authority over this day, in the name of Jesus. I decree that this day all the elements will cooperate with me. I decree that the elemental forces should refuse to cooperate with my enemies. I speak unto the sun, the moon and the stars, they must not smite me. I pull down every negative energy planning to operate against my life today. This is the day the Lord has made, I will rejoice and be glad in it. I dismantle any power uttering incantations to capture the day. I render such incantations and satanic prayer nuil and void. I retrieve the day from their hands, in the name of Jesus. Spirits of favour, counsel, might and power, come upon me, in the name of Jesus. I shall excel this day and nothing shall defile me. I shall poses the gates of my enemies. The Lord shall anoint me with the oil of gladness above others. The fire of the enemy shall not burn me. My ears shall hear good news I shall not hear the voice of the enemy. My future is secured in Christ, in the name of Jesus.

God has created me to do certain definite services. He has committed into my hands some assignments which He has not committed to anybody alse. He has not created me for nothing. I shall do good. I shall do His work. I shall be an agent of peace. I will trust Him in whatever I do and wherever I am. I can never be thrown away or downgraded. There will be no poverty of body, soul and spirit in my life. The anointing of God upon my life gives me favour in the eyes of God and men all the days of my life. I shall not labour in vain. I shall walk everyday in victory and liberty of the spirit. I receive the mouth and the wisdom which my adversaries are not able to resist, in Jesus' name.

1. I bind all evil spirits in me or that are attacking me, in Jesus' name.

2. O Lord, cause my whole heart to be at rest, trusting in You.

3. O Lord, keep me from leaning and relying on my own understanding and intelligence.

4. O Lord, deliver me from what seems right to me and deliver me to what is right to You.

5. O Lord, pull down imaginations and every high thing in my life that are not of God.

6. O Lord, purify my lips with Your holy fire.

7. O Lord, reveal to me those things that give my enemies advantage over me.

8. O Lord, let my fellowship with You become greater.

9. I draw upon heavenly resources today, in the name of Jesus.

10. O Lord, enable me to become the person You created me to be.

11. I surrender myself completely in every area of my life, in the name of Jesus.

12. I stand against every satanic operation hindering my prayer, in the name of Jesus.

13. Satan, I refuse your involvement in my prayer life, in Jesus' name.

14. Satan, I command you, to leave my presence with all your demons, in the name of Jesus.

15. I bring the blood of the Lord Jesus Christ between me and you satan.

16. Father Lord, open my eyes to see how great You are, in the name of Jesus.

17. I declare that satan and his wicked spirits are under my feet, in the name of Jesus.

18. I claim the victory of the cross for my life today, in Jesus' name.

19. Every satanic foothold in my life, be dismantled by fire, in the name of Jesus.

20. I put off all forms of weakness, in the name of Jesus.

21. Lord Jesus, come into my life by fire. Break down every idol, and cast out every foe.

22. Every wicked spirit planning to rob me of the will of God, fall down die, in the name of Jesus.

23. I tear down the stronghold of satan against my life, in the name of Jesus.

24. I smash every plan of satan formed against me, in Jesus' name.

25. I smash the stronghold of satan formed against my body, in the name of Jesus.

26. O Lord, let me be the kind of person that would please You.

27. Holy Spirit, bring all the work of resurrection and Pentecost into my life today, in the name of Jesus.

28. Every witchcraft power, I cast you into outer darkness, in the name of Jesus.

29. I confound every stubborn pursuer, in the name of Jesus.

30. I bind every power cursing my destiny into ineffectiveness, in the name of Jesus.

31. I strike every evil power siphoning my blessing with chaos and confusion, in the name of Jesus.

32. I nullify the incantations of evil spiritual consultants, in Jesus' name

33. I turn the evil devices of household witchcraft upside down, in the name of Jesus.

34. I render every local satanic weapon harmless, in the name of Jesus.

35. I receive deliverance from the spirit of anxiety, in Jesus' name.

36. I bind every spirit of mental stagnation, in the name of Jesus.

37. I release myself from the power and authority of any curse, in the name of Jesus.

38. I renounce any unholy covenants involving my life, in Jesus' name.

39. I grab every stubborn problem and smash it against the Rock of my salvation, in the name of Jesus.

40. I nullify every sacrifice to demons used against me, in Jesus' name.

41. Every power cursing my destiny, be silenced, in the name of Jesus.

42. I break the power of any incense burnt against me, in Jesus' name.

43. Every Python spirit, go into the hot desert and be burned, in the name of Jesus.

44. Let the blood of Jesus poison the roots of all my problems, in the name of Jesus.

45. I go back to Adam and Eve on both sides of my bloodline, and I cut off every evil root, in the name of Jesus.

46. I reverse every improper operation of body organs, in Jesus' name.

47. Every evil contract working against my life, be re-written by the blood of Jesus.

48. I reverse every satanic calendar for my life, in the name of Jesus.

49. Anything my ancestors have done to pollute my life, be dismantled now, in the name of Jesus.

50. I refuse to be in the right place at the wrong time, in Jesus' name.

51. I bind every negative energy in the air, water and ground working against me, in the name of Jesus.

52. Anything from the kingdom of darkness that has made it their business to hinder me, I single you out right now and bind you, in the name of Jesus.

53. Be bound with chains that cannot be broken, in the name of Jesus.

54. I strip off all your spiritual armour, in the name of Jesus.

55. Lose the support of other evil powers, in the name of Jesus.

56. Do not involve yourself with me again, in the name of Jesus.

57. Lord Jesus, I thank You for the victory.

58. I renounce any signing of my name over to satan, in Jesus' name.

59. I announce that my name is written in the Lamb's book of life, in the name of Jesus.

60. I renounce any ceremony regarding my being wedded to satan, in the name of Jesus.

CONFESSING AND PRAYING THE WILL OF GOD

- **PRAISE WORSHIP**

1. It is written, *For whosoever shall do the will of God, the same is my brother, and my sister, and my mother (Mk. 3:35; Matt. 12:50).* Therefore, I receive the power and the grace to always be obedient to the will of God for my life, in the name of Jesus.

2. It is written, *And that servant, which knew his lord's will, and prepared not himself, neither did according to his will, shall be beaten with many stripes (Lk. 12:47).* Therefore, I reject the spirit of unpreparedness. I refuse to go against the will of God. Anything in me that will make me receive many stripes, be roasted now by the fire of God, in Jesus' name.

3. It is written, *If any man will do His will, he shall know of the doctrine whether it be of God, or whether I speak of myself (John 7:17).* Therefore, I refuse to doubt the voice of the Holy Spirit in me, in the name of Jesus.

4. It is written, *Now we know that God heareth not sinners: but if any man be a worshipper of God, and doeth His will, him He heareth (John 9:31).* Therefore, I will not lay my hands on anything that will not make God hear me again, by His grace, in the name of Jesus.

5. It is written, *Not with eye-service, as men pleasers; but as the servants of Christ, doing the will of God from the heart (Eph. 6:6).* Therefore, I receive the grace of God to do His will always from the bottom of my heart. I refuse to depreciate to the level of pleasing men rather than God, in the name of Jesus.

6. It is written, *For ye need of patience, that, after ye have done the will of God, ye might receive the promise (Heb. 10:13).* Therefore, I receive of the Lord, the gift of patience that will always enable me obtain God's promises, in the name of Jesus.

7. It is written, *And the world passeth away, and the lust thereof; but he that doeth the will of God abideth forever (1 John 2:17).* Therefore, I will not fade away with this passing world. I obtain, by faith, the power in the word of God, that I will make me abide forever, in the name of Jesus.

8. It is written, *And this is the confidence that we have in Him, that, if we ask anything according to His will, He heareth us: And if we know that He hears us, whatever we ask, we know that we have the petition that we desired of Him (1 John 5:14-15).* Therefore, I reject and cast out of me every spirit that asks amiss. I receive the knowledge and power to always know the mind of God before opening my lips in prayers. By the grace of God, the word of God shall always enlighten the eyes of my understanding in the place of prayer, in the name of Jesus.

9. It is written, *And he that searcheth the hearts knoweth what is the mind of the Spirit, because He maketh intercession for the saints according to the will of God (Rom. 8:27).* Therefore, the intercessory prayers of Jesus, who is seated at the right hand of the throne of God, will not be in vain over my life, in the name of Jesus.

10. It is written, *But I know, that even now, whatsoever Thou wilt ask of God, God will give it Thee (John 11:22).* Therefore, because I am quickened from sin as Jesus was quickened from the dead, because I am a joint heir of the kingdom of God with Christ Jesus, and because I am seated with Christ in the heavenly places, I obtain by faith, similiar divine favour that was upon Jesus, which made Him receive speedy answers to all His requests while on earth, in the name of Jesus.

11. It is written, *And He went a little further, and fell on His face, and prayed, saying, O My Father, if it is possible, let this cup pass*

from me: nevertheless not as I will, but as Thou witt (Matt. 26:39).
Therefore, let my will be lost in the will of God. Let the will of God
always be my will. I obtain by faith, the grace, courage and strength to
always bear any pain necessary in order to fulfil the will of God for my
life. I receive the boldness and confidence to bear any shame in doing the will of God, in the name of Jesus.

12. It is written, **Thy kingdom come. Thy will be done on earth, as it is
in heaven (Matt. 6:10).** Therefore, let the will of God always prevail
over every other will in my life, in Jesus' name.

13. It is written, **And He said to them all, if any man will come after me,
let him deny himself, and take up his cross daily and follow Me
(Lk. 9:23).** Therefore, I receive divine grace and strength to take up
my cross daily and follow Jesus Christ. Let my weaknesses be converted to strength. Father Lord, raise up intercessors who will always
stand in the gap for me in times of need, in the name of Jesus.

14. It is written, **And be not conformed to this world: but be ye transformed by the renewing of your mind, that ye may prove what is
that good, and acceptable and perfect will of God (Rom. 12:2).**
Therefore, anything in my life stubbornly conforming to this present
evil world, be melted by the fire of God. Let the word of God I eat daily
wash, cleanse and always renew my mind. By faith, I possess the
divine energy to always do that which is good and abide by the perfect will of God, in the name of Jesus.

15. It is written, **And this they do, not as we hoped, but first gave their
own selves to the Lord, and unto us by the will of God (2 Cor.
8:5).** Therefore, I receive the spirit of readiness to always commit
myself to the will of God. I receive the zeal of God to always give
myself totally unto the things of God, in the name of Jesus.

16. It is written, **For it is God which worketh in me both to will and to
do of His good pleasure (Phil. 2:13).** Therefore, the hands of God
working in me to make me do His good will, will not be cut short by my
shortcomings, in the name of Jesus.

17. It is written, *Epaphras, who is one of you, a servant of Christ, saluteth you, always labouring fervently for you in prayers, that ye may stand perfect and complete in all the will of God (Col. 4:12).* Therefore, Father Lord, raise up for me my own Epaphras that will devotedly labour in prayer for me, in the name of Jesus.

18. It is written, *For this is the will of God, that ye should abstain from fornication (1 Thess. 4:3).* Therefore, every lust of the eyes, the flesh and the heart in my life, be washed away by the blood of Jesus. Every attempt of the devil to defile and pollute the temple of God in me, be frustrated, in Jesus' name.

19. It is written, *Rejoice evermore. Pray without ceasing. In every thing give thanks: for this is the will of God in Christ Jesus concerning you (1 Thess. 5:16-18).* Therefore, Father Lord, give me the testimonies that will always make me rejoice in You. Father Lord, give me the heart that will always appreciate every little thing You do for me. By faith, I receive the strength of prevailing prayers, in the name of Jesus.

20. It is written, *The Lord is not slack concerning His promise, as some count slackness; but is long-suffering to us-ward, not willing that any should perish, but that all should come to repentance (2 Pet. 3:9).* Therefore, any abit or besetting sin in me that is making the promises of God to slack in my life; I overcome you by the blood of the Lamb. Any power hindering the manifestations of the promises of God in my life, fall down and die and perish, in the name of Jesus.

21. Bless God for all answers to your prayer points.

BREAKING MINISTERIAL CURSE OF FAILURE

Eph. 1:3-10

- **To deal with every conscious and unconscious curse of ministerial failure.**

• CONFESSIONS

I am the manifestation, the product and the result of God's word. God has spoken into my life and I have become the manifest presence of Jehovah God on earth. I expressly manifest everything the word of God says I am. I am filled with the word of life.

The word of God is in me, not written in ink, but by the Spirit of the living God, not on table of stone, but on flesh-table of the heart.

The word of God in me is a quickening spirit and always keeping me alive. I have received the body and the blood of Jesus Christ; I am full of Him - He is the bread of life sent from heaven, I have eaten Him, I shall not hunger or thirst or die; because in Him is life, and life eternal.

I receive all the blessings that accompany the word of God. I decree that they become operational in my life and I ask for a speedy physical manifestation of the result in my life.

I am not an image of failure and I am not fashioned after the likeness of a god of the tail. I am the salt of the earth. On the inside of me is every excellency of the power of God. God has put this feature of His power in earthen vessels. This power is in me. My appearance is as the appearance of a horse. So I leap. I run like mighty men. When I fall upon the sword it cannot hurt me. The word of God has made me a brazen wall, a fortified city, an iron pillar. My presence terrifies the enemy. He trembles, feels much pain and travails at the sound of my voice which the Lord has empowered. For it is written, wherever the voice of the king is, there is authority.

With my heart I believe the power in the word of God. With my mouth I have made confessions. Therefore as I go into prayer let the word run swiftly to perform my requests and bring results, in the name of Jesus.

- **PRAISE WORSHIP**

1. *Yea, though I walk through the valley of the shadow of death, I will fear no evil: for Thou art with me; Thy rod and Thy staff they comfort me.* Every curse of untimely death operating in the lives of God's ministers, especially in this country; break and loose your hold over my life, in the name of Jesus.

2. *Mark the perfect man, and behold the upright: for the end of that man is peace.* My calling shall not be aborted, I will complete my assignment with peace, in the name of Jesus.

3. *For this God is our God for ever and ever. He will be our guide even unto death.* Every curse inspiring the ministers of God to leave his guiding light, I break you and loose myself from you, in Jesus' name.

4. *But God will redeem my soul from the power of the grave for He shall receive me.* Any power hunting to convert me to a living and walking corpse, fall down and perish, in the name of Jesus.

5. *My flesh and my heart fail but God is the strength of my heart, and my portion for ever.* Any power feeding on the anointing and strength of God's minister, be consumed over my life, in the name of Jesus.

6. *He will swallow up death in victory; and the Lord God will wipe away tears from off all faces; and the rebuke of His people shall He take away from off all the earth for the Lord has spoken it.* Let the precious blood of Jesus swallow every death sentence placed upon any member of my family, in the name of Jesus.

7. *I will ransom them from the power of the grave; I will redeem them from death: O death, I will be thy plagues; O grave, I will be thy destruction: repentance shall be hid from mine eyes.* Every curse of

death before success, every curse issued by occultists, witches, rulers of darkness and local wickedness against God's ministers in this country: I break you by the blood of Jesus over my life, in the name of Jesus.

8. *But thou shall remember the Lord thy God: for it is He that giveth thee power to get wealth.* Every curse of financial failure and poverty, be destroyed by the blood of Jesus.

9. *For the Lord thy God blesseth thee, as He promised thee: and thou shalt lend unto many nations, but thou shall not borrow.* Every curse of borrowing, lacking and wanting in the lives of God's ministers, I loose myself from your grip by fire, in Jesus' name.

10. *The Lord shall open unto thee his good treasure, the heaven to give the rain unto thy land in his season and to bless all the work of thine hand.* Any power shutting off good treasures of God from my life, fall down and perish, in the name of Jesus.

11. *For the Lord God is a sun and shield: the Lord will give grace and glory; no good thing will he withhold from them that walk uprightly.* Anything in me repelling the good things promised by God to His own; come out by fire, in the name of Jesus.

12. *That I may cause those that love me to inherit substance; and I will fill their treasures.* Any power in my family and locality creating difficulty for me in obtaining good substance, receive multiple destruction, in the name of Jesus.

13. *For the love of money is the root of all evil: which while some coveted after, they have erred from the faith, and pierced themselves through with many sorrows.* Every attack and manoeuvre of mammon making God's ministers easily diverted from the true gospel, be frustrated in my life and calling, in the name of Jesus.

14. *He that loveth silver shall not be satisfied with silver; nor he that loveth abundance with increase.* Every seed of mammon making God's ministers to lust after money and run after gains, be uprooted from my life and die, in the name of Jesus.

15. *Before destruction the heart of man is haughty and before honour is humility.* Every curse of failure and destruction of the ministers of God prospering through pride, I destroy you in my life, in the name of Jesus.

16. *Pride goeth before destruction and an haughty spirit before a fall.* Anything in my flesh putting up and exhibiting haughtiness against God and His people, die now, in the name of Jesus.

17. *A man's pride shall bring him low: but honour shall uphold the humble in spirit.* Every attack, plot, scheme, device, manoeuvre and operation of the enemy to bring me low (into the valley), be divinely frustrated to nothingness, in the name of Jesus.

18. *For by means of a whorish woman a man is brought to a piece of bread.* Every woman agent assigned as an open sepulchre to swallow me and my calling up, receive speedy judgment of destruction, in the name of Jesus.

19. *Now the works of the flesh are manifest, which are these, adultery, fornication, uncleanness, lasciviousness . . ..* Every work of the flesh being exploited by the enemy against me and my calling, die now, in the name of Jesus.

20. *Now these things became our examples to the intent that we should not lust after evil things as they also lusted.* I receive a special grace of God that will enable me escape ministerial pitfalls that swallowed the people before me, in the name of Jesus.

21. *Rejoice in the Lord always, for we can do all things through Christ who is our strength.* Bless the Lord for all answered prayers.

BREAKING ANCESTRAL EVIL HOLD

● CONFESSION

By natural heritage I was dead in trespasses, for I was brought forth in iniquity and conceived in sin in my mother's womb; and according to the law, I was preserved for the wrath of God that was to be revealed upon the children of disobedience, but now I am God's handiwork recreated in Christ Jesus, born anew that I may do those good works which God already predestined for me.

Through the blood of Jesus Christ; I, who was once far away, have been brought near to God. I am now engrafted in Christ my Messiah, I have become a new creature altogether. The previous moral and spiritual condition has passed away. Behold the fresh and new one has come.

Therefore, since I am declared righteous and given a right standing with God through faith, I have peace with god through Jesus Christ. Now, being justified by the blood of Christ, I shall be saved by Him from the wrath of God to come.

The person who is united to the Lord becomes one spirit with Him. Therefore, there is now no condemnation for those who are in Christ Jesus, who walk not after the dictates of the flesh but after the dictates of the spirit. For the law of our new being, which is the law of the spirit of life in Christ, has freed me from the law of sin and death.

I am separated by God through the redeeming power in the blood of Christ my Messiah, the author and finisher of my faith, from every tie with ancestral covenants, curses and guardian spirits.

My citizenship is now of heaven. I belong to the household of God. My life is hidden with Christ in God. I am washed in the blood of Him who loved me and gave His life for me. He has called me with a holy calling and by His name I am called.

As it is written: For it is he who delivered and saved me and called me with a calling in itself holy and leading to a life of consecration, a vocation of holiness. He did it not because of anything of merit that I have done, but because of and to further His own purpose, and grace which was given me in Christ Jesus.

As it were, I am now cut off from evil consequences, I am physically and spiritually separated from their dos and don'ts. I no longer belong to any generation upon whom God could visit the sins of their fathers. Christ has redeemed me from such curses of the law. I cannot labour any longer under the weight of such yokes and burden; I have received the yoke of Christ which is easy and His burden which is light.

Therefore, every interference of household wickedness and ancestral spirit disturbance in my life and in my ministry is a transgression against the covenant promises of God concerning me; For it is written; touch not my anointed and do my prophets no harm.

For this reason, as the God of heaven lives, let every manifestation and exhibition of rebellion from the ancestral and family spirits receive the undiluted anger of my God who is a consuming fire.

For it is written, it is a righteous thing for God to repay tribulation to those that trouble me: Therefore, let every association of wicked spirits assembled against me be shattered by God . Let its hold on my life and ministry be broken. Let its projections return back to it, Let its plotting, scheming, manoeuvring and operation, receive divine frustration and let their wickedness come to an end in my life.

I reject every evil family and ancestral name, I renounce and reject their praise poems ever sung for me, I break the power of any evil dedication ever placed on my head, every pledge, vow, promise or covenant ever made on my behalf with these spirits. I renounce and reject them and cut myself off from them with the blood of Christ.

Henceforth, let no ancestral or evil family spirit have any hold on me and my ministry. Let them not have any entry point into my life, for now I bear in my body the marks of the blood of the Lamb of God who has paid the price for my life and has bought me to belong to Himself eternally. Amen.

● **PRAISE WORSHIP**

1. Cover yourself properly with the blood of Jesus.

2. Stand against any power already assembled against this prayer.

3. Every grip of the evil consequences of the ancestral worship of my forefathers' god over my life and ministry, break by fire, in the name of Jesus.

4. Every covenant with water spirits, desert spirits, witchcraft spirits, spirits in evil sacred trees, spirits inside / under sacred rocks / hills, family gods, evil family guardian spirits, family / village serpentine spirits, masquerade spirits, inherited spirit husbands / wives, be broken by the blood of Jesus.

5. Every unconscious evil soul-tie and covenant with the spirits of my dead grandfather, grandmother, occultic uncles, aunties, custodian of family gods/oracles/shrines, be broken by the blood of Jesus.

6. Every decision, vow or promise made by my forefathers contrary to my divine destiny, loose your hold by fire, in the name of Jesus.

7. Every legal ground that ancestral/guardian spirits have in my life, be destroyed by the blood of Jesus.

8. Every generational curse of God resulting from the sin of idolatry on my forefathers, loose your hold, in the name of Jesus..

9. Every ancestral evil altar prospering against me, be dashed against the Rock of Ages, in the name of Jesus.

10. Every ancestral placental manipulation of my life, be reversed, in the name of Jesus.

11. Every evil ancestral life pattern designed for me through vows, promises and covenants, be reversed, in the name of Jesus.

12. Every hold of any sacrifice ever offered in my family or on my behalf, I break your power in my life, in the name of Jesus.

13. Any ancestral blood shed of animals, or human beings affecting me, loose your hold by the blood of Jesus.

14. Any curse placed on my ancestral line by anybody cheated, maltreated or at the point of death, break now, in Jesus' name.

15. Every garment of ancestral, infirmity, disease, sickness, untimely death, poverty, disfavor, dishonor, shame and failure at the edge of miracles passed down to my generation, be roasted by fire, in the name of Jesus.

16. Every evil ancestral river flowing down to my generation, I cut you off, in the name of Jesus.

17. Every evil ancestral habit and weakness of moral failures manifesting in my life, loose your grip and release me now, in Jesus' name.

18. Any power from my family background seeking to make a shipwreck of my life and ministry, be destroyed by the fire of God, in the name of Jesus.

19. Every rage and rampage of ancestral and family spirits resulting from my being born again, be quenched by the liquid fire of God, in the name of Jesus.

20. Any ancestral power frustrating any area of my life in order to discourage me from following Christ, receive multiple destruction, in the name of Jesus.

21. Every ancestral chain of slavery binding my people from prospering in life, you are broken in my life by the hammer of God, in the name of Jesus.

22. The right nobody has attained in my generation, I will reach, in the name of Jesus.

23. I recover every good thing stolen by ancestral evil spirits from my forefathers, my immediate family and myself, in Jesus' name.

24. Every ancestral embargo, be lifted; and let good things begin to break forth in my life and in my family, in the name of Jesus.

25. Bless God for all answers to your prayer.

POWER AGAINST SATANIC COUNTER ATTACK
Isa. 59:19

• CONFESSIONS

The Lord shall cause my enemies that rise up against me to be smitten before my face: they shall come out against me in one way, and flee before me seven ways.

For the Lord my God is He that goeth with me, to fight for me against my enemies to save me. They that hate me shall be clothed with shame; and the dwelling place of the wicked shall come to nought.

For in the time of trouble He shall hide me in His pavilion: in the secret of his tabernacle shall He hide me; He shall set me up upon a rock. And now shall mine head be lifted up above mine enemies round about me: therefore will I offer in his tabernacle sacrifices of joy.

Through God I shall do valiantly: for He it is that shall tread down my enemies.

For the rod of the wicked shall not rest upon the lot of the righteous; lest the plenteous put forth their hands unto iniquity.

I am not afraid of sudden fear, neither of desolation of the wicked when it cometh, for the Lord shall be my confidence and shall keep my foot from being taken.

Behold all that are incensed against me shall be ashamed and confounded: they shall be as nothing; and they that strive with me shall perish. I shall seek them, and shall not find, even them that contend with me, they that war against me shall be as nothing, and as a thing of nought.

Behold they shall surely gather together, but not by me: whosoever shall gather against me shall fall for my sake. But I will deliver thee in that day, saith the Lord: and thou shall not be given into the hand of men of whom thou art afraid. For I will surely deliver thee, and thou shall not fall by the sword, but thy life shall be for a prey for thee; because thou has thy trust in me, saith the Lord.

And shall God not avenge His own elect which cry day and night unto him, though he fear long with them.

He shall deliver me in six troubles: yea, in seven there shall no evil touch thee.

The angel of the Lord encampeth round about them that fear him and delivereth them.

For the Lord loveth judgement, and forsaketh not his saints; they are preserved forever, but the seeds of the wicked shall be cut off.

But the Lord is faithful, who shall stablish you, and keep you from evil.

For the eyes of the Lord are over the righteous, and his ears are open unto their prayers.

The Lord knoweth how to deliver the godly out of temptations and to reserve the unjust unto the day of judgement to be punished.

• PRAISE WORSHIP

1. Cover yourself properly with the blood of Jesus and stand against any power that is ready to resist you.

2. Any satanic agent pretending to be a counsellee in order to project evil into my life, be disgraced, in the name of Jesus.

3. Any spiritual arrow I have prayed out of anybody that is now in my family, be roasted by fire, in the name of Jesus.

4. Any demon of marital bondage the Holy Ghost has ever used me to cast out of peoples' marriages before, now oppressing my marriage, loose your hold by fire, in the name of Jesus.

5. Any demon of infirmity in my life or in my family as a result of my ministering to people possessed of it, get out now by fire, in the name of Jesus.

6. Any household witchcraft the Holy Ghost has used my ministry to and which is now affecting me or my family, be suddenly destroyed, in the name of Jesus.

7. Any marine witchcraft rage against me and my family as a result of destroying their works in people's lives, be silenced by the blood of Jesus.

8. Any member of my family being oppressed by any familiar spirit that was cast out through my ministry, receive divine deliverance, in the name of Jesus.

9. Every spiritual wickedness in the heavenlies reinforcing against me and my ministry, be disgraced by the blood of Jesus.

10. Every servient spirit assigned against me to be watching for my unguarded hour, receive thunderbolts of God and depart from me, in the name of Jesus.

11. Every assembly of local witchcraft formed against my ministry, receive baptism of multiple destruction, in the name of Jesus.

12. Any power divining against me and my ministry, fall down and perish, in the name of Jesus.

13. Any power circulating my name for evil as a result of my ministry work, fall down and die now, in the name of Jesus.

14. Any satanic agent that is already in the sheepfold purposefully to watch and report me back to the evil world, be exposed and be disgraced, in the name of Jesus.

15. Let every ministerial hazard I have ever suffered be healed by the blood of Jesus.

16. Every good thing carted away by raging demon from my marriage, financial life and my ministry, be restored a hundred-fold, in the name of Jesus.

17. Any demon assigned to be frustrating my success at the edge of breakthroughs, depart by fire, in the name of Jesus.

18. Any power creating difficulties for me in the ministry, be roasted by fire, in the name of Jesus.

19. Any power creating disfavour and diverting my divinely appointed helpers, be suddenly destroyed, in the name of Jesus.

20. Every arrow I have ever fired out that was returned to me, go back with a hundred-fold strength, in the name of Jesus.

21. I shield myself with the blood of Jesus against any evil reunion, re-gathering, reattaching and reinforcement, in the name of Jesus.

22. Affliction shall not arise a second time in my life, in the name of Jesus.

23. Henceforth, let no principality, power, ruler of darkness, spiritual wickedness in the heavenlies and local wickedness trouble me, for I bear in my body the marks of the Lamb of God.

POWER AGAINST MARINE WITCHCRAFT

Psalm 8:4-8, Isa. 27

- *To be used when seeking deliverance from a bondage of water spirit.*

Marine witchcraft is one of the most destructive evil powers. Children of God must learn to deal with it.

Nahum 3:1-3: *"Woe to the bloody city! it is all full of lies and robbery; the prey departeth not; The noise of a whip, and the noise of the rattling of the wheels, and of the pransing horses, and of the jumping chariots. The horseman lifteth up both the bright sword and the glittering spear: and there is a multitude of slain, and a great number of carcases; and there is none end of their corpses; they stumble upon their corpses:"*

Many nations and many lives will not advance unless this is dealt with. It is to be noted that practically in all nations there are people who worshiped bodies of water. These spirits are proud, mean, wicked, heartless, and stubborn. They try to control trade and commerce.

- **CONFESSIONS**

Ezek 29:1-3: *"In the tenth year, in the tenth month, in the twelfth day of the month, the word of the LORD came unto me, saying, Son of man, set thy face against Pharaoh king of Egypt, and prophesy against him, and against all Egypt: Speak, and say, Thus saith the Lord GOD; Behold, I am against thee, Pharaoh king of Egypt, the great dragon that lieth in the midst of his rivers, which hath said, My river is mine own, and I have made it for my-self."*

In the beginning God created man to subdue the earth and have dominion over all the fish of the sea, and over the fowl of the air and over everything creature that moveth upon the face of the earth.

The psalmist also confirms it as he wrote that God has made man to have dominion over all the works of His hands; thou has put all things under his feet. All sheep and oxen, yea and the beasts of the field, the fowl of the air, and the fish of the sea and whatsoever passeth through thee PATHS OF THE SEAS.

The mandate every man lost to devil through Adam's disobedience has been restored unto us by Jesus Christ. I am a workmanship of God, recreated in Christ as a priest and king to reign here on earth.

Jesus Christ was made manifest that He might destroy all the works of the devil and when He was going, He said that greater works than He did I shall do.

Therefore as I go into this prayer, I hold in my hand the victory Jesus Christ purchased on the cross at calvary, when He made an open show of principality and powers. I take my position in Christ as one given power to become a son of God, even joint heir with Christ of the kingdom of God, to execute judgment against every form of disobedience exhibited against the knowledge of God.

Greater is He that is in me than any power on earth and in the seas. I am born of God, and I have overcome the world with my faith.

In faith, I hand over my battle to God. In faith, I come against evil strongholds of any marine kingdom. In faith, I pollute your water with the blood of Jesus Christ. In faith, I overturn every queen enthroned against me. In faith, I trample upon her serpents and scorpions. In faith, I spoil her palace and set her captives free and bind her herself.

There shall be no reinforcement or evil reunion of this power against me. I seal my confessions with the blood of Jesus and I cover myself with the blood of Jesus. Amen.

- **PRAISE WORSHIP**

1. Any witchcraft practised under any water against my life, receive immediate judgment of fire, in the name of Jesus.

2. Let every evil altar under any water upon which certain evils are done against me, be roasted, in the name of Jesus.

3. Every priest ministering at any evil altar against me inside any water, fall down and die, in the name of Jesus.

4. Any power under any river or sea remotely-controlling my life, be destroyed by fire, and I shake myself loose from your hold, in the name of Jesus.

5. Let any evil monitoring mirror ever used against me under any water, crash to irredeemable pieces, in the name of Jesus.

6. Every marine witchcraft that has introduced spirit husband/wife or child in my dreams be roasted by fire, in the name of Jesus.

7. Every agent of marine witchcraft posing as my husband, wife or child in my dreams, be roasted by fire, in the name of Jesus.

8. Every agent of marine witchcraft physically attached to my marriage to frustrate it, fall down and perish now, in Jesus' name.

9. Every agent of marine witchcraft assigned to attack my finances through dream, fall down and perish, in the name of Jesus.

10. I pull down every stronghold of bewitchment, enchantment, jinx or divination fashioned against me by marine witches, in Jesus' name.

11. Let the thunderbolts of God locate and destroy every marine witchcraft covens where deliberations and decisions have ever been fashioned against me, in the name of Jesus.

12. Any water spirit from my village or the place of my birth, practising witchcraft against me and my family, be amputated by the word of God, in the name of Jesus.

13. Let every spiritual weapon of wickedness fashioned against me under any river or sea, be roasted by the fire of God, in the name of Jesus.

14. Any power of marine witchcraft holding any of my blessings in bondage, receive the fire of God and release them, in Jesus' name.

15. I loose my mind and soul from the bondage of marine witches, in the name of Jesus.

16. Any marine witchcraft chain binding my hands and feet from prospering, be broken and shattered to pieces, in Jesus' name.

17. Every arrow shot into my life from under any water by witchcraft powers, come out of me and go back to your sender, in the name of Jesus.

18. Any evil material transferred into my body through contact with any marine witchcraft agent, be roasted by fire, in the name of Jesus.

19. Every sexual pollution of marine spirit husband/wife in my body, be flushed out by the blood of Jesus.

20. Any evil name given to me under any water, I reject and cancel it with the blood of Jesus.

21. Every image constructed under any water to manipulate me, be roasted by fire, in the name of Jesus.

22. Any evil ever done against me through marine witchcraft oppression and manipulation, be reversed by the blood of Jesus.

POWER AGAINST EVIL NAMES, PRAISES AND THEIR ATTENDANT PROBLEMS

Isa. 62:2

God is concerned about names. Some human problems are tied to the names they bear. A born again Christian who bears a 'cursed name' would have unexplainable problems. Many Christians are now discovering how the meaning of their vernacular or other names speak plainly through their daily life experiences.

When genuine Christians bear names which glorify the devil, or suggest evil or misfortune, they do themselves a great harm by retaining such names. For Christians whose names specifically imply evil, a bold step should be taken to change such names. However, to make the change of any name spiritually effective, we must destroy the power and the effect of the former name through prophetic praying and prayers of deliverance.

• CONFESSIONS

1 Chr 4:9-10: *"And Jabez was more honourable than his brethren: and his mother called his name Jabez, saying, Because I bare him with sorrow. And Jabez called on the God of Israel, saying, Oh that thou wouldest bless me indeed, and enlarge my coast, and that thine hand might be with me, and that thou wouldest keep me from evil, that it may not grieve me! And God granted him that which he requested."*

Gen 17:5-6: *"Neither shall thy name any more be called Abram, but thy name shall be Abraham; for a father of many nations have I made thee. And I will make thee exceeding fruitful, and I will make nations of thee, and kings shall come out of thee."*

Gen 32:24-30: *"And Jacob was left alone; and there wrestled a man with him until the breaking of the day. And when he saw that he prevailed not against him, he touched the hollow of his thigh; and the hollow of Jacob's thigh was out of joint, as he wrestled with him. And he said, Let me go, for the day breaketh. And he said, I will not let thee go, except thou bless me.*

And he said unto him, What is thy name? And he said, Jacob. And he said, Thy name shall be called no more Jacob, but Israel: for as a prince hast thou power with God and with men, and hast prevailed. And Jacob asked him, and said, Tell me, I pray thee, thy name. And he said, Wherefore is it that thou dost ask after my name? And he blessed him there. And Jacob called the name of the place Peniel: for I have seen God face to face, and my life is preserved."

Matt 1:21: *"And she shall bring forth a son, and thou shalt call his name JESUS: for he shall save his people from their sins."*

● **PRAISE WORSHIP**

● **STRATEGY**

1. *Find out the meaning of your names and the history behind the name.*

2. *Change those names immediately, if they do not glorify the Lord Jesus Christ.*

3. *Carry out research into the praise names of your family and ancestors.*

4. *Take three days fast breaking at 7 p.m. each day.*

1. Father, I thank You for opening my understanding on this issue.

2. Father, I thank You for the new birth and for naming me after You.

3. I renounce every demonic name attached to me and my family, in the name of Jesus.

4. I dissociate my life from every name given to me under satanic anointing, in the name of Jesus.

5. Let any record of these names in the demonic world be wiped off by the blood of Jesus.

6. I break and smash to pieces every curse and evil covenant attached to these names, in the name of Jesus

7. I break the flow of any evil river coming into my life through these unprofitable names, in the name of Jesus.

8. I cancel every influence of family idols attached to these names, in the name of Jesus.

9. You . . . (mention the name), I renounce you. I reject you. I refuse you. You shall have no landing place in my life, in Jesus' name.

10. Every familiar and wicked spirit behind the names, get out of my life, in the name of Jesus.

11. I refuse to come under the control and domination of any satanic name, in the name of Jesus.

12. Every witchcraft naming, be dissolved from my fore-head and navel, in the name of Jesus.

13. Holy Spirit, take control of any negative situation these names have caused, in the name of Jesus.

14. My new name . . . (mention it) would bind me to the blood of Jesus and to prosperity, in the name of Jesus.

15. Holy Ghost fire, consume every evil label, mark, stamp or ordination of evil attached to my former names, in Jesus' name.

16. I receive the seal of the Holy Spirit upon my life, in Jesus' name.

17. Every hidden or silent name given to me to destroy my destiny on my naming ceremony day, I nullify you, in Jesus' name.

18. I receive deliverance from every satanic cage created for me by any evil name, in the name of Jesus.

19. Every good thing these names have destroyed in my life, be restored seven-fold, in the name of Jesus.

20. I re-name myself as follows . . . (mention your names), in the name of the Father, of the Son and of the Holy Spirit.

Below are examples of names to be considered for a change:

Names (Ibo)	Meaning
1. Njoku	a demon deity responsible for yam production.
2. Nwosu	a child belonging to a demon called 'osu'.

3. Nwagwu   a child belonging to a demon of stubbornness
4. Agu   Tiger

(Calabar)

5. Eseme   Lamentation
6. Nyong   Vagabond
7. Ekim   Darkness
8. Nsifon   Nothing is good

(Yoruba)

9. Ogunmuyiwa 'ogun' (god of iron) brought this
10. Fawole   'ifa' oracle has arrived
11. Iyabo   the dead mother has come back (re-incarnated)
12. Babatunde father has re-incarnated

(English)

13. Linda   snake
14. Diana   goddess of the hunt and of the moon

POWER AGAINST THE SPIRIT OF FEAR
Job 3:25

● CONFESSIONS

I announce that greater is the One that is in me than any devil on the side of my enemies. It is written, "The righteous is as bold as a lion." By my faith in Christ Jesus, I am righteous. I receive my divine boldness. The angels of the Lord encampeth round about them that fear Him. The angels of God are with me, I have no basis to fear any man, any evil, any evil spirit. Because the Lord of hosts is with me, I put my confidence in Him.

It is written ,"If God be for us who can be against us?" God is with me, I have no reason to fear, in the name of Jesus. It is written, "The Lord is my light and my salvation whom shall I fear? The Lord is the defence of my life" of whom shall I be afraid? Though a host of demons encamp against me, my heart will not fear; though war rises against me, even in this I shall be confident."The Lord is with me like a mighty terrible one. I am not afraid. I cannot be threatened. My persecutors shall stumble and fumble. Their everlasting confusion and disgrace shall never be forgotten. God has commanded me to fear not.

Of the 366 days in a year, no single day is allowed for me to fear. So, I refuse to be afraid of anything. You spirit of fear, you are not in God's agenda for me. I dismiss you from my life now, in the name of Jesus. Jesus said even the very hairs of my head are not only counted but numbered. Not one single strand can be removed without God's knowledge and permission. Therefore, I put my confidence in the Lord, Who takes so much care of me.

The Bible says whatsoever I desire when I pray, I should believe and receive, in the name of Jesus. Therefore, I pray now that, in Jesus' name, I am set free from every captivity or attack of negative speech from my mouth or thoughts from my heart against myself.

Let the word of God that is quick, powerful and sharper than any two-edged sword pierce through every negative thought or speech I have ever made and tear them down.

God wishes me above all things that I prosper, in Jesus' name. I receive prosperity, in Jesus' name. God has not given me the spirit of bondage again to fear. Therefore, every evil the spirit of fear has done to my life, I reject you. Be reversed and get out of my life.

In Jesus' name, I have the mind of Christ. I reject, refuse and bind negative thoughts and statements. Right now, I cast down every imagination and high thing exalting itself against the word of God in my life.

My God is the Father of faith. I ask and receive the faith in God to increase in my spirit, in my soul and in my body, in the name of Jesus.

I totally trust in the Lord, and I am not leaning on my own understanding. I fill my heart with the words of faith, I receive and speak the words of faith.

The perfect will of God for my life shall come to pass. I abide in the secret place of the most high God. He is my shelter and my refuge. Today, I begin to be what God says I am, and begin to walk in it, in the name of Jesus. I am a person of authority, power, dominion, grace and favour, in Jesus' name. I can do all things through Christ Who strengthens me. I can run through a troop. I can leap over a wall. I can crush principalities and power under my feet. I can pursue, overtake and break the necks of my enemies.

Henceforth, I refuse to live in fear, rather my fear and dread shall be upon all my enemies. As soon as they hear of me, they shall submit themselves unto me.

My confession is from the word of God, therefore it standeth sure.

• PRAISE WORSHIP

1. Begin to bless the Lord, Who has comforted you on all sides and satisfied your mouth with good things.

2. In the name of Jesus, I refuse to fear, because God has not given me the spirit of fear, but of power and of love and of a sound mind.

3. I bind the spirit of fear in my life, in the name of Jesus.

4. Every power behind every activity of fears in my life, receive the wrath of God and be consumed in it, in the name of Jesus.

5. Everything I have feared will not come upon me, in Jesus' name.

6. Everything I was afraid of will not come to me, in Jesus' name.

7. The local wickedness I have ever keen afraid of will not have a hold on me, in the name of Jesus.

8. The evil obtainable in my family background will not have hold on me, in the name of Jesus.

9. The evil everybody dreads in my family will not locate me, in the name of Jesus.

10. The failure and disappointment in marriage will not manifest in my marriage, in the name of Jesus.

11. The financial failure and embarrassment I have ever feared will not befall me, in the name of Jesus.

12. The fear of backsliding I have nursed or nurtured up in my life will not come upon me, in the name of Jesus.

13. The fear of not being spiritually fulfilled will not germinate in my life, in the name of Jesus.

14. Let the fear of being ministerially stunted get out of my vision, in the name of Jesus.

15. Let the fear of committing unpardonable sin be washed out of me by the blood of Jesus.

16. Let the fear of not being able to overcome any weakness in me dry to its roots, in the name of Jesus.

17. Let the fear of missing the rapture go back to the bottom of the pit, in the name of Jesus.

18. I bind and cast out every fear of compromising my faith, in the name of Jesus.

19. I bind and cast out every fear of losing my anointing and salvation, in the name of Jesus.

20. I break every evil covenant that has brought fear into my life, in the name of Jesus.

21. I command every terror of the night that has brought fear into my life to stop and move from my environment, in the name of Jesus.

22. You spirit of fear, loose your hold upon my life and my family, in the name of Jesus.

23. I command all human agents using the spirits of fear to terrify me in the night to stumble and fall, in the name of Jesus.

24. The fear and terror of the unbelievers shall not be my lot, in the name of Jesus.

25. My tomorrow is blessed is Christ Jesus. Therefore, you spirit responsible for the fear of tomorrow in my life, I bind you, in the name of Jesus.

26. My destiny is attached to God, therefore I decree that I can never fail, in the name of Jesus.

27. Every bondage that I am subjecting myself to by the spirit of fear, I break you, in the name of Jesus.

28. All negative doors that the spirit of fear have opened in the past, be closed now, in the name of Jesus.

29. Every disease, oppression and depression that came into my life as a result of fear, disappear now, in the name of Jesus.

30. I refuse to be intimidated by any demonic nightmare, in the name of Jesus.

31. Every enchantment and invocation of fear being made against me, I neutralise you and I command you to fail, in the name of Jesus.

32. Every confederacy of the enemies in my home with the enemies outside shall not stand, in the name o f Jesus.

33. All arrangements of the devil concerning my home shall not stand; neither shall they come to pass, in the name of Jesus.

34. I destroy all efforts of the enemy to frustrate my work, in the name of Jesus.

35. I nullify every writing, agreement or covenant against my work, in the name of Jesus.

36. Father Lord, increase my greatness and comfort me on every side, in the name of Jesus.

37. O Lord, as You delight in my prosperity, I pray that You bless me indeed in my work. Let no household enemy be able to control my wellbeing any longer, in the name of Jesus.

38. Let all those who are against me without a cause in my place of work turn back and be brought to confusion, in the name of Jesus.

39. I close every door through which the enemies have been working against my work, in the name of Jesus.

40. No weapon of satan and his agents fashioned against me shall prosper, in the name of Jesus.

41. My life is hid with Christ in God. Therefore nobody can kill me or harm me, in the name of Jesus.

42. I open wide all doors leading to my blessings, victory and breakthroughs which the enemies have closed, in Jesus' name.

43. Let every territorial spirit working against us in our neighbourhood be frustrated, bound and cast out, in the name of Jesus.

44. Let every power contrary to the power of God operating to suppress people in my area be neutralised, in the name of Jesus.

45. I bind every spirit of frustration, defeat, delayed blessing and fear in my environment, in the name of Jesus.

46. I banish every enemy of progress in my neighbourhood, in the name of Jesus.

47. I bind the spirit of death, armed robbery and assassination in my neighbourhood, in the name of Jesus.

48. I reject, renounce and destroy every evil agreement or covenant in the environment, in the name of Jesus.

49. By the blood of Jesus, I nullify the effects and operation of evil forces around my house, in the name of Jesus.

50. Lord, get all my stubborn pursuers occupied with unprofitable assignments, in the name of Jesus.

51. In Jesus' mighty name, I fire back every arrow, spiritual bullets and satanic missiles fired at me.

52. O Lord, reveal the secrets and expose all my enemies masquerading as my friends.

53. Father Lord, make it impossible for my enemies to use my foot marks, urine, faeces, hair, clothing, and shoes.

A

B

C

D

E

Eagle believers (193,194, 435, 599)
Earthquake (333)
Ease of passage (374, 449, 519, 531, 534)
Effect of dedication (130)
Egypt (159)
Embargo (34, 45, 113, 116, 170, 181, 237, 239, 261, 361, 375, 387, 444, 448, 456, 530, 542, 544, 558, 559, 561, 619) - - -
Employments (30, 31, 104, 183, 474, 604)
Empower to prosper (77, 84, 183, 215)
Enemy of God (16)
Engagements (122)
Enough is Enough (69, 408)
Enticement (220, 342)
Establishment (21)
Eternal perdition (148, 149, 150, 515, 527)
Every door (380)
Evil associations (118, 119, 147, 191, 294, 297, 298, 466, 508, 621)
Evil bands (73, 247, 309, 310, 348)
Evil bondage (344, 396)
Evil covenants (193, 194, 435, 505)
Evil decision (133, 304, 421, 456, 533, 576, 577, 585 586 587)
Evil decree (452)
Evil dedication (133)
Evil deposits (9, 40, 64, 159, 160, 196, 212, 265, 297, 308, 367, 398, 449, 519, 578, 581, 602)
Evil family altars (5, 12, 53, 125, 189, 467, 534)

Evil family pattern (378)
Evil family patterns (39, 193, 194, 512, 552)
Evil family rivers (193, 194)
Evil flow (193, 194)
Evil growth (396)
Evil hands (12, 48, 51, 122, 125, 192, 219)
Evil handwriting (268, 357, 377, 456, 464, 528)
Evil inheritance (29, 133, 268)
Evil linkage (39, 62, 243)
Evil marital magnets (378)
Evil marks (53)
Evil powers (166, 288, 533)
Evil reinforcement (32, 46, 63, 144, 146, 195, 216, 253, 259, 282, 307, 339, 357, 363, 378, 445, 504, 592 619)
Evil spirits (313, 534)
Evil stones (21, 67, 131, 159, 212, 235, 311, 382, 582, 589, 604)
Evil strategies (473, 498)
Evil streams (43, 283)
Evil stubborn growth (47, 276, 346, 378)
Evil umbrella (122)
Evil weapons (193, 194)
Evil wisdom (357)
Evil words (248, 284, 449, 475)
Examination (167, 176, 211, 225, 465, 546)
Excellent spirit (89, 410, 454, 557, 561)
Excellent wisdom (77, 178, 215, 583)
Excitement (215)
External forces (223)

F

Failure (413, 420)
Faith   (4, 10, 18, 19, 30, 31, 66, 79, 88, 96, 109, 118, 119, 132, 135, 137, 143, 144, 152, 163, 184, 186, 192, 192, 193, 194, 199, 204, 213, 208, 221, 233, 245, 260, 269, 270, 271,

278, 291, 294, 300, 301, 312, 316, 320, 326, 328, 330, 347, 368, 362, 367, 398, 404, 415, 421, 424, 425, 443, 452, 453, 454, 456, 471, 476, 478, 490, 493, 494, 501, 502, 517, 528, 533, 540, 543, 545, 557, 558,

G

I

M

N

O

Obedience (558)
Obedient child (352, 364, 390, 443, 449, 516)
Objectives (183)
Obsessive affection (541)
Obstruction (407)
Olympus complex (130)
Open doors (407)
Open heavens (89, 180, 181, 209, 545)
Open mind (323, 324, 329, 403)
Open Shame (92)
Opportunities (304, 318)
Opposition (147, 226, 237, 480, 482, 485, 532, 544, 545)
Oppressed (43, 52, 83, 101, 145, 181, 218, 238, 239, 254, 331, 372, 450, 452, 455, 470, 475, 539)

Oppressive forces (219, 607)
Order (239)
Ornament of grace (11, 34, 45, 66, 84, 103, 104, 110, 117, 127, 130, 148, 181, 272, 275, 291, 319, 321, 368, 387, 398, 401, 422, 444, 455, 465, 500, 501, 502, 523, 524, 547, 560, 567, 575, 595, 604, 606)
Other tongues (215)
Our plans (165, 558, 560, 561)
Our ways (223)
Ovarian cysts (223)

P

Package of salvation (49)
Palm (522)
Paralyse (530)
Parental dedication (19, 26, 48, 49, 71, 72, 83, 84, 101, 102, 104, 113, 118, 141, 142, 143, 145, 146, 156, 162, 163, 166, 175, 180, 186, 189, 190, 190, 198, 216, 208, 220, 221, 222, 250, 252, 253, 259, 276, 277, 279, 280, 283, 289, 305, 311, 313, 315, 317, 322, 323, 324, 329, 330, 333, 334, 338, 343, 354, 372, 402, 425, 430, 450, 451, 457, 459, 460, 472, 476, 479, 491, 495, 500, 515, 518, 529, 531, 532, 539, 560, 582)
Partner (159, 508)
Past questions (53, 106, 114, 163, 173, 232, 412, 416, 418, 427, 433, 538, 548, 552, 553, 554)
Path of love (558)
Perfect deliverance (423)
Perfect marriage (39)

Perfect will (423)
Perfection (232, 595 618)
Performance (66, 221, 298, 439)
Permanent Change (212, 550, 555)
Perpetual frustration (548)
Persecutions (410)
Personal deliverance exercises (507)
Personal deliverance programme (208)
Pharaoh (34, 45, 46, 239, 275, 301, 373, 387, 444, 445, 506, 619)
Pharaohlike pursuers (89)
Physical progress (34, 45, 46, 239, 275, 301, 360, 387, 444, 445, 506, 619)
Pity (239)
Place (203)
Placenta (104, 548)
Pleasures (2, 3, 13, 38, 39, 42, 48, 53, 57, 66, 78, 88, 91, 97, 121, 126, 130, 135, 136, 151, 155, 175, 198, 201, 207, 208, 210, 211, 212, 224, 241, 243, 253, 263, 267, 276, 280, 283, 303, 318, 328, 340, 346, 370,

S

Y

Made in United States
Troutdale, OR
10/01/2023

13331756R00365